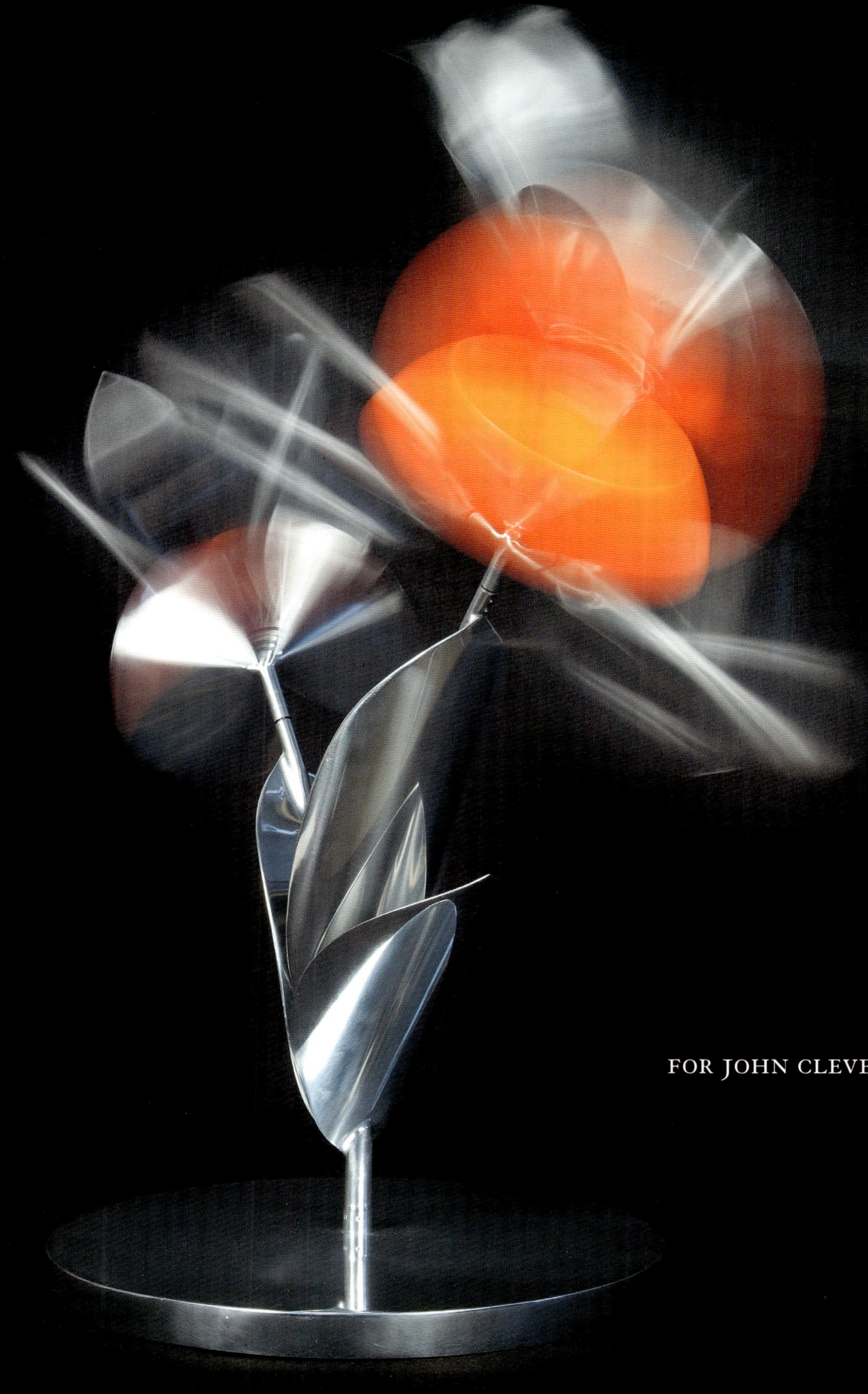

FOR JOHN CLEVELAND

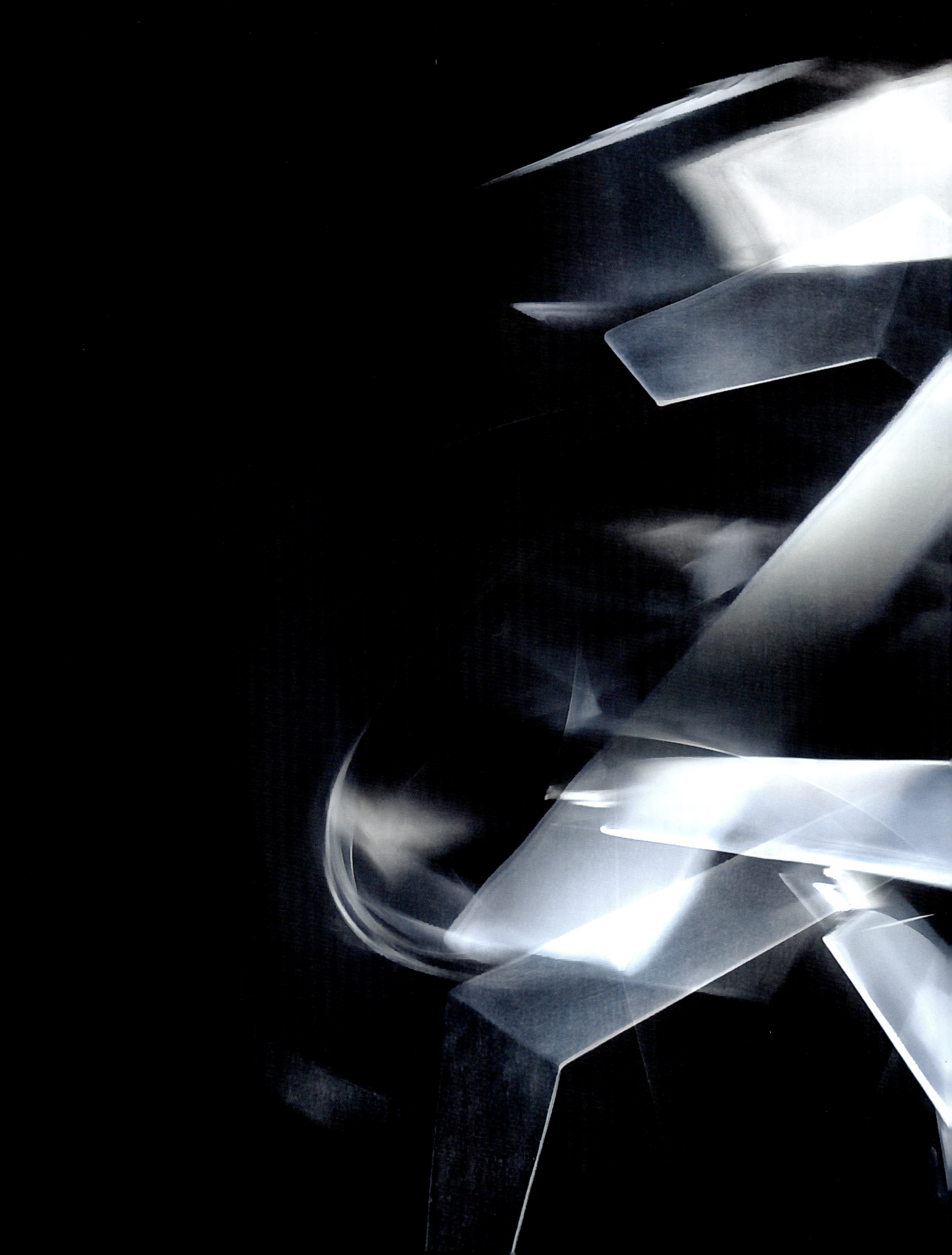

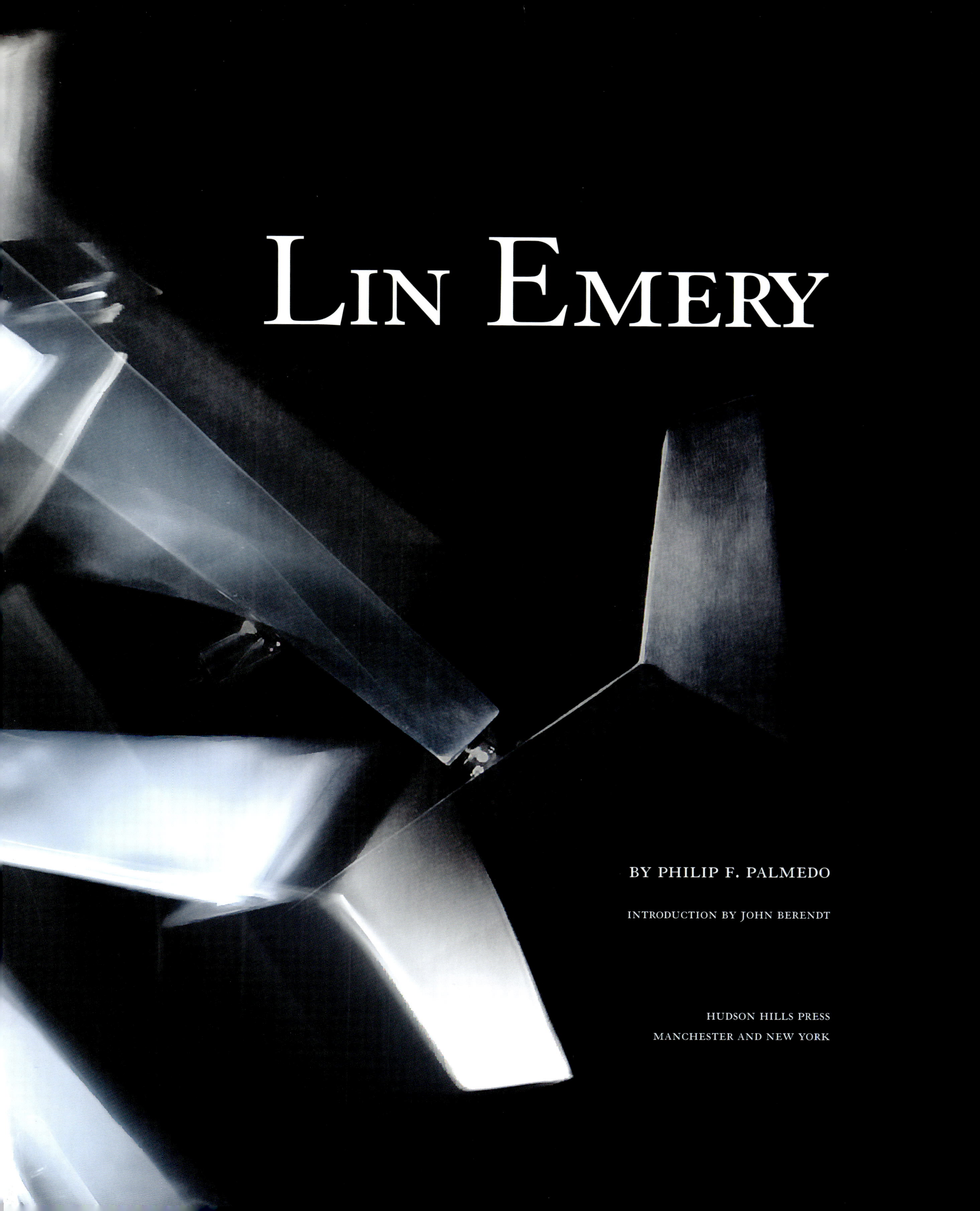

LIN EMERY

BY PHILIP F. PALMEDO

INTRODUCTION BY JOHN BERENDT

HUDSON HILLS PRESS
MANCHESTER AND NEW YORK

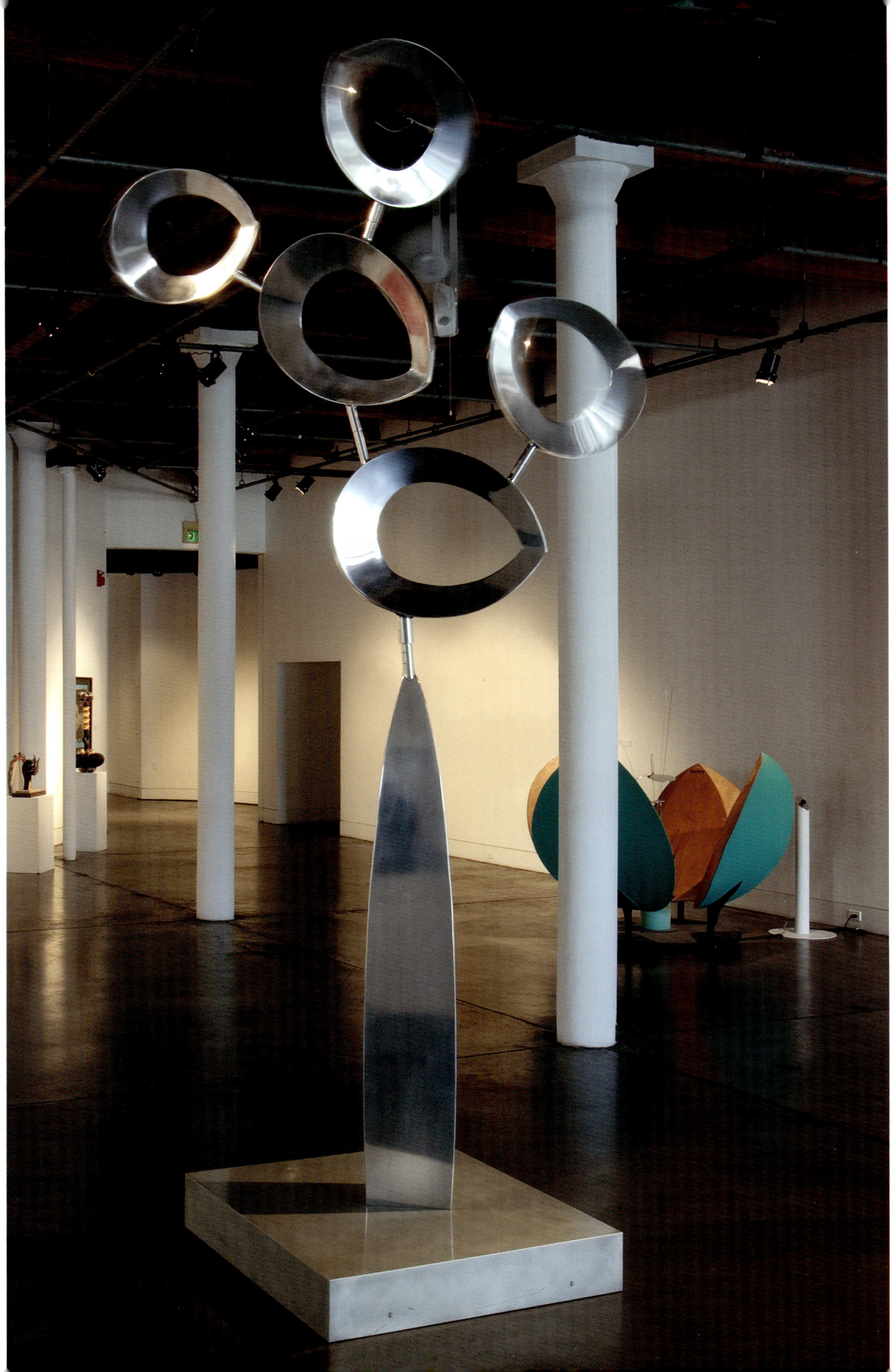

Contents

opposite page
Lin Emery, Rondelet, *2010. Aluminum, 14 feet, orbit 9 feet (4.2 m, orbit 2.7 m). Private collection.*

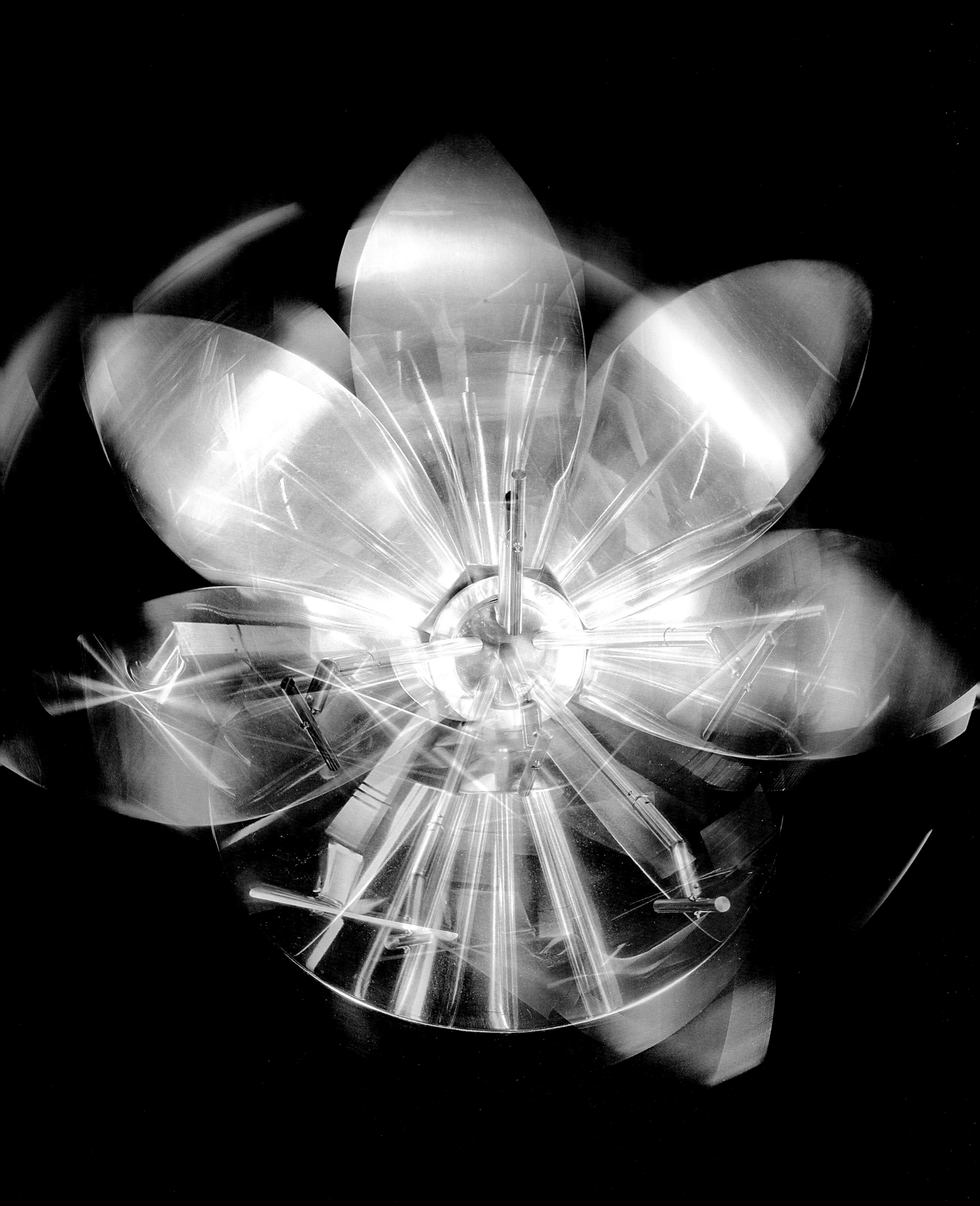

Encounters with Lin Emery

I fell under Lin Emery's spell for the first time six years ago while watching one of her kinetic sculptures in action. It was ten inches high, made of aluminum, and polished to a mirror finish. Its five moving pieces resembled the leaves of a broadleaf plant. The leaves were poised, one above the other, connected by stems that swiveled freely, allowing each leaf to rotate independently of the others. A current of air or a gentle push was all it took to set the works in motion.

I pushed it, and to my surprise the leaves began to twirl and tumble in all directions—swooping, soaring, diving, rolling, and weaving in and out unpredictably. For all its chaotic convolutions, however, the sculpture moved with a remarkably fluid grace.

And it moved in silence. There were no sounds of parts scraping against one another, or of joints turning. The leaves of this metal plant swirled like feathers caught in a draft.

Leaf Dance still resides where I first laid eyes on it: in a baronial drawing room on the second floor of the Beaux-Arts clubhouse designed by Stanford White for the Century Association in New York. The room is filled with art created, like the building itself, by members of the Century over the past 150 years.

A small watercolor by Winslow Homer hangs at the entrance to the room. The walls within are adorned with paintings by John Singer Sargent, Alfred Bierstadt, Asher B. Durand, John Frederick Kensett, George Inness, and John LaFarge. *Leaf Dance* sits below the Bierstadt on top of a bookshelf, facing two sculptures at the far end of the room: a bas-relief by Augustus Saint-Gaudens and a maquette of Karl Bitter's *Pomona*, the centerpiece for the Pulitzer fountain in front of the Plaza Hotel.

A few years later, I had a chance encounter with a second Emery sculpture, this time in New Orleans.

I had spent an afternoon at the Ogden Museum of Southern Art, walking from gallery to gallery, and when I finally stepped out onto the roof terrace I found myself looking at a ten-foot sculpture of polished aluminum with four wedge-shaped pieces swirling above a base of three tall reeds. I knew without looking at the name card that it was an Emery. One of the curators volunteered the information that Ms. Emery lived in New Orleans and was still turning out

opposite page
Lin Emery, Lilyflower *(in motion), 2010 (detail). Aluminum, 15 inches, orbit 28 inches (38.1 cm, orbit 71.1 cm). Artist's studio.*

sculptures. Several were on public display, and three were within a few blocks of where we were standing.

Indeed, virtually around the corner from the Ogden, I found *Flight* installed on a plaza overlooking Lee Circle. Its long, aerodynamic streaks of aluminum rose and fell with regal calm, suggesting an airplane or a dignified bird in flight. Inside the lobby of an adjacent building, *Variations* mimicked the swaying of saw grass. Four blocks down Camp Street, in front of St. Patrick's Cathedral, stylized pieces of a deconstructed Maltese cross twirled like jewels in the sun.

The best-known Emery sculpture in New Orleans was the one with the most dramatic setting: *Wave*. It stood at the end of a tree-lined allée, rising above a circular pool in front of the Neoclassical façade of the New Orleans Museum of Art.

Wave performed admirably in its place of honor. Its eight silvery crests depicted a changing seascape—undulating in the wind, becalmed in still air, shimmering on sunlit days, and turning gray under lowering skies. People often paused to watch it as they passed. Its message, especially to children, seemed to be that serious art did not have to be static, and that abstract art need not be incomprehensible.

Eventually, I got in touch with Lin Emery herself and then visited her on the leafy uptown street where she lived and worked. Her single-storey house and studio lay cloistered behind walls and vegetation, looking inward on a central garden and pool. A twelve-foot, broadleaf sculpture stood on a patio among real palms and shrubs, looking very much at home.

"Please forgive the mess," Lin Emery said as she welcomed me into her studio. The room was filled with works in progress, some nearly finished, some in the cardboard mock-up stage. Tools of the sculptor's craft were scattered everywhere: hand implements, metalworking machines, sheets of scrap metal. This was a combination atelier and industrial machine shop.

It is difficult to describe Lin Emery without seeming to compare her with her sculptures. She was tall and slender, verging on frail. Her movements and her speech were unhurried and—like her sculptures—graceful. The idea of this gentle lady operating a welding machine or a metal lathe in goggles and asbestos gloves was incongruous to say the least. But she had been doing that for fifty years, and by the look of things in this room, she was still at it.

She took me around the studio, explaining the function of various machines and showing me several pieces she hoped to finish in time for a show in New York eight months away. "I need a deadline to finish anything," she said.

I asked her how she developed ideas.

"I sketch in three dimensions," she said. She picked up one of the glued-together paper models. "It starts with these. At each stage in the process I make adjustments. The movement of the pieces depends on an infinite number of variables: points of balance, the center of gravity of each element, and the changing flow of wind or water or whatever the driving force may be."

We were standing in front of a table that had five gleaming new sculptures on it.

"May I?" I asked.

"Yes, of course," she said.

I tapped one of them, sending its four spikelike pieces into a series of sinuous gyrations that sparkled as they caught the light. Then I tapped the others and recognized in every one of them that same beguiling, and by now familiar, silent and supple movement.

"What accounts for the silky-smooth action?" I asked.

In answer, she showed me a hand-drawn schematic of the swiveling stems that connected the rotating parts. And there it was: each stem was made of two pieces—a shaft that rotated inside a sheath that was fitted with ball bearings.

"I started to use bearings in the seventies," she said. "They reduce resistance, so the pieces glide as they rotate. When I made my first kinetic sculptures, I used the flow of water to move the pieces, then hidden motors with magnets. But with ball bearings, wind became more reliable than either water or magnets."

I gave the sculptures a few more twirls, and then we left the studio and walked through the garden to the living room for tea. A handsome collection of art and artifacts, many of them primitive carvings, was arranged around the room with care. Light poured in through large plate glass windows that framed a view of the garden.

As we spoke, Emery made a point of stressing that the context of her work had been all-important—the context being New Orleans itself.

"I could never have done any of this anywhere else," she said, "especially as a woman. New Orleans was the only place where sculpture was thought of as something for women to do. When I was starting out, living in a ground-floor apartment in the French Quarter, I set up welding equipment in my bedroom, and no one objected. On the contrary, people were very supportive and always have been.

"I had so much help from industry. This is a boat-building, ship-building city, and for a sculptor in need of special materials and expertise, that was a great advantage. I used propeller shafts for one piece. The Kaiser Aluminum plant in Chalmette provided the aluminum for a piece installed in front of City Hall. International Nickel commissioned a sculpture made with an experimental metal they were developing for use in space. It was a combination of stainless steel and nickel they called Incoloy®. When I welded it, it screamed."

I well understood, after being in New Orleans for only a short time, that artists were the princes of the city. That is, artists in the broad sense of the word: painters, sculptors, musicians, writers, actors, street performers, and—especially in New Orleans—chefs. These were the creative ones, the people New Orleans held in highest regard. And, according to the *Times-Picayune*, Lin Emery was the "queen of Crescent City artists."

The natural environment of New Orleans shaped her work as surely as her machine tools and welding rods. Though her subject might be water, clouds, or trees, the reference would more than likely be specific to New Orleans.

"One of my favorite things to do," she told me shortly before I left that day, "is to walk to the levee and watch the tops of the trees on the far side, swaying in the breeze."

A week or so later, I happened to see Lin Emery's devastating homage to Katrina. The subject was water, as it had been in others of her sculptures, but

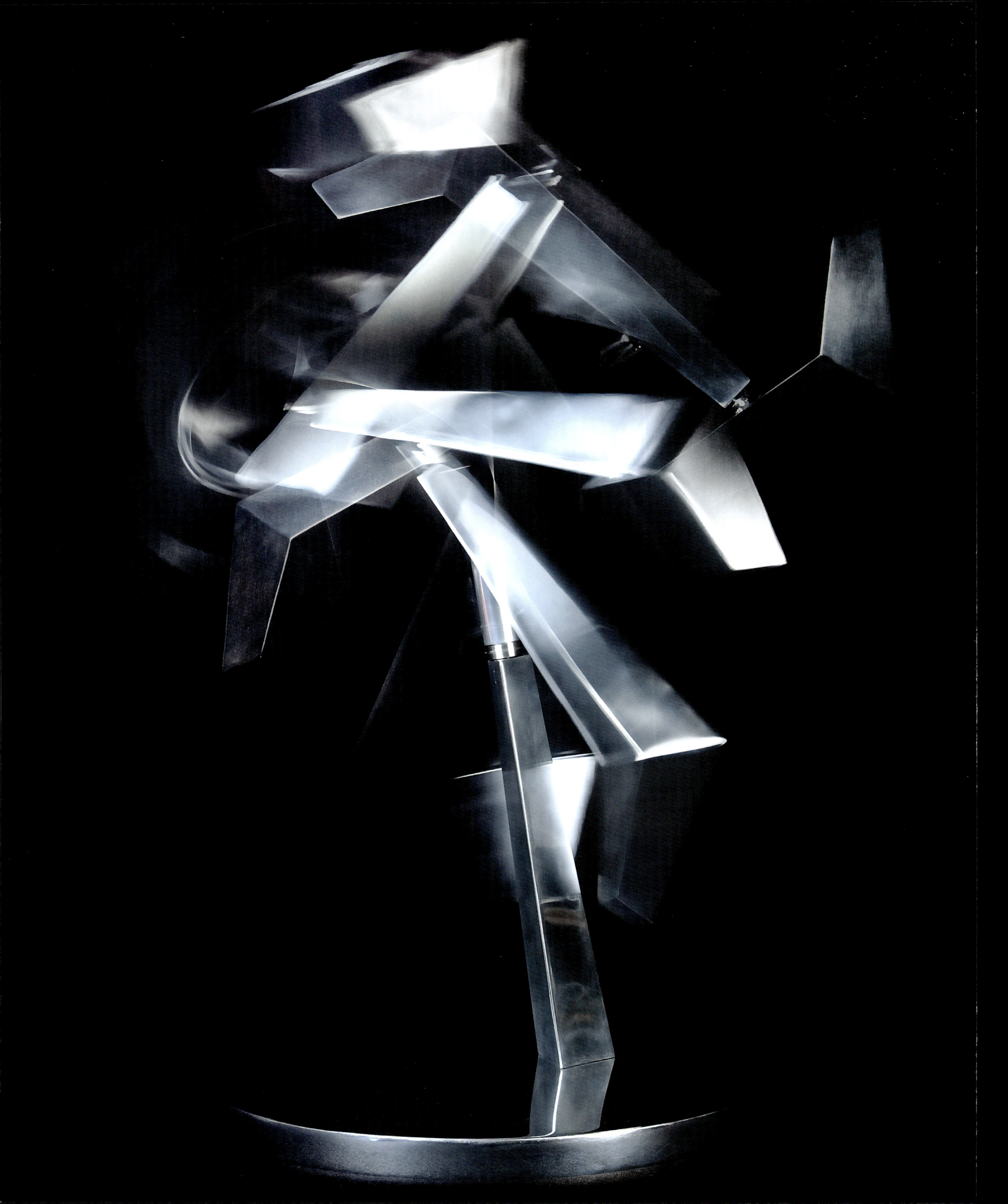

Katrina's three waves were blunt, choppy, and brutal. They bore no resemblance to the graceful, rolling ocean swells of *Wave*.

Nonetheless, I gave it a push and set it in motion, and as it dipped and pitched and swung around, I couldn't help but watch it, captivated, falling under Lin Emery's spell one more time.

JOHN BERENDT

NOTE
The remarkable movements of Lin Emery's sculptures present a serious challenge to any writer who tries to put them into words. I'm not sure I've succeeded. Fortunately, anyone who wants to watch the action can go online at arthurrogergallery.com, click on "Artists," then "Lin Emery," and watch the videos.

opposite page
Lin Emery, Acrobat *(in motion), 2001. Aluminum, 16 inches, orbit 12 inches (40.6 cm, orbit 30.5 cm). Private collection.*

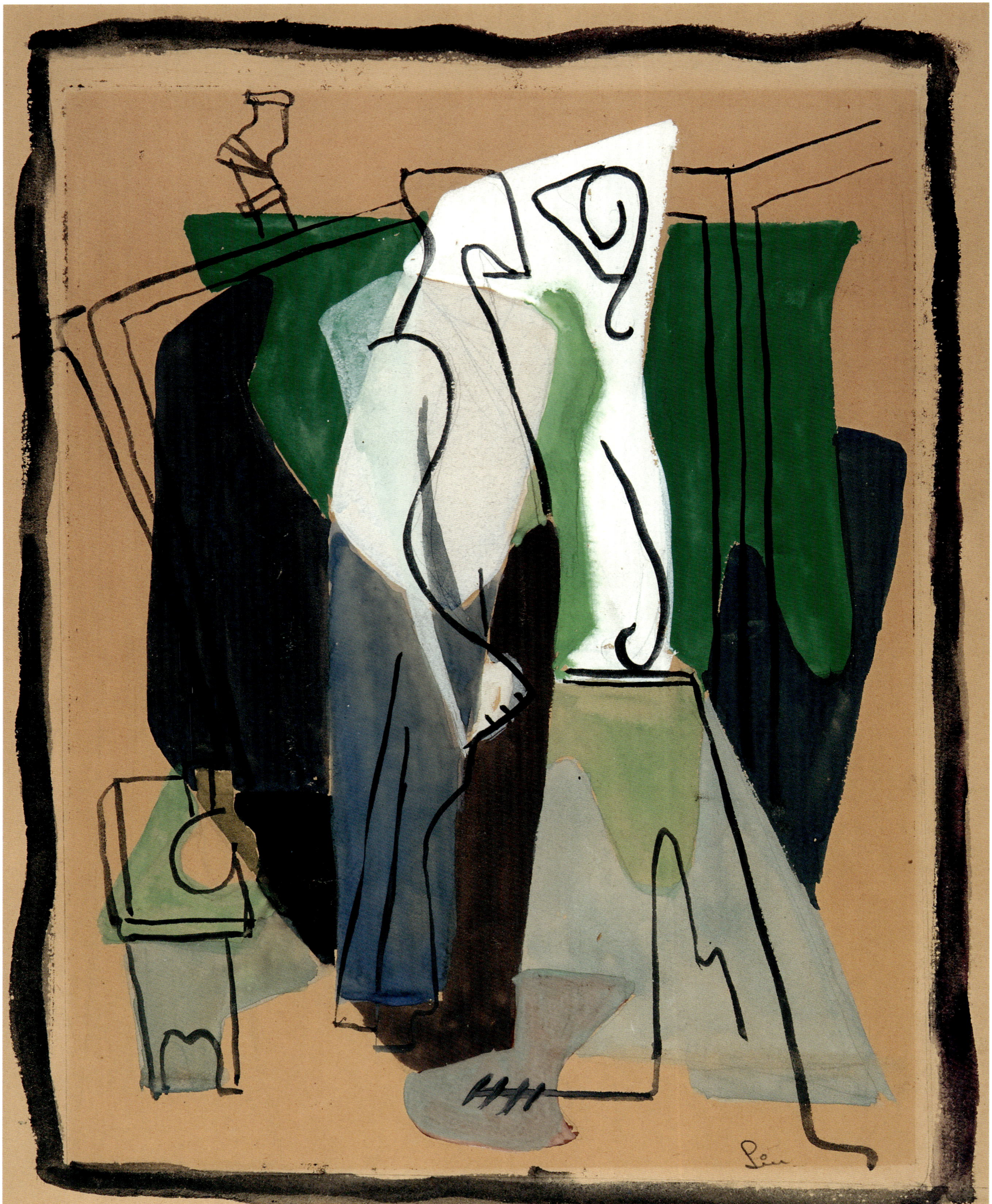

CHAPTER I

Clay: The Formative Years

Man walks in the forest of his being.

—Ossip Zadkine, as quoted by Lin Emery

The first thing Lin Emery noticed when she entered Ossip Zadkine's teaching studio on the rue de la Grande Chaumière in Paris was the seductive smell of wet clay, earthy and slick. It was 1949 and the 21-year-old Emery was living across the street at the modest Hôtel des Académies et des Arts, earning a few francs writing for a disreputable Paris paper. Although she had drawn and painted a little, as upper-class American girls do, her main interest now was writing, and her journalist boyfriend had gotten her the freelance position. Most of her articles were simply translated from *TIME* magazine, but that day she needed to get some background for an article on sculpture, and the studio across the street seemed a convenient source.

She explained to Zadkine that she wanted to learn about sculpture, which he interpreted as an interest in learning to sculpt. Emery formed a quick impression of the sculptor as a male chauvinist, and thought that he took her on as a student in part because he needed the money, but also because he saw her as the ultimate challenge: untutored, unskilled, and a woman to boot. Emery also took the situation as a challenge. The seductive perfume of clay, the young, eager students (all male), the purposeful atmosphere in the studio, and the imperious sculptor-instructor constituted an opportunity she couldn't resist. The winter session started the next day and she signed on. For some years, Emery had pursued an unusual, very personal educational path following the lead of her independent, bright, inquiring mind. In Zadkine's studio, she saw an opportunity not only to learn about something new but also to learn to *do* something new.

Lured by the smell of the clay, the feel as she kneaded it was not disappointing. Born left-handed, she was forced as a girl to write right-handed and it felt good simply to be able to work the sensuous clay ambidextrously. Emery was inquisitive and intelligent and had for years been seeking forms of stability in a highly unsettled existence. In Zadkine's studio she would find the stable, lasting interest of her life and the first foundation stones of her career.

There is a certain fittingness to the fact that Emery eventually became a kinetic sculptor, considering the erratic and unstable character of her early life. Even her given name was unsettled at first. On her birth certificate it was Leonor, the name of her father's first, adored, wife. The choice didn't sit well with Emery's mother,

opposite page
Lin Emery, Chicago Fantasy: Sculpture Studio, *1944. Poster paints on poster board, 13 x 10 inches (33 x 25.4 cm).*

who changed it to Lenore. Emery preferred a less formal name and, as soon as she could, changed it legally to Lin.

Emery remembers little of her father; he died when she was 3. Cornell Emery had set the precedent of changing names, changing his from Imre when he emigrated from Hungary at the age of 20. The son of a banker, he found business success in New York first in shipping and then as a member of the Curb Exchange (the predecessor of the American Stock Exchange). A patron of the arts, he was a significant donor to the Metropolitan Museum and decorated his comfortable house in Larchmont, New York, with paintings and sculpture. Lin's mother, Jean Weill Emery, a cousin of Kurt Weill, had been Cornell Emery's secretary, and the dispute over their daughter's name was emblematic of a troubled marriage. In the months before he died, Cornell Emery was trying to divorce his wife and arrange for a close friend to take custody of Lin and his two sons by his first wife. Lin has a vague memory of sitting in the office of a judge or a lawyer when her mother was granted custody of her and was allowed to stay in the house in Larchmont. Part of the agreement required Mrs. Emery to account for every penny spent on her daughter out of a trust set up by Lin's father.

Lin's relationship with her mother was no better than her father's had been. She now tries to understand her mother's behavior by noting the resentment she must have felt at the requirement for financial accounting. In retrospect, Emery feels that her mother must have felt love for her only child, but could not express it. Lin's early memories are of a beautiful woman who was more interested in parties than in motherhood, an "unfriendly" mother who, when she did take an interest, was severely critical. At times her criticism mounted to a terrifying rage. Jean Emery's mental instability led her stepsons to attempt, without success, to have her committed to a mental institution.

A saving stability and a powerful influence arrived in Lin's life when her mother hired Mrs. Bertha Oliver to be her governess. It is not clear why this widow from a wealthy Irish family from Galway answered Jean Emery's ad in the paper and took the job. Lin's only explanation is that she was fascinated by her mother, and found her "extraordinary." The diminutive, elegant Mrs. Oliver, who was rarely seen without her pristine white gloves, shared a bedroom with her charge, in a separate area of the house. Lin's fear of her mother produced a recurrent nightmare in which she forgot to lock the door of their living area, with undefined, but horrible consequences.

A total contrast to Lin's mother, Mrs. Oliver read avidly, was highly intelligent and socially concerned, and a staunch believer in broad culture, specifically as applied to the education of young women. In England she had been a member of the Fabian Society and had known one of its leading lights, George Bernard Shaw. Founded in 1884, the Fabians formulated and advocated the programs of a democratic socialist state in Great Britain. In contrast with the revolutionary socialism of Hegel and Marx, the Fabians espoused evolutionary socialism. Education, publications, and public debate were central to their advocacy, and well before women won the vote, the Fabian Women's Network argued for gender equality.[1]

Schools and school friends often provide stability in an otherwise unsettled life. Not so for Lin; for three months in the middle of every school year her mother would take her to Florida and place her in a different school. Mrs. Oliver did her best to round out what she considered a thin education. She arranged for Lin to study French and Latin with tutors and to take painting lessons. Later, Mrs. Oliver persuaded Lin's mother to enter Lin into the Edgewood School in Westchester, which was based on the educational theories of Rudolf Steiner. Steiner's curriculum aimed at the creation of liberated human beings who knew how to direct their own lives, and emphasized the development of the student's own innate sense of morality. This positive and intellectually generous atmosphere, and Steiner's broader philosophy, anthroposophy, would become important components of Emery's own philosophical outlook.

Lin's relationship with her mother came to a violent climax one night in 1941 when her mother flew into an exceptionally fierce rage. The child thought that her mother, foaming at the mouth, was going to kill her. At Mrs. Oliver's urging, Lin, in her underwear, fled the house and ran to the family doctor's house, two blocks away. The doctor went back to sedate Lin's mother, and Mrs. Oliver came with Lin's clothes and some money and took the child to a hotel in New York City.

At the age of 15, Lin was essentially on her own. Her one close friend and surrogate parent was Mrs. Oliver, but she felt she had to take care of Lin's mother. Emery remembers bathing in the bathrooms of Grand Central Station and spending at least one night in Central Park. Eventually, Mrs. Oliver felt free to come to New York and arranged to rent two small apartments for herself and Lin on West 10th Street. Lin signed up for the Dwight School, a selective private school on the Upper West Side, took the College Board exams, and gained the highest score ever recorded in Latin.

The restlessness that had been imposed on her as a child had become a need, and she began a peripatetic educational journey of personal discovery as advocated by Rudolf Steiner. That first summer in New York she spent time at the Public Library reading Helena Blavatsky and Annie Besant. Blavatsky, a Russian who had trained in Tibet, founded the Theosophical Society in 1875. Annie Besant, an ardent activist for women's and workers' rights, birth control, and Fabian socialism, became the head of one branch of the Theosophical Society on Blavatsky's death in 1891. Initially, Theosophy (literally "knowledge of the divine") dealt with mediumistic phenomena, but it evolved into a belief system that emphasized the universality of mankind, compassion, and codes of behavior underlying all religions. In this system, and the related philosophy of anthroposophy (literally "human wisdom"), all aspects of the universe, subatomic particles, animals, humans, planets, and galaxies are interconnected through the divine, and the seeking of unbiased truth—including through scientific research—is part of human destiny. Rudolf Steiner characterized anthroposophy as "a path of knowledge which leads the spiritual in the human being to the spiritual in the universe."[2]

Initially explored by Lin in her teenage years, this skein of nonreligious but pan-spiritual ideas, combined with elements of social concern, would be enriched over time through her studies of the Bahai faith, Zen Buddhism, and Christian Science, among others. But the foundations of her personal philosophy, which would ultimately find reflection in her art, were built during those early years.

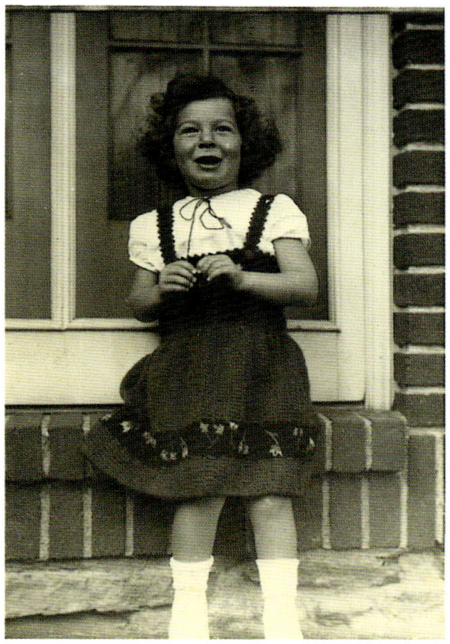

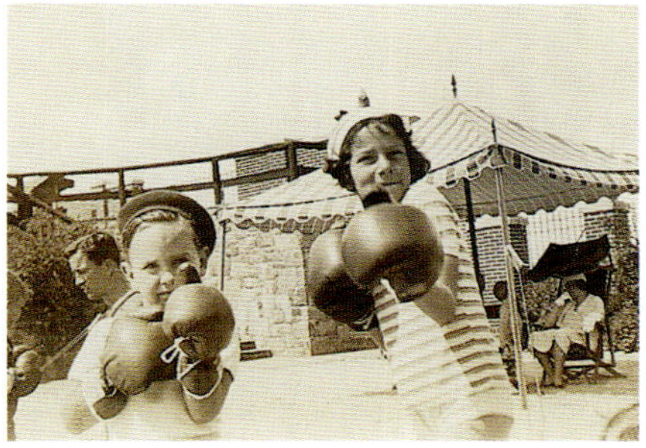

Lin, 2 years old.

Lin, 7 years old (boxing lesson with Edward Albee).

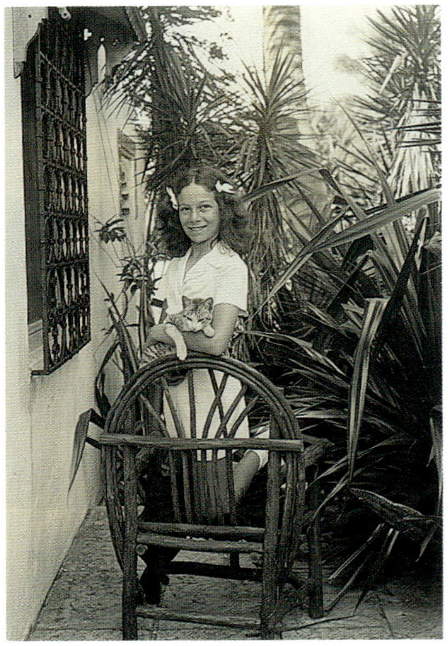

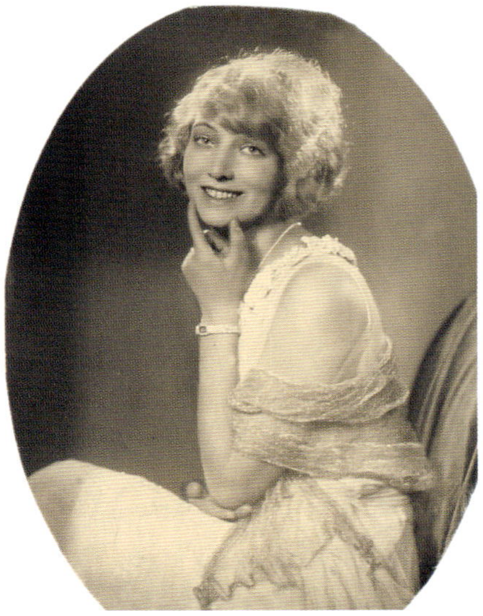

Lin, 10 years old (with cat).

Lin's mother, marriage portrait.

Despite the fact that her only diploma was from the fourth grade, Lin applied to and, based on her exceptional test scores, was accepted by Columbia University, where she entered a period of voracious, peripatetic learning. In her own words, she had a "greed to learn as much as I could about as many things as possible." At Columbia, she studied Russian and mathematics. After a semester, in part to get farther away from her mother, Emery transferred to Syracuse University, where she took courses in comparative religion, German, and social sciences. She left after one term. The unsettled pattern of Emery's early life, bouncing between houses and schools, seems to have become a deeply ingrained restlessness. By the time Lin left Syracuse, Mrs. Oliver had moved to New Orleans, and when she invited Lin to visit she contributed another major element to the structure of Emery's life: New Orleans would eventually become the principal setting for her life and career.

From New Orleans, Mrs. Oliver traveled with Lin to Mexico City, where Lin took courses at the university and signed up for Diego Rivera's school, where she lasted only one day. All the other students were boys, and Lin was chagrined to find that they spent most of the day, unguided by the master, flipping pennies. After returning from Mexico, Lin decided to move to Chicago. At that time her interests were writing and theater, and she signed up for the Goodman School of Drama (now the Theatre School at DePaul University) and entered the University of Chicago. There, she found highly sympathetic the idea-rich, cross-disciplinary Great Books program instituted by Robert Maynard Hutchins.

In keeping with the tenets of Mrs. Oliver's Fabians and Theosophy, Lin's evolving intellectual interests were complemented by social concerns. In the slums of Chicago she volunteered with an idealistic group of young people who were attempting to wean teenagers away from gangs. There she met a diversely talented divinity student, Chris Joslyn, with whom she entered into a kind of marriage of convenience. A new trustee for the trust fund set up for Lin by her father had ruled that she could not receive disbursements from the trust until she was 21, or married. The solution was obvious, but she agreed with Joslyn that their marriage would last only three years, until she was 21. In fact, she left him sooner, but continued to take care of him through his bouts of mental illness. After spending time in New Orleans with her new husband and Mrs. Oliver, Lin joined a friend to go to Paris, where, following her well-established pattern, she signed up for courses at the Sorbonne. Soon she had found her way by chance to the studio of Ossip Zadkine.

When Emery arrived at Zadkine's studio in 1949, his work was recognizable as a direct descendant of the Cubism that had flourished in Paris beginning in 1910. Starting with Picasso and Braque around 1907, and with inspiration from Cézanne and tribal sculpture, Cubism's first radical experiments were carried out on canvas. As the word *cubism* implies, however, there was a three-dimensional quality to the concept from its inception, and it wasn't long before Picasso was exploring the implications of sculptural Cubism. Picasso's 1909 *Head of a Woman* (fig. 1.1) is generally considered the first Cubist sculpture, and Ossip Zadkine arrived in Paris at about the time that Picasso was completing this seminal work. Born in Belarus in 1890, Zadkine was part Scottish through his mother, and he received much of his artis-

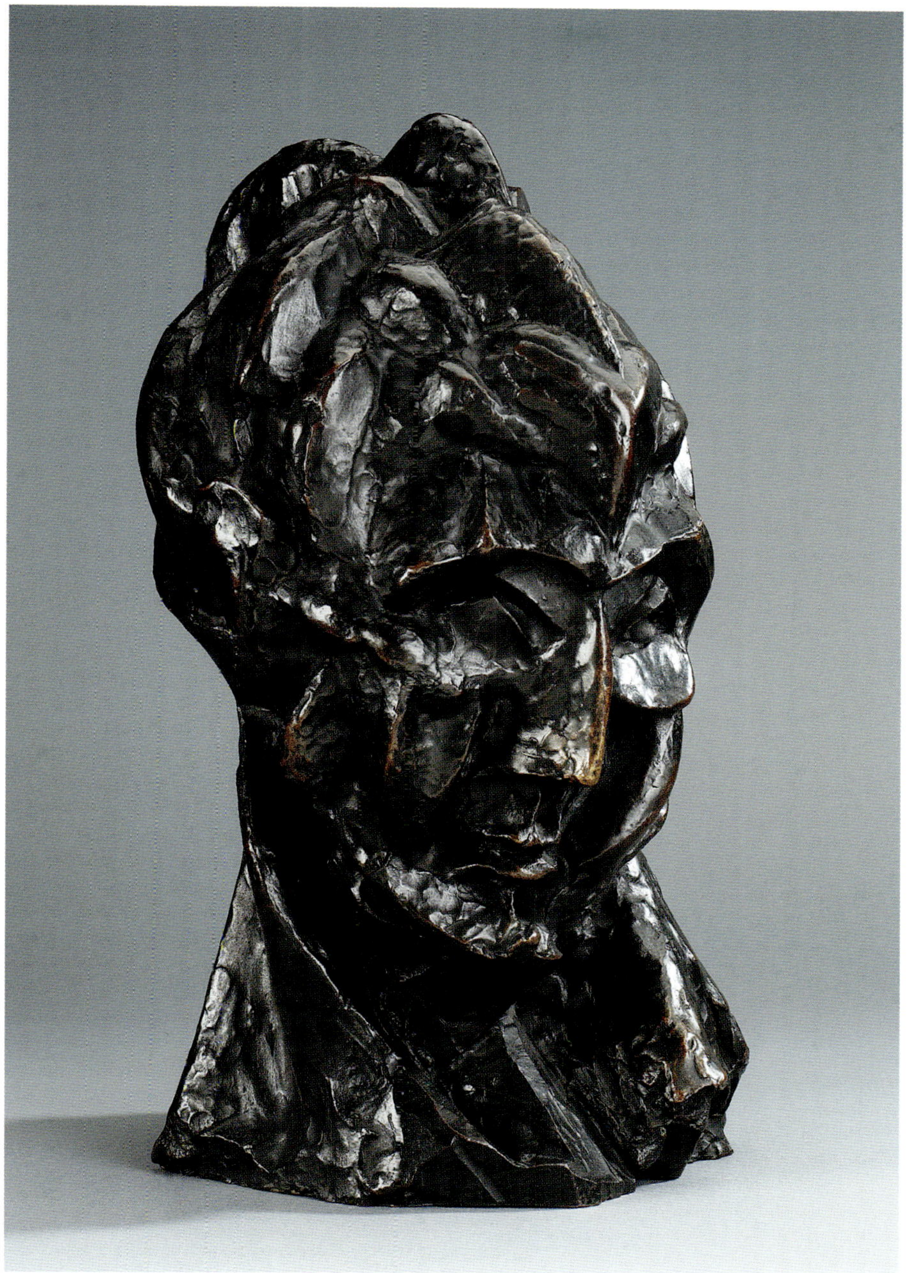

FIG. 1.1 *Pablo Picasso (Spanish, 1881–1973),* Head of a Woman (Fernande), *1909. Bronze, 16½ x 10⁵⁄₁₆ x 10½ inches (41.9 x 26.1 x 26.7 cm). Art Gallery of Ontario, Canada. Purchase, 1949. © 2011 Estate of Pablo Picasso/Artists Rights Society (ARS), New York.*

tic training in London. In Paris, Zadkine joined a cluster of Eastern European artists that included Marc Chagall, Chaim Soutine, Jacques Lipchitz, and Alexander Archipenko. The Italian artist Amedeo Modigliani was also part of this group and became a close friend of Zadkine. Along with Picasso, they all at one time or another had studios in a dilapidated building in Montparnasse called La Ruche (the "hive").

After completing his *Head of a Woman*, Picasso concentrated on painting, and when he returned to sculpture three years later, he worked in the entirely different genre of assemblage. Meanwhile, among the many sculptors exploring the territory opened up by Cubism were Henri Laurens, Raymond Duchamp-Villon, and Henri Gaudier-Brzeska.[3] Zadkine's most immediate rival was Lipchitz and, in a reliable

Ossip Zadkine (French, b. Russia, 1890–1967), Forms and Light (Mother and Child), *1918. Marble, 23⅝ x 16½ x 8 inches (60 x 41.9 x 20.3 cm); base: 2½ x 18 x 9 inches (6.4 x 45.7 x 22.9 cm). Gift of Joseph H. Hirshhorn, 1966. Photograph by Lee Stalsworth, Hirshhorn Museum and Sculpture Garden, Smithsonian Institution. © 2011 Artists Rights Society (ARS), New York/ADAGP, Paris.*

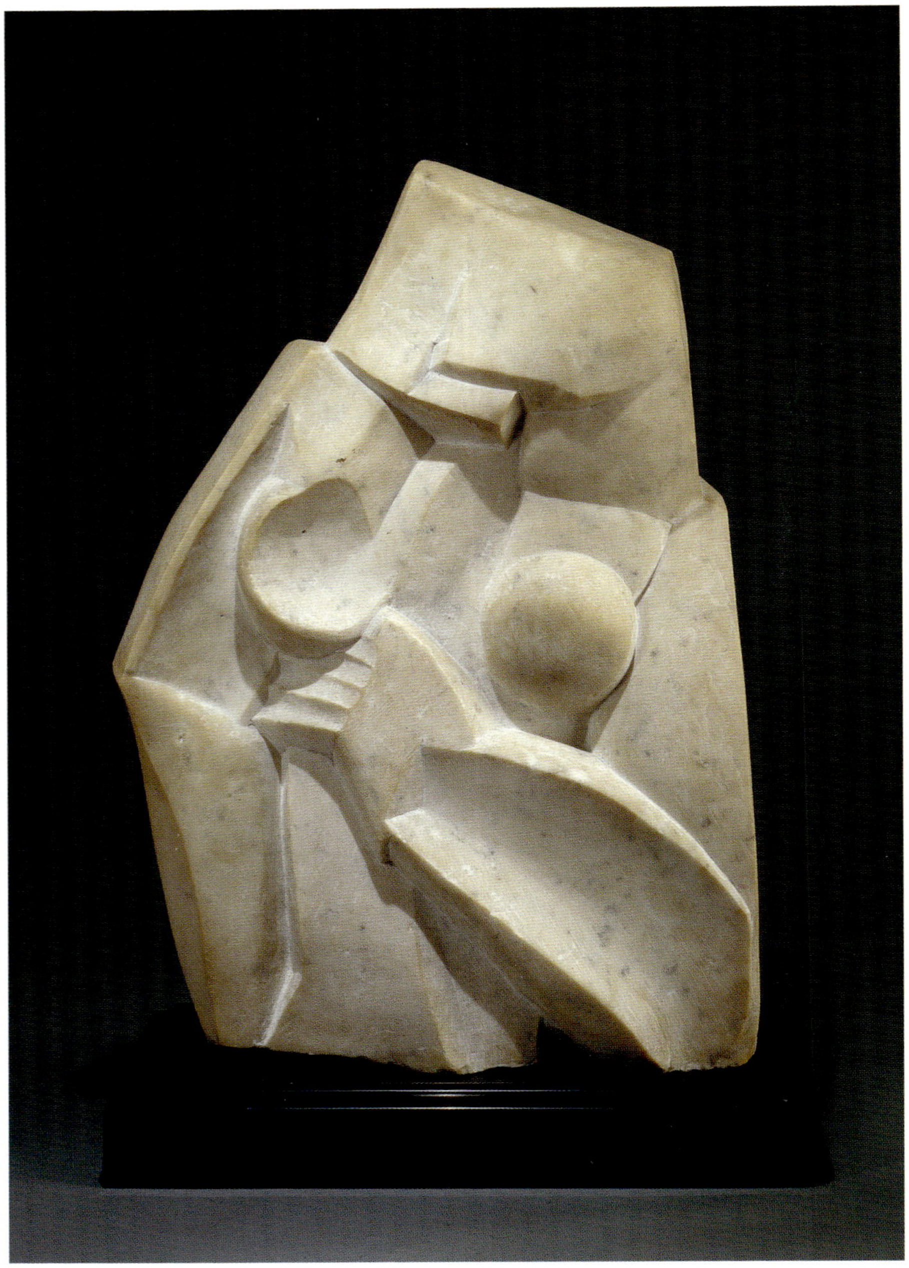

indication of artistic competitiveness, Zadkine ardently contended that Lipchitz stole his sculptural ideas. They both employed concave surfaces to represent convex shapes, but once again it was Picasso who had first used that device. A highly inventive and skilled artist, Zadkine was once considered a leader of European Cubist sculptors, but over time his star has been eclipsed by those of his peers.[4]

Every week, Zadkine's students would develop a classical, figurative work in clay from a model and, at the end of the week, take it apart, only to start over again on Monday. Outside of class time, Emery tried her hand at portrait busts. One of Carla Esser (*Carla Esser*, fig. 1.2), the friend with whom she had come to Paris, and one of a boyfriend (*Portrait of Bob*, fig. 1.3) reveal a rapidly developing skill for translating sensitive perceptions into clay.

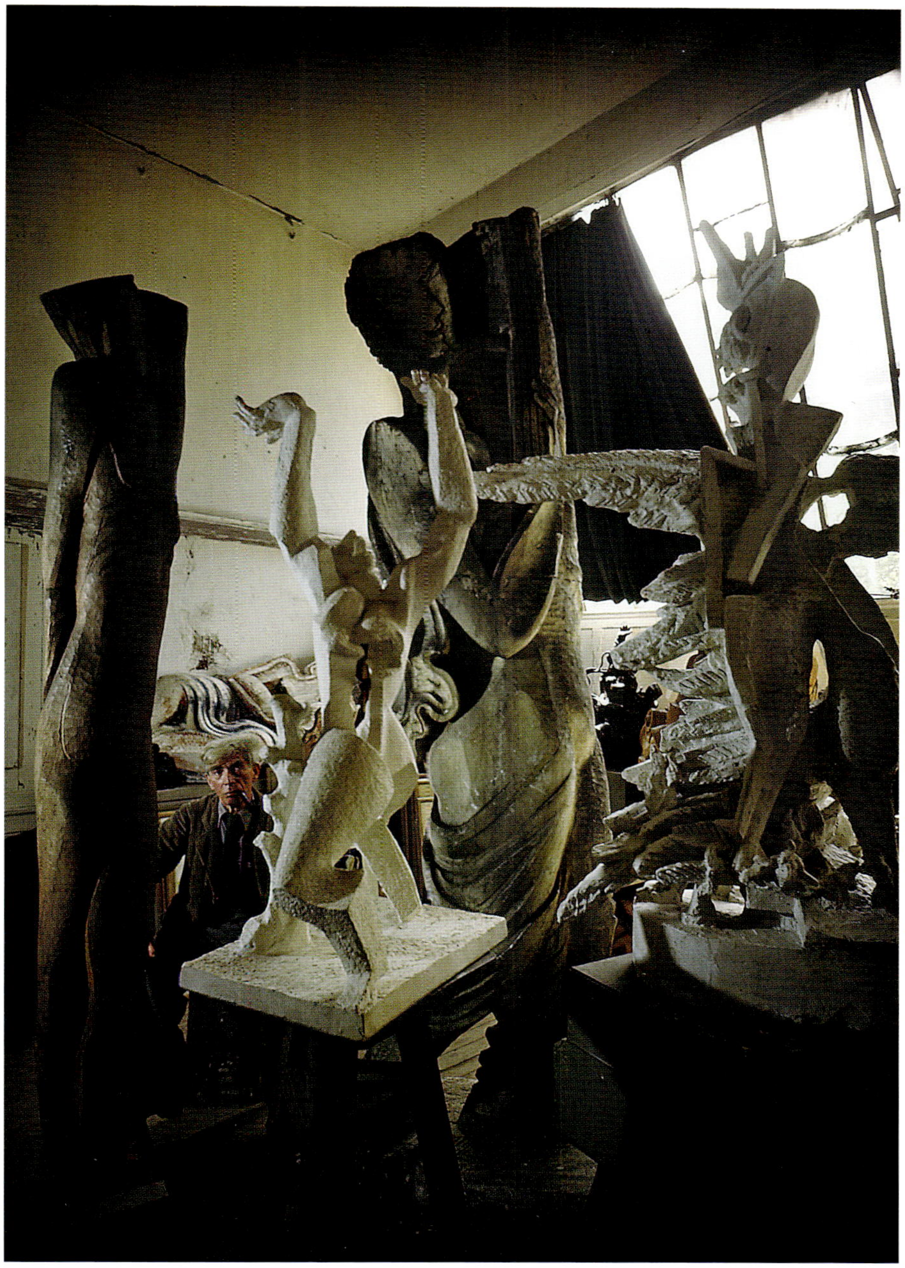

Gjon Mili (American, b. Albania, 1904–1984), Ossip Zadkine in His Studio, *1948. Photographic print on paper, 14 x 11 inches (35.6 x 27.9 cm). Gjon Mili/Time & Life Pictures/Getty Images. Zadkine Art © 2011 Artists Rights Society (ARS), New York/ADAGP, Paris.*

In his teaching, Zadkine emphasized a realism chastened by simplicity. Zadkine and other Cubists were strongly influenced by archaic and tribal sculpture, and to his students he elevated Egyptian art as the ideal. Simplicity of form was the guiding principle, and Emery and her fellow students were puzzled by the extreme difference between what he taught and the Cubist sculpture he made. Zadkine also emphasized movement, in the sense of the changing aspect of a work as a viewer moved around it, and the importance of a satisfactory composition from every angle.[5] He claimed that he—and Michelangelo—could create the illusion of the sculpture moving faster than a viewer moving around it, a reflection of a lively articulation of surface. Over time, Emery gained Zadkine's respect, which he expressed, in his paternalistic manner, by allowing her to sharpen his wood-carving tools.

FIG. 1.2 *Lin Emery,* Carla Esser, *1949. Clay, 14 x 8 x 8 inches (35.6 x 20.3 x 20.3 cm). Location unknown.*

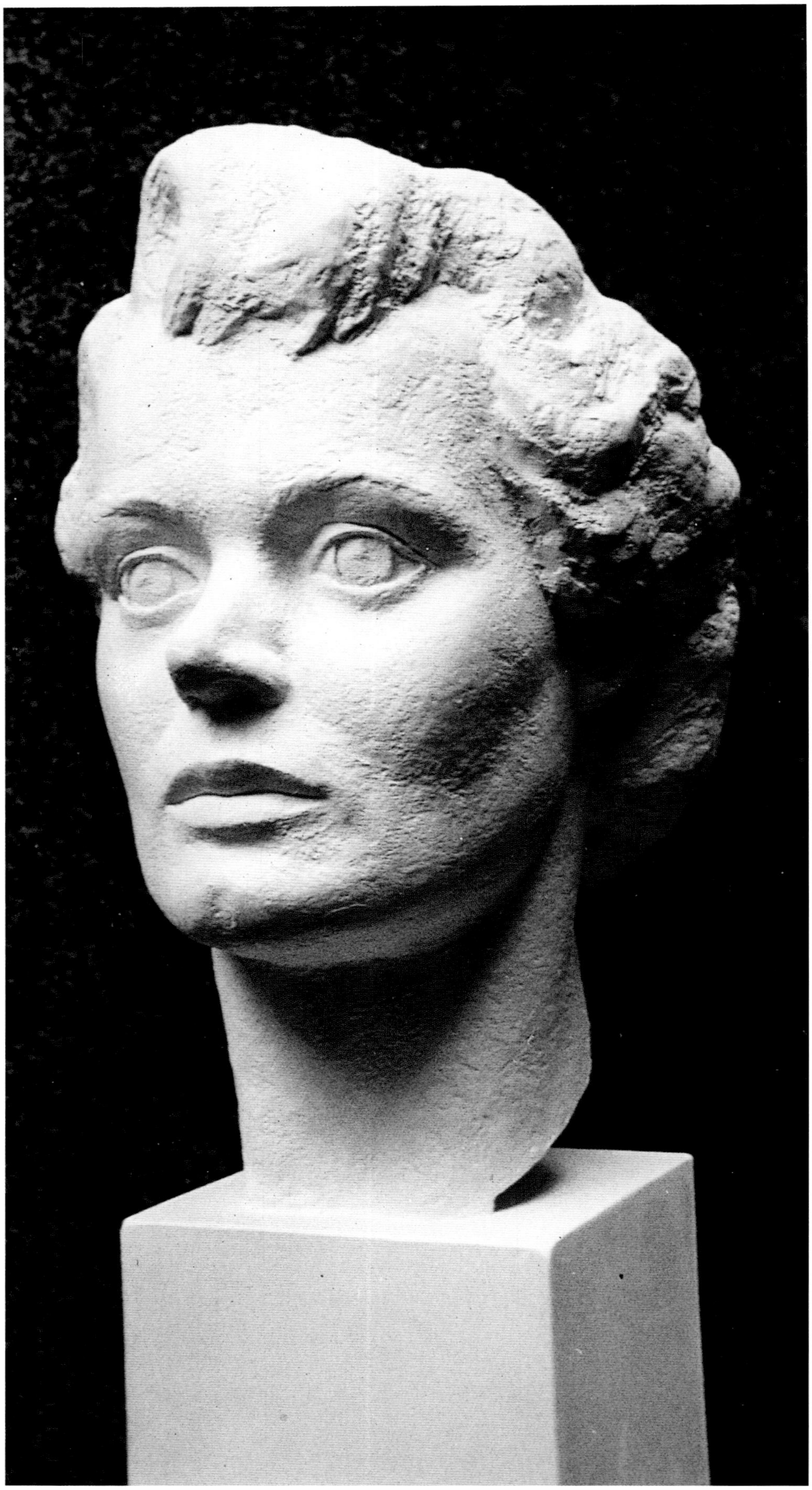

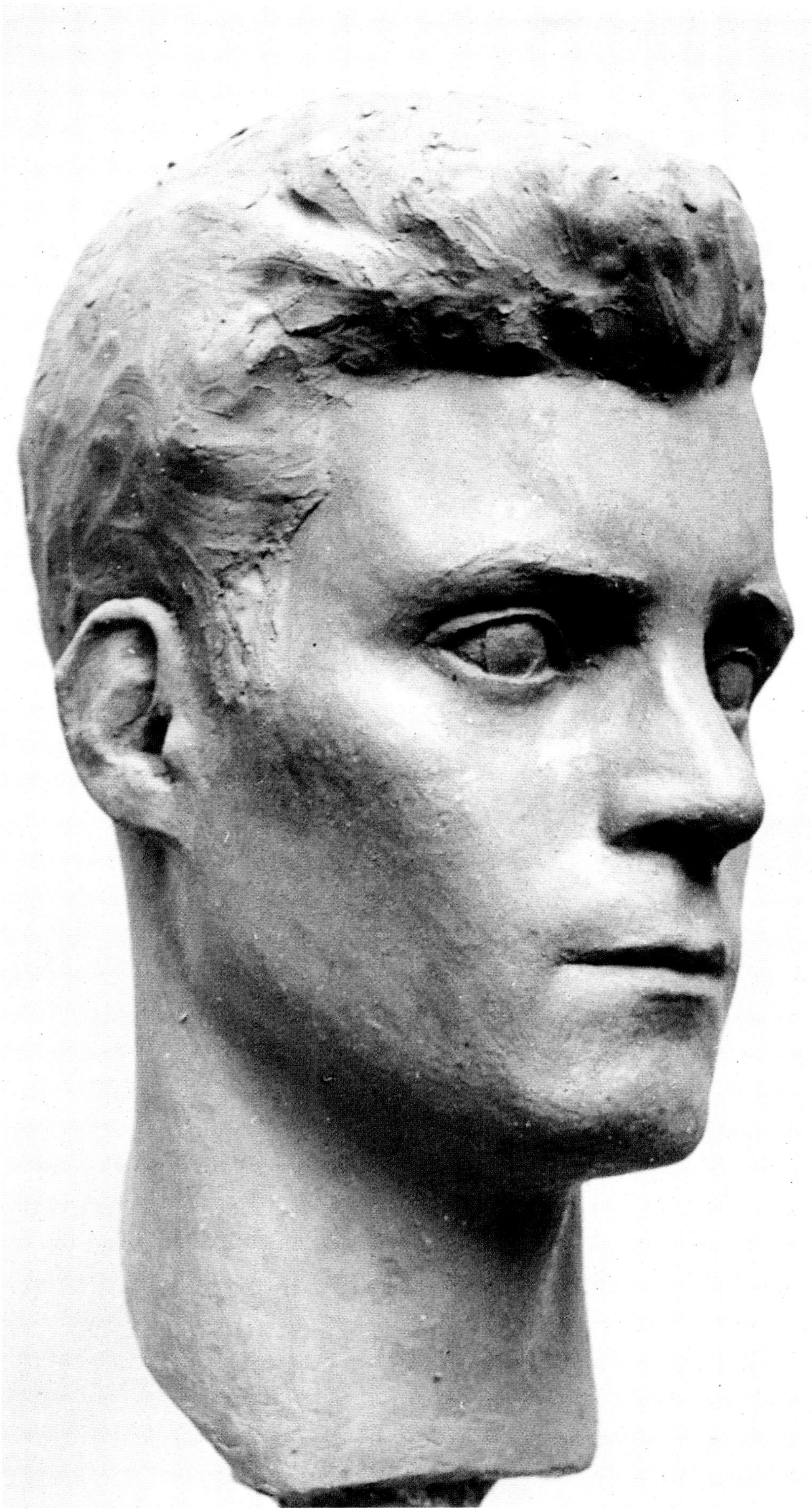

FIG. 1.3 *Lin Emery,* Portrait of Bob, *1949.*
Clay, 14 x 8 x 8 inches (35.6 x 20.3 x 20.3 cm).
Location unknown.

Although she didn't realize it, when Emery happened into Zadkine's studio, he was well known as a teacher. Two of the Americans who were there at the same time as Emery were Harold Tovish and his wife, sculptor Marianna Pineda. Tovish, who through a long career continued to explore representations of the human form, would also have a distinguished teaching career.

As Emery learned the techniques of sculpture in Zadkine's studio, her personal stylistic approach was also being formed. Zadkine's emphasis on Egyptian simplicity of form was reinforced by Emery's weekend visits to the Musée de l'Homme, whose holdings of "primitive art" had profoundly affected Picasso, Matisse, and Braque—and Zadkine himself. In this immensely diverse museum (its modest ambition was to gather in one site everything that defines the human being), Emery was particularly affected by casts of Romanesque ecclesiastical sculpture. These works from the eleventh and twelfth centuries used an economical sculptural language, bordering on the naive, to communicate a sincerity of spiritual belief. That artistic concept would later profoundly inform Emery's own work.

Emery was becoming a sculptor. No matter how satisfying, for a young woman with Emery's restless, inquiring intelligence, sculpture may also at some level have seemed limiting. That may explain the importance she attributes to meeting André Bloc in Paris and learning of the breadth of his work. Originally trained as an engineer, Bloc was also a highly successful architect, sculptor, and editor of architecture and art journals. He would later publish Emery's work in his prominent *Art d'Aujourd'hui*. With a group of like-minded artists and urbanists, in 1951 Bloc formed the Group Espace, which, in the spirit of Russian Constructivism and the Bauhaus, espoused the role of painting, sculpture, design, and architecture in social progress. Of particular interest to Emery was Bloc's "habitable sculptures," which integrated architecture and sculptural form.

Emery spent only eight months in Zadkine's studio. She describes her discovery of sculpture as being remarkably quick, but it was also convincing, with a completeness and intimation of durability very different from the earlier restless activities of her life. In Paris she had been exposed to the Cubist-derived currents of modernism as well as some the sources of modernism's urge to simplicity: Egyptian, African, and Romanesque art. And she had also seen, in André Bloc's ideas, a reassuringly broad social context for sculpture.

Soon after Zadkine closed his teaching studio for the summer of 1950, Emery left Paris for New Orleans, for a new phase of her life, but with an unusually secure sense of what the future would contain.

NOTES

1. The society continues today as the principal think tank of Britain's Labour Party. See fabians.org.uk.

2. Rudolf Steiner, *Anthroposophical Leading Thoughts: Anthroposophy as a Path of Knowledge* (London: Rudolf Steiner Press, 1998), p. 13. Originally published 1924.

3. Zadkine didn't consider himself to be a Cubist. In his view, his stylistic innovations, notably his use of concave surfaces to represent the convex, constituted advances beyond Cubism. However, Cubism was such a revolutionary innovation, its realm so large, that minor stylistic extensions couldn't be considered to move beyond it.

4. In his book *The Meaning of Modern Sculpture* (Boston: Beacon Press, 1932), R.H. Wilenski describes Zadkine as "the most agile-minded and technically adventurous figure in the whole field of European sculpture" (p. 164).

5. This is an old idea, of course, elaborated on, for example, by Leonardo da Vinci and Benvenuto Cellini, who considered that there were "more than forty" views of a sculpture that had to be graceful.

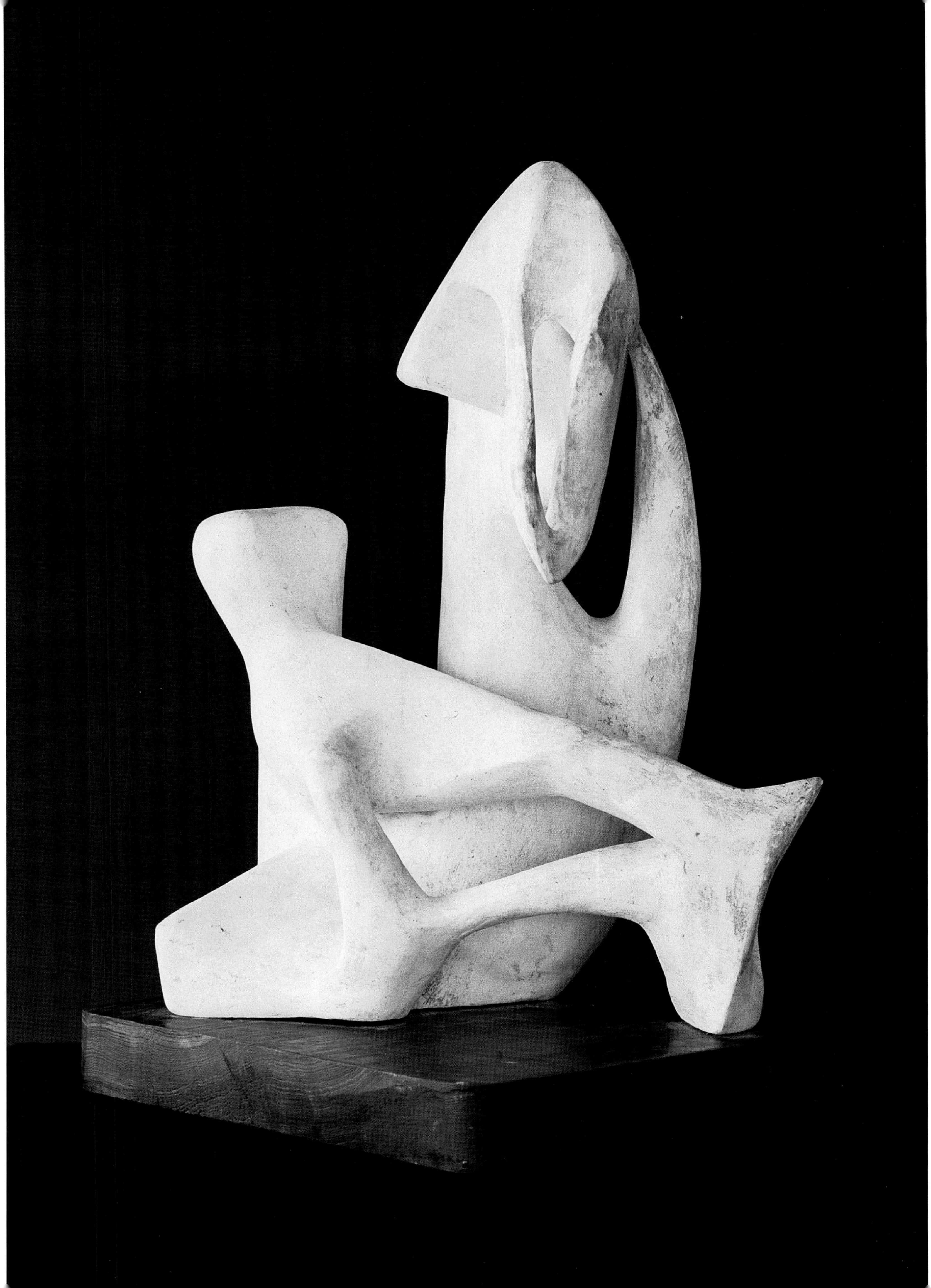

CHAPTER II

From Clay to Bronze

Develop an infallible technique, and then place yourself at the mercy of inspiration.

—Zen maxim

When Zadkine closed his teaching studio for the sacrosanct August vacation in 1950, Emery returned to New Orleans, firm in the conviction that she would become a sculptor. She found a ground-floor apartment on Barracks Street and set up her first studio there. Since Emery's only training in sculpture had been in Zadkine's studio, she had not experienced the years of student experimentation that are a sculptor's usual formative process, and she now set out to create that experience. She sought out a prominent sculptor in New Orleans at the time, Enrique Alferez, and became his studio assistant. A colorful Mexican-born veteran of Pancho Villa's army, Alferez had settled in New Orleans in 1929, and many of his Art Deco–style sculptures were sited prominently around the state. Although Alferez's muscular, Mexican-influenced work didn't match Emery's sensitivities, she responded to his love of tools and his devotion to his work, two attributes that would become her own. Emery's work in the early 1950s constitutes a restless exploration of material, technique, and style. For the most part, these early sculptures also show a surprisingly mature sculptural intelligence at work as well as an inventive bravado. Those characteristics, along with rapidly acquired technical skills, resulted in some early commercial success.

One of the earliest examples of Emery's work in this period is her 1951 *Pieta* (fig. 2.1). There were two major paths of sculptural development in the first half of the twentieth century. One originated with the Constructivists and, from the beginning, consisted of pure abstraction, with sculptures typically fabricated from industrial materials. The other path, pioneered by the post-Cubists, was forged by artists such as Constantin Brancusi, Jean Arp, Amedeo Modigliani, and, perhaps most relevant to Emery's early work, Henry Moore. These artists maintained a reference to the figure, but in some simplified, yet significant, form. In her *Pieta* and other works of the period, Emery trod firmly in that path. In simplifying its figures and eliminating the specifics of personality, Emery accomplishes two objectives: the creation of gracious abstract forms and the direct communication of the pathos of the Virgin's mourning. There are no details of clothing or facial expressions, no gestures or colors to complicate the expressive image. This artistic strategy is possible

opposite page

FIG. 2.1 *Lin Emery,* Pieta, *1951. Plaster, 15 x 12 x 8 inches (38.1 x 30.5 x 20.3 cm). Destroyed 1957. Photograph: John Kuhlman.*

FIG. 2.2 *Lin Emery,* Archangel Michael, *1952. Magnesite, 36 x 20 x 6 inches (91.4 x 50.8 x 15.2 cm). New Orleans Museum of Art, New Orleans, LA. Photograph: Owen Murphy.*

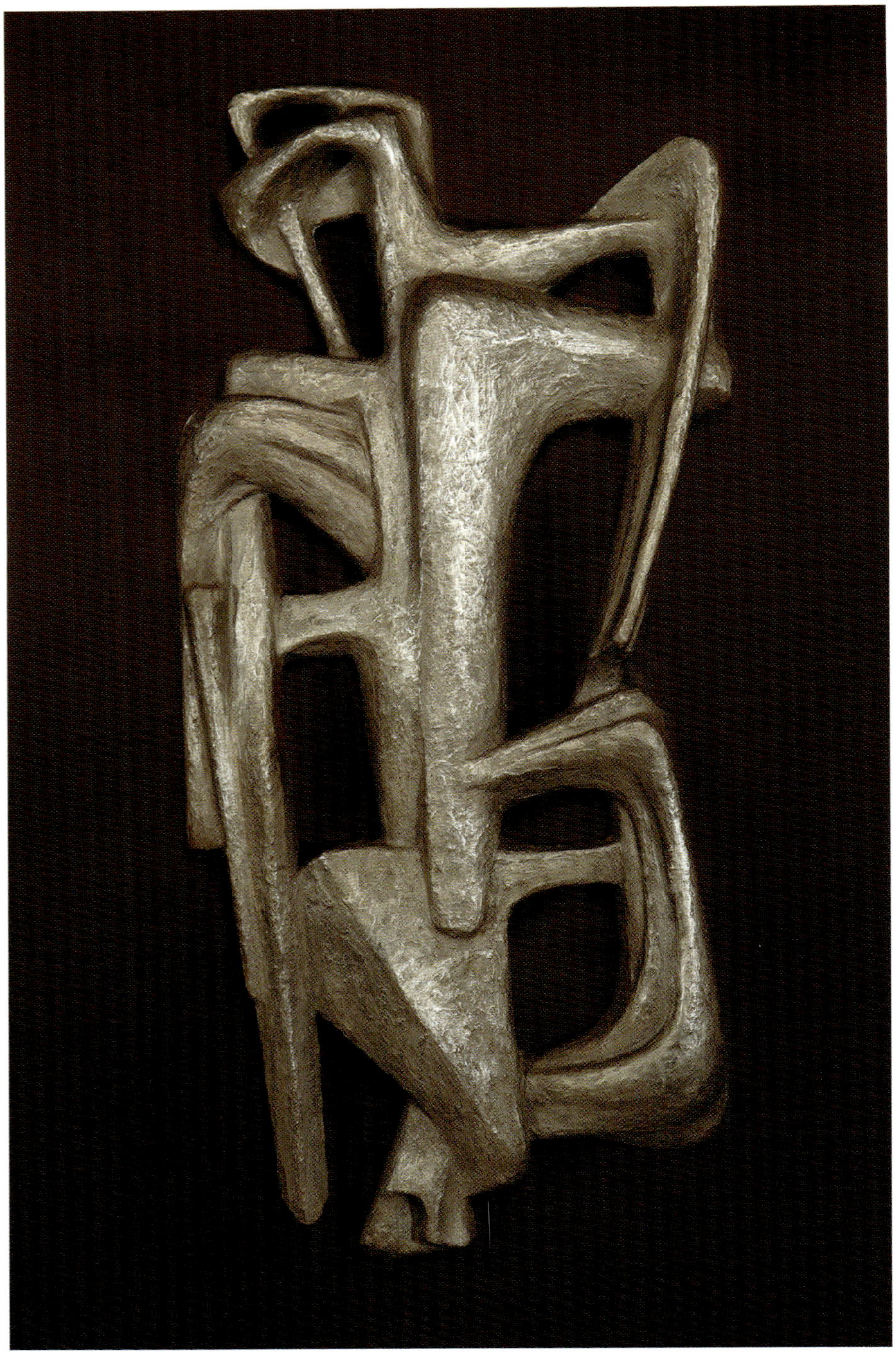

because we have seen the Pieta represented many times; we recognize the form. Emery in effect refers to our collective memory and evokes the common elements of specific images, similar forms, and emotional content.

Two other works of this period, the relief sculpture *Archangel Michael* (fig. 2.2) and *Torso* (fig. 2.3), are close in aesthetic spirit to Emery's *Pieta*. As does the earlier work, both combine a tight, self-contained compositional structure with an unambiguous representational content. The masculine strength of the *Archangel* contrasts with the seductive femininity of *Torso*. Emery may have been experimenting during this

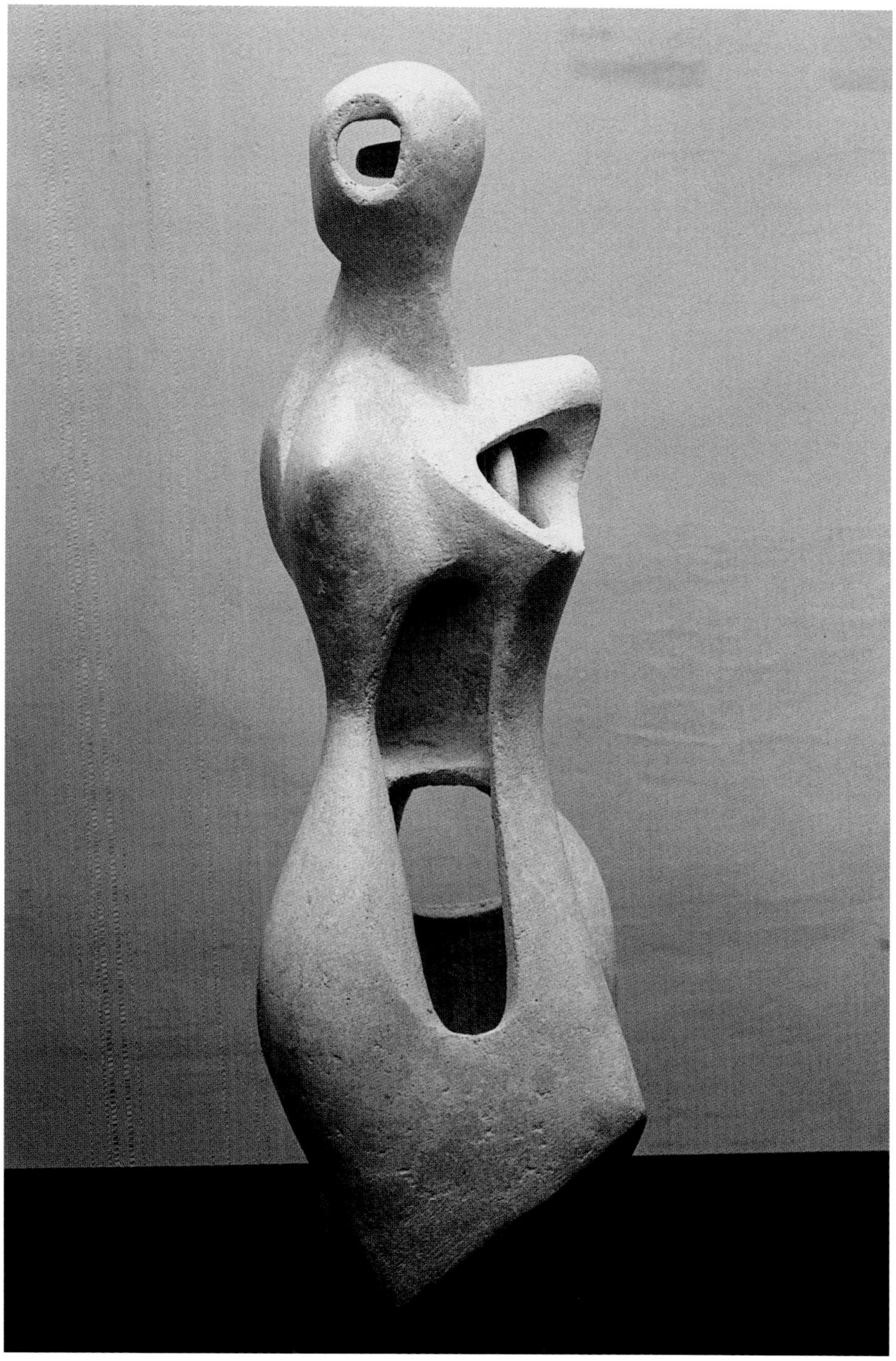

FIG. 2.3 *Lin Emery,* Torso, *1952. Magnesite and asbestos, 38 x 13 x 13 inches (96.5 x 33 x 33 cm). Private collection.*

time, but there is nothing immature or unsure about *Torso*. Any well-conceived three-dimensional sculpture invites you to move around it. *Torso* also draws you inside.

A small piece of luck can make an outsize difference to a young artist. Not long after Emery set up her studio, the architect James Lamantia just happened to see her sculpture of Archangel Michael in a show at the Delgado Museum, and just happened to be completing the design of a new church, the St. James Major Roman Catholic Church in the Gentilly area of New Orleans. He commissioned the neophyte Emery to produce seven religious figures (*St. James Major Altar*, fig. 2.4), to be

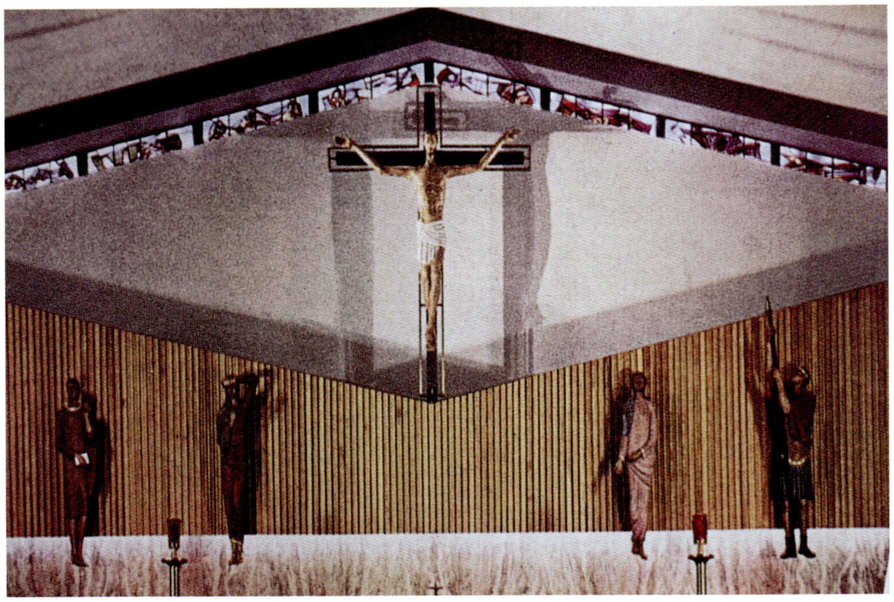

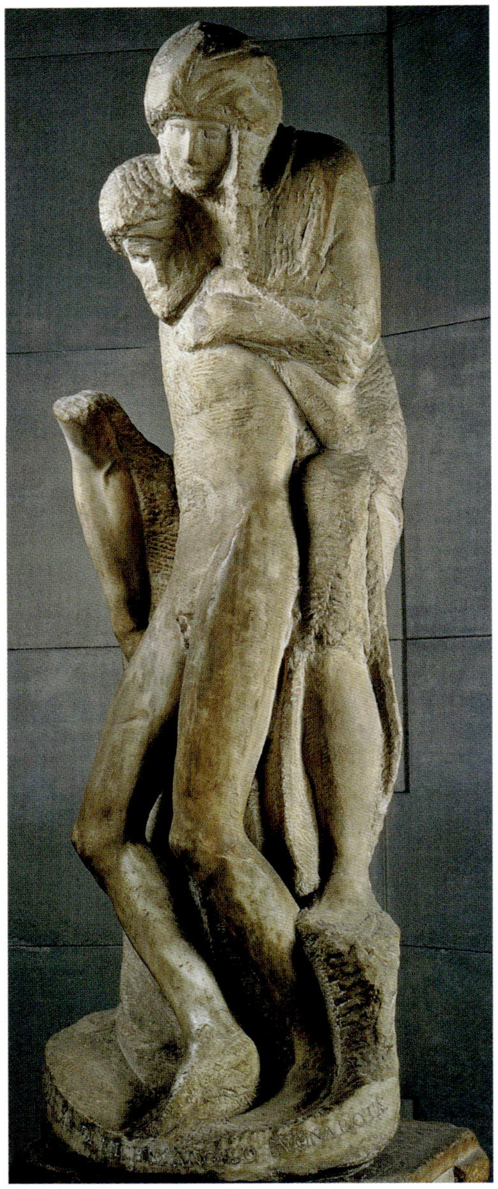

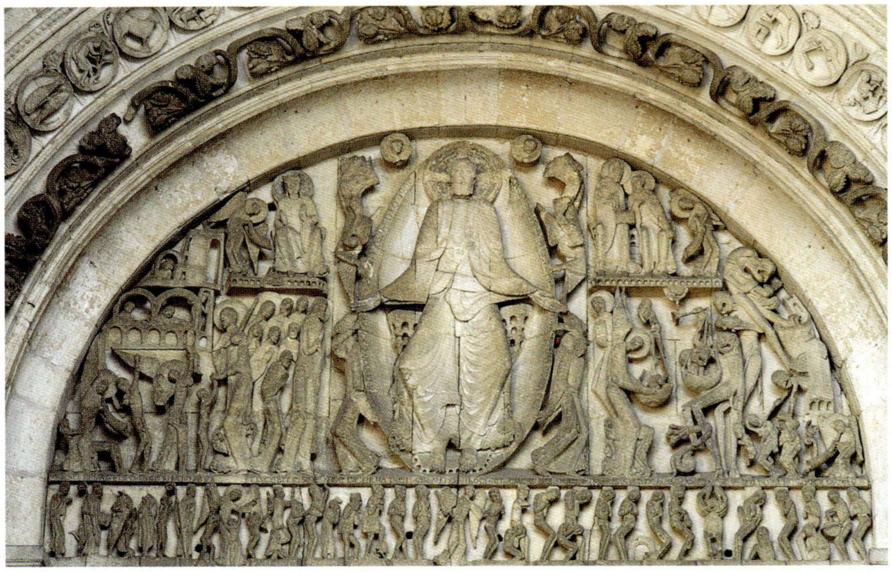

top left

FIG. 2.4 *Lin Emery,* St. James Major Altar, *1952. Wood, paint, and bronze; seven models: 34 x 6 inches (86.4 x 15.2 cm). Enlarged by Da Prato Studios in Italy. St. James Major Church, Gentilly, New Orleans, LA. Photograph: Mike Smith.*

right

Michelangelo (Italian, 1475–1564), Pietà Rondanini, *c. 1555–1564. Marble, 76 13/16 x 22 1/4 inches (195 x 56.3 cm). Sforzesco Castle, Milan, Italy. Photograph © Alinari Archives/The Image Works.*

bottom left

Gislebertus (French, active 1100–1150), The Last Judgment, *c. 1130–1135. Limestone, 11 15/16 x 20 15/16 feet (3.6 x 6.3 m). West Portal, Tympanum, Cathedral of Saint Lazare, Autun, France. Photograph © Hervé Champollion/akg-images/ The Image Works.*

placed in prominent positions in the church. In creating those works, Emery drew on her memories of the Romanesque sculpture that had impressed her in the Musée de l'Homme in Paris.

Emery consciously shied away from later Gothic or Northern Renaissance models of religious art, for she found them too violent, too bloody. The Romanesque combines an immediately affecting naïveté with a confident serenity. In her attraction to the Romanesque, Emery was responding to an artistic expression at the center of the modern movement. The power of the Romanesque stems from its eloquent simplicity. The lack of elaboration expresses a kind of honesty in the maker and in the making. In this kind of sculpture the meaning is beneath the surface. To Romanesque simplicity, Emery added her own stylistic element: a suave attenuation of form. In *Corpus* (fig. 2.5), the overlapping of the feet, characteristic of the Gothic rather than the Romanesque, accentuates the verticality of the figure.

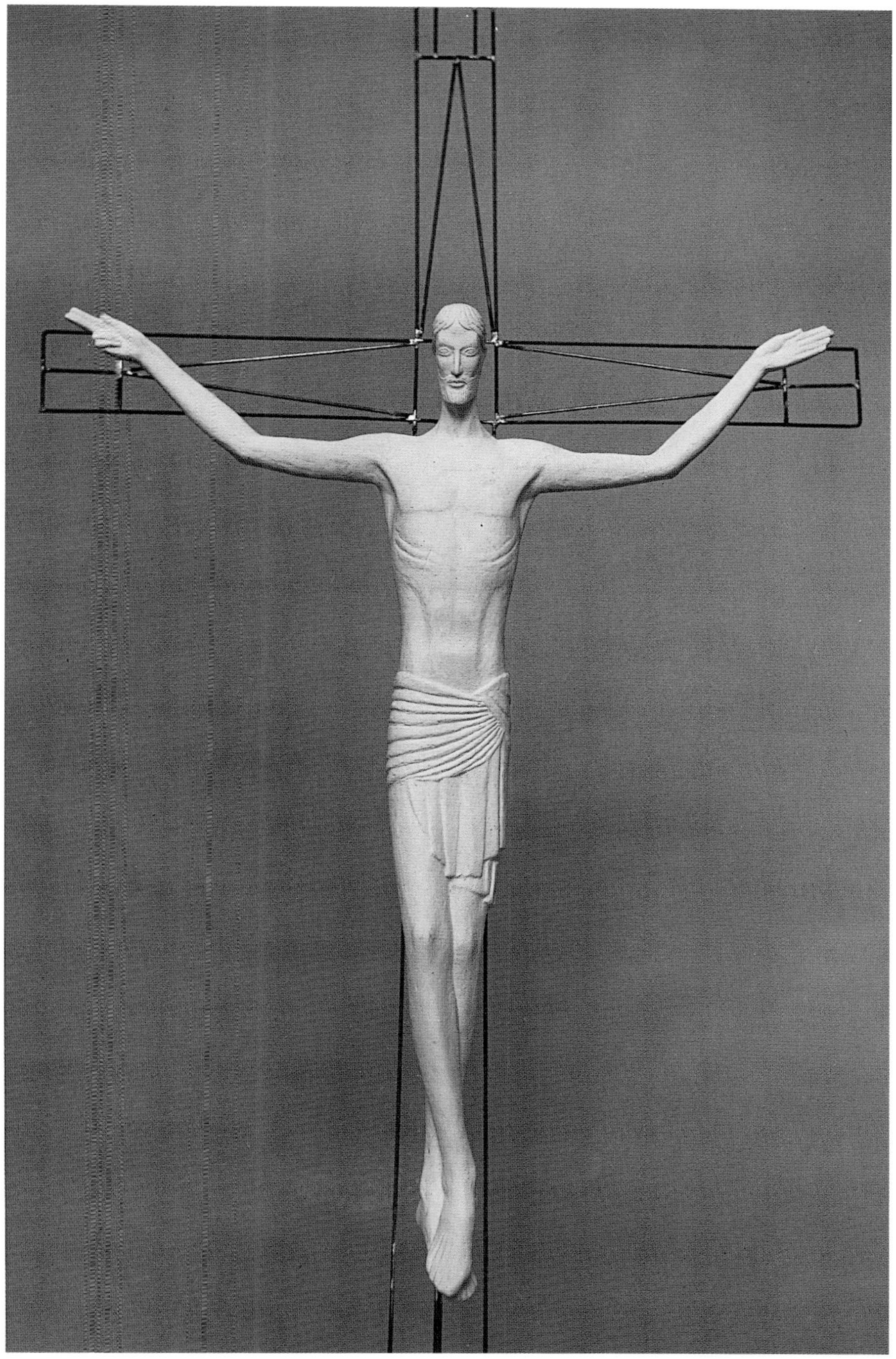

FIG. 2.5 *Lin Emery,* Corpus, *1961. Hydrocal and bronze, 33½ x 28 x 10 inches (85.1 x 71.1 x 25.4 cm). St. Philip Neri Church, Metairie, LA.*

The drapery is a matter of formal delight, rather than representational accuracy. In a radical transformation of iconography, Emery's Christ ascends and blesses rather than hanging from the cross.

Although Emery may have projected some of her own tall elegance into these religious sculptures, a deeper concept is at work here. Tallness is widely associated with status.[1] Whether conscious or not, there is also something spiritual about an elongated figure, perhaps because it bespeaks the ascetic and transcendent. Near the end of his life, Michelangelo became increasingly religious. During his last days, in 1564, he was working on a Pieta whose extraordinary ethereal quality owes much

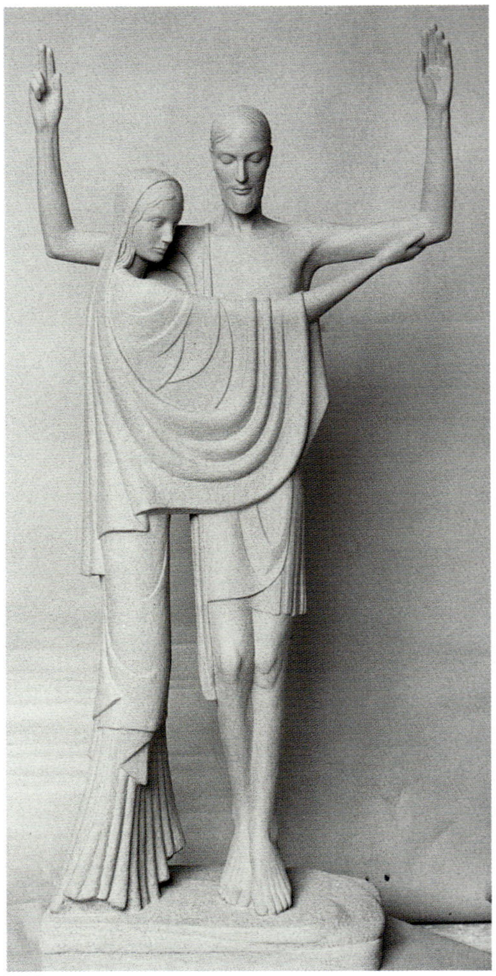

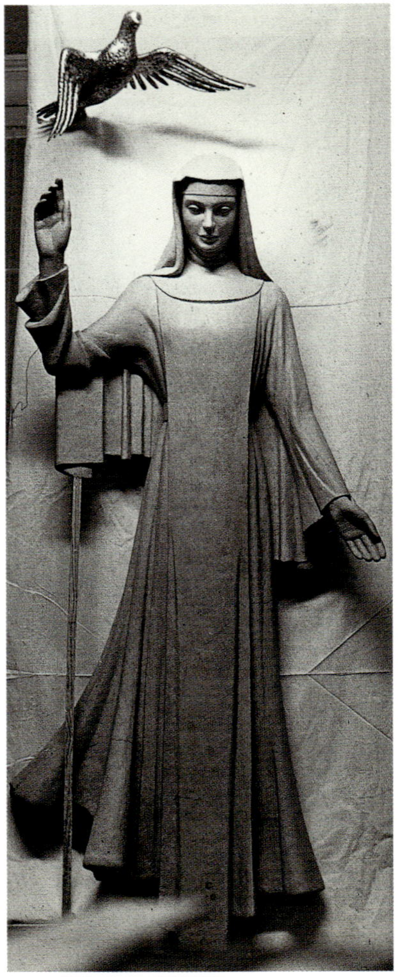

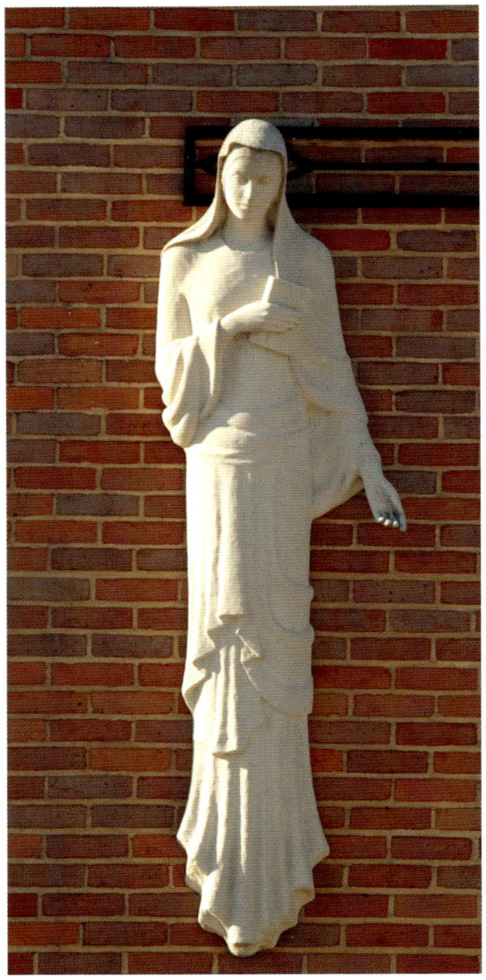

Lin Emery, Holy Cross Pieta, *1955. Cast stone, 80 x 50 x 20 inches (203.2 x 127 x 50.8 cm). Holy Cross High School, New Orleans, LA. Photograph: Myles De Russy.*

FIG. 2.6 *Lin Emery,* St. Scholastica, *1956. Cast stone and bronze, 90 x 30 x 15 inches (228.6 x 76.2 x 38.1 cm). St. Scholastica Academy, Covington, LA. Photograph: Jeremiah Russell.*

FIG. 2.7 *Lin Emery,* St. Gertrude, *1959. Cast stone, 72 x 30 x 15 inches (182.9 x 76.2 x 38.1 cm). St. Gertrude Catholic Church, Des Allemands, LA. Photograph: Frank Lotz Miller.*

to its elongated proportions (in contrast to the pyramidal version of 1499). Part of the modern agenda is to alter the form of things, not arbitrarily, but for communicative effect. Simplification is perhaps the dominant strategy, but exaggeration is close behind. In 1931, Picasso explored multiple forms of sculptural exaggeration in portraying his mistress, Marie-Thérèse Walter, including radical elongation in sculptures carved from pieces of wood stretcher.[2] His inspiration may have been the extremely attenuated Etruscan figures said to represent the lengthened shadows of late afternoon that also inspired Giacometti.

The publicity that surrounded Emery's work for the St. James Major church led to other figurative church commissions, including its namesake saint for St. Scholastica Academy in Covington, Louisiana (*St. Scholastica,* fig. 2.6), St. Gertrude for a church in Des Allemands, Louisiana (*St. Gertrude*, fig. 2.7). In 1955, Emery and her first New Orleans mentor, Enrique Alferez, were approached by the Father Judge Mission Seminary to carry out important elements for their church in Monroe, Virginia. For the seminary church, Emery was to create the baldachino, a metal canopy over the altar (*Baldachino*, fig. 2.8), and Alferez was to produce fourteen relief sculptures of the Stations of the Cross. When the priest in charge came to Emery's studio to see models of their proposed work, Alferez, who enjoyed being

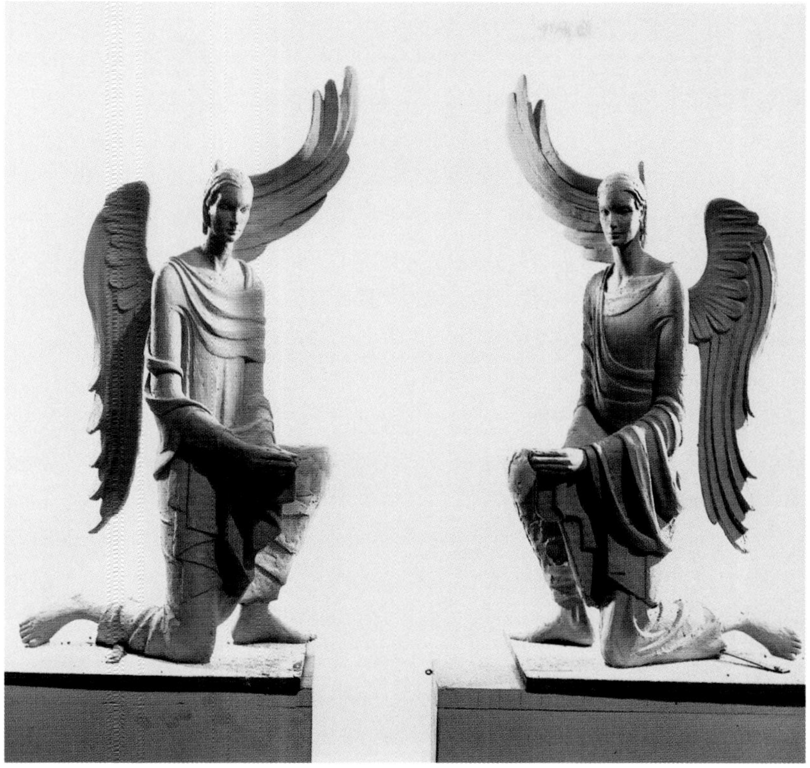

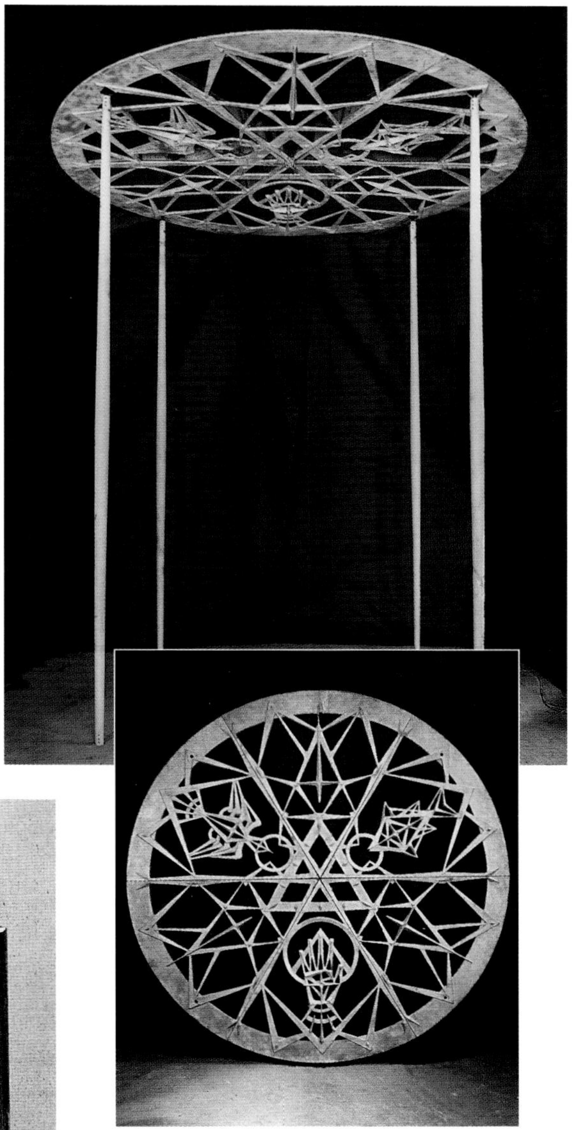

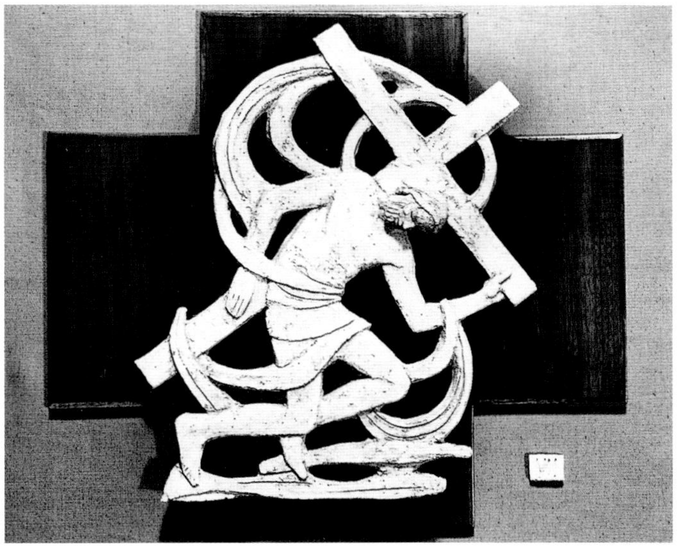

top left

Lin Emery, Tabernacle Angels, *1958. Cast bronze, 33 x 16 x 15 inches (83.8 x 40.6 x 38.1 cm). St. Catherine of Siena Church, Metairie, LA.*

top right

FIG. 2.8 *Lin Emery,* Baldachino, *1961. Gold-leafed aluminum, 15 x 11 x 11 feet (4.5 x 3.3 x 3.3 m). Father Judge Mission Seminary, Monroe, VA. Photograph: Stuart Lynn.*

bottom

FIG. 2.9 *Lin Emery,* Stations of the Cross, *1961. Terra-cotta, each 16 x 16 x 2 inches (40.6 x 40.6 x 5 cm). Father Judge Mission Seminary, Monroe, VA.*

outrageous, made the mistake of referring to the Stations of the Cross, representing Christ's progression to Calvary, as a comic strip. Given the role of early religious art in preliterate societies, the analogy was quite apt, but the priest was not amused. Alferez was dismissed on the spot and the entire commission given to Emery (*Stations of the Cross*, fig. 2.9).

Emery's religious figures of the 1950s constituted an isolated period of her sculptural career. While they would not be repeated, these works provide a revealing insight into the sculptor's artistic inclinations, which emphasize simplified and expressive forms whose meaning is internal. Those characteristics would appear decades later in quite a different guise.

The New York Sculpture Center

When Emery returned to New Orleans from Paris, organized her studio, and began to sculpt intensively, her abiding interest in learning was augmented by an acutely felt need to acquire the techniques of her art. She received what turned out to be a suggestion of great consequence from an unexpected source. Emery's mother had heard of her marriage in Chicago to Chris Joslyn and because of either that or other events in Mrs. Emery's life, her attitude toward her daughter changed abruptly, from cold to warm, from uninterested to caring. It was she who, perhaps in a gesture of reconciliation, suggested in 1951 that Emery consider attending the Sculpture Center in New York.

Founded as the Clay Club in 1928 by sculptor Dorothea Denslow, the Sculpture Center played an important role in the mid-twentieth century by training young sculptors and introducing the American public to modern sculpture. This was particularly the case after World War II as American art was in the ascendant. For Emery, the center was the most fertile of fields both to learn techniques and to exhibit her work. There was an inverted class structure at the center. The serious sculpture students looked down on the society women who were learning to model clay, but it was they who subsidized the typically impoverished students and, in difficult financial times, kept the center afloat. One of those women was Lizette Sarnoff, the wife of radio and television pioneer and founder of NBC, David Sarnoff.

There was no art school bohemianism allowed at Denslow's center. Louise Nevelson was there, working in terra-cotta and marble at the same time as Emery, and was repeatedly reprimanded by Denslow for wearing low-cut and revealing blouses. The sculptor Barbara Lekberg was also a student at the Sculpture Center in the early 1950s. She recently recalled her early impression of Emery as "very elegant in every way, in everything she did. She was very composed. Things were always difficult for me, but they always seemed easy for Lin. I was very unsure of myself but she never seemed to be. She was in a different sphere; I envied her."[3] Emery's recollections of her feelings in those years tell a different story. When Dorothea Denslow invited her "adopted" students to go out for Dutch-treat dinners, Emery would feel ill with panicked insecurity. Her early school experience, bouncing between two elementary schools, and having no normal teenage years stole from her the opportunities for early socialization. Despite outward appearances, it took her years to feel comfortable in social circumstances.

The first floor of the Sculpture Center was devoted to exhibition space, and the second floor to clay, ceramics, and stone carving. When a student such as Emery was recognized as being serious she was allowed upstairs to the third floor to learn to weld and cast metal. When Emery climbed those stairs and came under the tutelage of Sahl Swarz, it was an event as important to her evolution as a sculptor as when she walked into Ossip Zadkine's studio. Rather than the seductive smell of clay, here it was the light and heat of the oxyacetylene flame and the transformative power of the welding torch that excited the young sculptor.

Emery's first objective in learning to weld was to create armatures for her religious sculptures. Once a clay sculpture grew beyond a foot or so in height, it required an armature, a metal skeleton to give it structural strength. Welding

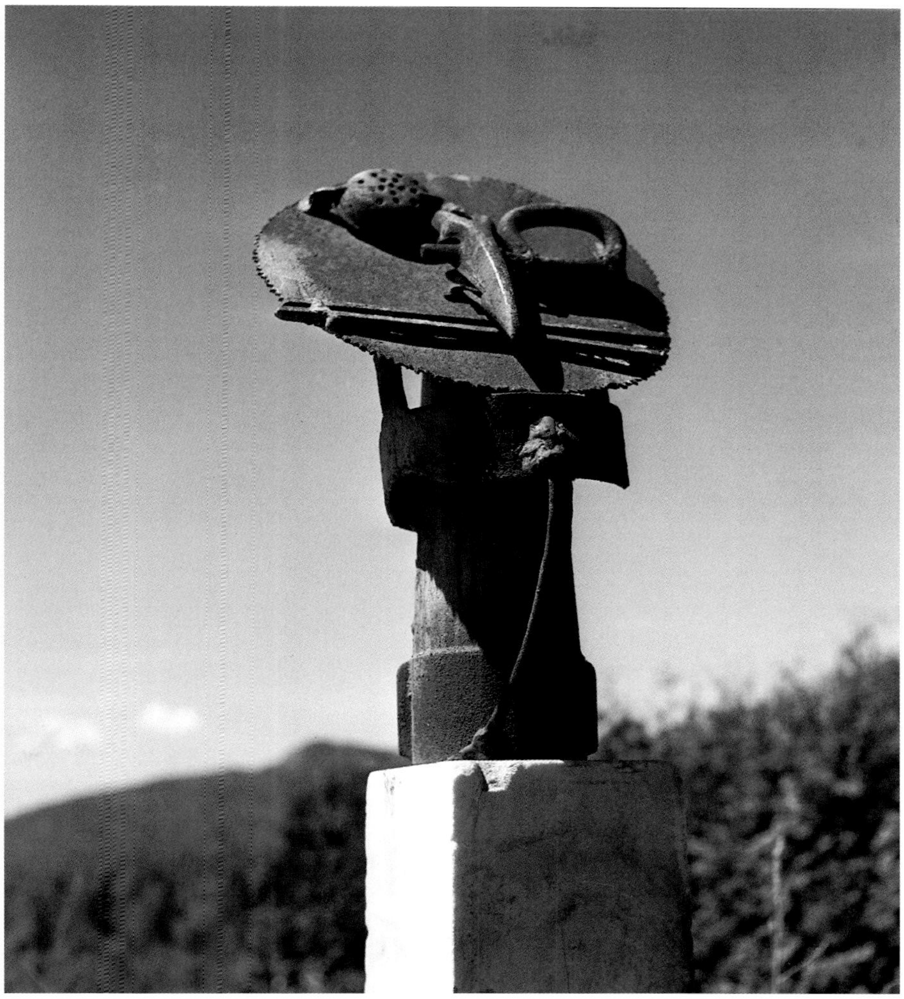

David Smith (American, 1906–1965), Saw Head, *1933. Iron and bronze, painted, 18½ x 12 x 8¼6 inches (47 x 30.5 x 21 cm). The Estate of David Smith, on extended loan to Tate Modern, London. Photograph taken by David Smith at Bolton Landing, NY. Art © Estate of David Smith/Licensed by VAGA, New York, NY.*

became the means of creating not only the armatures for her religious work but also the crosses behind *Corpus* and *St. Gertrude*, and the dove that accompanies *St. Scholastica*.

For Emery, metal rapidly became much more than the stuff of armatures. Cast metal, particularly bronze, has been a valued medium for sculpture across civilizations and centuries. Metal was also the material with which modernist sculptors revolutionized the art, but rather than casting valuable metals, they used the industrial techniques of welding to construct sculptures out of common metals such as steel, aluminum, and copper.

It was Picasso who, in 1931, after being taught to weld by his fellow Spaniard Julio González, set welded sculpture on its storied course. Two years later, David Smith, then primarily a painter and commercial artist, saw photographs of Picasso's work and set out to establish welding as a central path of American sculpture in the twentieth century. (Dorothy Dehner, a painter and sculptor, was married to Smith between 1927 and 1952. When she moved to New York after her divorce, she worked at the Sculpture Center along with Emery.) By the time Emery learned to weld in 1952, a rich tradition of abstract American metal sculpture had been established.[4]

The form of welding taught at the Sculpture Center was invented in 1895 by Henri Le Chatelier and involved the controlled burning of acetylene and oxygen in a metal-tipped torch. To achieve higher temperatures, another form of welding, also developed in the nineteenth century, created an electric arc between a metal rod and the metal to be joined. Emery attempted to learn electric arc welding in New Orleans, but the welding school there refused to accept a woman. She persuaded a trade school in New York to accept her, but was looked on with suspicion by her fellow students, who were convinced she was a social worker or a spy from a government agency.

While Emery's early welded works created in bronze and steel at the Sculpture Center were primarily abstract, they generally had strong references to the figure, as suggested by their titles. A piece such as *Icarus* (fig. 2.10) shares an attenuated elegance with her religious sculptures.

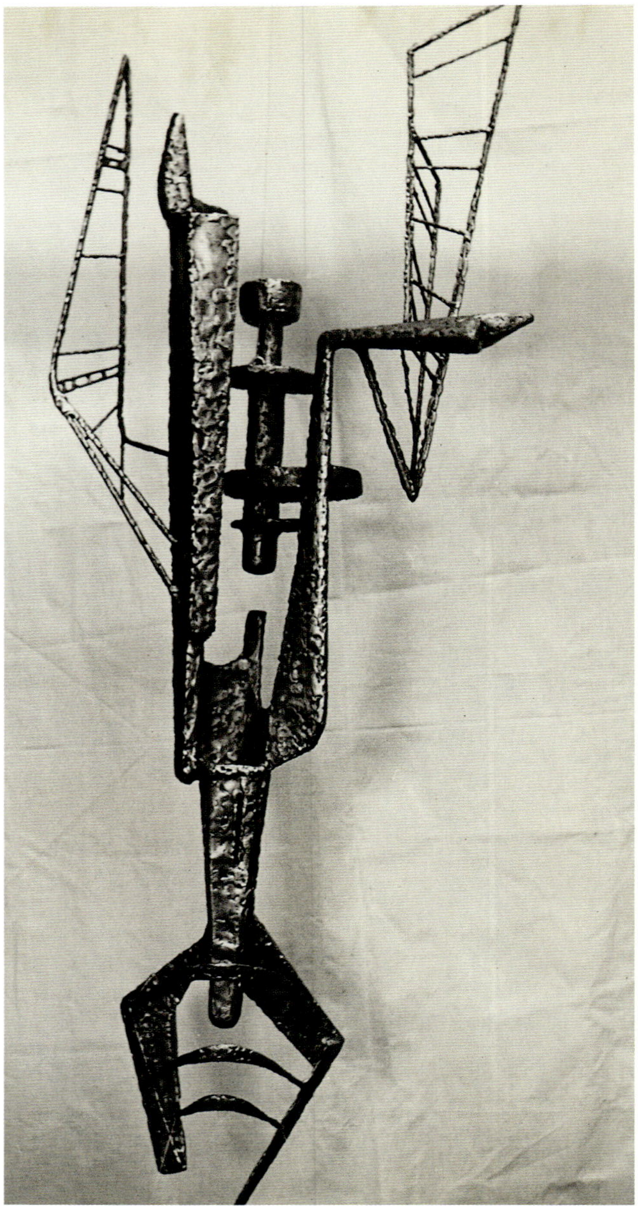

FIG. 2.10 *Lin Emery,* Icarus, *1954. Welded bronze, 48 x 10 x 12 inches (121.9 x 25.4 x 30.5 cm). Collection of Mrs. Robert Reisfeld, New Orleans, LA.*

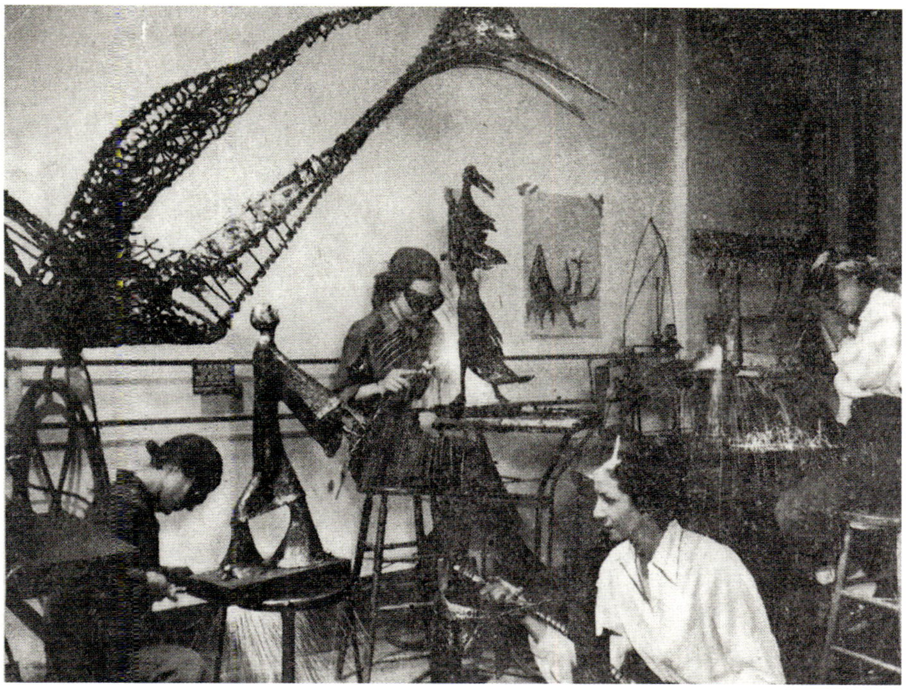

Photo of Lin Emery with colleagues at the Sculpture Center.

There were a number of metal sculptors active in and around New York who provided inspiration for Emery and other up-and-coming sculptors: David Smith, of course, but also Herbert Ferber, Ibram Lassaw, Theodore Roszak, and David Hare. The most directly influential for Emery was Seymour Lipton. In the 1950s and early 1960s, Lipton created his forms with steel or Monel® metal, using bronze and, later, nickel silver as a surface coating. Employing a similar technique, Emery

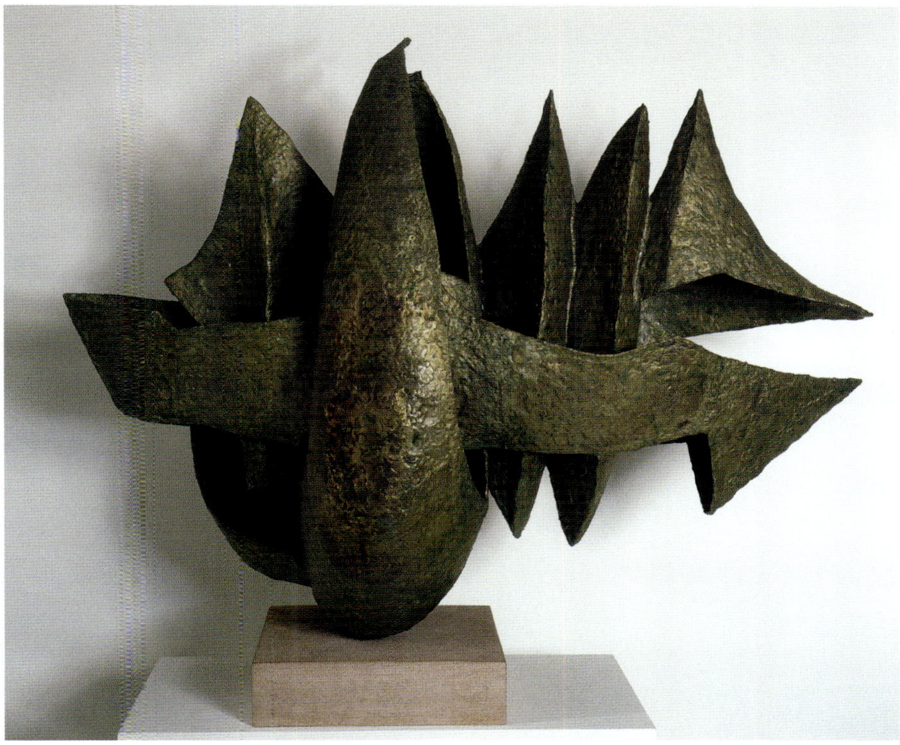

Seymour Lipton (American, 1903–1986), Sea King, *1955. Nickel silver over Monel® metal, overall: 30 ½ x 41 13/16 x 20 inches (77.5 x 106 x 50.8 cm). Albright-Knox Art Gallery, Buffalo, NY. A. Conger Goodyear Fund, 1956. Photograph: Albright-Knox Art Gallery/Art Resource, NY. © The Estate of Seymour Lipton; courtesy Michael Rosenfeld Gallery, LLC, New York, NY.*

FIG. 2.11 *Lin Emery,* Titan, *1956. Welded copper and bronze, 33½ x 43 x 18 inches (85.1 x 109.2 x 45.7 cm). Private collection. Photograph: Jeremiah Russell.*

FIG. 2.12 *Lin Emery,* Warrior, *1955. Welded copper and bronze, 52 x 24 x 24 inches (132.1 x 61 x 61 cm). Private collection. Photograph: Jeremiah Russell.*

FIG. 2.13 *Lin Emery,* Genesis, *1956. Welded copper and bronze, 49 x 24 x 22 inches (124.5 x 61 x 55.9 cm). Collection of Mrs. Evie Annenberg Hall. Photograph: Jeremiah Russell.*

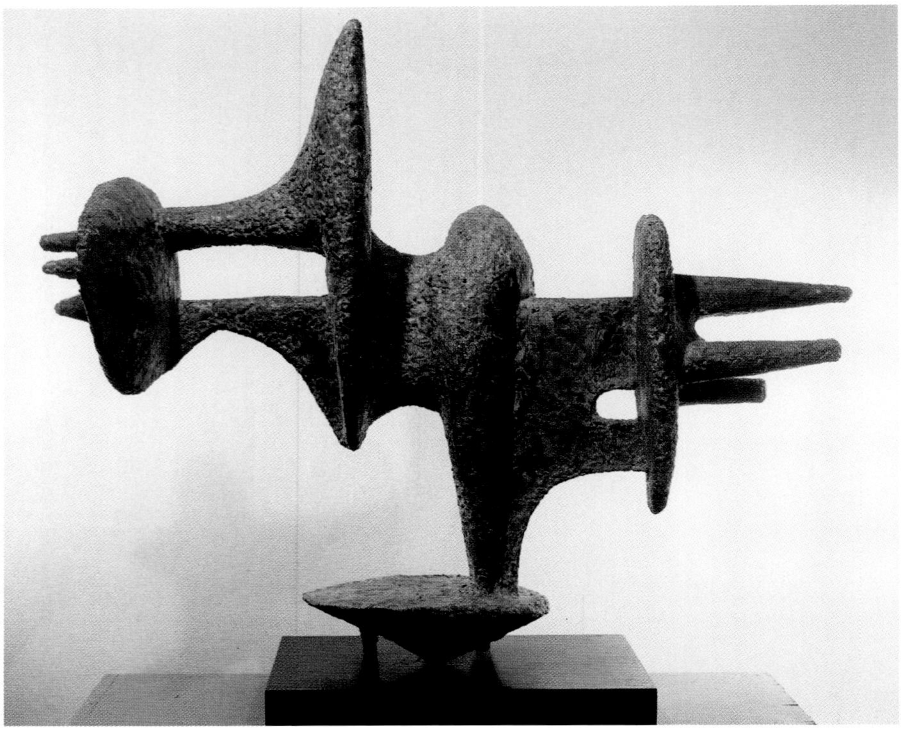

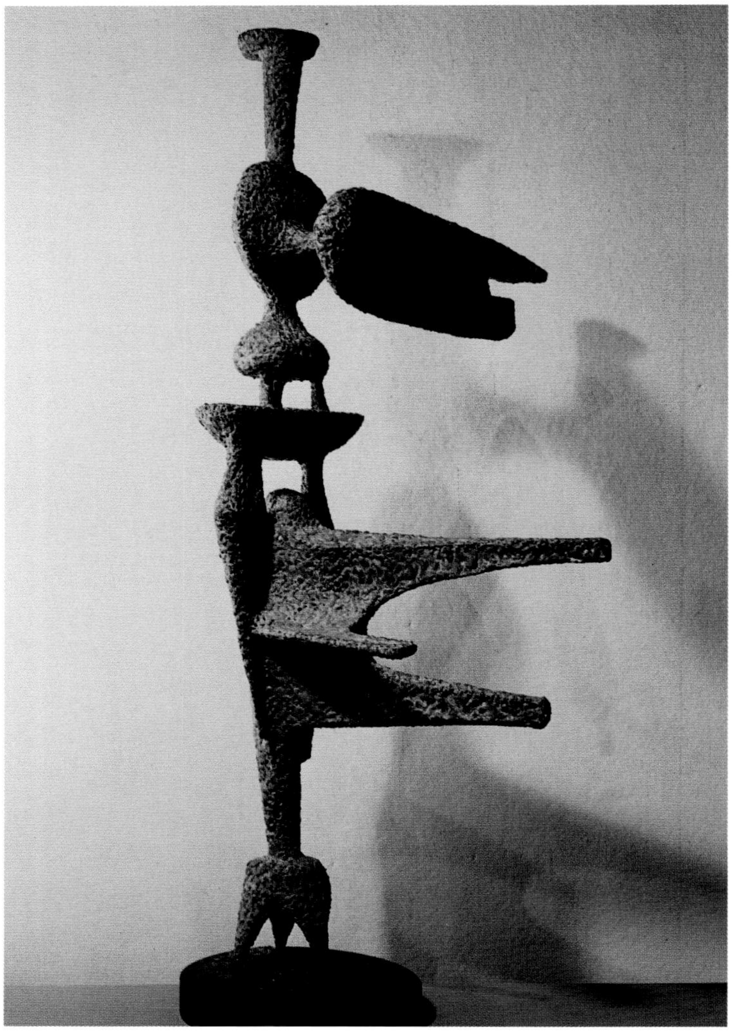

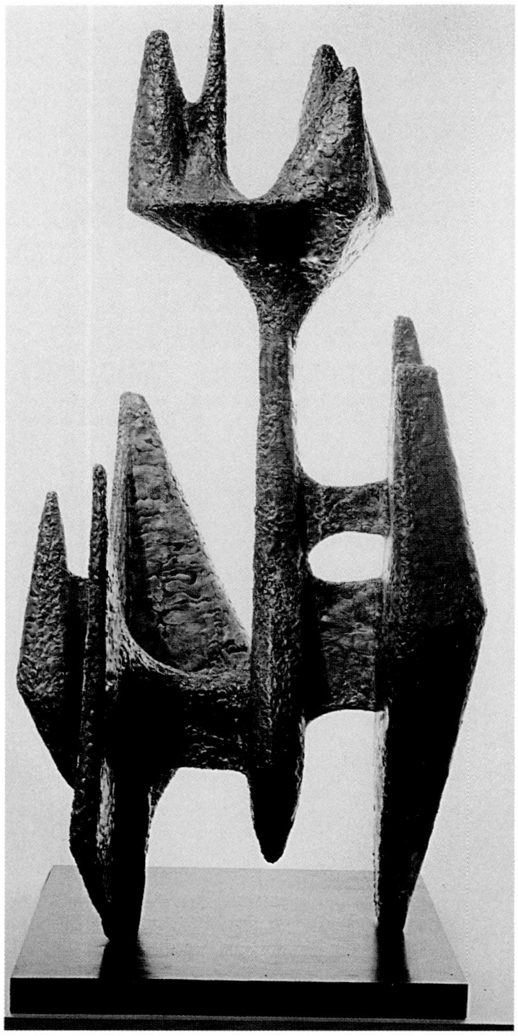

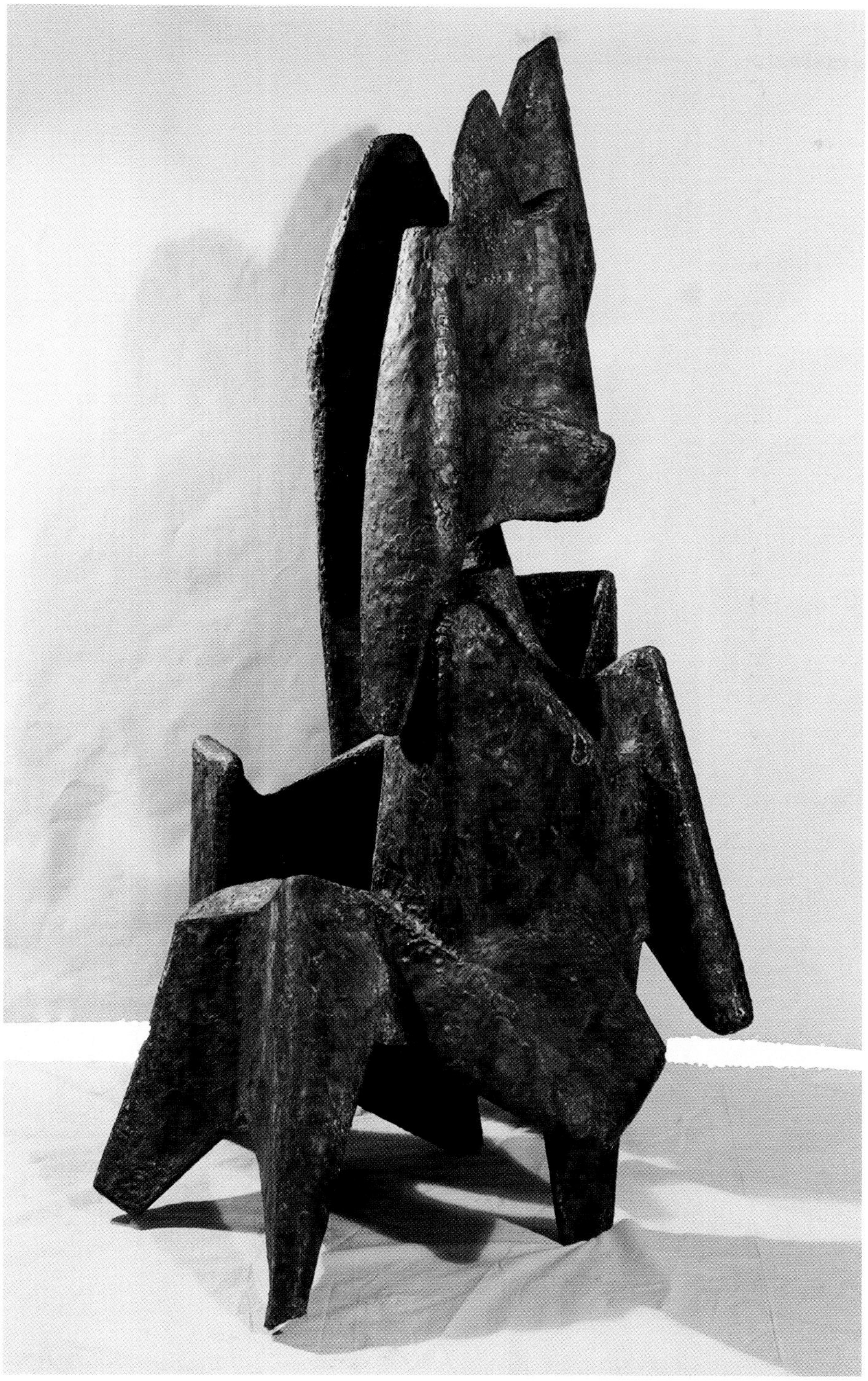

Lin Emery, Sanctuary, *1961. Phosphor copper, 58 x 38 x 32 inches (147.3 x 96.5 x 81.3 cm). Private collection.*

created the basic form of works such as *Titan* (fig. 2.11), *Warrior* (fig. 2.12), and *Genesis* (fig. 2.13) by shaping sheets of copper, tack welding them, and puddling—or brazing—bronze onto the surface with a welding torch, which gave the surface both texture and color.

During these years, Emery traveled back and forth between New York and her adopted city of New Orleans. She could not be long in New Orleans without finding a place where she could weld. She describes the place she found as "a real

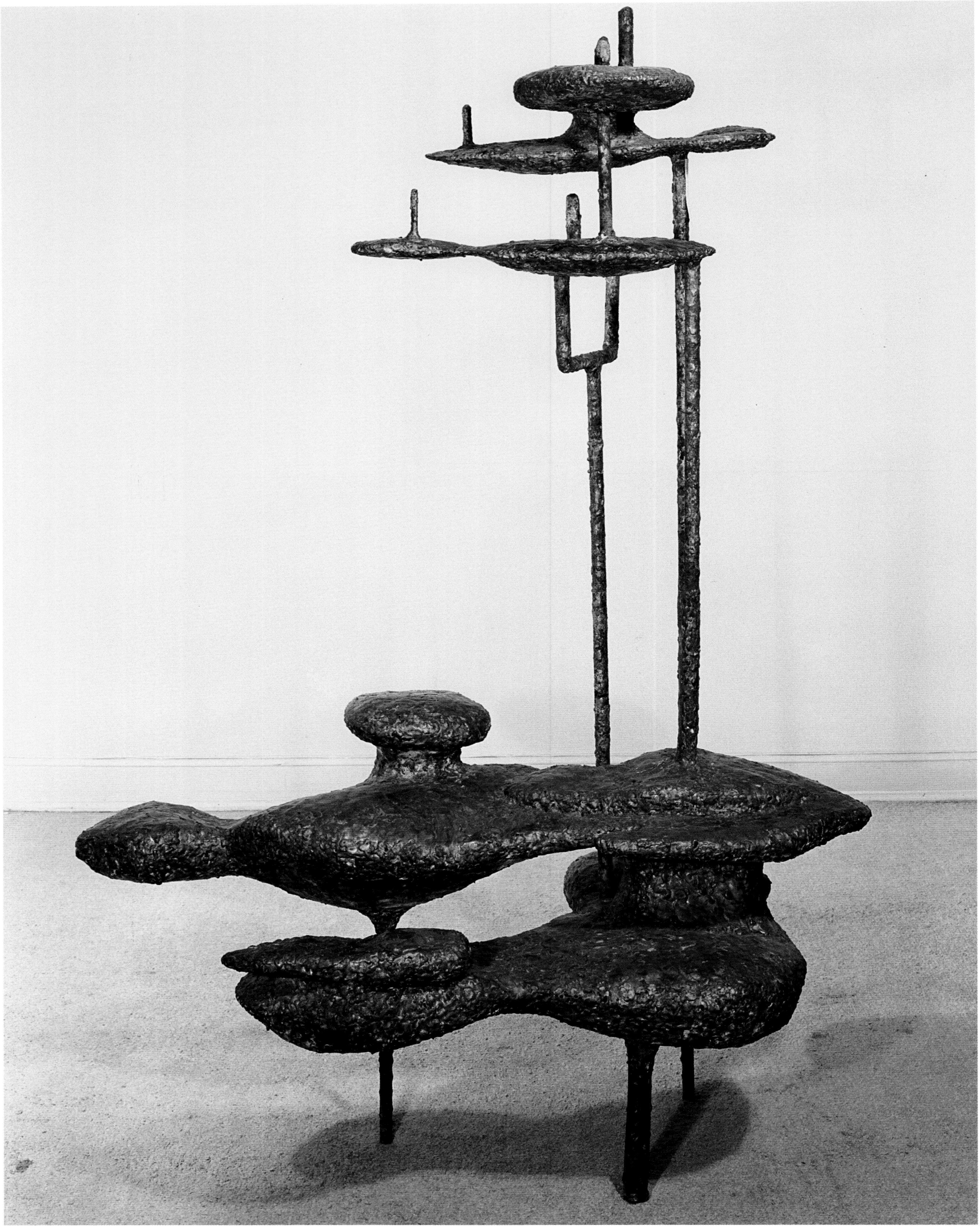

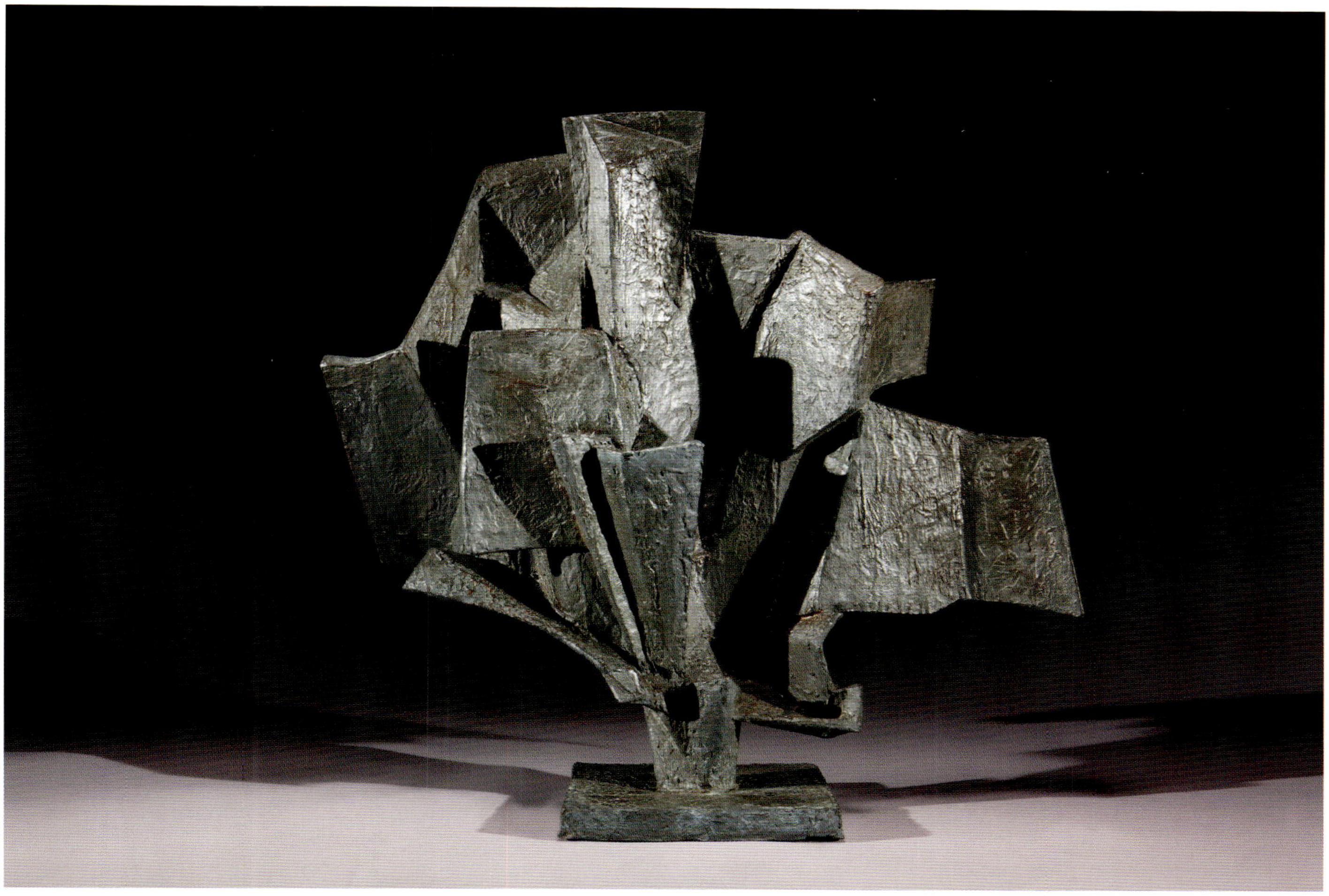

Cajun place, a blacksmith shop that made oyster tongs and things like that." Typically, she grasped the opportunity to learn blacksmithing as well as doing her welding. She set up in a corner of the shop and the customers were encouraged to watch her while they waited for their oyster rakes or tongs.

Quite rapidly, Emery received widening recognition for her work in New Orleans, which led to unusual opportunities. One day during the summer of 1957 a truck arrived at Emery's studio door and delivered a jail cell door. The city of Pensacola had decided to turn a jail into a museum and commissioned five sculptors to convert the doors into works of art. Emery's 6-foot-high work invoking cloudlike forms was titled *Freedom* (fig. 2.14). *Life* magazine had picked up on the story, but unfortunately, the jail-to-art spread was preempted by the launch of Sputnik on October 4.

In addition to learning oxyacetylene welding, Emery learned to cast metal at the Sculpture Center using the traditional lost wax technique. As she had with welding, Emery took naturally to casting, realizing satisfaction from the process as well as from the creative potential. The casting facilities at the Sculpture Center were minimal, but in 1963 Emery joined with two other sculptors to build a full-scale foundry in New Orleans, with massive burn-out kilns. They called it the

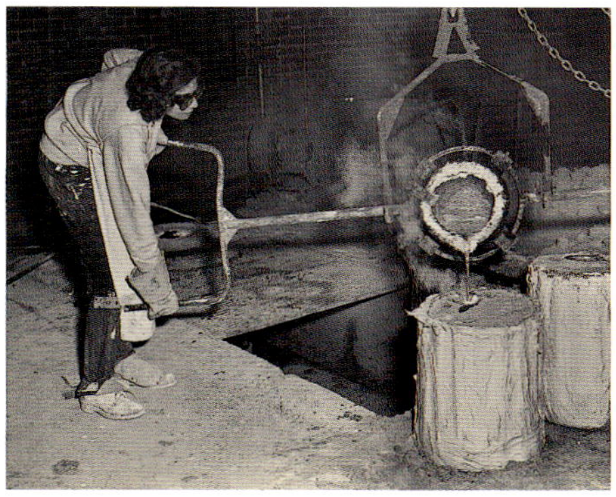

above

Lin Emery, Futile Cloak, *1964. Cast bronze, 25 x 25 x 11 inches (63.5 x 63.5 x 27.9 cm). New Orleans Museum of Art, New Orleans, LA.*

Photograph of Lin Emery pouring bronze, Orleans Workshop, 1963.

opposite page

FIG. 2.14 *Lin Emery,* Freedom, *1957. Steel, bronze, and copper, 71 x 49 x 30 inches (180.3 x 124.5 x 76.2 cm). Collection of Huntingdon College, Montgomery, AL. Photograph: Stuart Lynn.*

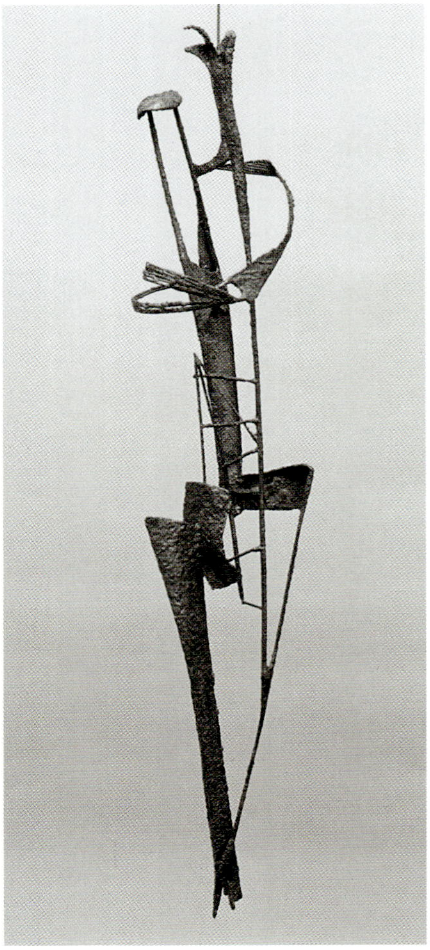

Orleans Workshop. The cast-bronze sculptures that Emery created in the 1950s and 1960s in New York and at her own foundry constitute a diverse and artistically substantial body of work.

In addition to being a place of learning, the Sculpture Center provided Emery with her first significant exhibitions. The year after she became a student there, in 1952, her *Ballet Dancer* (fig. 2.15) was included in a show where David Smith's *Stainless Network* and a piece by José De Rivera were also shown. The next year she took part in an exhibition of women welders. The newspaper headline managed to offend both incipient feminists and orthographers as it declared, "Cutting Fancy Figures: Gal sculpters [*sic*] now weld steel into works of art."[5] Over the years until 1972, Emery was included in several exhibitions at the center, including one-woman shows in 1957 and 1962.

New Orleans

For all of the importance the Sculpture Center held for Emery, during the late 1950s and early 1960s her relationship with the city of New Orleans continued to deepen. Given her restless, inquiring, and culturally open view of the world, it is quite natural that Emery found New Orleans to be a sympathetic place. Founded in 1718 by French Canadians and built by slave labor, New Orleans was the original American melting pot. During its first fifty years, Louisiana was under French and then Spanish rule, had a large indigenous Natchez Indian population, and experienced major immigrations from Germany, Nova Scotia, Haiti, and Cuba. France

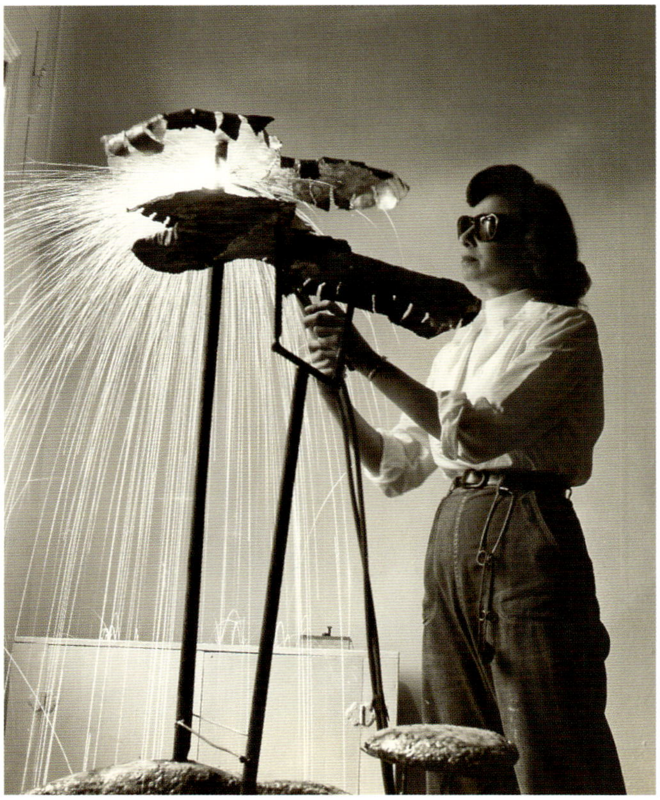

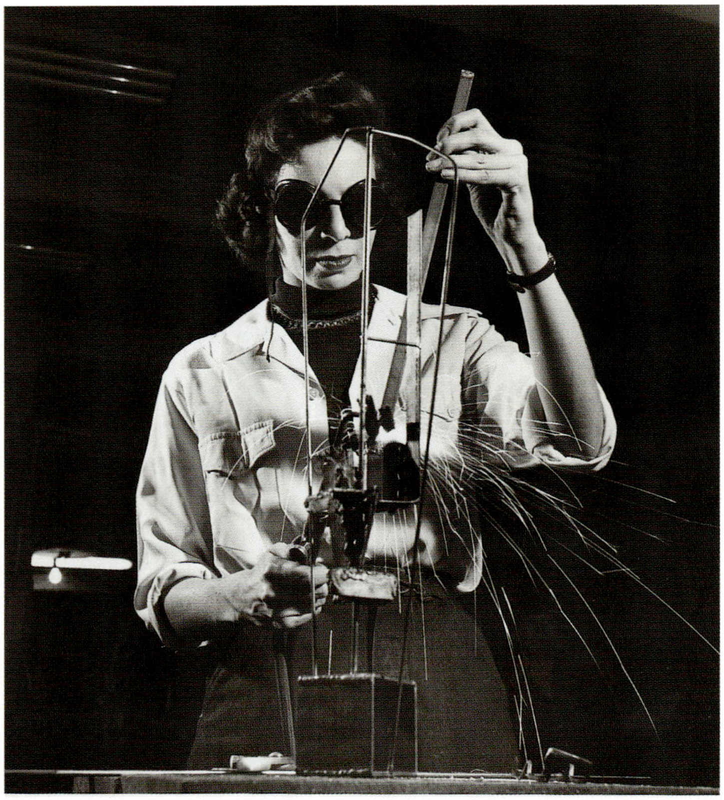

had the habit of deporting its criminals and prostitutes there, as well. But by the early nineteenth century, New Orleans had become the most urbane and fashionable city in the South. With its two opera houses the city was referred to as "Paris on the Mississippi." The Civil War brought the city's opulence to an end, but present-day New Orleans retains some of its early vibrancy and style, as well as a tolerance that comes from deep-rooted diversity. It is no accident that jazz, an inspired mix of popular music of the 1890s, spirituals, and work songs, was born in New Orleans. In a recent review of an exhibition of Emery's kinetic sculpture at the Arthur Roger Gallery, critic Chris Waddington speculated on why New Orleans was particularly fond of kinetic sculpture, noting that New Orleans was the "only U.S. city in which sensuality is not considered taboo."[6]

Emery attributes part of her early acceptance in New Orleans to the lack of prejudice against women artists. Unlike in other regions of the country, in that part of the Deep South, art was women's work. Newcomb College, established in 1886 as the first degree-granting college for women in the country and coordinate to Tulane, included a consequential art school. By the 1890s, a number of women artists were active in the city.[7] When Emery settled in New Orleans, one of the city's most prominent sculptors was Angela Gregory, a student of Antoine Bourdelle; she was a graduate of Newcomb and an artist in residence there who cast large architectural reliefs and hewed stone with the best of them. A group from the feminist art group the Gorilla Girls once attended a meeting of the board of Newcomb College and was prepared to protest angrily the male domination of art in New Orleans, only to be disappointed to find out there was no male domination.

From her early days there, Emery was an active, contributing member of the New Orleans arts community. In 1956, she and six other artists founded the Orleans Gallery, the city's first cooperative gallery, and one of the first in the South. One of the young artists that Emery attracted to the galley was John T. Scott. Born in the Ninth Ward, Scott, who would later earn a MacArthur Fellowship, combined in his sculptures aspects of his African American heritage and the colors and rhythms of New Orleans.

In 1962, another bond between Emery and New Orleans was forged in Mexico. Emery had formed a close friendship with Shirley Braselman, a successful businessman from an established New Orleans family, and they and some New Orleans friends went on a vacation to Mexico City. One day the group decided to go to Puebla for the day, but Emery wasn't feeling well and decided to stay at the hotel. Braselman stayed back to keep her company. Wondering what they could do that would be interesting, on a lark they decided to get married. Emery's memory of the event at the Municipal Building is selective and vivid: the cast the judge had on her arm, as well as the woman registering her baby and the man named DeLeon who were asked to be witnesses. She also remembers the fun of surprising their friends with the news when they came back from Puebla.

Emery's marriage to Braselman opened her eyes to aspects of New Orleans life she had only vaguely acknowledged. Through her mother, Emery is part Jewish, and she soon came up against a virulent anti-Semitism behind the smiles in Braselman's social circle. She realized that her Jewish friends left New Orleans dur-

opposite page, clockwise top to bottom

FIG. 2.15 *Lin Emery,* Ballet Dancer, *1952. Welded steel, 47 x 11 x 8 inches (119.4 x 27.9 x 20.3 cm). Private collection.*

Newspaper photograph "Cutting Fancy Figures," New York Times, *November 7, 1953.*

Newspaper photograph "The Sparks Fly," Sun Times, *May 30, 1954.*

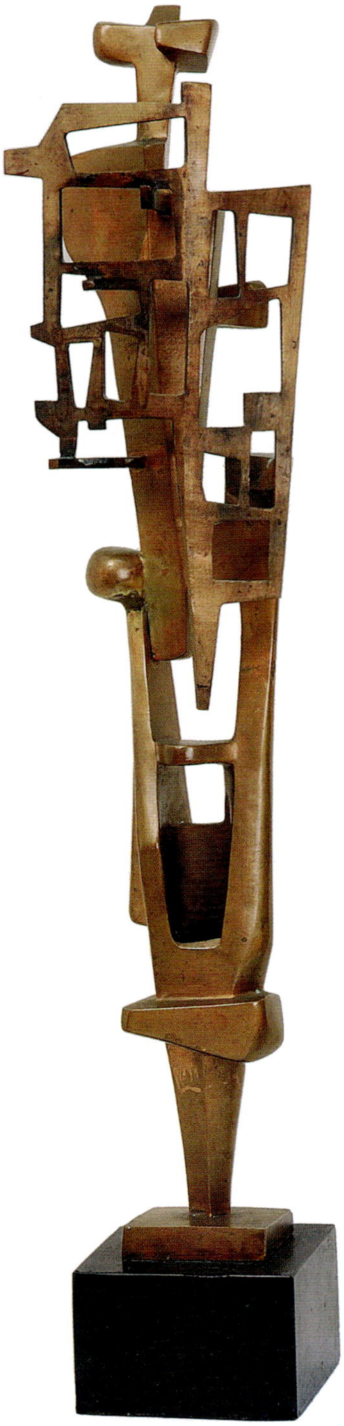

FIG. 2.16 *Lin Emery,* Figure*, 1954. Cast bronze, 21 x 4½ x 5 inches (53.3 x 11.4 x 12.7 cm). Farnsworth Art Museum, Rockland, ME.*

ing Mardi Gras. Braselman had business interests overseas and Emery was an interested and positive companion on his trips to Greece, Hawaii, Japan, and Mexico. In 1969 they adopted a son, Brooks, who is now an actor. A board member of various arts organizations in New Orleans, Braselman was more enthusiastic about the arts in general than about Lin's long hours in the studio. A combination of alcoholism and heart disease led to ten years of declining health until his death in 2001.

In her broad-ranging and avid sculptural explorations in the 1950s and early 1960s, Emery built the technical and conceptual foundation for her career. Her work during this period spans a vast diversity of form, material, and technique, from figurative religious pieces in plaster to welded and cast-metal abstractions. Any common formal characteristic that is evident in this diversity is revealing of something fundamental to the artist's vision, whether conscious or not. A highly controlled compositional purity would be a prevailing characteristic of her work. Another trait that is discernible in many of Emery's works in this period is a certain lightness of being. The welded steel *Ballet Dancer* (fig. 2.15) and the cast-bronze *Figure* of 1954 (fig. 2.16) share an elongated, ethereal quality with the figure of Christ in *Corpus* (fig. 2.5). Emery seems to seek lightness through floating and open forms, as in *Icarus* (fig. 2.10) and *Flight* (1961; fig. 2.17). Two years later, *Flight* (1963; fig. 2.18) is even lighter; it desperately wants to levitate from its base. The floating clouds at the top of *Freedom* (fig. 2.14) epitomize the work's title. All of this anticipates Emery's discovery, a decade later, of a more dramatic way of capturing the ethereal qualities of lightness—and motion—with her kinetic work.

The foundation that Emery built during these years also had mechanical strength, in the techniques that she so eagerly mastered. The steps in working metal by cutting, shaping, casting, and welding were not only those required to create the final product but pleasures in themselves, pleasures that contributed to natural mastery. Those skills and pleasures would, some years later, become manifest in Emery's wind-driven sculpture.

But the next immediate phase in Emery's career would start on a more frivolous note, with an eminently mundane incident.

NOTES

1. Painting, from El Greco to European royal portraiture, systematically exaggerates tallness. Dennis Dutton makes the case that women's preference for tall men is an evolutionary trait. See Dennis Dutton, *The Art Instinct* (New York: Bloomsbury Press, 2009), p. 143.

2. John Richardson, *A Life of Picasso: The Triumphant Years, 1917–1932* (New York: Alfred A. Knopf, 2007), p. 422.

3. Barbara Leckberg, interview with the author, September 15, 2009.

4. For an excellent summary of welded sculpture in the United States, see Judy Collischan, *Welded Sculpture of the Twentieth Century* (New York: Hudson Hills Press, 2000).

5. *Sunday News*, May 30, 1954.

6. Chris Waddington, "Lin Emery's Sculptures Sizzle with Kinetic Energy," *The Times-Picayune*, June 16, 1995.

7. Judith Bonner, "Women Artists in Louisiana, 1825–1965: A Place of Their Own," *Arts Quarterly* (April/May/June 2009): 10.

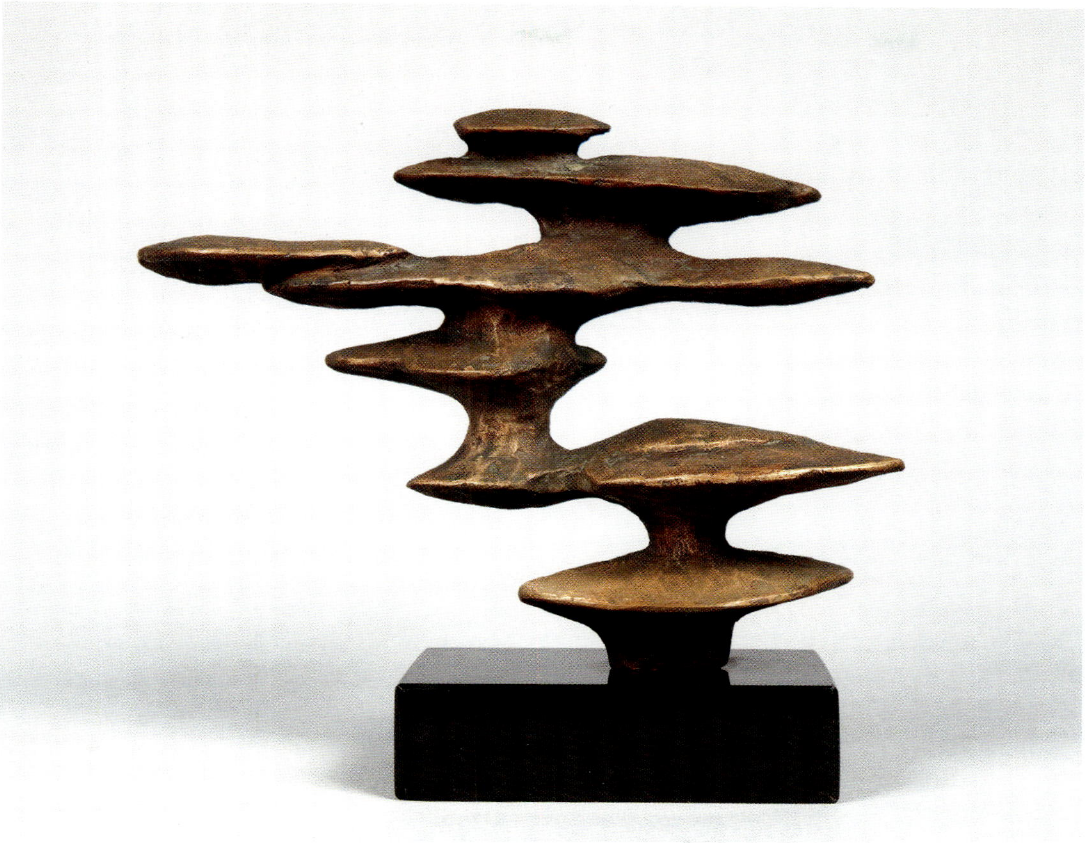

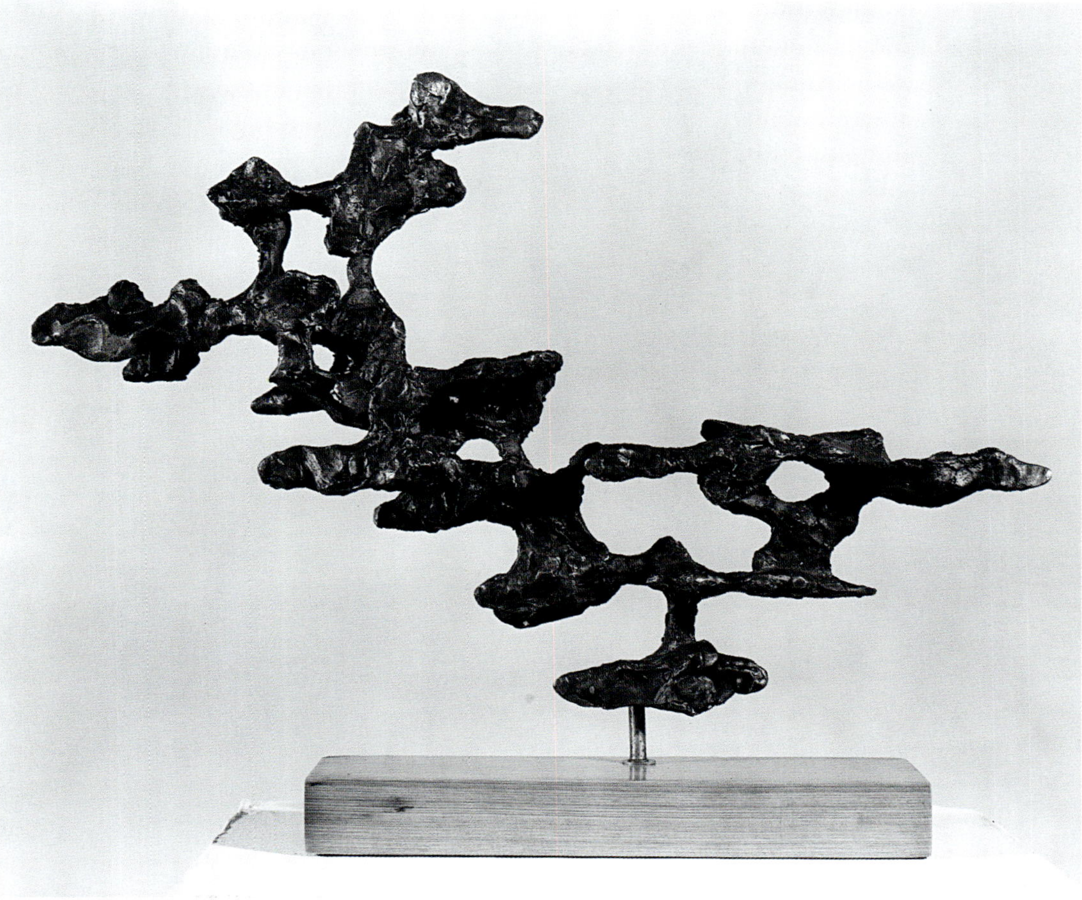

FIG. 2.17 *Lin Emery,* Flight, *1961. Cast bronze, 7 x 9½ x 4 inches (17.8 x 24.1 x 10.2 cm). Collection of C. Kohlmeyer.*

FIG. 2.18 *Lin Emery,* Flight, *1963. Cast bronze, 10½ x 15½ x 3 inches (26.7 x 39.4 x 7.6 cm). Private collection.*

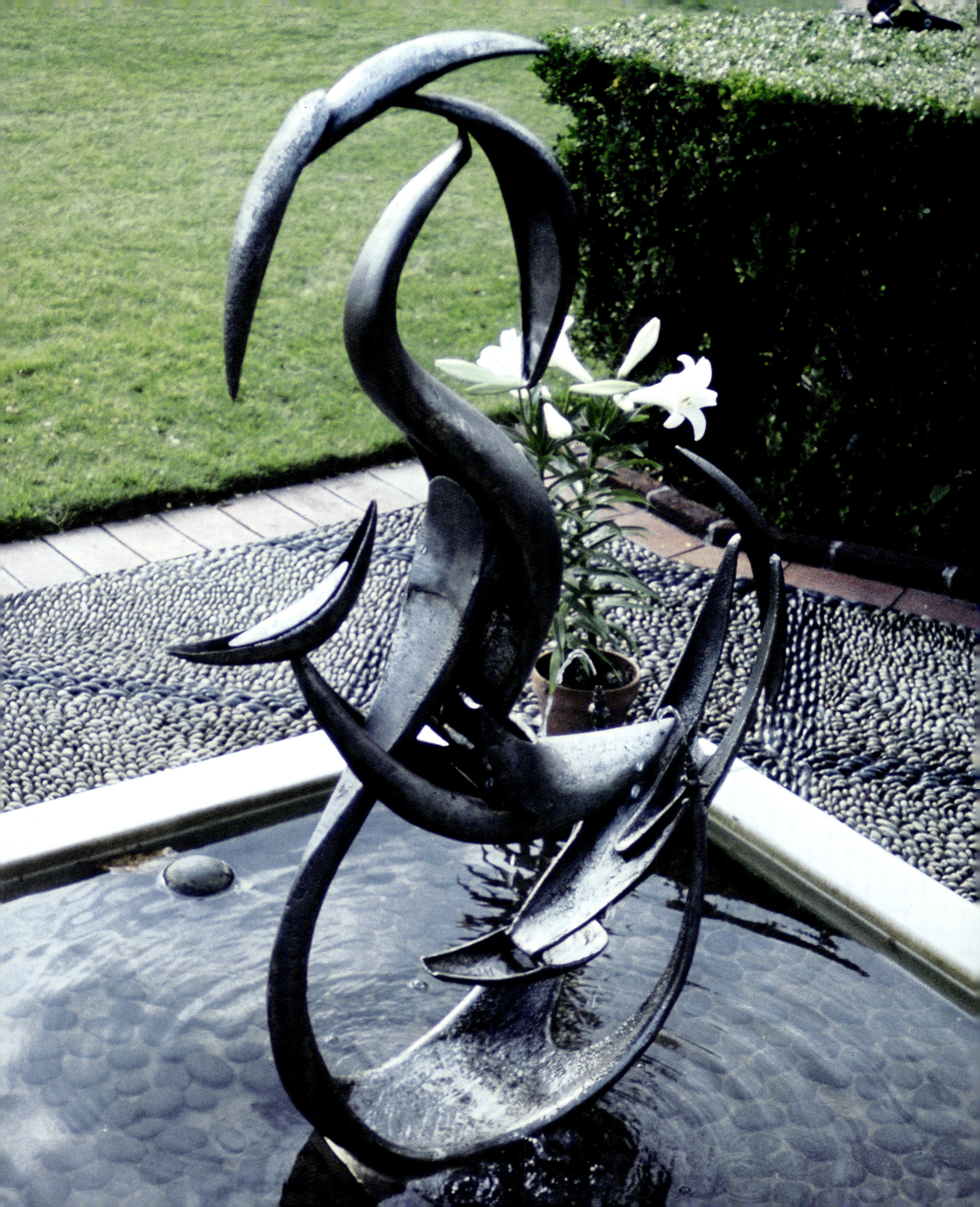

CHAPTER III

Water

Recently, a close friend of Emery's observed that she views the entire visual world primarily as a source of sculptural ideas. That was certainly the case in 1954 when she was washing dishes in her small kitchen in New Orleans. Water was dripping onto a spoon balanced on the edge of a cup, rocking the spoon up and down. In that mundane chance event Emery saw a sculpture, although she had little inkling of the range of work that would, over the years, emerge from that chance occurrence. At that point Emery saw water only as a source of movement and her first "aquamobiles," as she termed them, were playful toys that turned out to have serious implications, not unlike the circus animals that initiated Alexander Calder's kinetic work.

In moving water the earthly world thus allows the ever changing life in the universe of the stars to flow into the course of its own life.

—Theodor Schwenk[1]

In the early stages of her career, in her figurative sculptures as well as her cast and welded work, Emery felt a responsibility to seriousness, as if to declare her deep commitment to her new profession. The titles of her sculptures, such as *Pieta* (see fig. 2.1) and *Stations of the Cross* (see fig. 2.9), communicate the conceptual weightiness that characterized even her purely abstract work. At the same time, when inspired by a teaspoon, she felt confident enough to pursue a more frivolous path in parallel with her serious work. Ironically, in succumbing to the freedom of irresponsibility she discovered the defining characteristic of her mature work: movement.

First she embarked on works of fantasy and humor in which water provided the motor power. She became a plumber of the miniature, scouring the shops along Canal Street in lower Manhattan to find her little fittings and pumps. Her notebooks started to fill with sketches of the intricate workings of increasingly elaborate aquamobiles (fig. 3.1). The precise drawings work out the details of tubes, pumps, and cascades of water, and the pivot rods and bearings that allow flowing water to move delicately balanced pieces of metal. These sketches express ingenuity, attention to detail, and above all a delight in the combination of engineering and art.

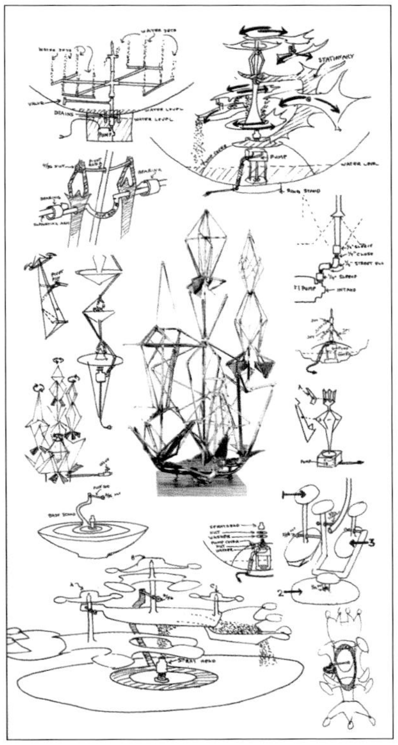

FIG. 3.1 *Lin Emery, sketches of aquamobile parts, c. 1962.*

opposite page
Lin Emery, Arabesque, *1967. White bronze with water system, 52 x 32 x 7 inches (132.1 x 81.3 x 17.8 cm). Longue Vue House and Gardens, New Orleans, LA.*

In an early example of an aquamobile, the 1954 *King and Queen at the Beach* (fig. 3.2), the toy welded metal figures stand regally on either side of a twirling toy. Although lighthearted, Emery's early aquamobiles, such as *Daphne and Apollo* of 1958 (fig. 3.3), had an intelligent and deft esprit. This modestly sized work repre-

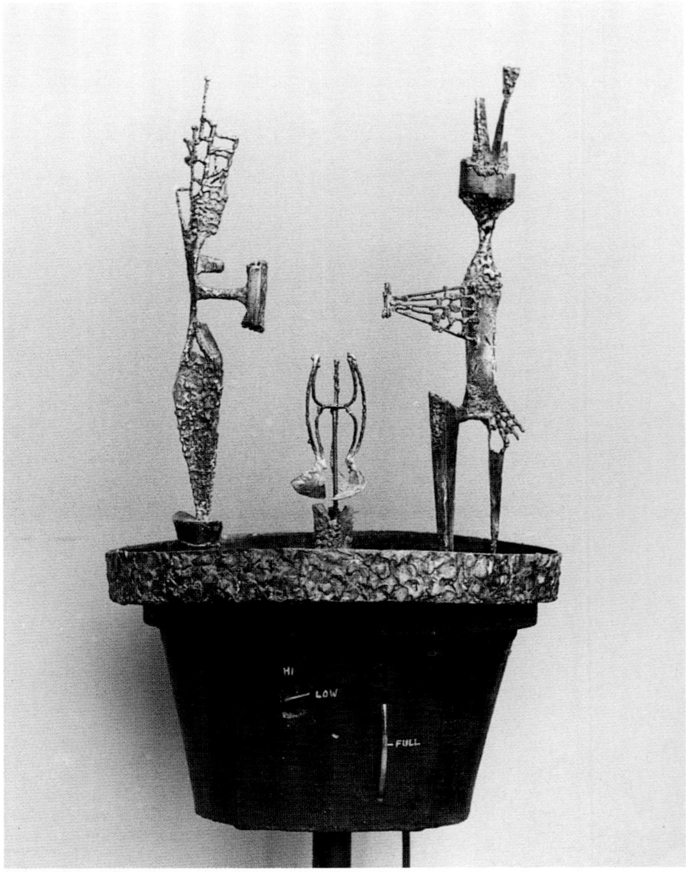

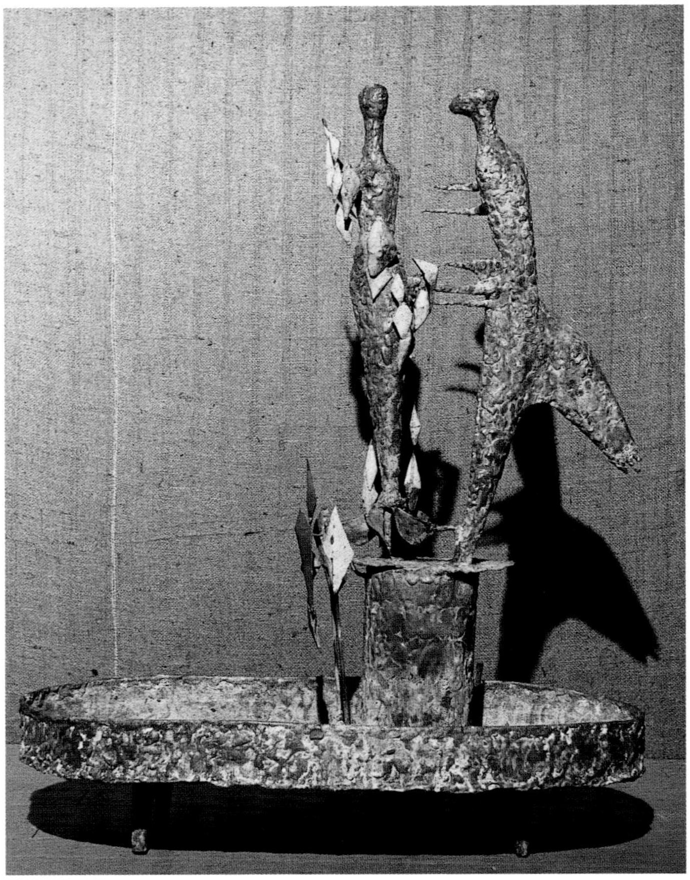

FIG. 3.2 *Lin Emery,* King and Queen at the Beach, 1954. *Welded bronze, water, and pump, 24 x 19 x 13 inches (61 x 48.3 x 33 cm). Private collection. Photograph: Neal Auction, New Orleans, LA.*

FIG. 3.3 *Lin Emery,* Daphne and Apollo, *1958. Bronze on copper, water, and pump, 30 x 16 x 16 inches (76.2 x 40.6 x 40.6 cm). Collection of Mrs. Alwyn Puriton, East Liverpool, OH.*

opposite page, clockwise

FIG. 3.4 *Lin Emery,* Busy Blossom, *1960. Welded bronze, copper, water, and pump, 66 x 30 x 30 inches (167.6 x 76.2 x 76.2 cm). Flint Institute of Arts, Flint, MI.*

FIG. 3.5 *Lin Emery,* Busy Garden, *1960. Welded bronze, copper, enamel, water, and pump, 10 x 22 x 21 inches (25.4 x 55.9 x 53.3 cm). Private collection.*

Lin Emery, Mixed Quartet, *1961. Welded bronze, water, and pump, 28 x 12 x 12 inches (71.1 x 30.5 x 30.5 cm). Artist's studio.*

Lin Emery, Rain Cloud, *1960. Welded bronze, copper, water, and pump, 9 x 3 x 2 feet (2.7 x 0.9 x 0.6 m). Imperial House Restaurant, Tampa, FL.*

sents Apollo, smitten with love for the nymph Daphne, who loved the woods, the chase, and her independence. As Apollo gains on her in pursuit, Daphne entreats her father, a river god, to change her form. Just as Apollo reaches her, she is transforming into a laurel tree. In Emery's sculpture, water pressure makes Daphne spin and wobble. When she wobbles closer to Apollo, the god catches her and she stops, but then she spins away and becomes a blurred object that could be a woman or a tree. We look on this work of sculptural fantasy and recall our pleasure as children at the movement of a wind-up toy. The joke is enhanced by recalling one of the greatest sculptures of the Italian Renaissance, Gian Lorenzo Bernini's *Apollo and Daphne*. In her title, Emery puts Daphne first.

Emery's use of water was liberating both in form and in subject matter. Water flowed, pulsed, dripped, spouted, and poured. Under its influence metal pieces spun, bobbed, and rotated. The linear dripping of water suggested works that hung from the ceiling. Emery's aquamobiles were first shown at the Sculpture Center, and the public was enchanted. Emery also recalls that all that rushing water sent a crush of visitors to the restroom. As Emery started to sell her water-driven sculptures, she was led to take seriously her frivolous sculptural escapade. As though nourished by water, forms of nature such as flowers and leaves started to appear in her work for the first time. The center of *Busy Blossom* (fig. 3.4) rotated while the petals opened and closed. Emery coated the leaves in *Busy Garden* (fig. 3.5) with yellow, green, and blue enamel, and activated them with jets of water from below.

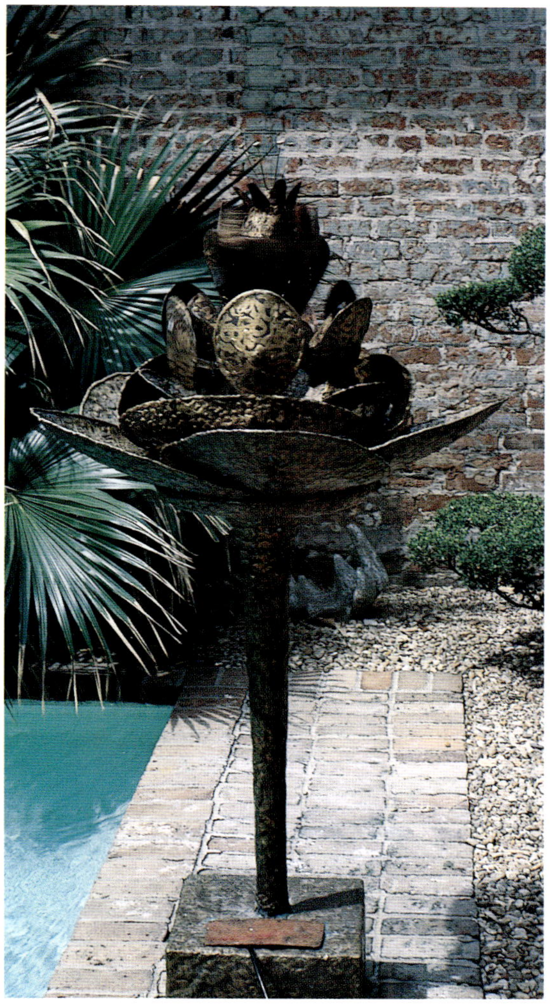

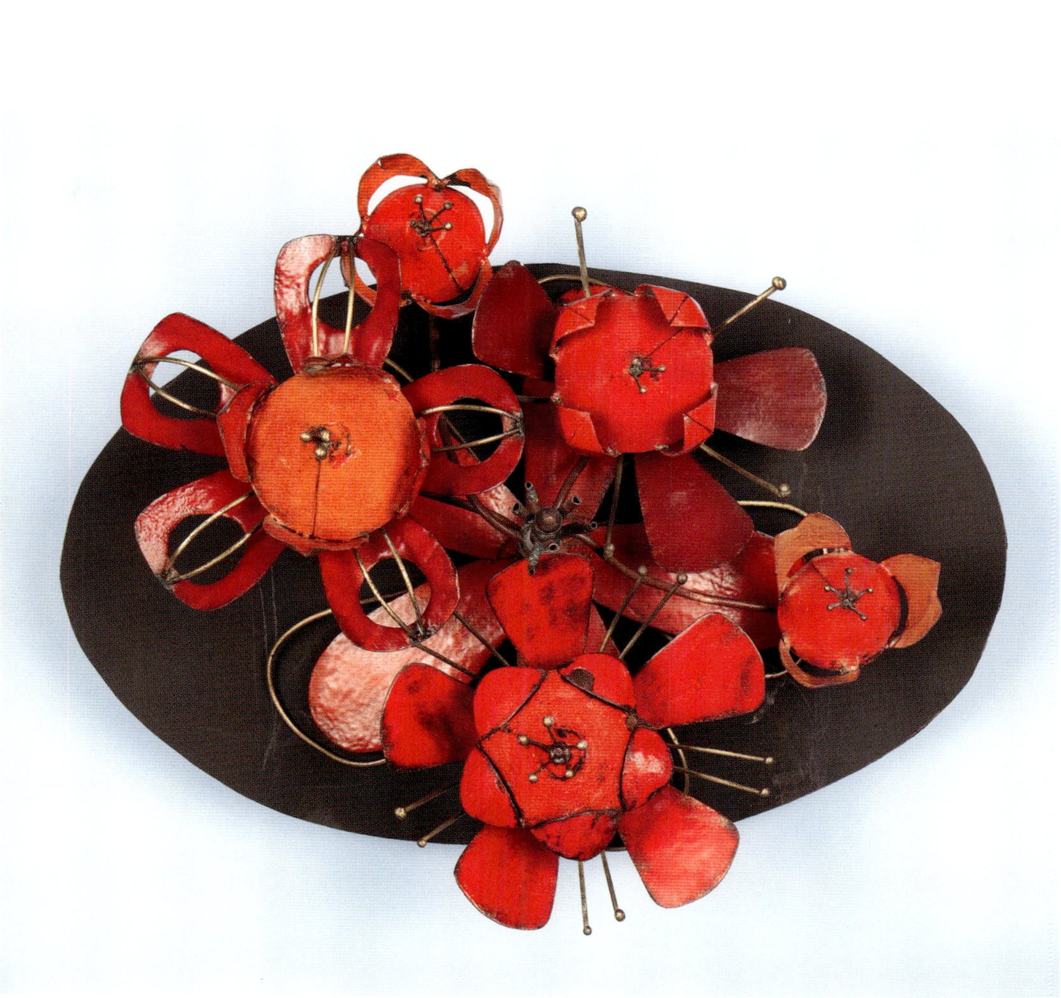

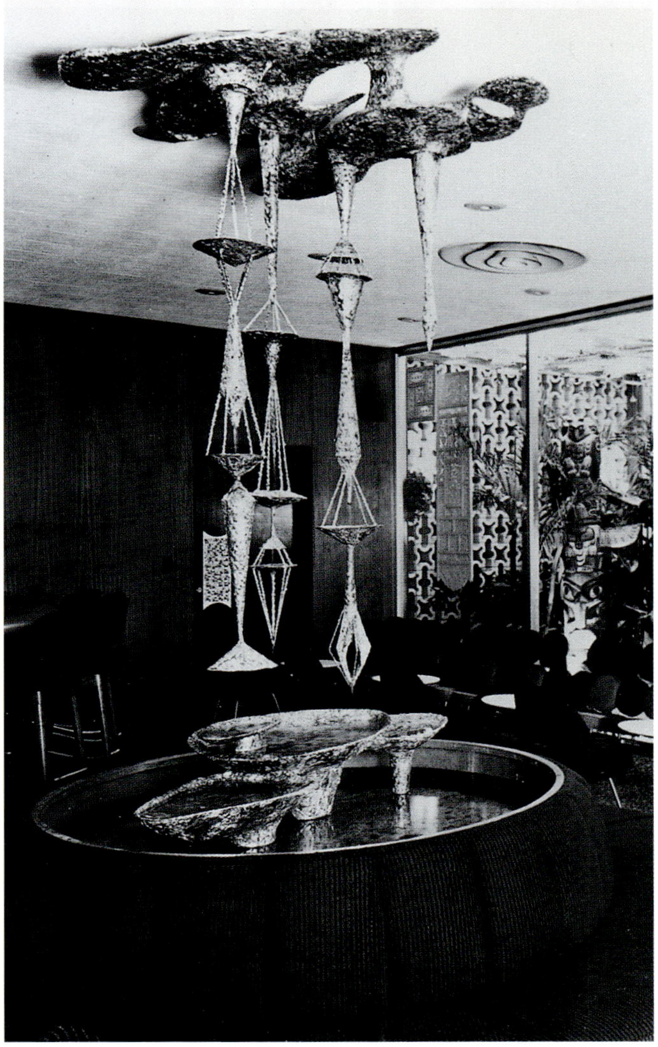

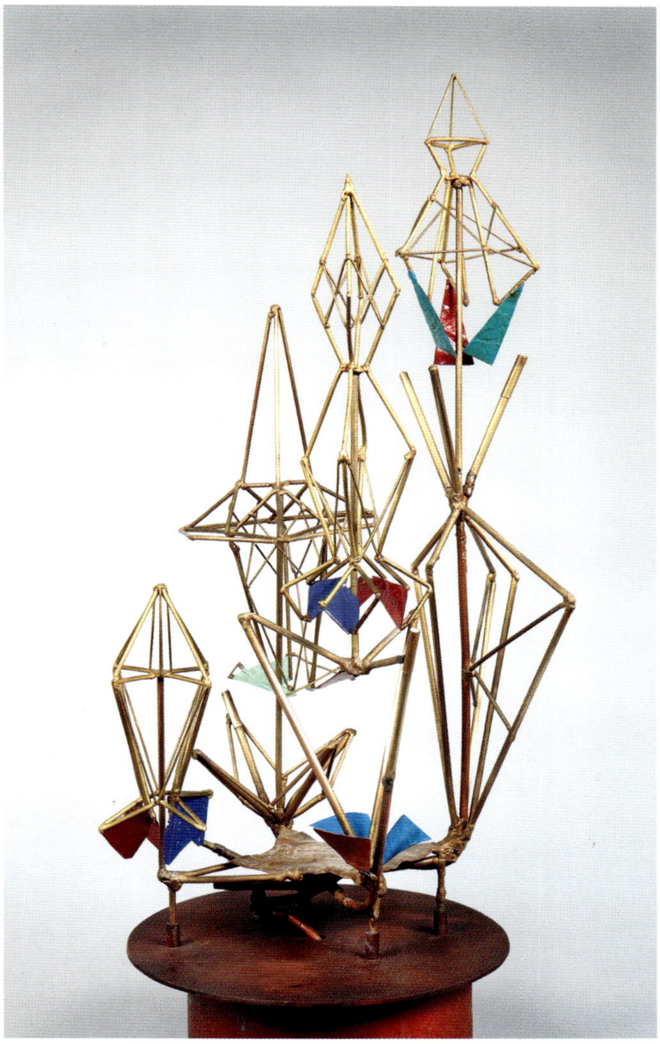

Lin Emery, Aquamobile, *1963. Bronze, water, and pump, 40 x 12 x 12 inches (101.6 x 30.5 x 30.5 cm). Texas Instruments, Inc., Dallas, TX.*

Lin Emery, Jack & Jill *(still), 1963. Cast bronze, water, and pump, 25 x 22 x 18 inches (63.5 x 55.9 x 45.7 cm). Royal-Athena Galleries, New York.*

Lin Emery, Jack & Jill *(in motion), 1963. Cast bronze, water, and pump, 25 x 22 x 18 inches (63.5 x 55.9 x 45.7 cm). Royal-Athena Galleries, New York.*

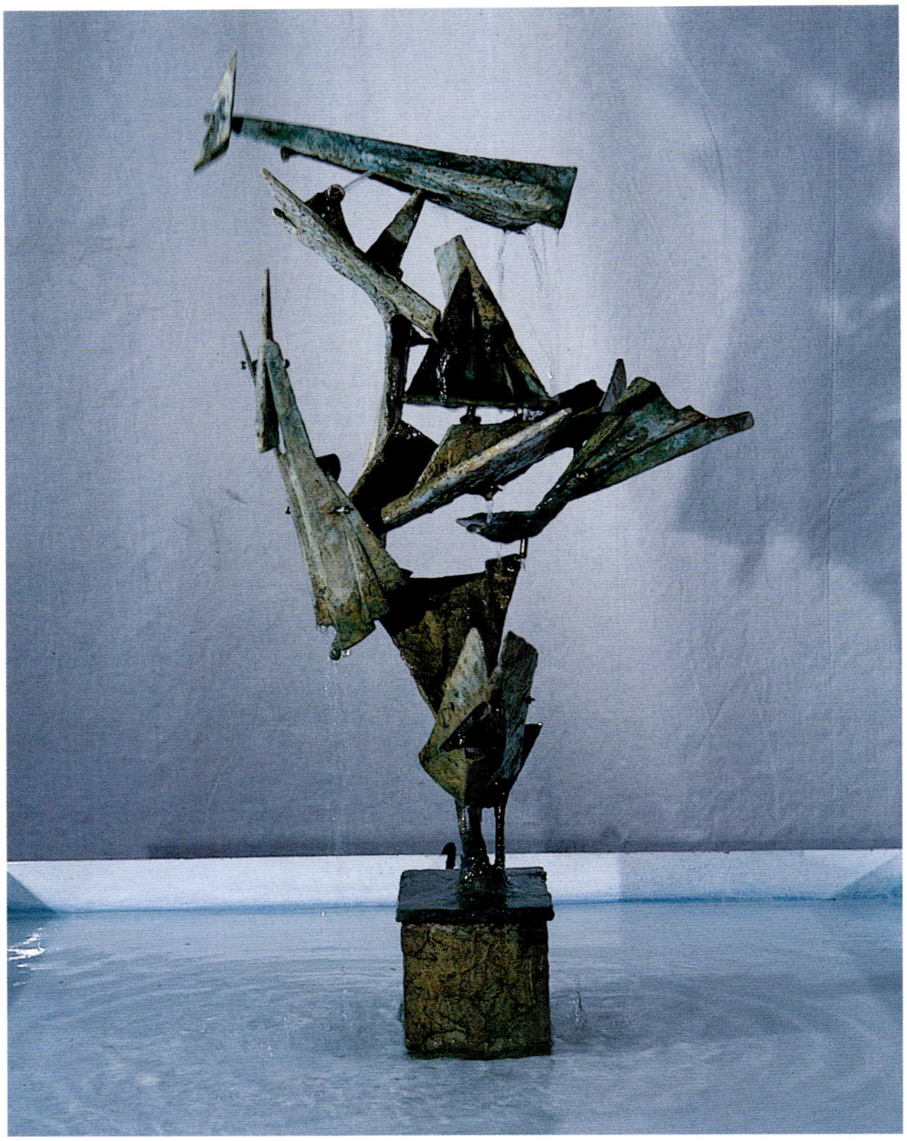

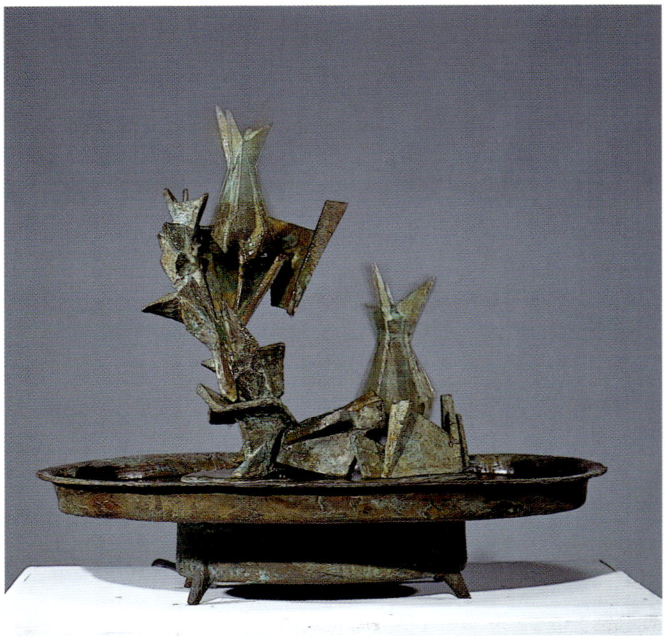

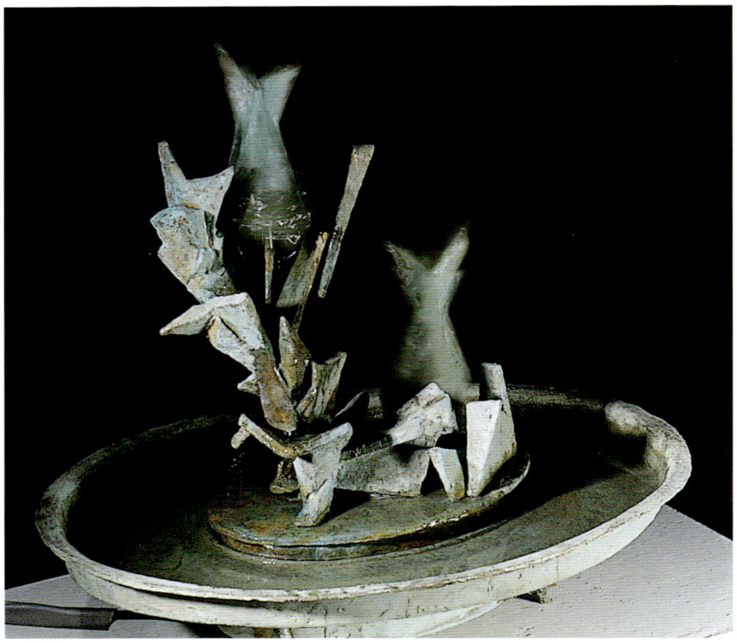

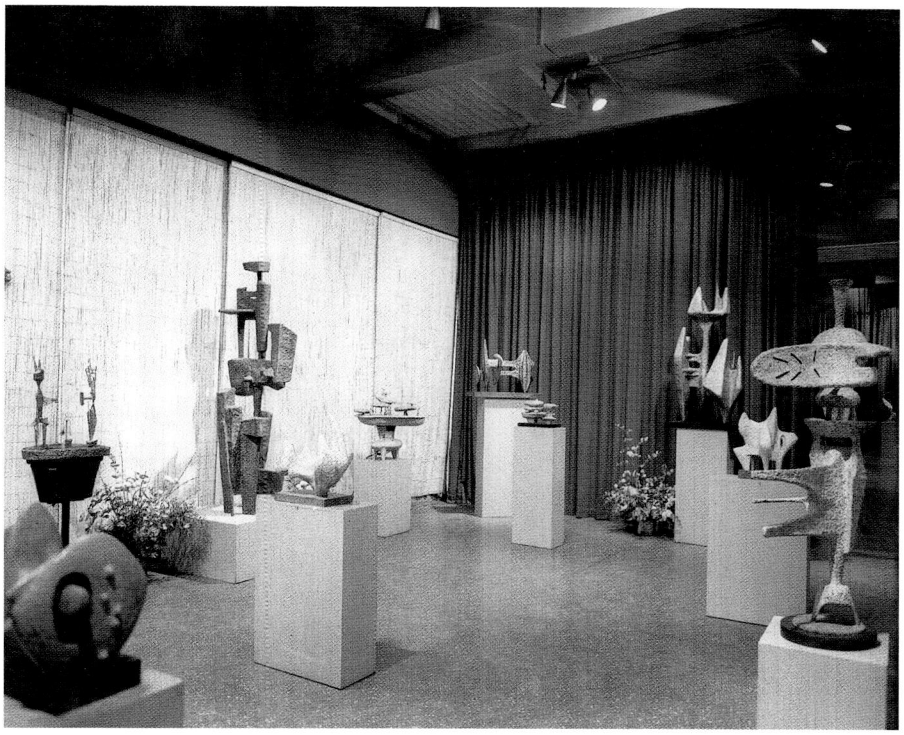

Photograph of show at the Sculpture Center, New York, NY, including aquamobiles.

In 1954, the Delgado Museum in New Orleans (later the New Orleans Museum of Art) gave Emery a solo show of her aquamobiles, which traveled to museums in Birmingham, Chattanooga, Columbia, South Carolina, and the Norton Museum in West Palm Beach. Emery was confronted with a perennial irony of art, the inverse relationship between popularity and artistic "worth," as defined by critics and so often associated with seriousness of form or subject. The irony was resolved naturally as her water-based work increased in both scale and formal integrity. In the 1960s, Emery's aquamobiles traveled to shows in Paris as well as Dallas and Miami.

Emery's interest was now engaged at a more serious level and she developed what she calls "a passion for water." She began to think more deeply about the significance of water and to investigate its historic role in sculpture. When she entered the Engineer's Library in New York, opposite the United Nations, she was greeted by a wall-size picture of the grandiose waterworks of Salomon de Caux. Born in 1576, the French engineer and physicist de Caux invented a device that used steam pressure to force water into jets to create fountains. Emery devoured his manuscripts and traced the basic principles of water-driven devices back to Hero of Alexandria, who, during the first century CE, used hydraulics to miraculously open temple doors and to activate theater pieces, and who demonstrated the first steam engine.[2] In a piece written to accompany an exhibition of her aquamobiles, Emery linked water-powered mobile sculptures back to the water clocks of the Arab world and China. She wrote that the Renaissance brought "the apogee of aquamobiles" and noted the great delight that the Dukes of Bourbon took in their "jets d'eaux of water toys, with articulated figures and animals."

When considering the philosophical aspects of water, Emery naturally turned to the framework of anthroposophy and found a book published by the Rudolf

Steiner Press, *Sensitive Chaos,* by Theodor Schwenk.[3] The text would have a strong influence on Emery's thinking and both her water-based work and the kinetic sculptures that followed. In the foreword to the book, Schwenk expresses his regret that man has lost "the knowledge and experience of the spiritual nature of water." Water was perhaps the most prevalent primordial element in creation myths across cultures and centuries. Sacred springs, rivers, and lakes abounded and some even carry their mystical character into modern times. Emery, who always seeks underlying truths—the sacred rather than the religious—readily accepted the spiritual nature of water.

Schwenk points out that the way forms arise out of liquid or gaseous elements is by movement, and the importance of water to life means that these are the "archetypal forms of movement." As described by the laws of fluid dynamics, those forces and movements produce the meanders of rivers, arching wave forms, and the curlicues of rising smoke. These forms, particularly the vortex spiral that appears in many natural organisms, such as the shell of the nautilus, are represented in some of man's earliest artistic expressions and have become deeply embedded in Emery's sculptural vocabulary.

Despite the precedence of Alexander Calder and George Rickey, the sculptor who most deeply influenced Emery during her formative years was Isamu Noguchi—a less obvious choice, but, on reflection, not surprising. She calls him "superb in every aspect of sculpture," and they became good friends when they first met in 1963. Noguchi introduced her to his supplier of fountains, welcomed her to his apartment and studio, and served on panels she organized about architecture and sculpture. There are similarities at multiple levels between the two artists. Noguchi also had a peripatetic childhood, traveling between Japan and the United States, and a disorienting family life. His father left the family before Isamu was born and shunned the youngster when Isamu traveled to Tokyo to connect with him. Both Noguchi and Emery were outsiders, he as a Japanese American during World War II, she as a woman entering the male-dominated world of public sculpture. More telling is a similarity of philosophical attitude, perhaps related to their backgrounds and expressed through their art. In their youth, both Noguchi and Emery had a rootless restlessness and an inquisitiveness that led them to explore alternative belief systems. Just as Emery did in New York, when Noguchi was a young man in Paris, he took a month off to read about Asian philosophies at the British Library in London. There, in addition to books on Zen Buddhism, he read Helena Blavatsky's books on Theosophy. Eventually, they both delved below the tenets of dogmatic belief systems to an underlying reality intertwined with the structures and forces of nature. Noguchi was strongly affected by Zen Buddhism both as an attitude to life and as manifested in works of art: simple abstract forms, inwardness, stones, gardens, water. He often expressed the desire to "see nature through nature's eyes."

As with Emery, some of Noguchi's most potent expressions of his aesthetic philosophy use water as a principal ingredient. In Dore Ashton's phrase, the garden was Noguchi's reigning metaphor,[4] and water was, in the tradition of Japanese stroll gardens and Persian and Western gardens, a frequent component. In his circular *Sunken Garden* (fig. 3.6) for the Chase Manhattan Bank in New York, Noguchi

opposite page

FIG. 3.6 *Isamu Noguchi (American, 1904–1988),* Sunken Garden, *Chase Manhattan Bank Plaza, 1961–1964. Black river stone and granite paving, diameter 60 feet (18.3 m). Photograph: Arthur Lavine/JPMorgan Chase. Courtesy JPMorgan Chase Art Collection, New York. © 2011 The Isamu Noguchi Foundation and Garden Museum, New York/Artists Rights Society (ARS), New York.*

FIG. 3.7 *Isamu Noguchi,* The Well (Variation on a Tsukubai), *1982. Basalt and water, 38¾ x 31 x 33 15/16 inches (98.4 x 78.7 x 86 cm). The Isamu Noguchi Foundation and Garden Museum, New York. © 2011 The Isamu Noguchi Foundation and Garden Museum, New York/Artists Rights Society (ARS), New York.*

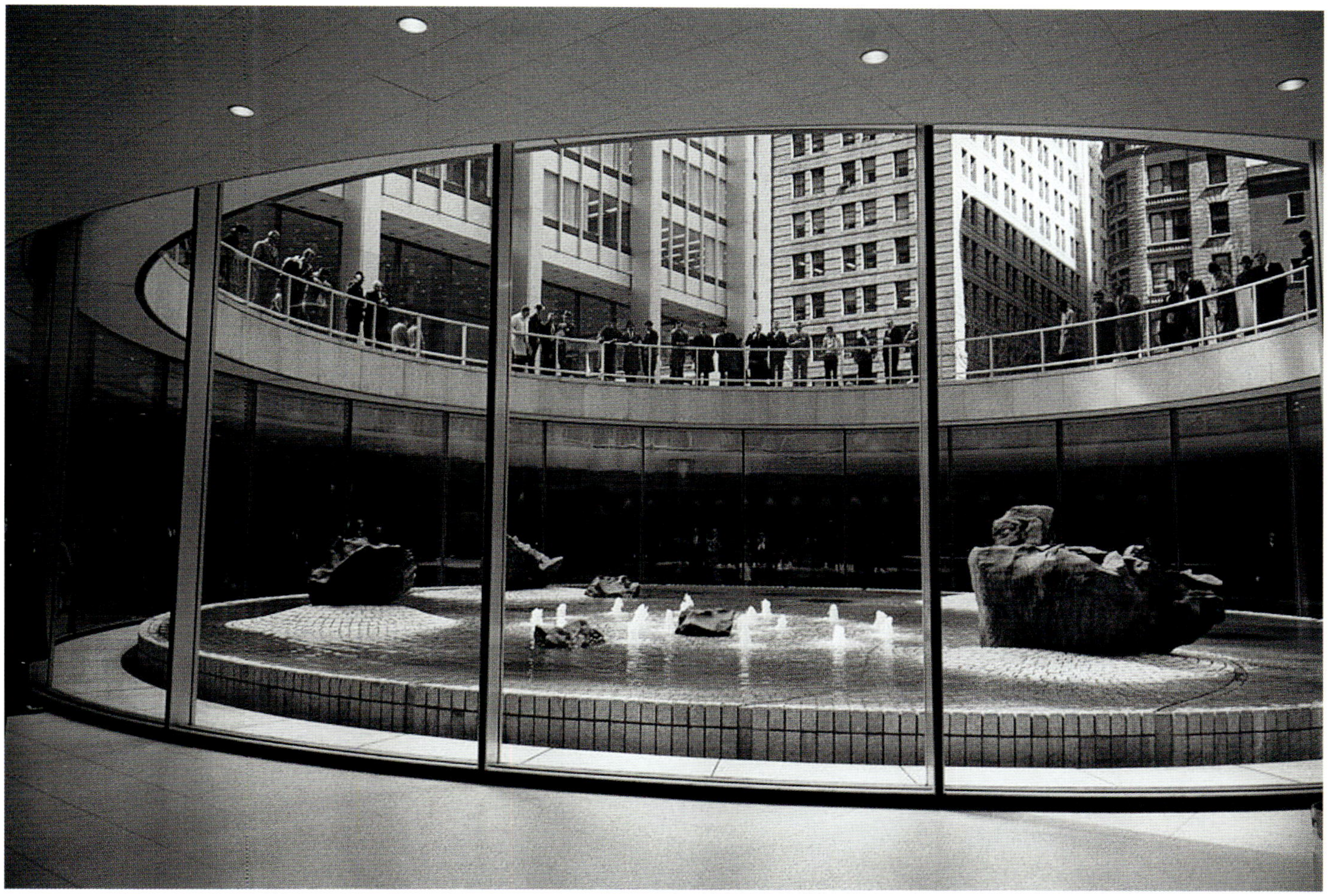

placed water-sculpted river stones from Japan on arrays of paving stones. A thin sheet of shimmering water takes the place of the raked gravel that is traditional in Zen meditation gardens. In his calmly stunning *The Well* (fig. 3.7), water flows mysteriously out of a circular opening, as though from the center of the earth, and glides over the rough and smooth surfaces of a brown basalt block. All of these works eloquently express a unity between nature, expressed through its most primal materials, and man, expressed through a creative act.

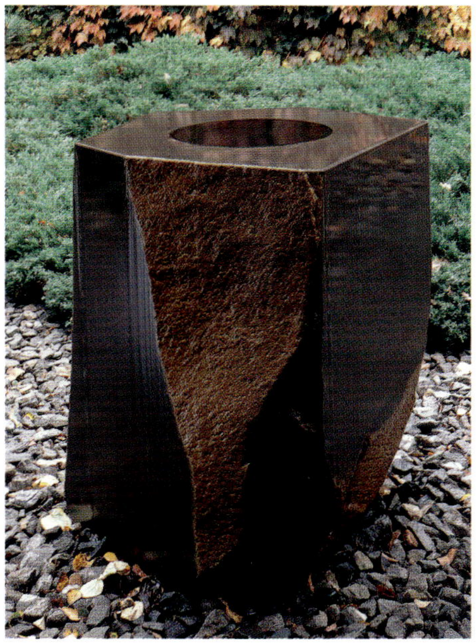

In 1966, Emery was able to incorporate her deepened attitude toward water into a significant sculptural work and at the same time contribute to the visual appeal of her adopted city. She doesn't know exactly how she was chosen by the city of New Orleans to create a memorial to Mayor deLesseps Morrison after his death in a plane crash. She had submitted a brochure on her new foundry to the selection committee, hoping to be able to cast the winning piece, and apparently on that basis was asked to design the memorial. A popular reformist politician and ambassador to the Organization of American States, Morrison was a hard-driving and effective catalyst of New Orleans's economic development. One of the projects that he pushed through, much in the style of Robert Moses in New York, was the New Orleans Civic Center, the site of Emery's memorial. Knowing that Morrison had in

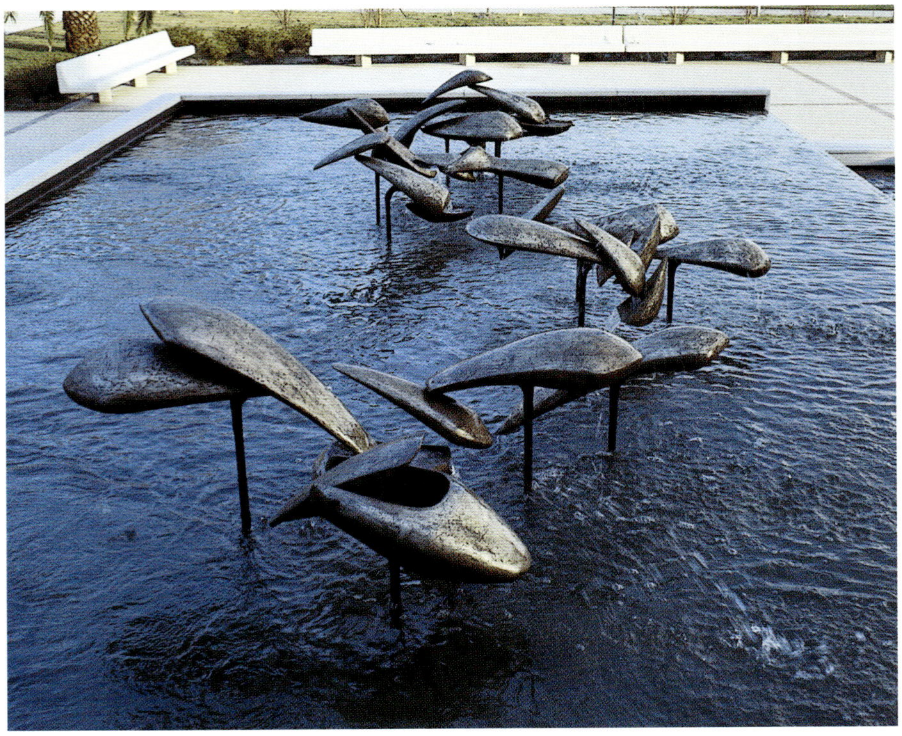

FIG. 3.8 *Lin Emery,* Morrison Memorial Fountain, *1966–1967. Cast nickel silver with water system, 5 x 25 x 10 feet (1.5 x 7.6 x 3 m). Stolen, 2010.*

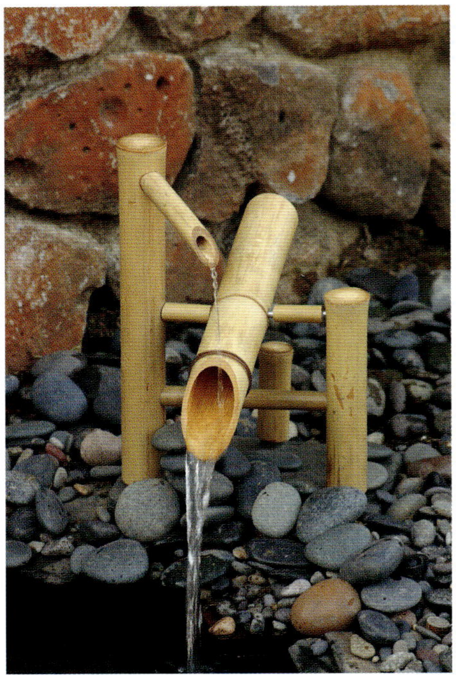

Hiromi Faibisch (Japanese, b. 1964), Japanese Deer Chaser (Shishi Odoshi), *2008. Bamboo spout, submersible pump, water, and river rocks, 12 x 7 x 9 inches (30.5 x 17.8 x 22.9 cm). Photograph © Hiromi Faibisch. Courtesy Bamboo Accents, San Rafael, CA.*

mind a pool for the Duncan Plaza of the Civic Center, she designed one with two levels and a long shallow waterfall that created an animating band of flowing water between them (*Morrison Memorial Fountain*, fig. 3.8).

Sculptural memorials come in two categories. In the first, the sculptor uses conventional portrait forms—the general on horseback or a standing figure—to commemorate the individual. In the second, common in modern times, the representation is indirect. The sculptor receives a commission when he or she is excited by independent sculptural ideas, and uses those ideas as a vehicle for testimony. That was the case for Picasso's two memorials to Guillaume Apollinaire, one a bronze of a woman's head, the other an abstract open metal construction, and it is true of Emery's Morrison Memorial. A combination of fountains and simplified water-driven porpoise shapes animate a rectangular pool in the courtyard of the Civic Center. James Smith Pierce described it well: "These silver creatures, awesome in their powerful movements as they slowly bow and spurt and rise, are apparently driven by wills of their own."[5] Emery is very explicit about her desire to achieve realistic, lifelike movement. Her Morrison fountain has a natural vitality that no figure on a horse could ever muster.

For the mechanisms in her Morrison Memorial, as well as many subsequent water sculptures, Emery drew on a traditional Japanese device, the *shishi odoshi*, or deer chaser. This elegantly simple device was originally developed by Japanese farmers to scare off deer and is often seen in Japanese-style gardens. Water flows into a long section of bamboo that pivots around an axis below its midpoint. As it fills, the section tips over, spilling its contents and rocking back to accept more water. As it rocks back and forth one or both ends hit a stone, creating a rhythmic, hollow knocking sound. Emery appreciates the irregular, nonmechanical variations in velocity of the deer chaser's movement. But there is a considerable technical distance between bamboo deer chasers and sleek, 5-foot-long dolphins. The Morrison Memorial provides a revealing example of Emery's hands-on philosophy and personal integration of the engineering and artistic aspects of her work. If there is no practical way for her to do something herself she will contract out an element of a project. Rather than a chore, learning new science or new skills is an integral and pleasurable part of being a sculptor. For the Morrison project she studied hydraulics at the Tulane School of Engineering and used the hydraulics laboratory to design a weir for the pool. She experimented for months to develop combinations of water tubing and sleeve bearings for the bobbing dolphins, and she cast the dolphins at her own foundry in nickel silver melted down from flatware that she bought from the Roosevelt Hotel when it changed hands.

The Morrison Memorial had a second component, a 40-foot-high, 5-ton tower of cast aluminum (*Morrison Monument*, fig. 3.9). The surface of the tower is enlivened by a Cubistic set of planes and cast sections containing words and dates relevant to Morrison's life. In her use of words on the surface of the tower, Emery may have been inspired by the giant Egyptian obelisk inscribed with hieroglyphics commemorating Ramses II that commands the center of Place de la Concorde in Paris. In contrast to the obelisk, the Morrison tower increases gradually in width toward the top, magnifying the power of its presence. The bright surfaces and deep shadows produced by the fretwork of numbers and words contribute a rich texture to the surface. Emery's life-size portrait of Morrison stands in a niche high in the tower, an integral part of the tower, as of the city that he so affected.

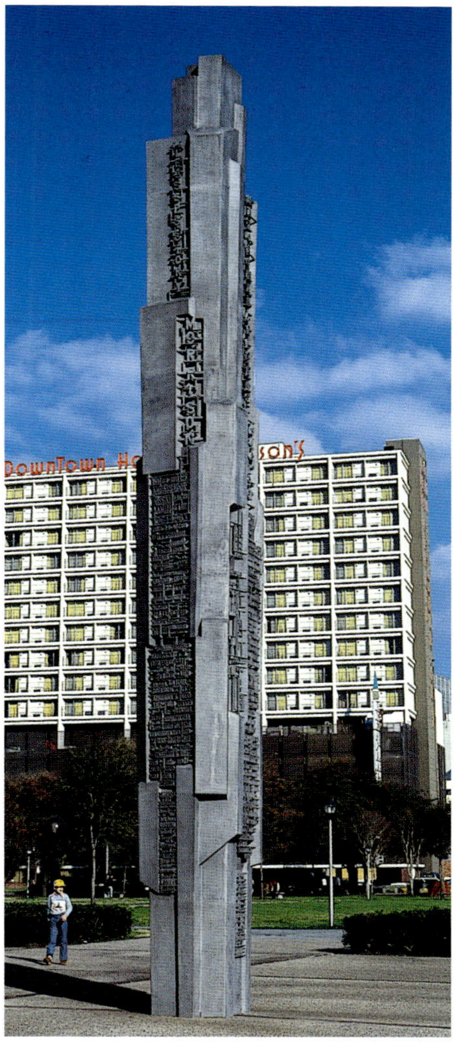

FIG. 3.9 *Lin Emery,* Morrison Monument, *1965–1971. Cast aluminum, 40 feet (12.1 m). City Hall Plaza, New Orleans, LA. Photograph: Mike Smith.*

The positive reception of the Morrison Memorial sparked interest in other large-scale water-based sculptures. At least one was too large. The 9-foot high *Flight of Fancy* (fig. 3.10), commissioned by a bank, couldn't make it through the front door but was eventually installed and ultimately made its way into a private collection when the bank closed. Emery's *Cupriflora Mobilia* (fig. 3.11) formed the basis for the design of a fountain commissioned by another bank, Fidelity Bank in Oklahoma City (subsequently owned by the Bank of Oklahoma after the failure of Fidelity). The plaque created for the dedication displayed the title in the Cherokee language and maintained that the cluster shape was inspired by the state flower, the mistletoe, and the forked forms derived from the state bird, the scissor-tailed flycatcher. Fabricated from bronze plate, the moving elements balanced on knife-edge bearings, similar to those used by George Rickey in his early work. In her *Aquamobile* (see p. 48) and *Flight of Fancy* of 1963, and in *Cupriflora Mobilia*, despite the reference to state flora and fauna, Emery abstracted natural forms well beyond representation to a delicate point of balance between the organic and the geometric. This creature of spilling and spurting water and tipping and bobbing metal was formidably alive, but unlike any natural being. For the first time the forms and seriousness of Emery's earlier bronze works, such as *Genesis* (see fig. 2.13) and *Futile Cloak* (see p. 39), had found their way into the aquamobiles. The whimsy of *King and Queen at the Beach* (fig. 3.2), the representational fancy of *Busy Blossom* (fig. 3.4), and the fragile structures of *Mixed Quartet* (see p. 47) were left behind for more refined and substantial stuff.

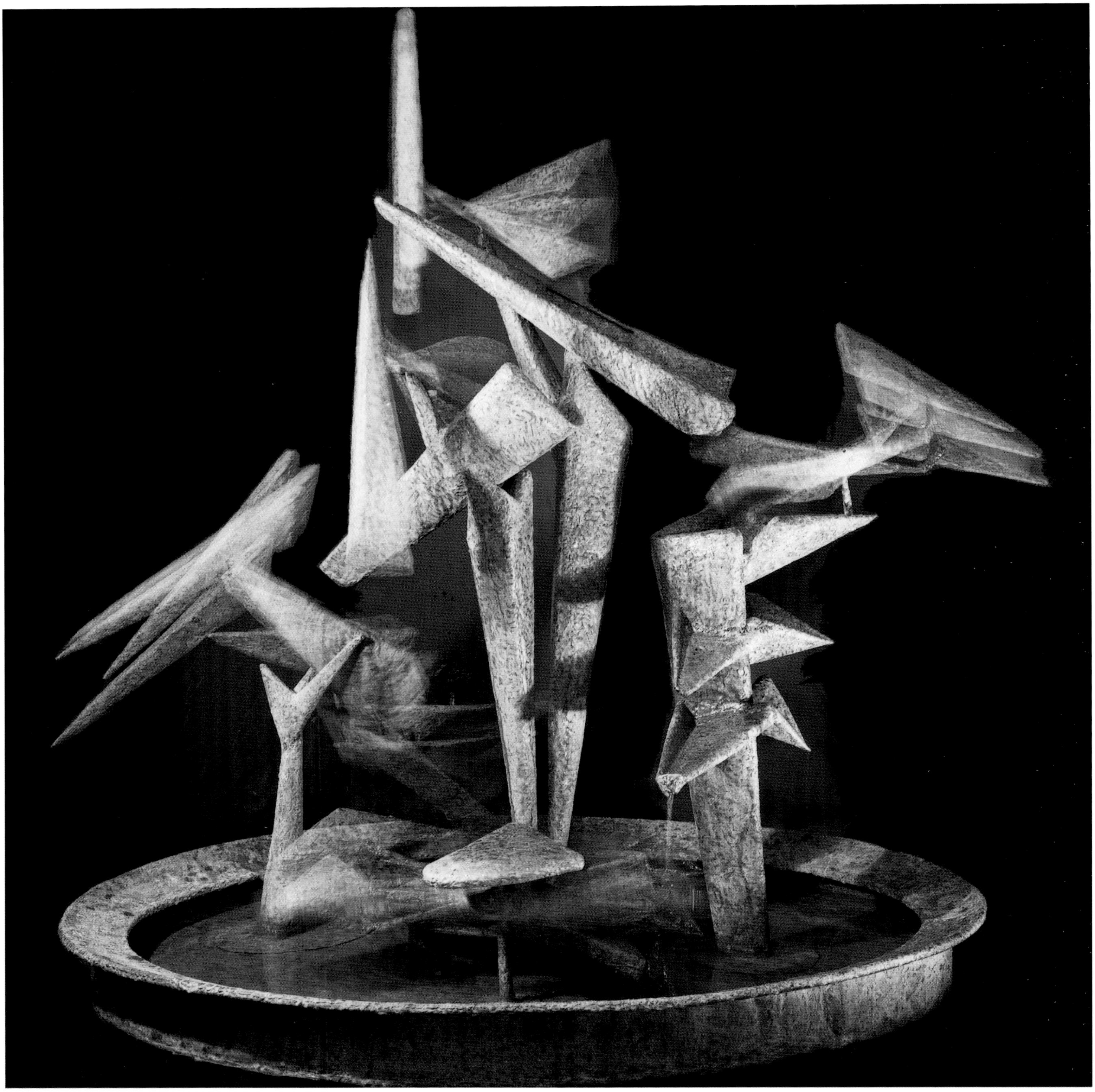

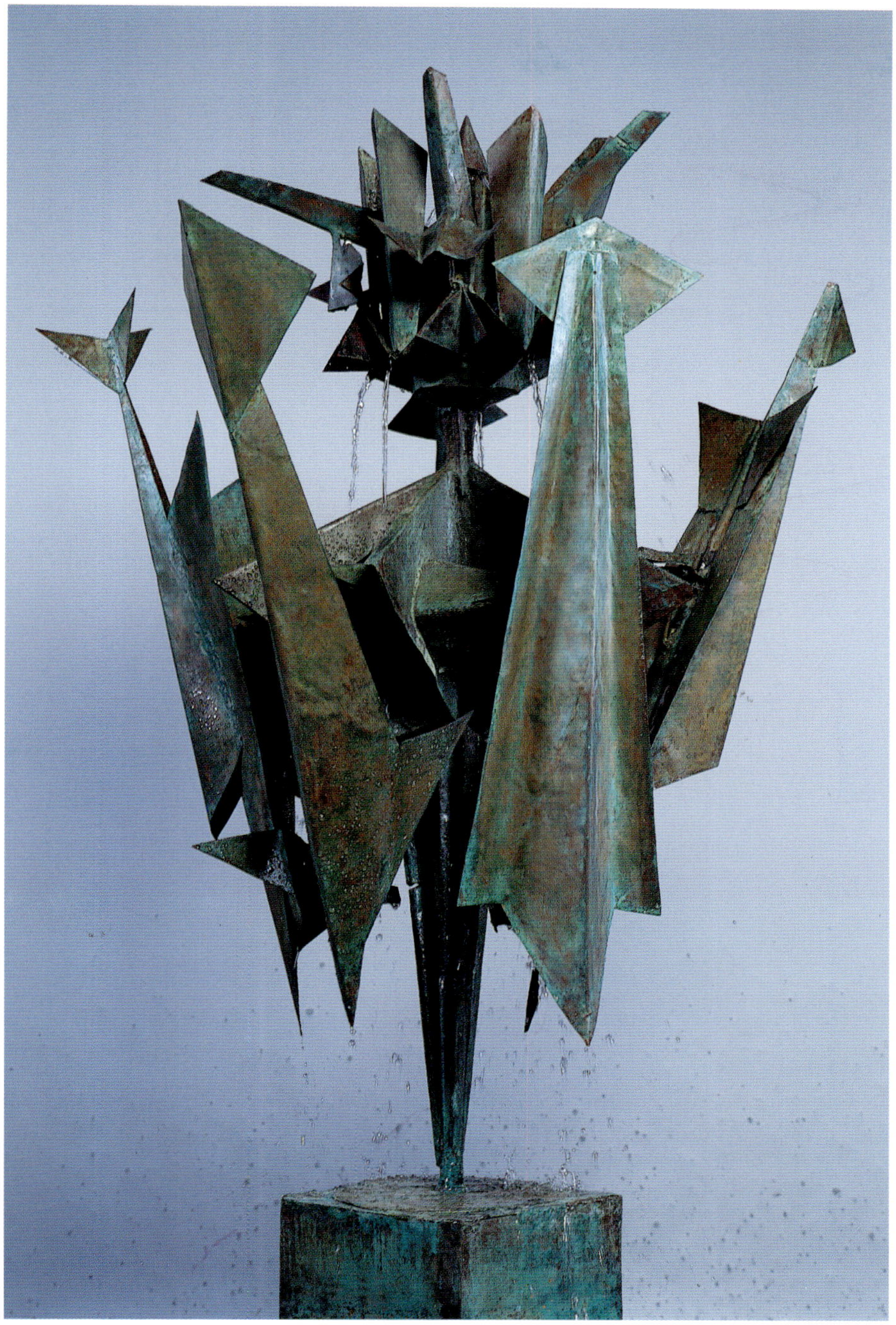

opposite page

FIG. 3.10 *Lin Emery,* Flight of Fancy, *1963. Brazed copper, water, and pump, 9 x 9 x 7 feet (2.7 x 2.7 x 2.1 m). Germantown Savings Bank, Philadelphia, PA.*

FIG. 3.11 *Lin Emery,* Cupriflora Mobilia, *1962. Brazed copper, water, and pump, 53 x 38 x 28 inches (134.6 x 96.5 x 71.1 cm). New Orleans Museum of Art, New Orleans, LA.*

Emery continued to explore new materials for her large works. When she was commissioned to design an aquamobile for the student center at the University of South Carolina, she used the structural techniques of modern boat-building—plastic foam injected onto a welded armature and coated with a fiberglass resin. In this dashing work (*Untitled*, fig. 3.12), Emery captures the spirit of one of the great sculptural objects of our time: the racing sailboat.

For her next major fountain commission, for the Tulsa-based energy company Helmerich & Payne, Emery created a group of eighteen linked bronze troughs that filled, spilled, and bobbed and were surrounded by independent jets of water

Lin Emery, Falling Water, *1972. Bronze with water system, 20 x 12 x 12 feet (6 x 3.6 x 3.6 m). Bank of Oklahoma, Oklahoma City, OK.*

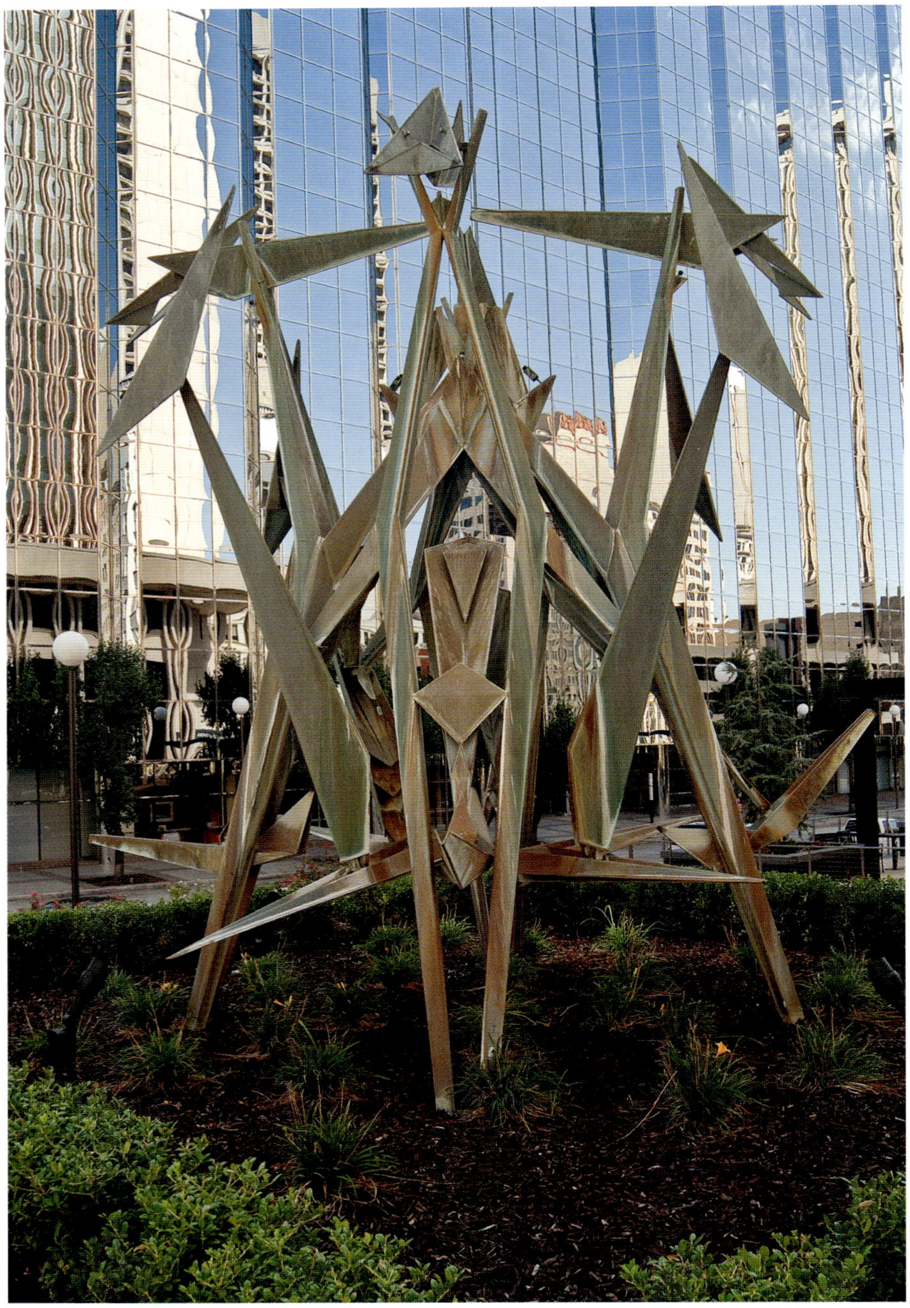

opposite page

FIG. 3.12 *Lin Emery,* Untitled, *1974. Steel armature, Styrofoam, and fiberglass with water system, 8 x 28 x 20 feet (2.4 x 8.5 x 6 m). University of South Carolina, Columbia, SC.*

FIG. 3.13 *Lin Emery,* Free Enterprise, *1977. Welded sheet bronze with water system, 15 x 20 x 20 feet (4.5 x 6 x 6 m). Helmerich Park, Tulsa, OK.*

(*Free Enterprise,* fig. 3.13). By placing the elements farther apart than in the Oklahoma City fountain, Emery created a community, with the work's vitality deriving from a shared dynamic, as if all the members of the community are inspired by a common idea. Emery avoids machine-like movements, aiming for distinct forms of vital movement (distinguishing her aquamobiles from, say, those of Jean Tinguely) that she achieves through engineering design:

> "I don't like mechanical movement. It's so repetitive. What I try to do is control the rhythms and timing of the movement by adjusting the relationships of the pivot point and the center of gravity to get a natural, realistic movement, to get a motion that's related to life."

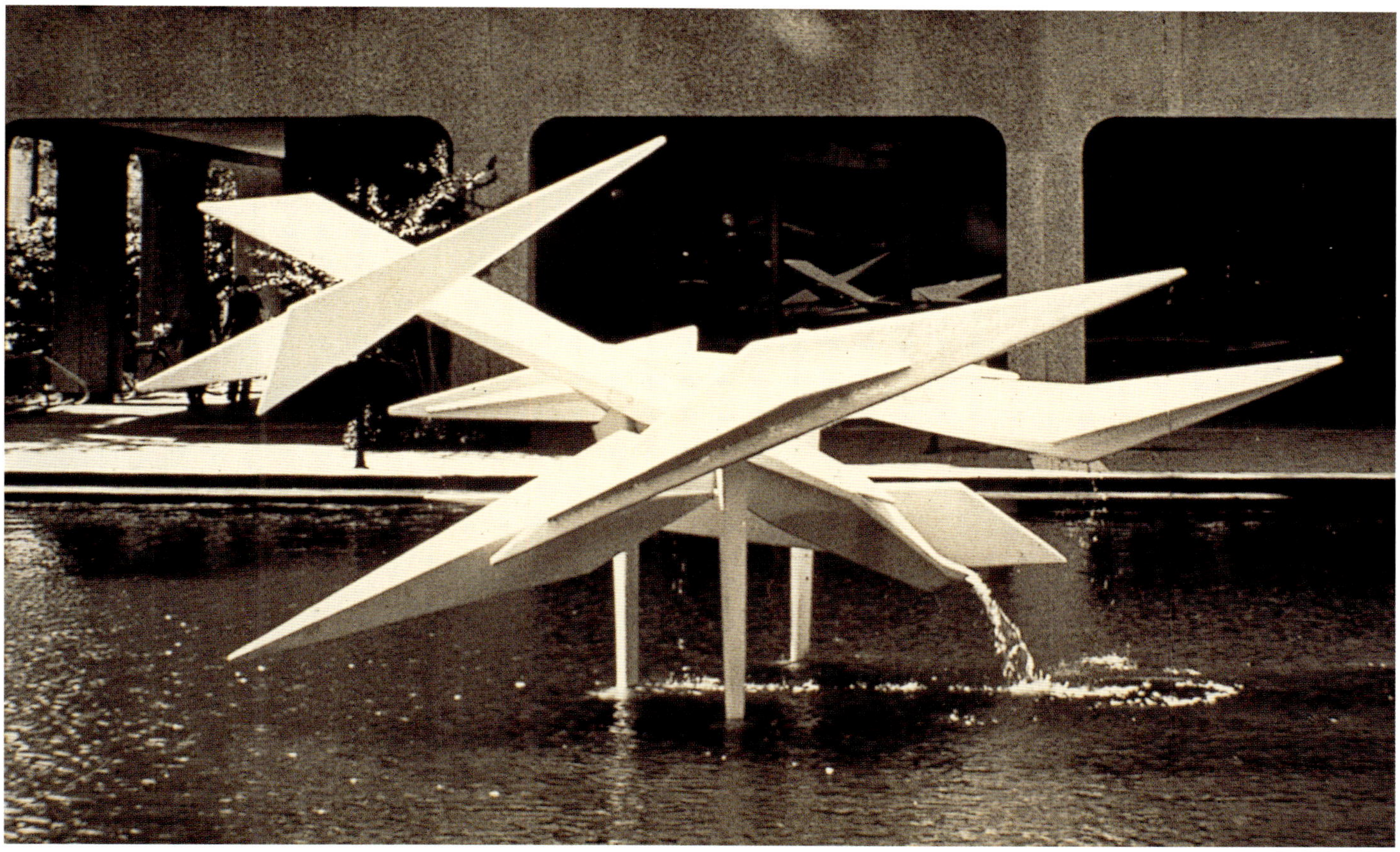

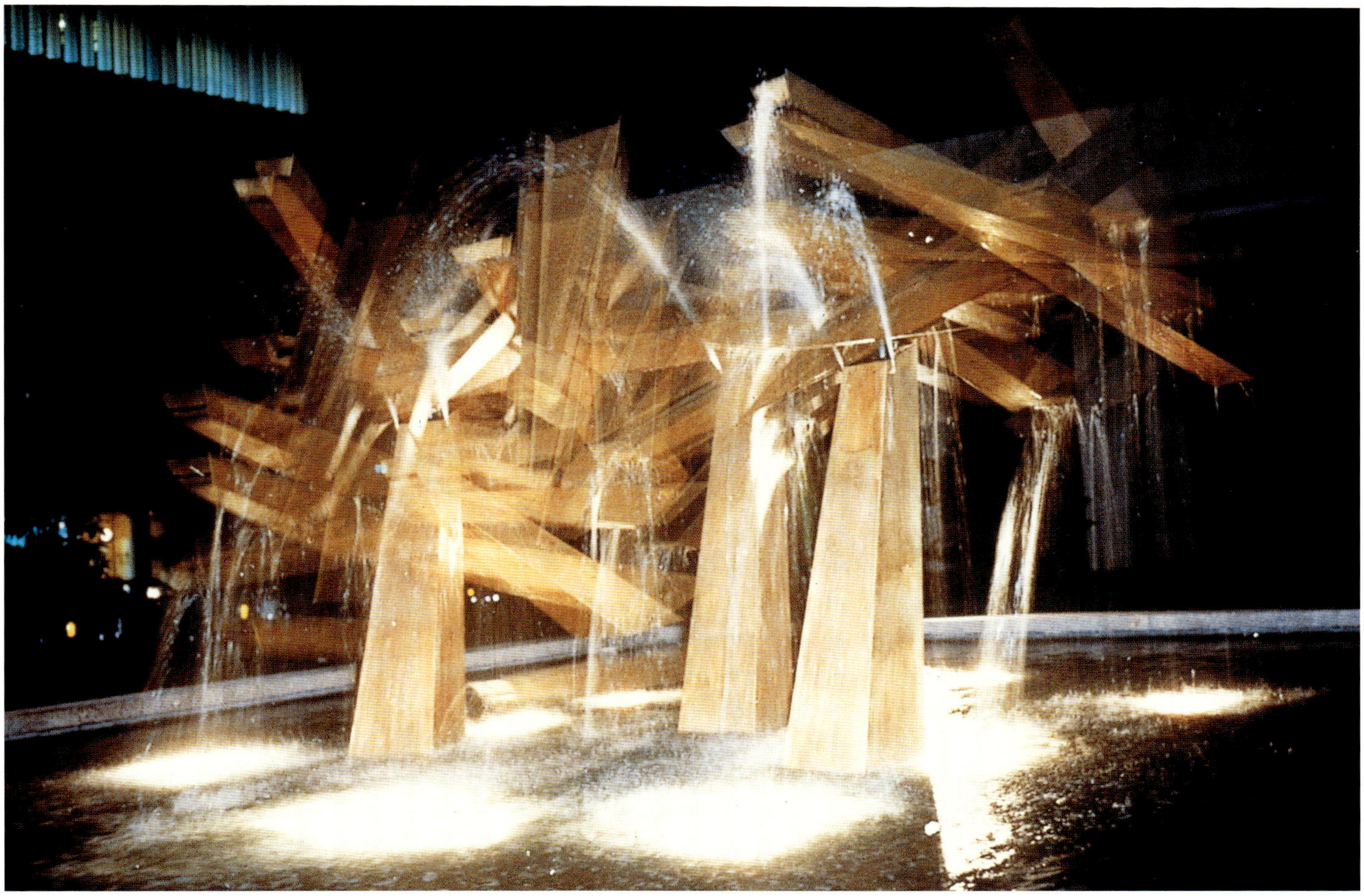

FIG. 3.14 *Lin Emery,* Reflexions, a Play with Water, *1980. Water, wood, and plastic, dimensions variable. The Levee, River Road, Jefferson, LA.*

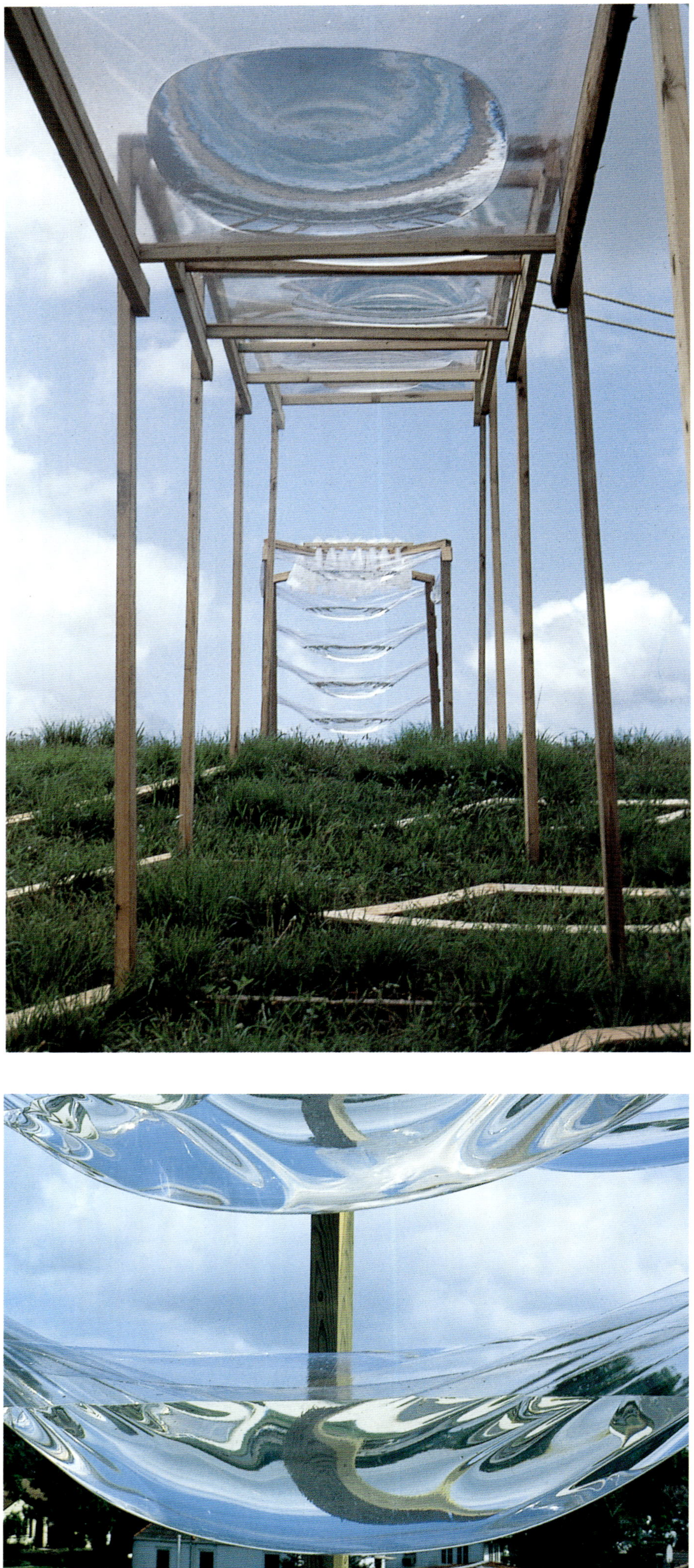

Emery's enthusiasm for water and her zeal for movement were soon confronted by the unfortunate tendency of mechanical systems to fail. Even mechanical systems designed by engineers for purely mechanical purposes fail. A system with artistic objectives poses an even greater provocation to Murphy's Law. The only component of the Morrison Memorial Fountain that Emery didn't manage herself was the main pump. The state's contractors had neglected to install a sump, guaranteeing that the pump failed whenever it rained. When the state didn't correct the problem, Emery removed her dolphins in protest. They were stolen from her Apple Street studio in 2010 and presumably sold for scrap.

The dedication of the Oklahoma City fountain occurred during a bitter cold spell and its water was frozen solid. Later, the anchor bolts started to fail and it was found that the engineers installing the piece had used ordinary steel rather than the stainless steel bolts that Emery had specified. Now reinstalled, the sculpture is stationary and surrounded by groundcover rather than water. For 20- or 30-foot works of sculpture, the risk of the unpredictable starts with the installation. For the University of South Carolina fountain, Emery specified that a forklift be used for the installation. To save money, the university enlisted members of the football team to do the lifting, but they managed to drop one of the largest elements—on the sculptor. Emery's shoulder was operated on back in New Orleans. Her inclination for experimentation and innovation has its own perils. In 1970, her stock of nickel silver depleted, she experimented with a new alloy called white bronze, provided by Asarco, using it for a 15-foot-high caduceus on the side of a hospital. The alloy turned out to be unstable, and when the manganese leached out, the wall of the hospital was streaked with black.

Most of these failures could be corrected, in the case of the hospital with a coat of paint, but Emery's sensitivity and centered dedication to her work mean that any failure affects her deeply. Inevitably, as she continued to innovate and as her work became more ambitious, mechanical failures continued to occur and their importance, exaggerated in her own mind, would constitute the most trying aspect of her career as a sculptor.

Despite the diversity of Emery's aquamobiles, she sought more direct ways of displaying water's deeper nature. She installed a work on a levee of the Mississippi intending to represent water as "reflection, as illusion, as symbol, as wishing well, as oracle" (*Reflexions*, fig. 3.14). By building overhead pools of water on transparent plastic, Emery created an experience of seeing light through water and with fresh eyes. Sparkling clear plastic bags of water hung in bunches, and children were invited to spear the bags like piñatas; a small shower of water, heated by the sun, would rain down.

Although Emery made no more large aquamobiles after 1990, the movement and qualities of water remained a central part of her aesthetic consciousness. The dynamics of water have found their way into many of her kinetic works, and in 2003 she had a charming reprise of her aquamobiles in the form of a kinetic wall sculpture in the Renaissance Arts Hotel in New Orleans (*Leaf Dance*, fig. 3.15). Activated by the flow of water, five pairs of leaf forms wave back and forth as in a breeze and water flows out of their stems into a shallow basin with a calm splashing

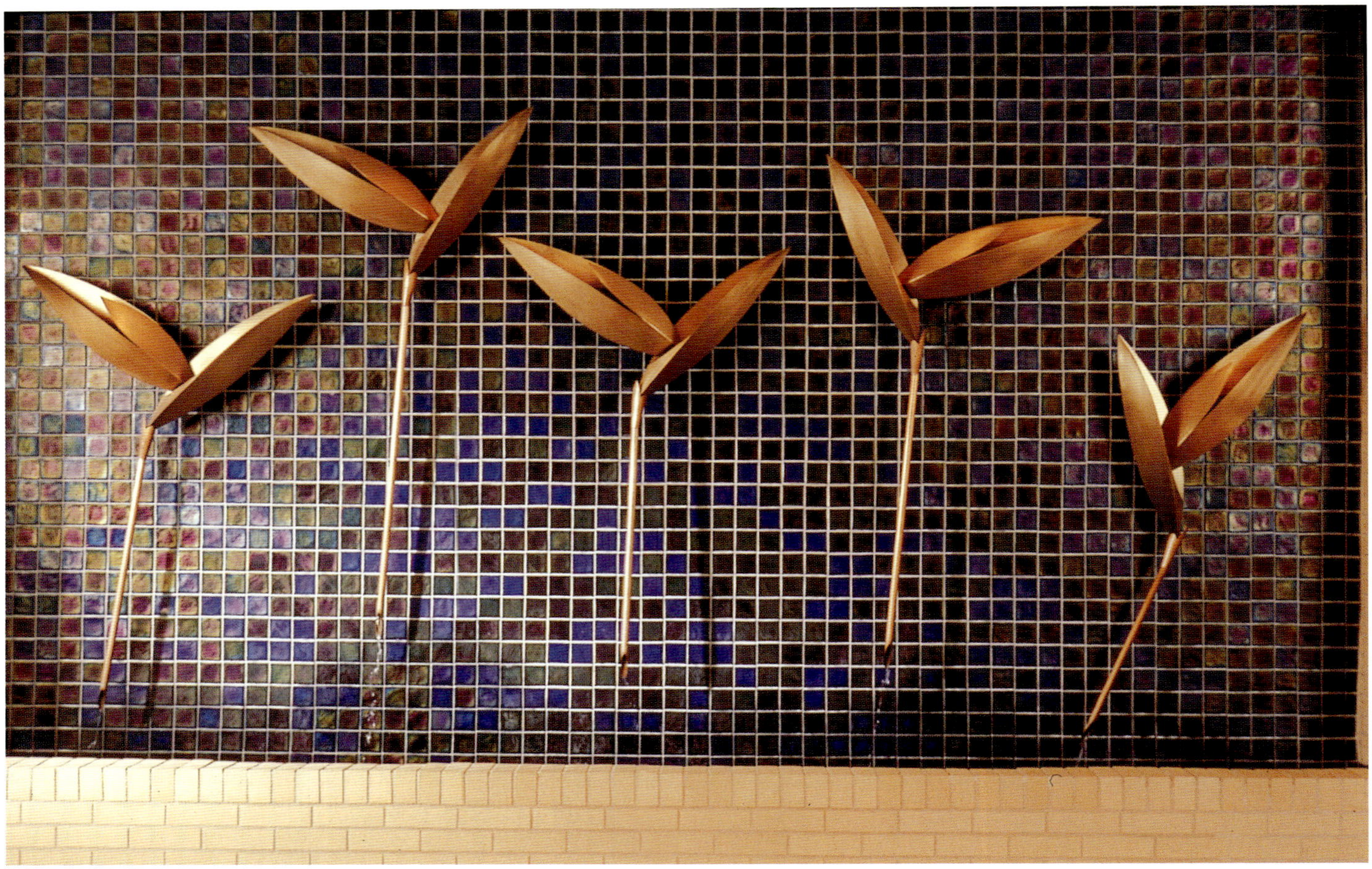

Fig. 3.15 Lin Emery, Leaf Dance, *2003. Bronze with water system, 10 x 15 x 1 feet (3 x 4.5 x 0.3 m). Renaissance Arts Hotel, New Orleans, LA.*

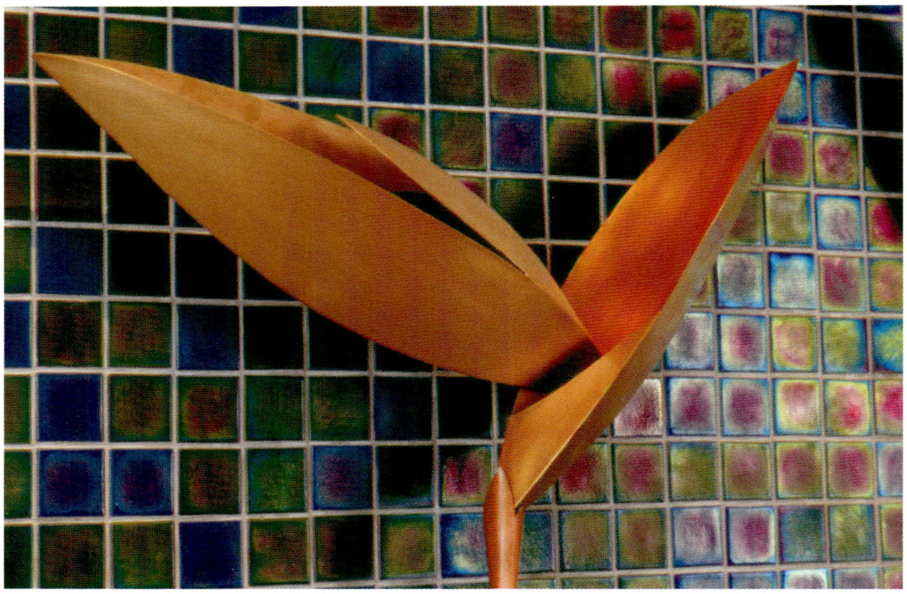

sound. The friezelike shallow alignment of the leaf forms produces a compositional formality unusual in Emery's aquamobiles.

Perhaps not as dramatic as the day that Emery entered Zadkine's studio, the moment she observed the teaspoon rocking up and down on the cup under the spell of water was a critical moment in the evolution of her work. That chance event led to her water-based sculpture, initially fanciful, then serious, and at all times highly appealing. While Emery is now best known for her wind-driven kinetic works, her series of large fountains in the 1960s and 1970s constitutes one of the most substantial integrations of water and modern sculpture in our times. Fountains of the nineteenth and early twentieth centuries provided a natural context for figurative sculpture, but the concerns of modernism isolated and elevated the abstract sculptural object from the "real world," and water seemed incompatible with that vision. Noguchi's connection with nature made him an exception, but only in isolated works. Many other sculptors have worked effectively with water, but Emery's series of grand and lively fountains constitute an exceptional and coherent synthesis of the qualities of water, abstract shapes, and vital movement.

NOTES

1. Theodor Schwenk, *Sensitive Chaos: The Creation of Flowing Forms in Water and Air* (London: Rudolf Steiner Press, 1965), p. 67. The title derives from the eighteenth-century German romantic writer Georg Philipp Friedrich von Hardenberg, who took the nom-deplume Novalis.

2. If patents had been around in the first century, Hero would have been a rich man. He could make the case that he invented not only the steam engine but also the vending machine. A contraption described in his *Mechanics and Optics* dispensed a controlled amount of holy water when a coin was inserted in a slot on top.

3. Schwenk, p. 126.

4. Dore Ashton, *Noguchi East and West* (New York: Alfred A. Knopf, 1992), p. 6. See also Ana Maria Torres, *Isamu Noguchi: A Study of Space* (New York: Monacelli Press, 2000), chapter 5.

5. James Smith Pierce, "Lin Emery's Aquamobiles," *Art International*, 13, no. 1 (January 1969): 34–35.

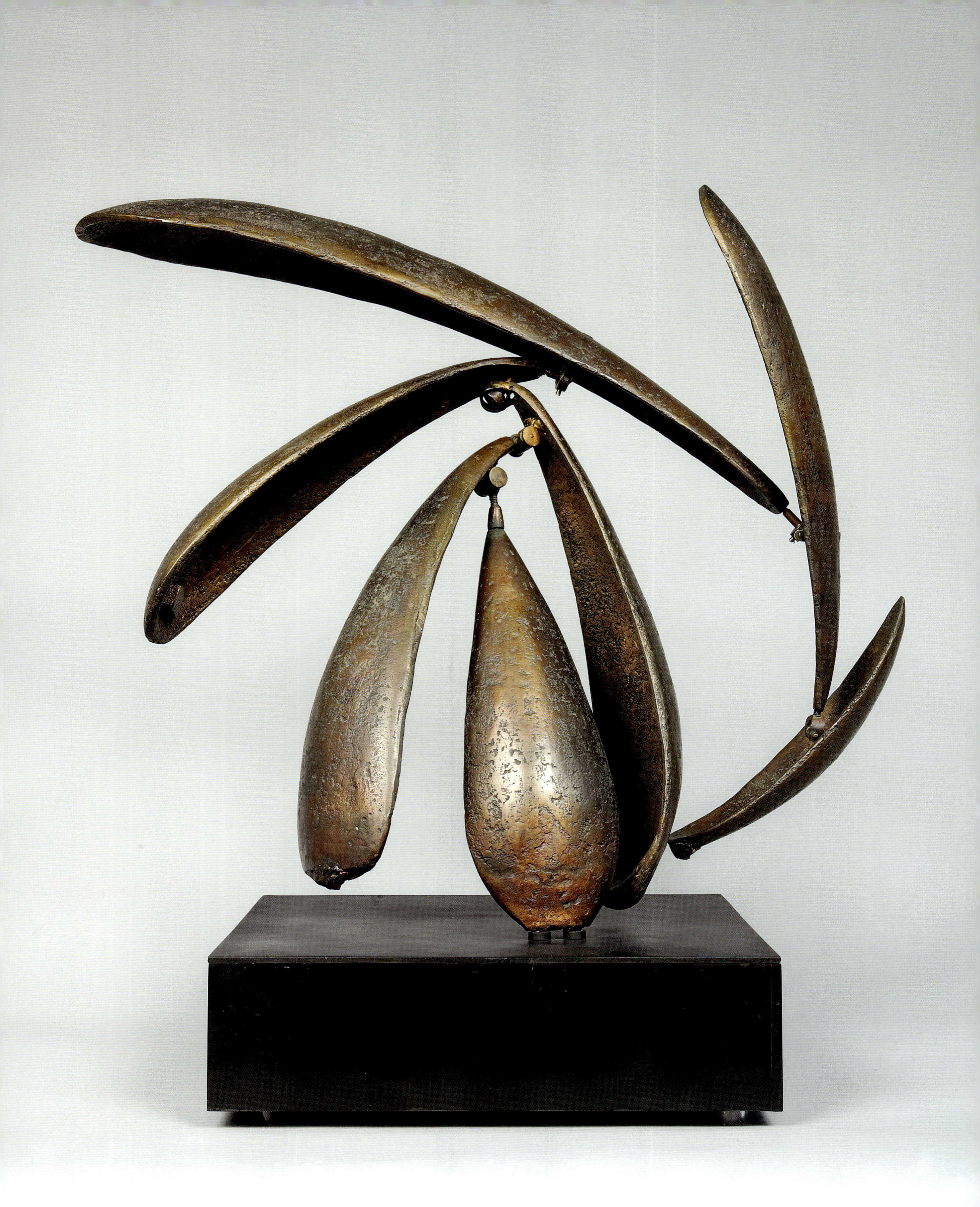

CHAPTER IV

Magnets

A machine become a poem . . .

—Isamu Noguchi[1]

Despite the great success of Emery's use of water as an integral part of her sculpture, there were problems of various kinds. Full of mythological and philosophical significance, water is in principle a powerful aesthetic medium, but it is very difficult to embody those concepts in serious sculptural work. There were also the ornery practical problems of failing pumps, rusting mechanisms, and freezing water. In the early 1970s, Emery was using only journal bearings, cylinders rotating in tubes. Not only did this limit the movement of the individual elements to one plane, but the balancing of heavy metal elements was annoyingly difficult. There was another reason for Emery to move on from her water-driven work: her inveterate restlessness, once geographical and now technical and aesthetic.

In addition to her restless desire to innovate, from an early age Emery had a ferocious appetite to learn. She is very conscious of the fact that, with the exception of her partial year with Zadkine and her time in New York at the Sculpture Center, she had no academic grounding in sculptural methods. Having no dominant mentor may have been a good thing. Brancusi, when he turned down the opportunity of being Rodin's apprentice, famously said, "Nothing grows in the shadow of great trees." In Zadkine's studio, Emery learned classical techniques of figure sculpture but never came under the influence of his Cubism. Growing up on her own aesthetically and, for the most part, away from New York kept her at a distance from other artists' shadows. Emery has always been an independent thinker, wary of dogma, and her aesthetic development had all the signs of hard-won independence. Her magnetic sculptures are a case in point.

Emery's learning was concentrated on technique, which she put into the service of her own developing aesthetic ideas. In 1960, she discovered a perfect vehicle for that kind of learning, a biennial series of hands-on conferences devoted to sculptural techniques. Although she missed the first National Sculpture Casting Conference, organized by the University of Kansas, she eagerly attended the second one, in 1962, and over the years became increasingly involved. Initially, the three-day meetings concentrated on metal casting, but they gradually expanded to include all aspects of sculptural practice and beyond. In 1968, for the fifth conference, "Cast-

opposite page

Lin Emery, Fledgling, *1965. Bronze, magnets, and motor, 21 x 25 x 15 inches (53.3 x 63.5 x 38.1 cm). Collection of Arthur Roger.*

Lin Emery, Leaf Play, *1968. Bronze, magnets, and motor, 16 x 16 x 8 inches (40.6 x 40.6 x 20.3 cm). Mobile Museum of Art, Mobile, AL.*

opposite page
Lin Emery, Variations, *1978. Aluminum, magnets, and motor, 7 x 4 x 1½ feet (2.1 x 1.2 x 0.5 m). K&B Plaza, New Orleans, LA.*

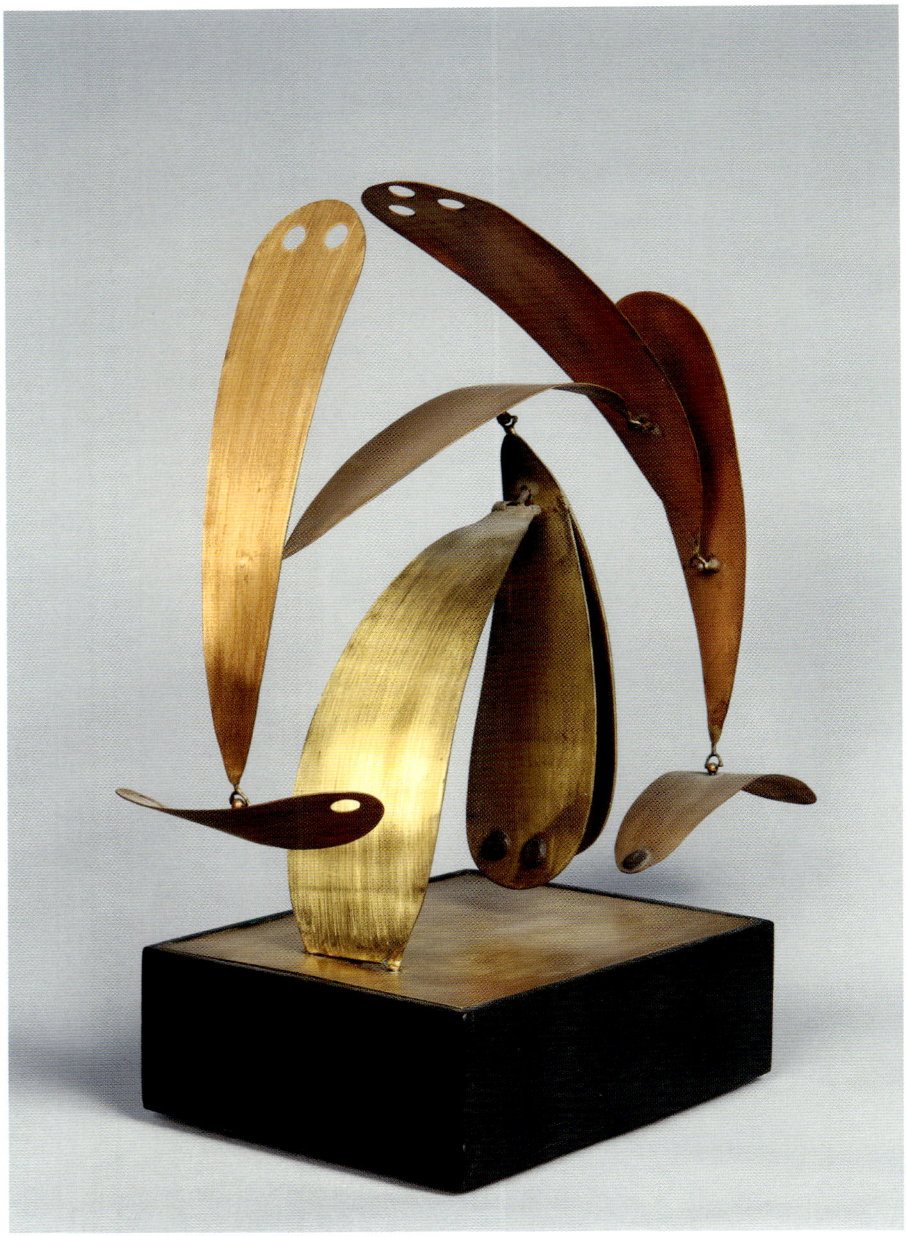

ing" was dropped from its name and that year's conference included sessions on plastics, light, and kinetics. At subsequent meetings, panels discussed architecture, urban planning, environmental art, and sculpture in theater, sound, and education, as well as practical methods of working in ferro-concrete, stone, plastics, and glass. The subjects were expanding exponentially and, as though concerned about its hubristic implications, during one conference Jack Burnham gave a lecture titled "The Limits of Art."

As their reputations grew, the conferences attracted more of the country's sculptural elite to show slides of their latest work, exchange technical methods, complain about their galleries, brag about their commissions, contemplate the future of their art form, and just schmooze. For the sculptural community, these

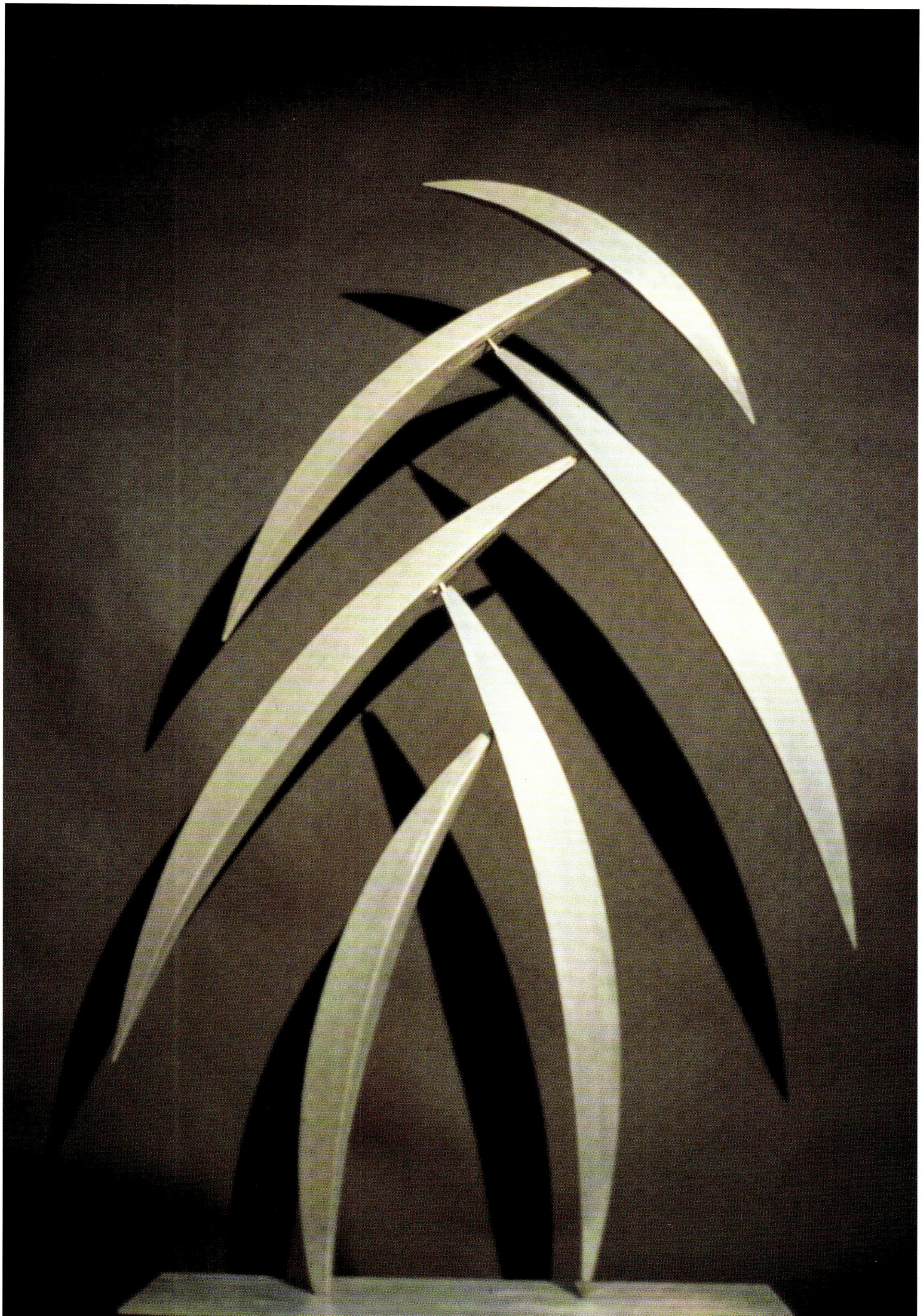

biennial conclaves combined the high-mindedness of the Athenian Academy, the purposefulness of a trade school, and the clubbiness of a lodge of the Loyal Order of Moose—with women allowed. In 1975, Emery joined the board of the conference, and in 1976 she undertook the year-long organizational toil of bringing the ninth conference, now with "International" in its name, to New Orleans. The roster of speakers she was able to attract once again elevated the status of the conference: sculptors Yaacov Agam, Elizabeth Catlett, Dmitri Hadzi, Clement Meadmore, Constantino Nivola, Beverly Pepper, George Sugarman, Seymour Lipton, critics Hilton Kramer and Irving Sandler, and many others. During those four days in 1976, a good fraction of the renowned, normally bustling sculpture studios in the nation were silent.

At the conclusion of her highly successful meeting, one that actually made money, Emery discovered that little disasters could plague conferences as well as complex sculptures. A professor from the University of Kansas, who had organized the preceding conference, drove home with all the proceeds.

By the time of the New Orleans conference, Emery had gotten to know Isamu Noguchi. She persuaded him to come to New Orleans and later to join a panel on architecture and sculpture that she moderated at a conference in Washington. The sculpture conferences continued for several years with Emery's active involvement, and then came under the purview of the International Sculpture Center. When the ISC had financial problems, the conferences were discontinued. Emery tried to restore the program with a small conference in New Orleans in 2004, attracting Antony Gormley as the keynote speaker, but a falling-out with ISC management ended her involvement with the conferences. They have now been revived by the ISC as the biennial International Sculpture Conferences.

In the mid-1960s, frustrated by the difficulties and limitations of water as a motive force, Emery was searching for a new way of activating her sculptures. One of the publications she read to feed her curiosity about scientific and mechanical devices was a catalogue called *American Science and Surplus*. In an issue that featured enticing descriptions and pictures of magnets, Emery recognized a possible solution to her problem. She didn't realize at the time that magnets and sculpture had an ancient liaison: Pliny the Elder, in the first century CE, reported that an architect in Alexandria used lodestone (a natural magnetic ore) in the vaulting of a temple with the idea of suspending an iron statue in midair. When Emery came up with the idea of using magnets, a few other artists were experimenting with them. The Greek French sculptor Vassilakis Takis, for example, took delight in suspending objects in the air using magnetic and electromagnetic forces. At his exhibition at the Iris Clerc Gallery in Paris in 1960, he persuaded his writer friend Sinclair Beiles to read his Magnetic Manifesto, which began with the words, "I am a sculpture," and then to jump into the air, where he hung for an instant suspended by magnets in his belt. This was the spirit of much of the avant-garde art of the 1960s, in which novelty was the dominant criterion of artistic worth. The conceptual, the outrageous, self-mutilation—everything was in vogue except the traditional sculptural object, or any kind of object. Emery was aware of all this and she also pursued the novel, but as evolution rather than revolution, remaining within the canon of

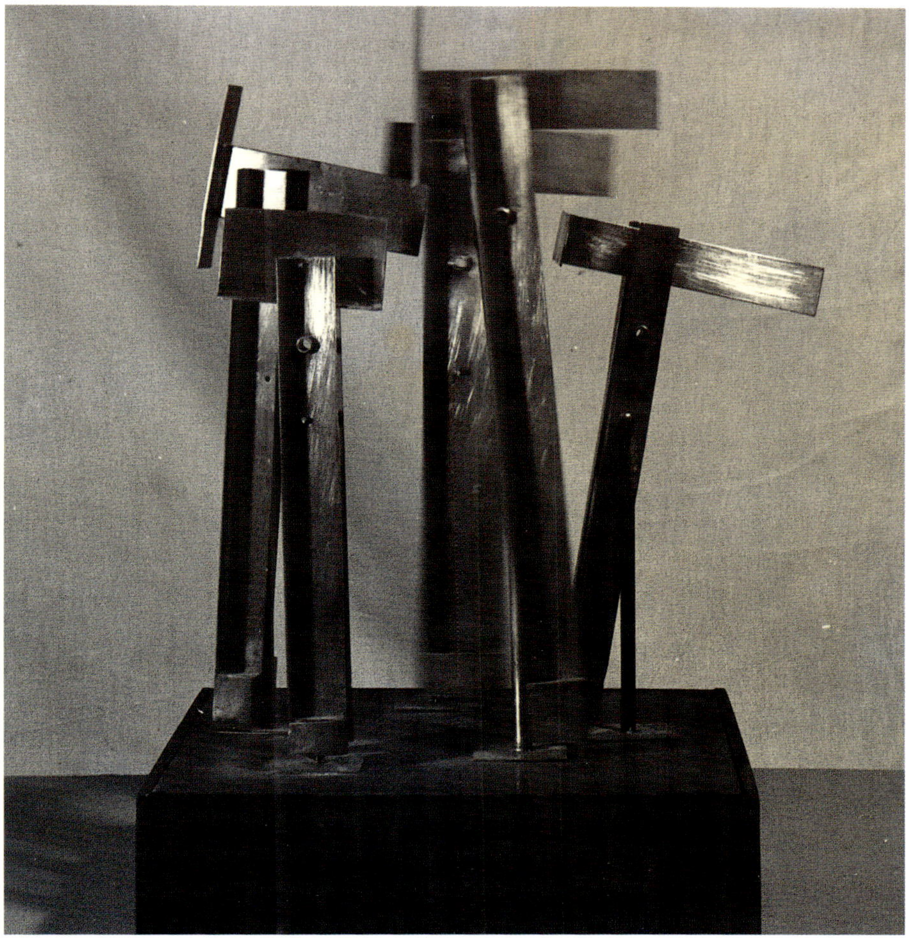

FIG. 4.1 *Lin Emery,* Protest March, *1968. Bronze, magnets, and motor, 12 x 6 x 8 inches (30.5 x 15.2 x 20.3 cm). Private collection.*

modernism. Like Takis, she used magnets, but hers were hidden and all the more effective. The important innovation was that her magnets weren't merely suspending something; she attached the driving magnets to a turntable or other machine hidden in the sculpture's base and hid other magnets in the various elements of the sculpture. Thus, she created seemingly spontaneous, mystical movement.

Emery called her magnet-driven sculptures magnetmobiles, and the first ones, made in 1965, used abstracted leaf forms. Alnico magnets on a small, hidden turntable in the base interacted periodically with magnets embedded in the bronze leaves, attracting, moving, letting go, and attracting again. Emery likes this kind of irregular movement, closer to the movements of actual leaves and flowing water than to the predictable movement of machines.

When inspired by social concern and world events, Emery could abandon the movements of nature for those of humans. Her *Protest March* of 1968 (fig. 4.1) responded to the unprecedented series of strikes and protests that engulfed France that year, ignited by student riots in May. Each abstracted figure in *Protest March* has a magnet for a foot, and each moves at a different rhythm with its head bobbing. Even more complex in form and motion, *Prisoner* (fig. 4.2) was created five years later. Also activated by magnets in a turntable within its base, the movement of the figure is driven by powerful magnets in its knees. Through its multiple linkages, as the knees flex, the body, hips, head, and arms move in an oddly natural way.

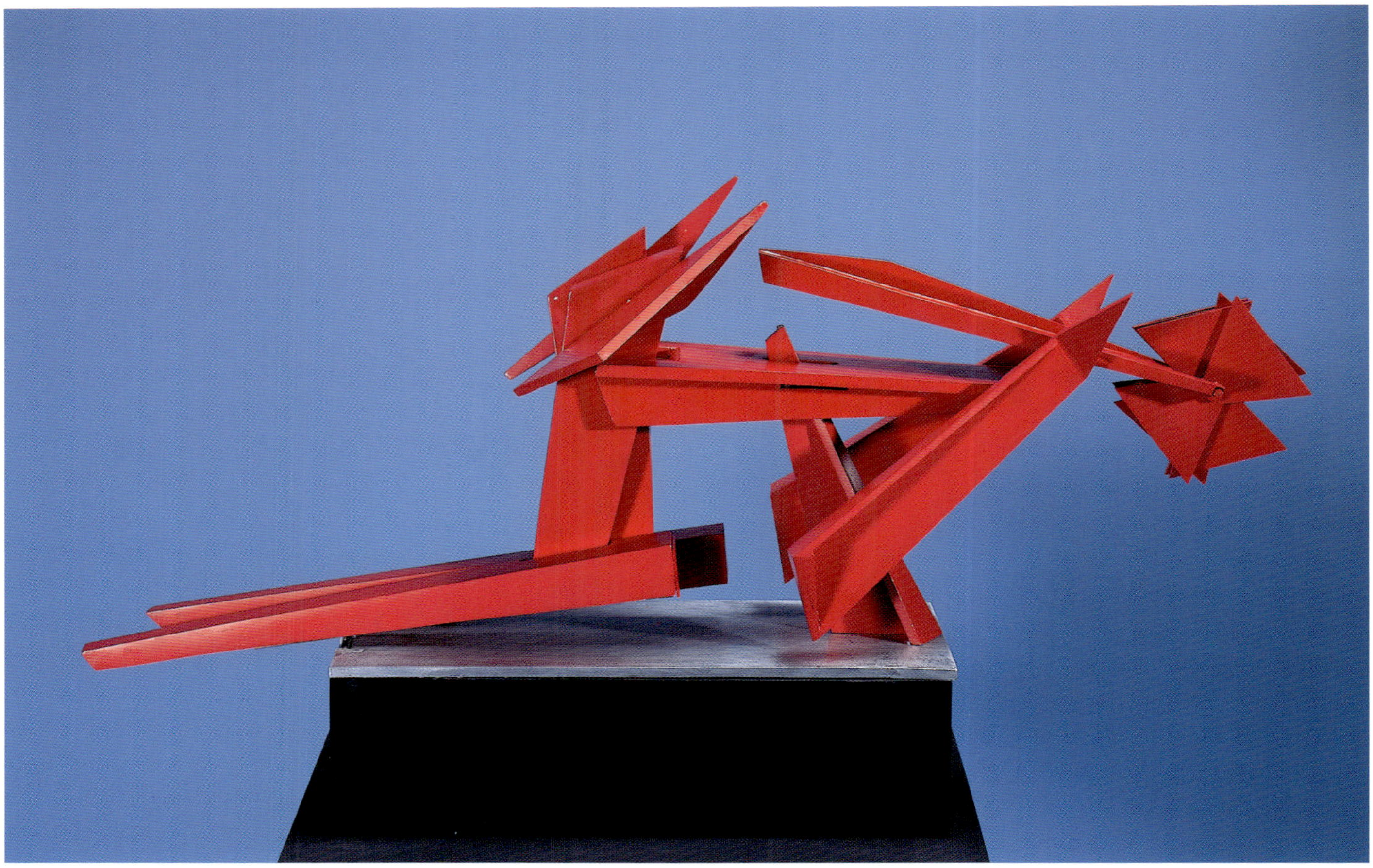

FIG. 4.2 *Lin Emery,* Prisoner, *1973. Aluminum, magnets, and motor, 26 x 48 x 10 inches (66 x 121.9 x 25.4 cm). Artist's studio.*

opposite page
FIG. 4.3 *Lin Emery,* Magnetmobile, *1973. Fiberglass, aluminum powder, magnets, and motor, 30 x 12 x 10 feet (9.1 x 3.6 x 3 m). South Central Bell Building, Birmingham, AL.*

Emery's magnetmobiles were first exhibited in a group show at the Oklahoma City Art Center in 1973. In that same year, she won a competition to create a large sculpture (*Magnetmobile*, fig. 4.3) for the atrium of the headquarters of the South Central Bell Company in Birmingham, Alabama (now the AT&T City Center building). Inspired by discussions at a National Sculpture Conference, Emery decided to consider plastic for the podlike elements of her 30-foot-high sculpture. As though the use of magnets and plastic wasn't sufficiently innovative, Emery opted to use a new material invented by a friend, William Seemann. Appropriately named, Seemann was a sailor and boat builder, and had recently developed a technique of constructing custom boats using a novel fiberglass fabric strengthened with longitudinal fiberglass rods that he called C-Flex®. The material could be shaped and saturated with a slow-curing resin, which allowed rigid and light fiberglass forms to be built inexpensively and avoided the complexity of casting. In creating her magnetmobile, Emery built the shaped pods with C-Flex and coated them with a mixture of resin and aluminum powder to provide a metallic finish. In this unprecedented work, two vertical clusters of pods rise from the floor and descend from the ceiling, moved by magnets located in hidden rotating disks in the floor and ceiling. The upper and lower sections are not connected; attracted by magnetic force, they almost touch, in the most emotionally charged, empty half-inch of the

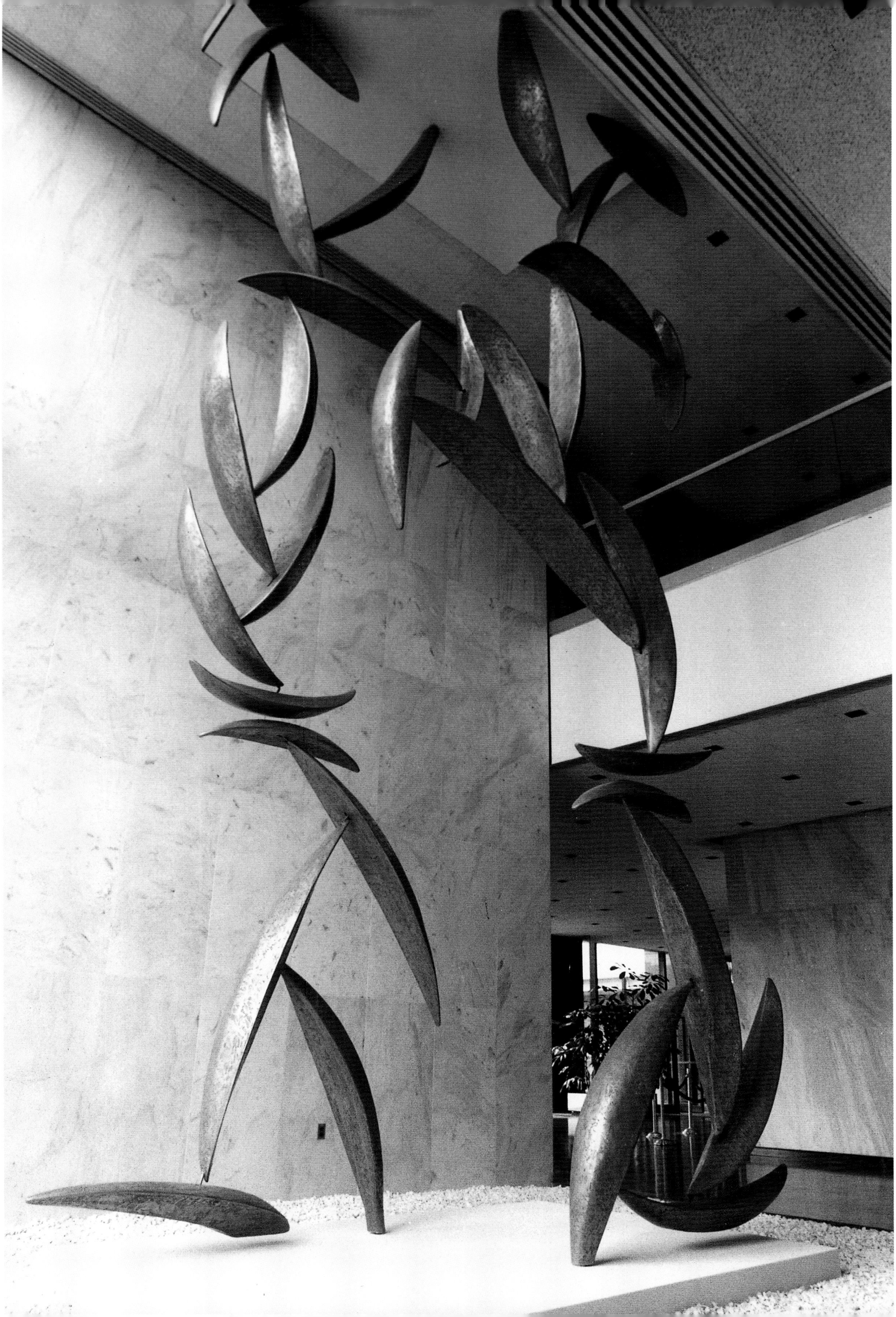

entire two-storey composition. The near-natural shapes of the pods, the lightness of the composition, and the sculpture's slow movement make it seem as though the elements are caught between falling and floating in a soft breeze.

The South Central Bell sculpture is exemplary of Emery's art. Strikingly original and finely crafted, every element of the sculpture serves the work's spirit, which derives from its forms and movement. Because of its dramatic presence and clarity of design, the work imposes itself on your consciousness immediately. Like one of her early inspirations, Hero of Alexandria, Emery hides her technical feats. Her complex craft, her hard-won engineering, is invisible.

Emery had moved to magnetically driven sculptures in part because of the practical problems of working with water. But the South Central Bell sculpture had a problem of its own, related neither to its magnets nor to its innovative fiberglass construction technique. When the work was first activated, the Bell engineers noticed that the entire ceiling structure started to move. The work's principal movement was created by a large motorized wheel containing the magnets hidden in the ceiling. It turned out that the period of the wheel exactly corresponded to the natural frequency of the ceiling beams, causing a sympathetic vibration. A slight adjustment in the wheel's movement solved the problem, and Emery was spared the embarrassment of bringing down South Central Bell's headquarters with a sculpture.

The mid- to late 1970s show Emery in full inventive command, using her hidden magnets to urge her sculptures on to increasingly elaborate feats. But the elaboration was in the movement, not the basic forms. The geometric components of *Acrobat* (fig. 4.4), 1975, rise, fall, and flip in response to a hidden turntable containing magnets in its base. In the 5-foot-high *Pipe Dream* (fig. 4.5), simple rods are the acrobats. The composition of *Cane Dance: Maquette* (fig. 4.6) reflects the symmetry inherent in many plant forms. As in nature, the basic symmetry of the sculpture breaks as the forms move, as if in the wind, and periodically return to their restful, symmetrical state. Based on the small version, the General Services Administration commissioned Emery in 1977 to produce a 28-foot-long version of *Cane Dance* for a federal building and post office in Houma, Louisiana (fig. 4.7). Emery had conceived the piece to be akin to a picket fence that a child could run along, activating its movement with a stick, but the government wouldn't let children near the work.

Because of her affection for technical innovation, Emery is constantly facing practical difficulties, always from unexpected places. In 1975, she heard about a new, stronger permanent magnet made from rare earth alloys. The exceptional magnetic properties of rare earths had only been discovered in 1966, and magnets using the materials had just become commercially available from the Crucible Magnetics Division of Colt Industries when Emery started to use them—too early, as it turned out. She had used the new magnets in several welded works, and they started to crumble and turn to dust. Crucible redesigned the magnets, Emery replaced hers, and they are still functioning.

Emery made no more magnetmobiles after 1977. As had happened before, the next step in her artistic evolution was dictated by something mechanical that

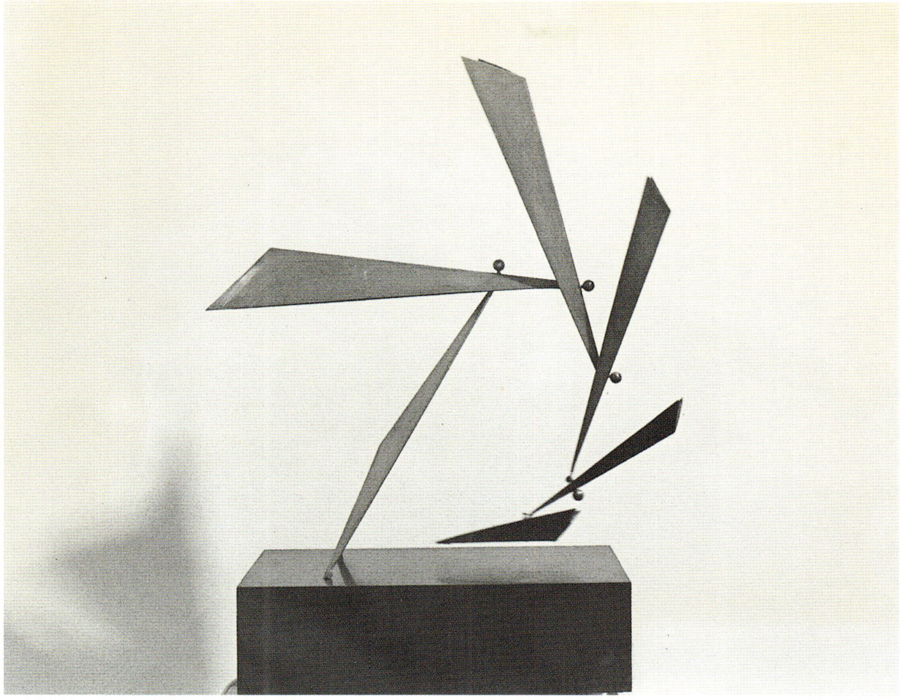

FIG. 4.4 *Lin Emery,* Acrobat, *1975. Aluminum, motor, and magnets, 16 x 10 x 3 inches (40.6 x 25.4 x 7.6 cm). Private collection.*

FIG. 4.5 *Lin Emery,* Pipe Dream, *1975. Aluminum, motor, and magnets, 60 x 60 x 15 inches (152.4 x 152.4 x 38.1 cm). Private collection.*

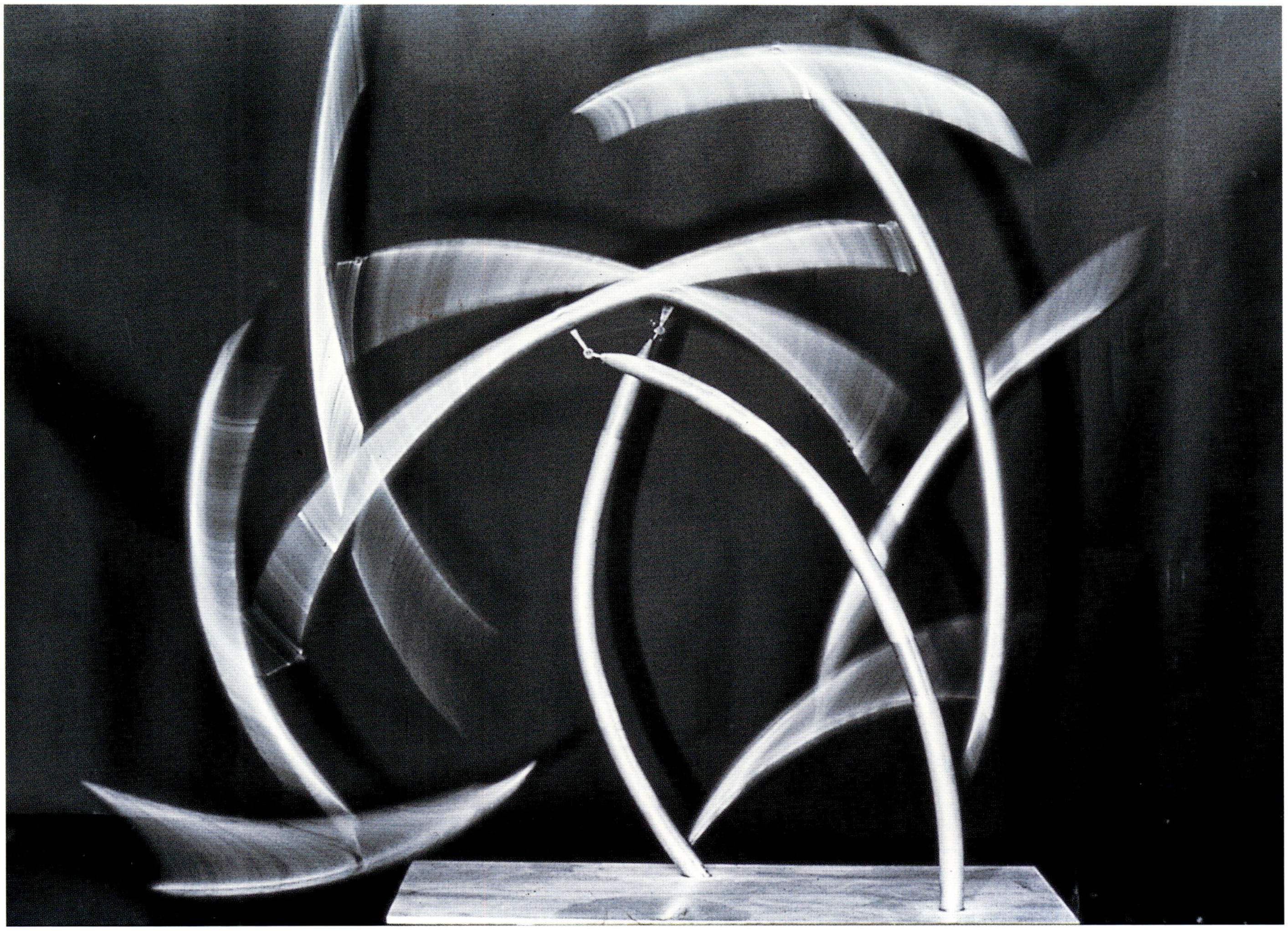

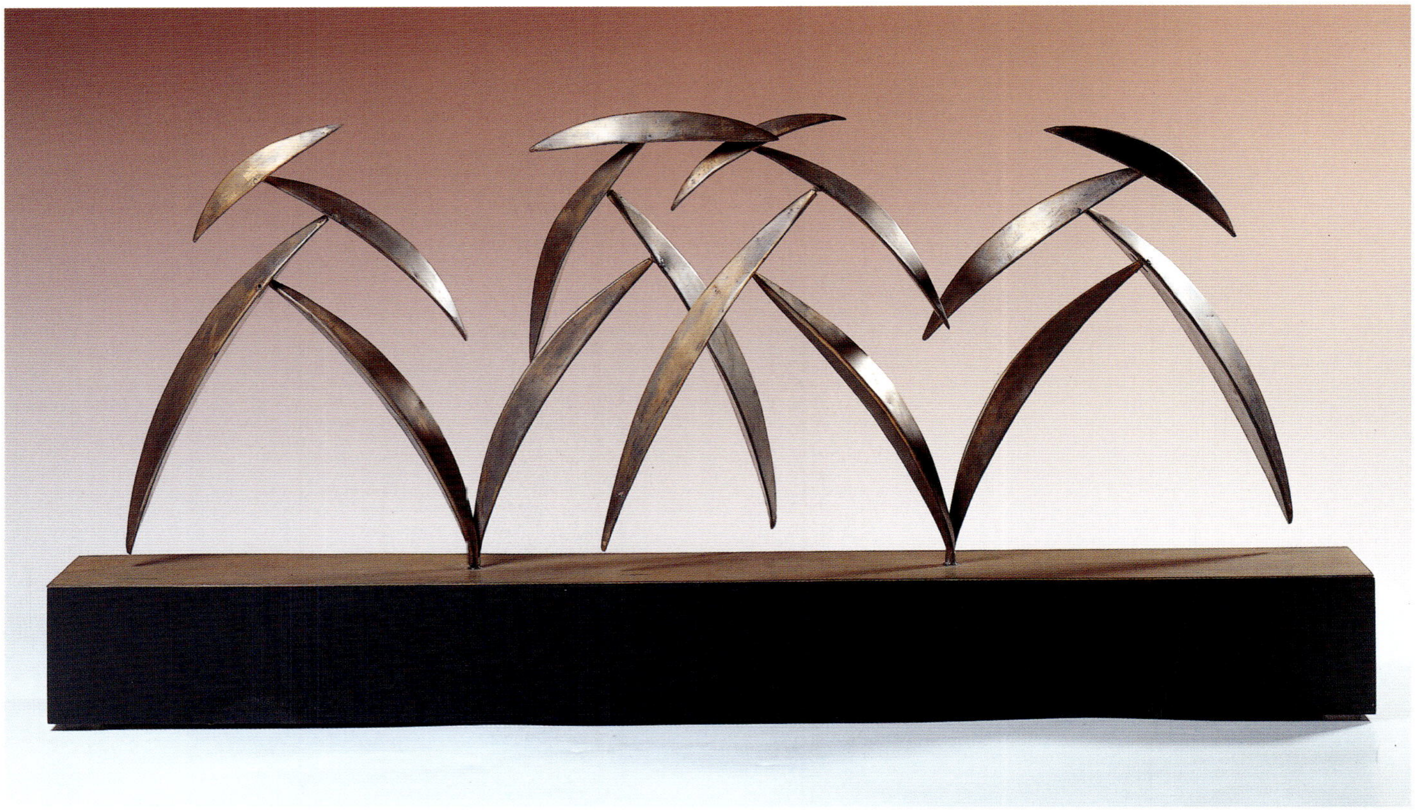

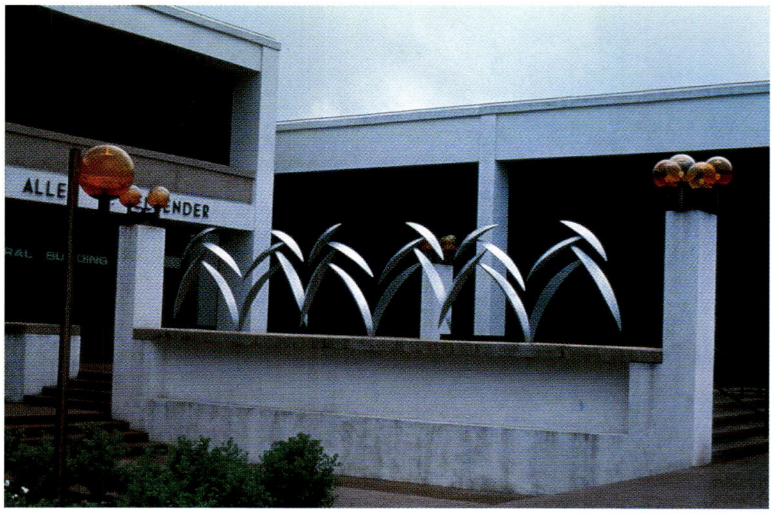

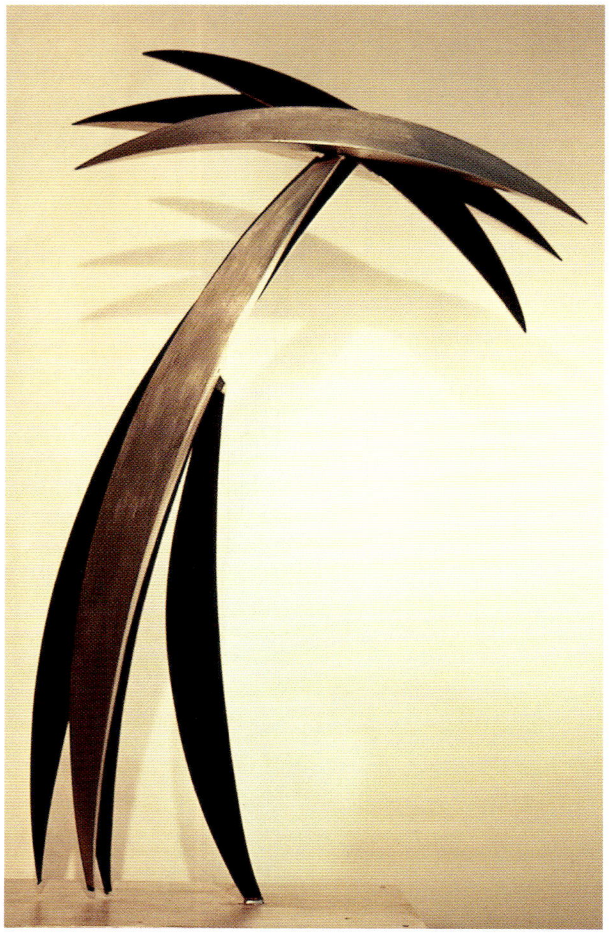

FIG. 4.6 *Lin Emery,* Cane Dance: Maquette, *1976. Welded bronze, laminated base with electric motor, and magnets, 18 x 48 x 10 inches (45.7 x 121.9 x 25.4 cm). Smithsonian American Art Museum, Washington, DC.*

FIG. 4.7 *Lin Emery,* Cane Dance, *1977. Aluminum, 8 x 28 x 3 feet (2.4 x 8.5 x 0.9 m). Allen J. Ellender Federal Building and U.S. Post Office, Houma, LA.*

Lin Emery, Alter Image, *1975. Aluminum, magnets, and motor, 60 x 36 x 14 inches (152.4 x 91.4 x 35.6 cm). Artist's studio.*

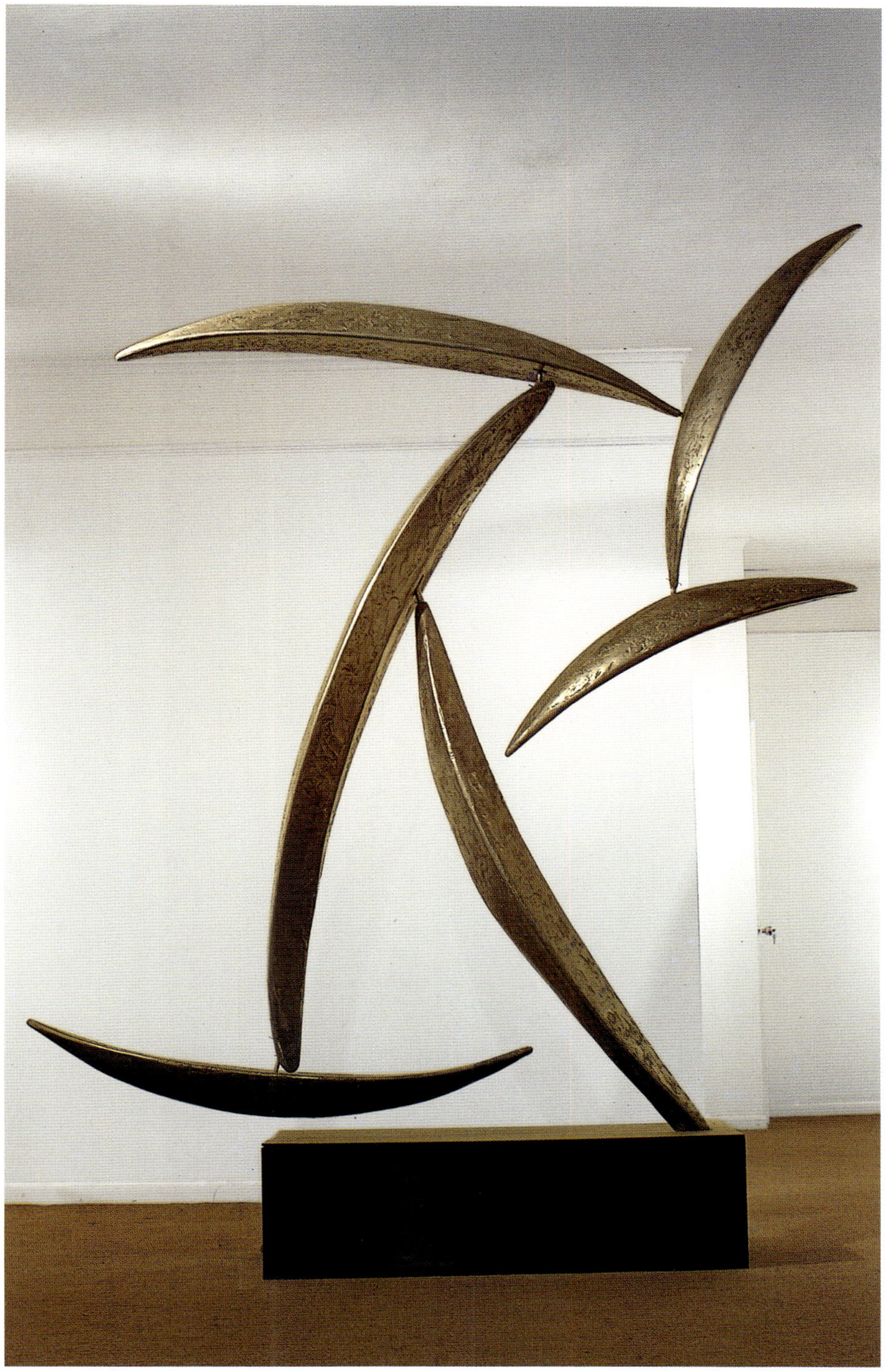

Lin Emery, Leaf Dance*, 1974. Fiberglass, bronze powder, magnets, and motor, 65 x 45 x 18 inches (165.1 x 114.3 x 45.7 cm). Guajardo Bottling Company, Monterrey, Mexico.*

she saw as an opportunity, and by her inveterate artistic restlessness. Her next step would be an important one, leading to the largest and most commanding series of sculptures of her career.

NOTE

1. Isamu Noguchi in a proposal for the Civic Center Plaza in Detroit, 1971, as quoted by Dore Ashton in *Noguchi East and West* (New York: Alfred A. Knopf, 1992), p. 25.

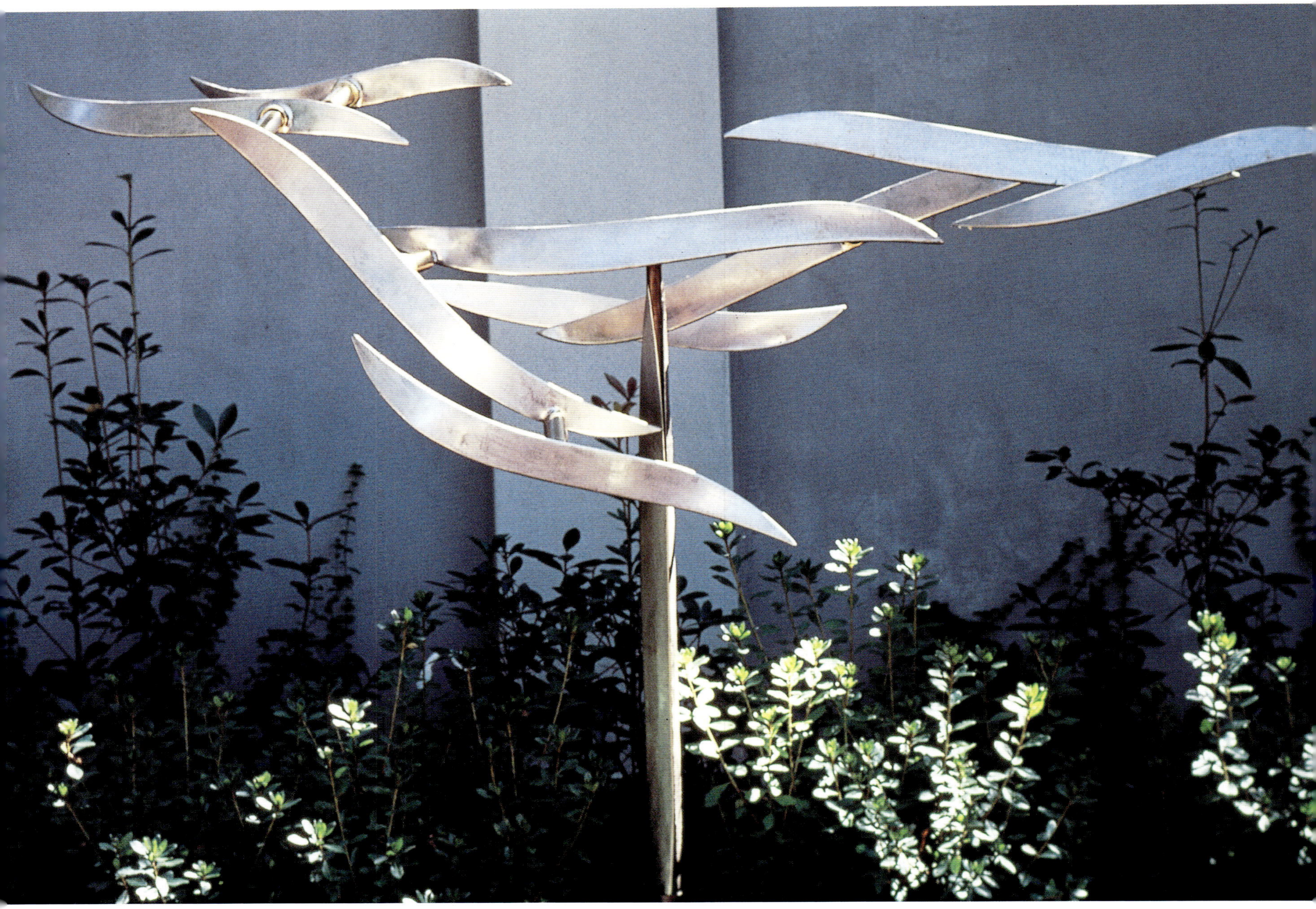

CHAPTER V

Wind

While Emery's pieces are abstract . . . they seem to become that which we fancy: birds in flight, a school of fishes, or—at least to my eye and mind—a ballerina in full twirl.

—Edward Albee[1]

There are many themes in Emery's sculptural evolution, but the one that is overarching is her quest for pure sculptural forms wedded to natural modes of movement. That objective was a major contributing factor to her decision to give up the complexities of using water and adopt hidden magnets to guide her magnetmobiles. And it was very much the motivation in the late 1970s when she first learned about ball bearings. Since they required much less force to turn, they gave her the impetus to try wind-driven sculptures.

It is quite amazing that Emery, with her talent for things mechanical, only learned about ball bearings in the 1970s. It was George Rickey who introduced her to this ancient invention. Sophisticated self-aligning ball bearings were in manufacture by 1907 and in wide use by the 1920s. But those are the vagaries of self-education. At one moment Emery is at the cutting edge, adopting the latest rare earth magnets or a recently invented fiberglass construction technique. At the next moment she is discovering a device whose invention goes back to Galileo. Nevertheless, for Emery the discovery of ball bearings came at an opportune time. Her artistic vision had matured to the point where she knew what she wanted to accomplish and immediately recognized the means to do so.

On the surface it may not seem like much of a distinction, but there is a profound difference between a sculpture that is driven by a mechanical device and one that moves naturally. Emery shuns regular, deterministic movements. By using the principle of the deer chaser in her large aquamobiles, she converted a steady flow of water into irregular bobbing motions. Then, in her magnetmobiles, by constraining the degrees of freedom of the elements, she converted the regular rotation of the driving motor into far more quixotic movements. But all of those works were dependent on engines or pumps or electric power. They were well-disguised compromises. When her discovery of ball bearings allowed her to make sculptures that were moved by the wind, Emery crossed the divide into natural, autonomous movement. When her sculptures were no longer tied to a machine, the door to nature was flung open and her works could revel in nature's dynamics and its beautiful quirks and accidents.

opposite page

FIG. 5.1 *Lin Emery,* Bernard (Nashville), *1962. Bronze, 32 x 36 x 8 inches (81.3 x 91.4 x 20.3 cm). Collection of Mr. and Mrs. Harold Bernard, Nashville, TN.*

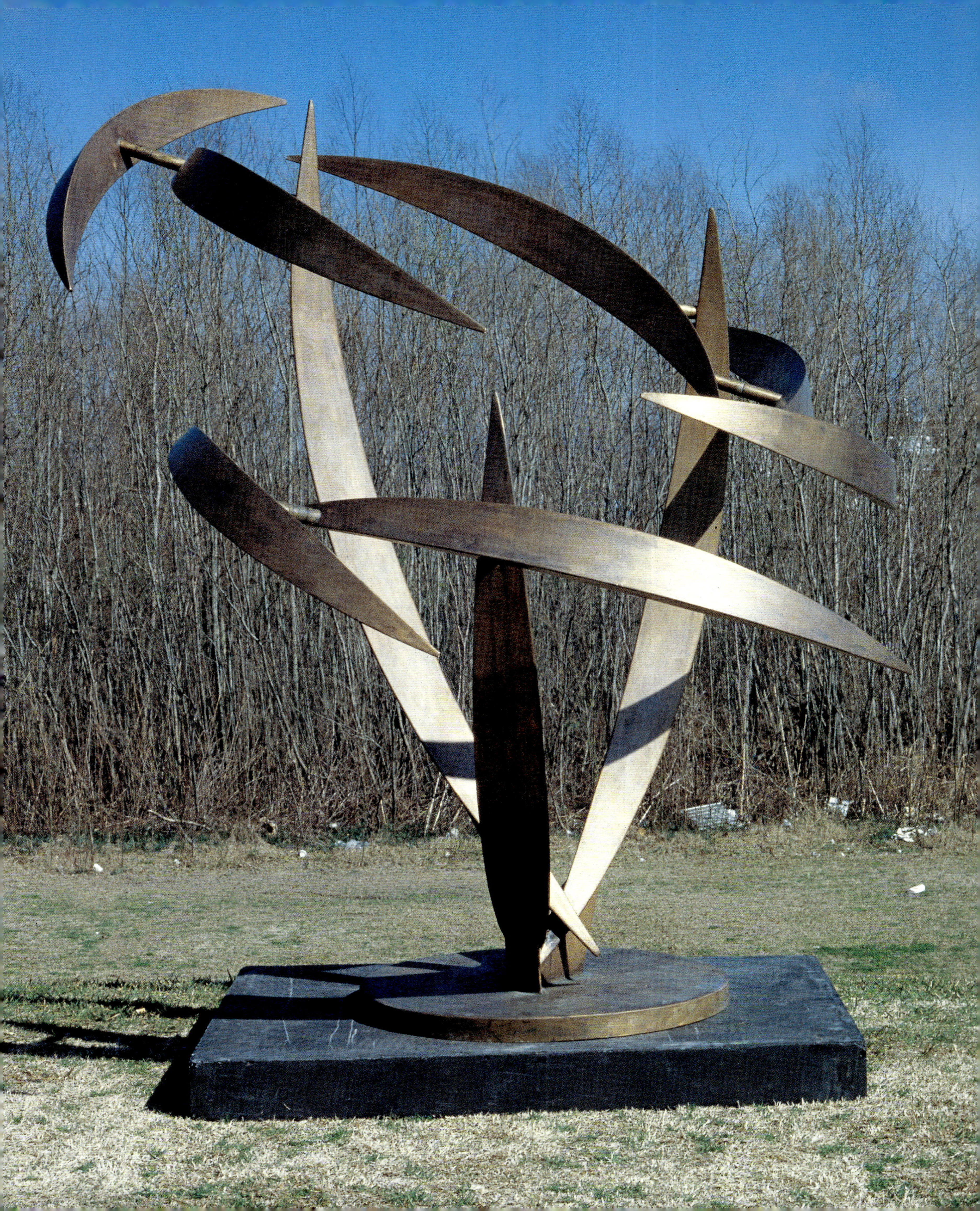

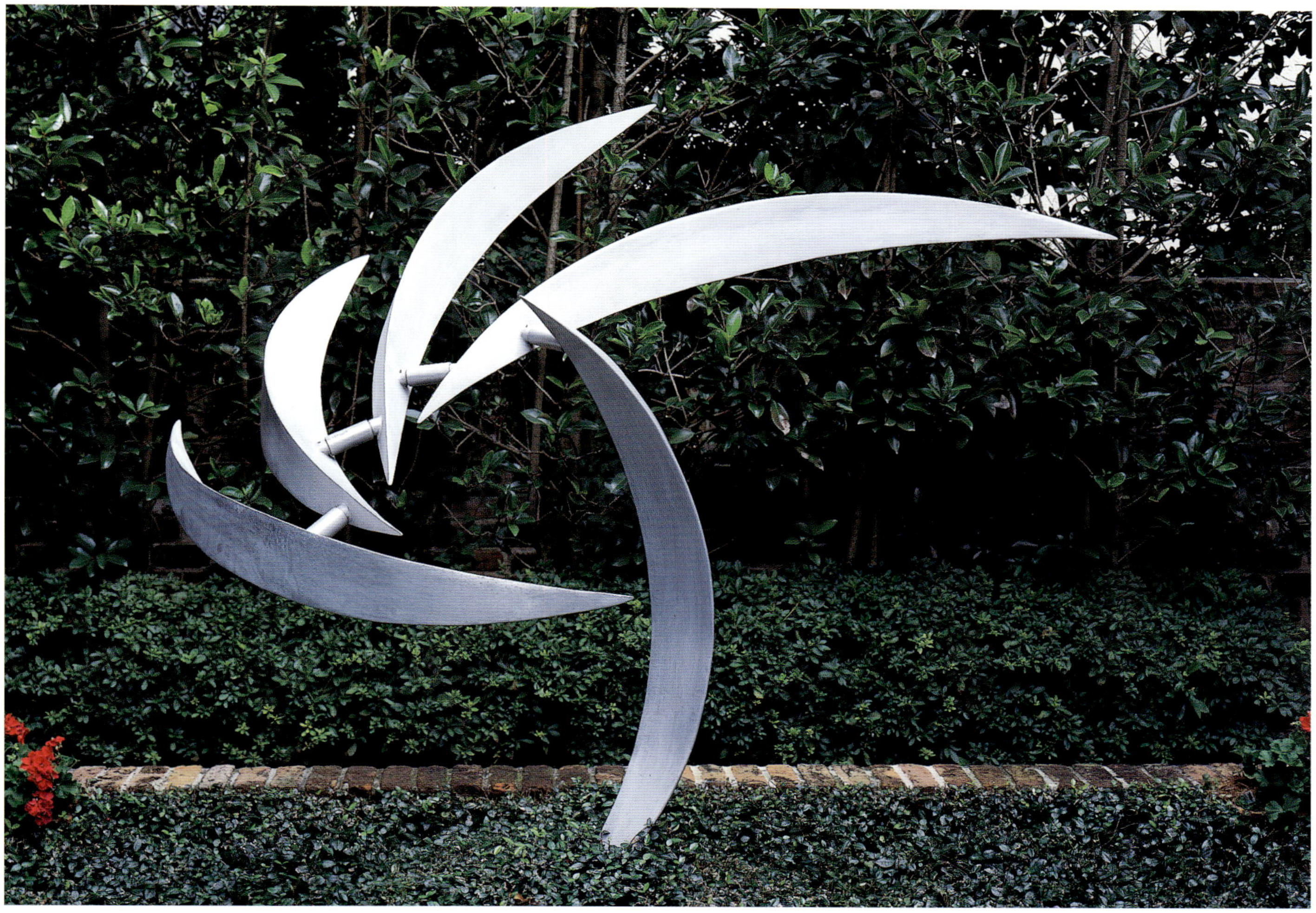

While Emery's dedication to movement in sculpture may seem a characteristically modern quest, its roots are as old as sculpture itself. Even for realistic sculpture, a fundamental challenge is to endow inanimate matter with life, and movement is the clearest evidence of vitality. The challenge intrigued the earliest sculptors, those carving horses in the Paleolithic Dordogne caves, the etchers of cylinder seals in fourth-millennium BCE Mesopotamia, and the genius who carved the Nike of Samothrace. Rodin called the expression of movement in something at rest the "revelation of the great mystery."[2]

The fascination with actual movement is widespread through societies and through cultures. Every civilization has its fountains, or automata, or animated clocks. One of the staples of early American folk art—the art of the people—was the whirligig. Many of these wind-driven sculptures portrayed soldier-patriots, with blades for arms rotating around a rod passing through the figure from shoulder to shoulder. Washington Irving described one in 1819: Balt did sit smoking his evening pipe...watching the achievements of a little wooden warrior, who, armed with a sword in each hand, was most valiantly fighting the wind on the pinnacle of the barn.[3]

Lin Emery, Spiral, *1971. Aluminum, 60 x 48 x 48 inches (152.4 x 121.9 x 121.9 cm). Collection of Mr. and Mrs. Richard Freeman, Folsom, LA.*

opposite page

Lin Emery, Hoist, *1968. Bronze, 7 x 6 x 6 feet (2.1 x 1.8 x 1.8 m). Collection of Dr. and Mrs. Roland Holst, San Diego, CA.*

opposite page

FIG. 5.2 *Lin Emery,* Flight, *1978. Aluminum, 18 feet, orbit 12 feet (5.4 m, orbit 3.6 m). K&B Plaza, New Orleans, LA.*

In other whirligigs, ducks flapped their wings, boxers boxed, bicycle wheels spun, and roosters or fish turned weathervanes into the wind.

Our fascination with movement is deeply held, rooted perhaps in our genes, and shaped by natural selection.[4] Alexander Calder demonstrated that movement greatly expands the appeal of abstract sculpture. Our instinct to ask what a work means is superseded by the sheer enjoyment of watching the flowing motions of colorful pieces of metal. We react to movement as we react to music, and as with music we experience a work of art most deeply, not when it is incidental, but when it is the subject of our rapt attention. With all of the distractions in our surroundings, not to mention in our minds, that kind of attention is rare. Kenneth Clark once said that the enjoyment of a pure aesthetic sensation could last no longer than one can enjoy the smell of an orange; for him, less than two minutes.[5] Particularly because of the complexity of their movements, Emery's sculptures grab our attention and hold on; the scent of the orange lingers, and as the aesthetic experience is prolonged, it is deepened.

Emery's innovations of the 1970s were anticipated more than a decade before. Even by her energetic standards, 1962 was a particularly busy and hectic year for Emery. In addition to getting married, she produced several complex aquamobiles and some deeply thought-out bronzes. In the spring she participated in the second National Sculpture Casting Conference and became a member of the professional society for welders, the American Welding Society. She had one-person shows at the Sculpture Center in New York and the Tennessee Fine Arts Center in Nashville, and she was included in a show at the Raymond Cordier Gallery in Paris and a traveling exhibition organized by the American Federation of Arts. Her career was well under way.

Also in 1962, Emery produced a work on commission (fig. 5.1) that might be missed in the flood of other seemingly more substantial accomplishments, a 32-inch-high work titled *Bernard (Nashville)*. In its simple movement and the clean profile of its welded bronze elements, this sculpture was an abstraction of the flight of birds and, dependent neither on water pressure nor on magnets, was unlike anything she had produced before. Although somewhat awkward in the integration of the supporting pole and wings, and incorporating simple journal bearings, this work contained the seed of a sculptural idea that would blossom ten years later when Emery discovered ball bearings.

One of Emery's first wind-driven works using ball bearings was *Flight* (fig. 5.2), completed in 1978. The title represents the phenomenon embodied in the sculpture, but it could just as well stand for the time in Emery's career when her work freed itself from connections to machines or power cords and took flight. The natural environment of her new sculptures was the sky.

There is no mistaking a wind-driven sculpture by Lin Emery. They all reflect a common, original artistic vision, but within that vision one can distinguish several themes. Following in the spirit of *Flight*, a distinct group of sculptures over the years combines two kinds of movement. One is inherent in its composition, a virtual upward and outward thrust visible even in a still photograph. The other is the

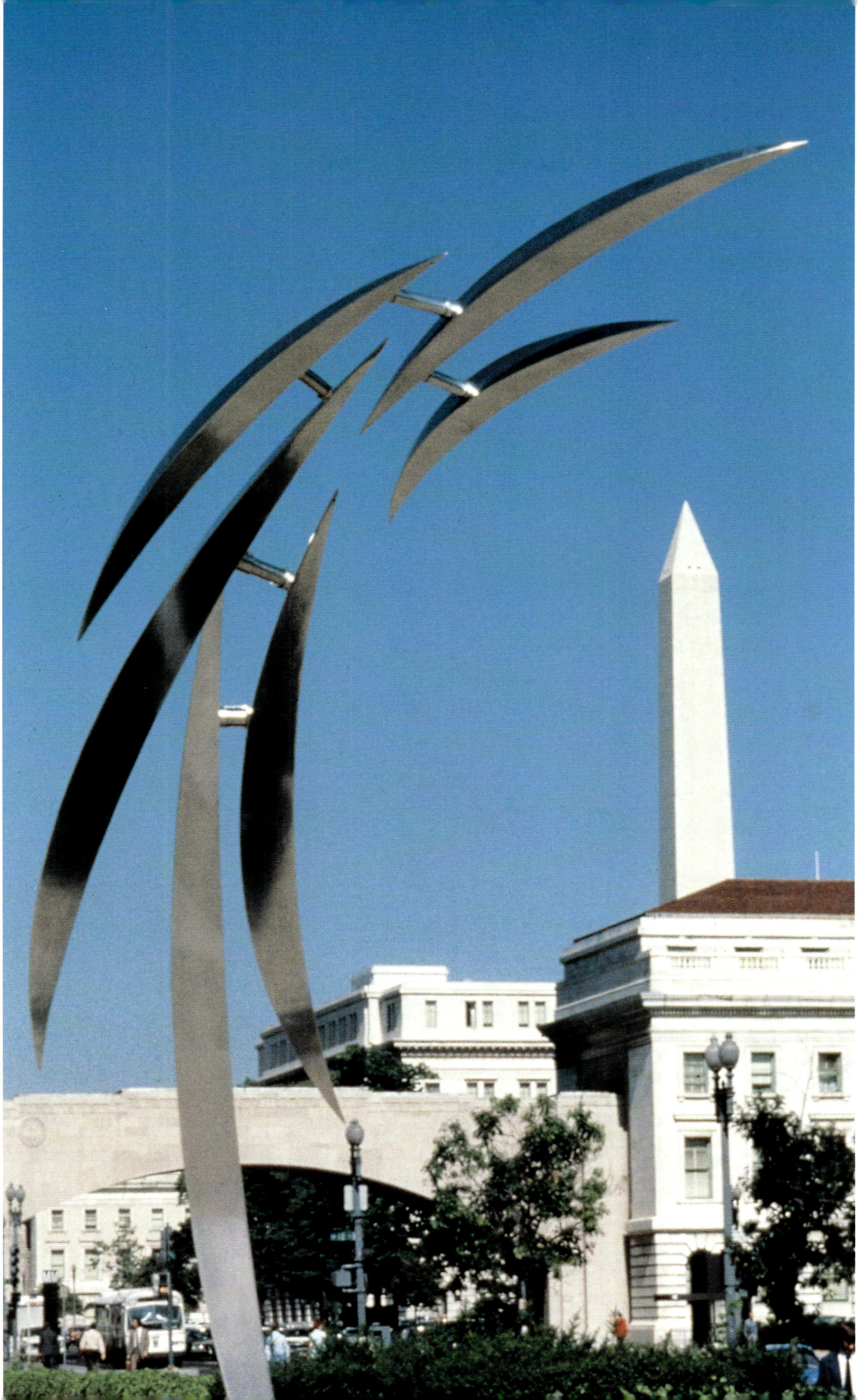

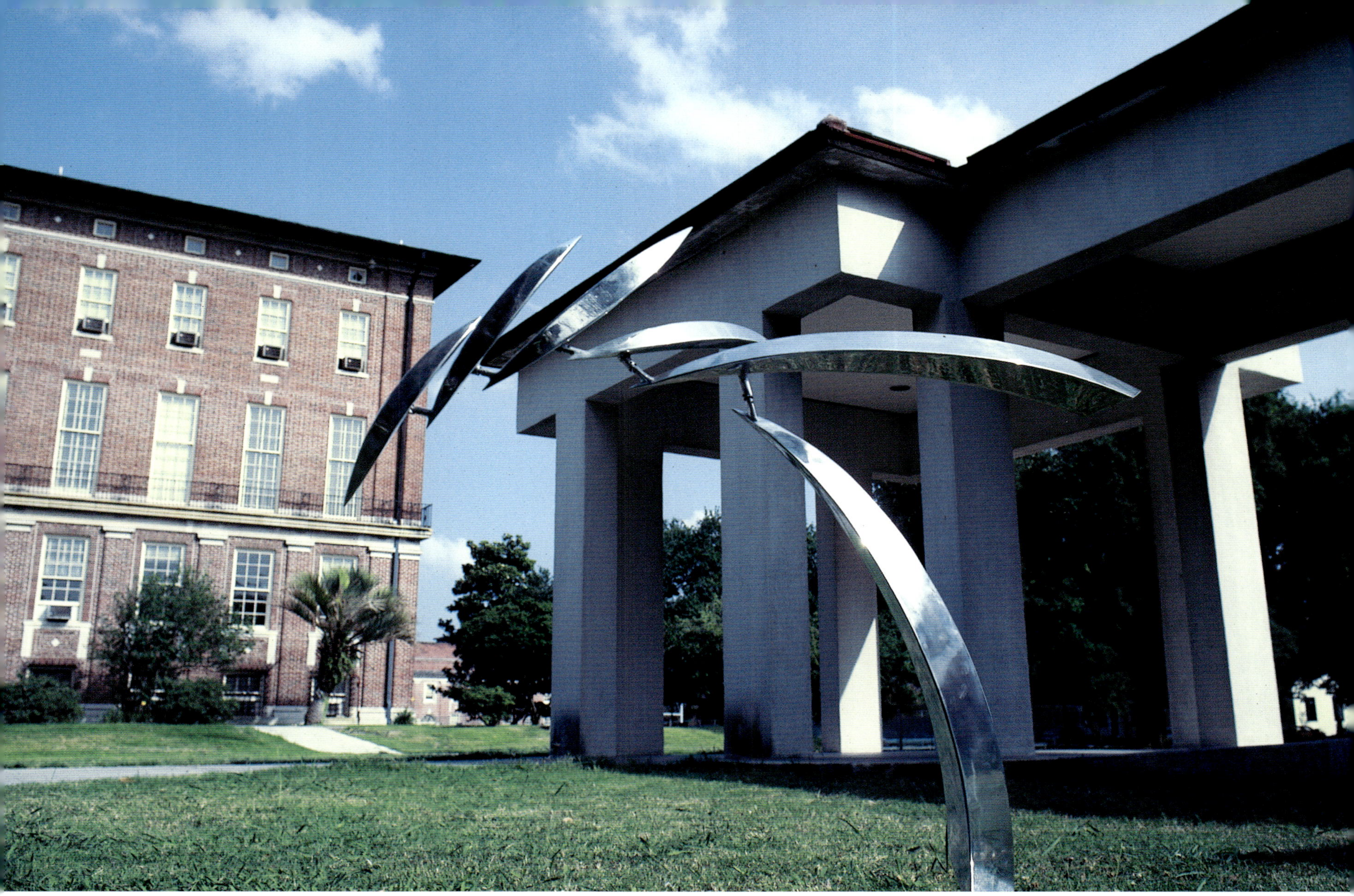

above

Lin Emery, Chassée, *1981. Aluminum, 36 x 42 x 34 inches (91.4 x 106.7 x 86.4 cm). Collection of Mr. and Mrs. Gus Reynoir, New Orleans, LA.*

right

Lin Emery, Anthem, *1982. Aluminum, 14 feet, orbit 12 feet (4.2 m; orbit 3.6 m). State Library of Louisiana, Baton Rouge, LA.*

opposite page

Lin Emery, Cadence, *1986. Aluminum, 18 feet, orbit 14 feet (5.4 m, orbit 4.2 m). Arboretum Lakes, Lisle, IL.*

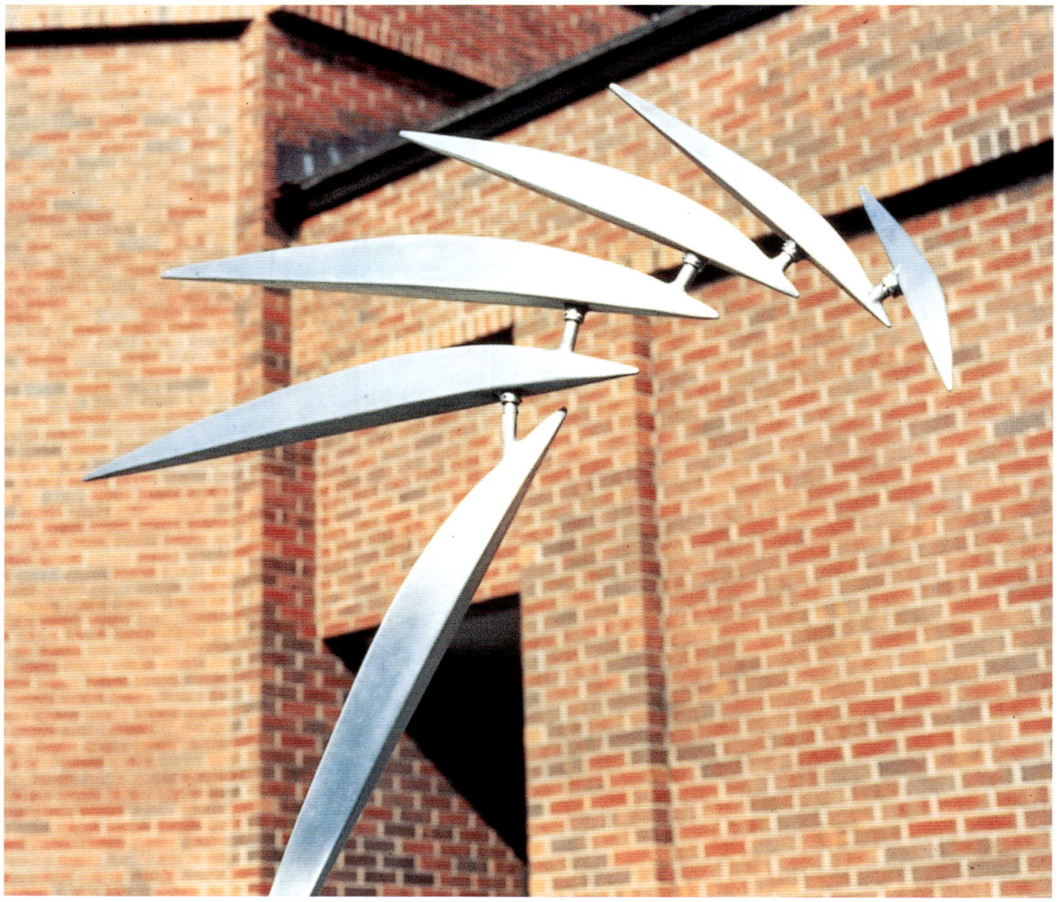

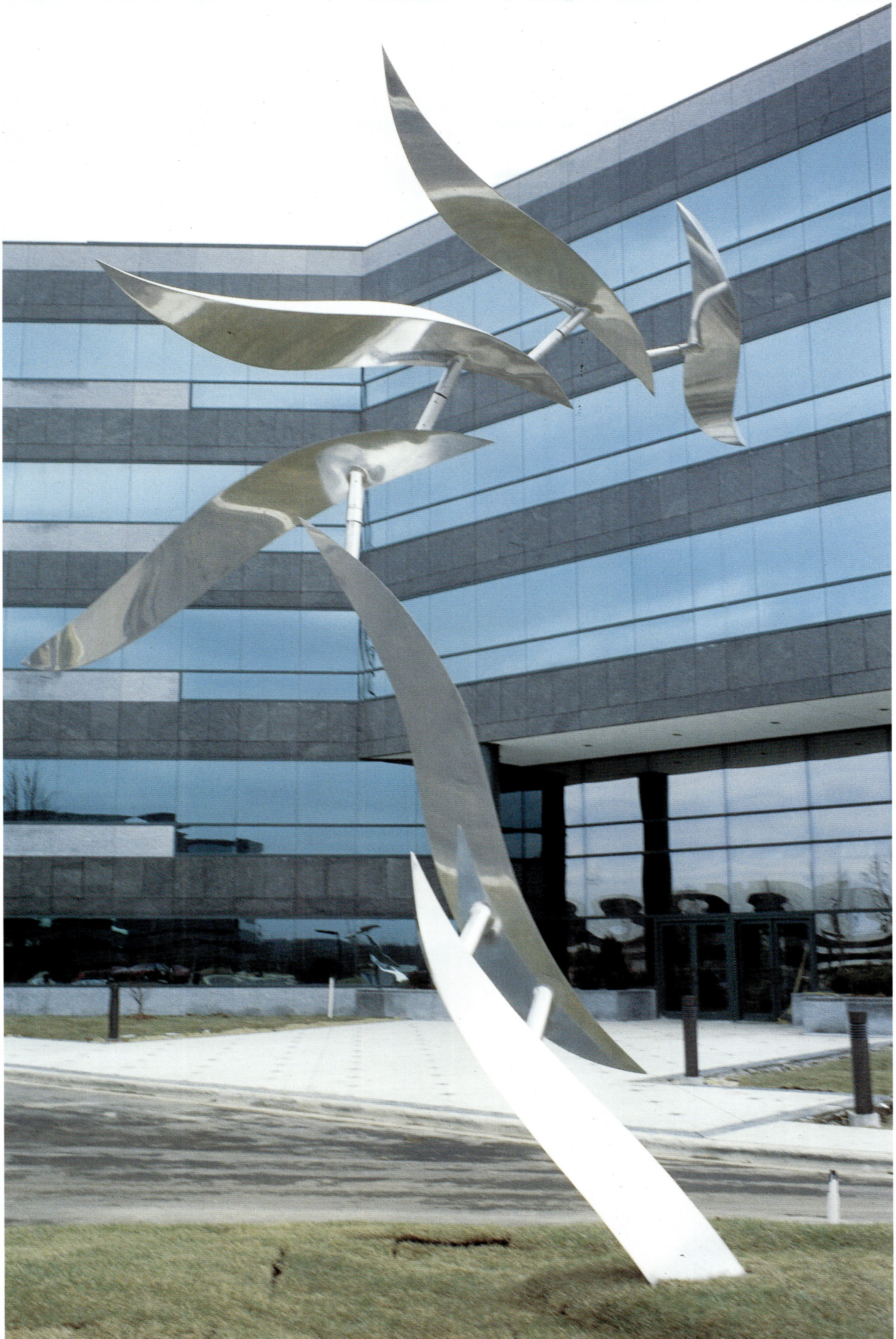

Lin Emery, Ariel/Dancer, *1988. Aluminum, 15 feet, orbit 9 feet (4.5 m, orbit 2.7 m). Delaware Art Museum, Wilmington, DE.*

opposite page

Lin Emery, Palmetto *(in motion), 1966. Aluminum, 5 feet, orbit 4 feet (1.5 m, orbit 1.2 m). Private collection.*

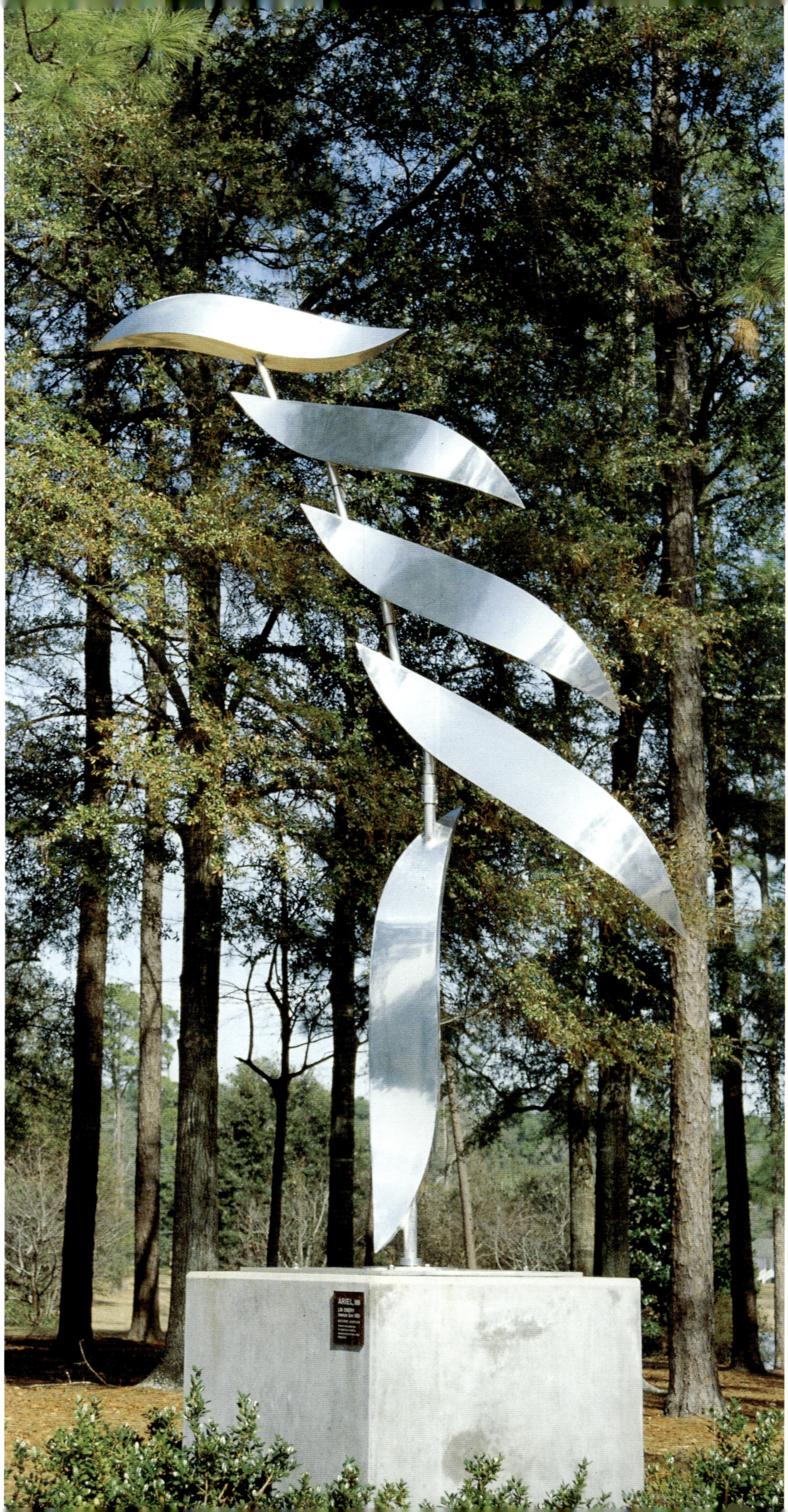

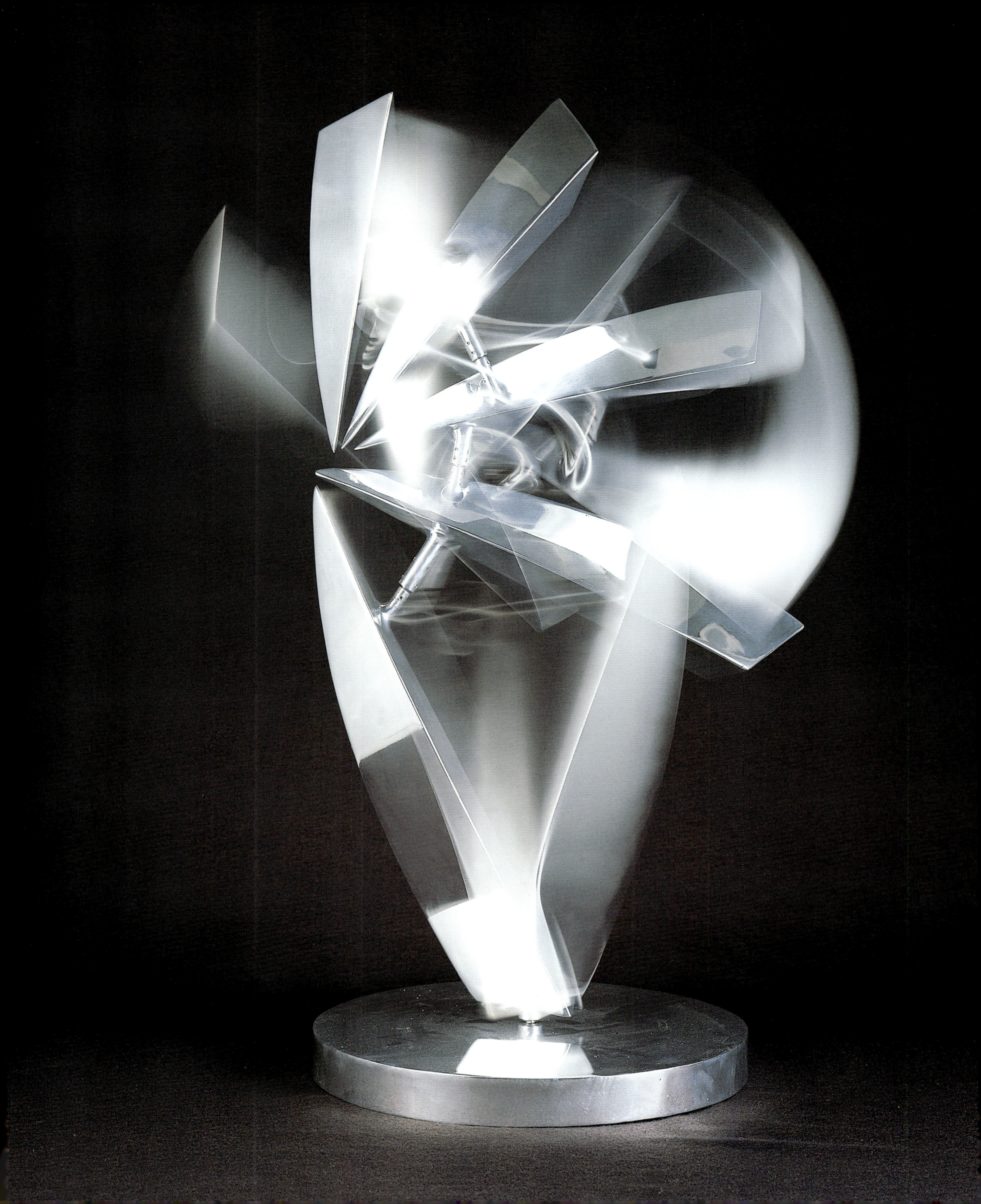

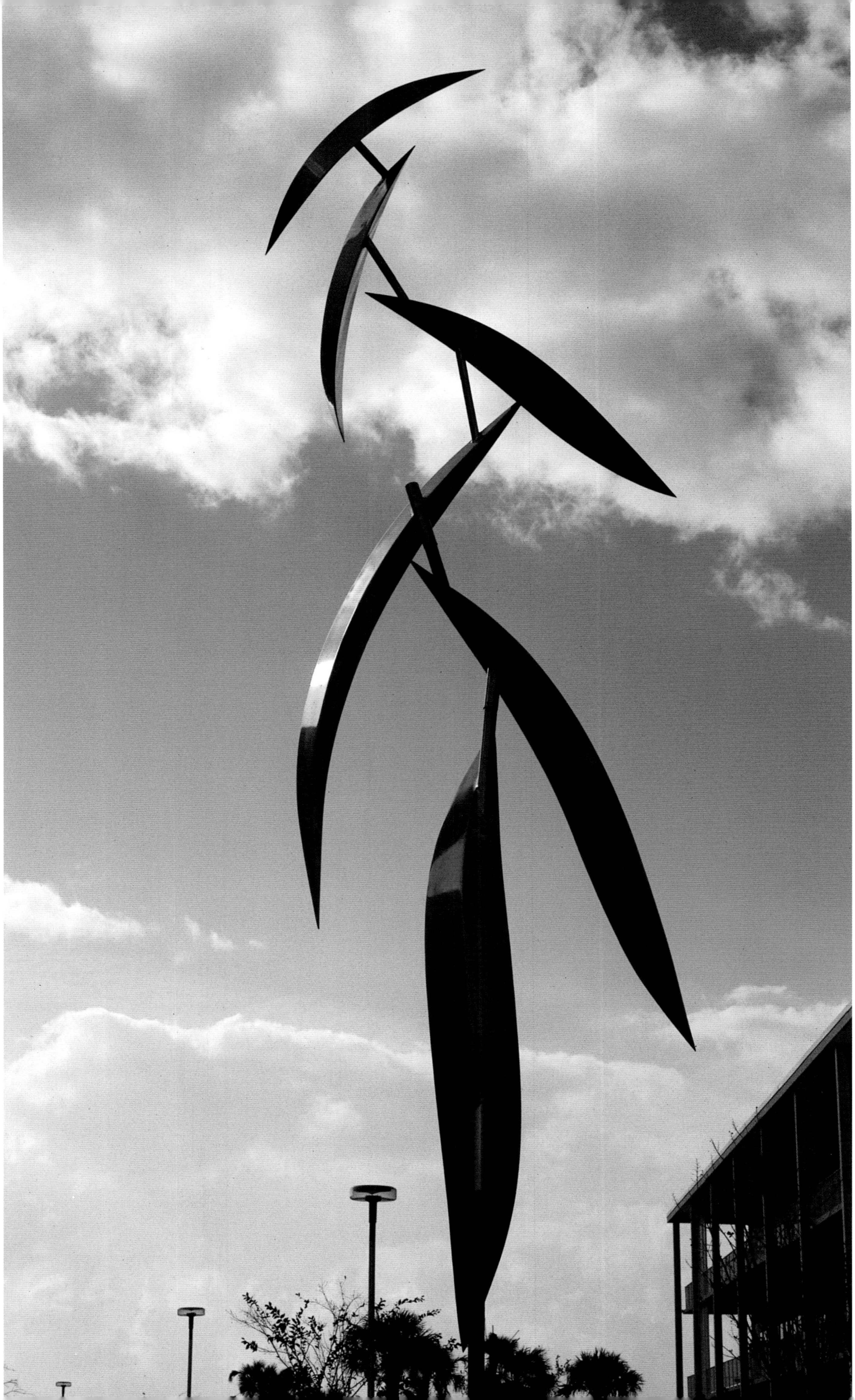

independent movement of the individual elements. In many of these works, the forms derive directly from nature. In others, such as *Cadency* (fig. 5.3) and *Mobius* (fig. 5.4) with their sharp-edged elements, the reference is less to leaves or stalks than to the wind itself. But in all of them there is a complete integration of and an energizing interaction between the movement of the parts and the dynamics of the whole, as with the limbs and body of Albee's "ballerina in full twirl."

opposite page
FIG. 5.3 *Lin Emery,* Cadency, *1988. Aluminum, 9 feet, orbit 5 feet (2.7 m, orbit 1.5 m). Private collection.*

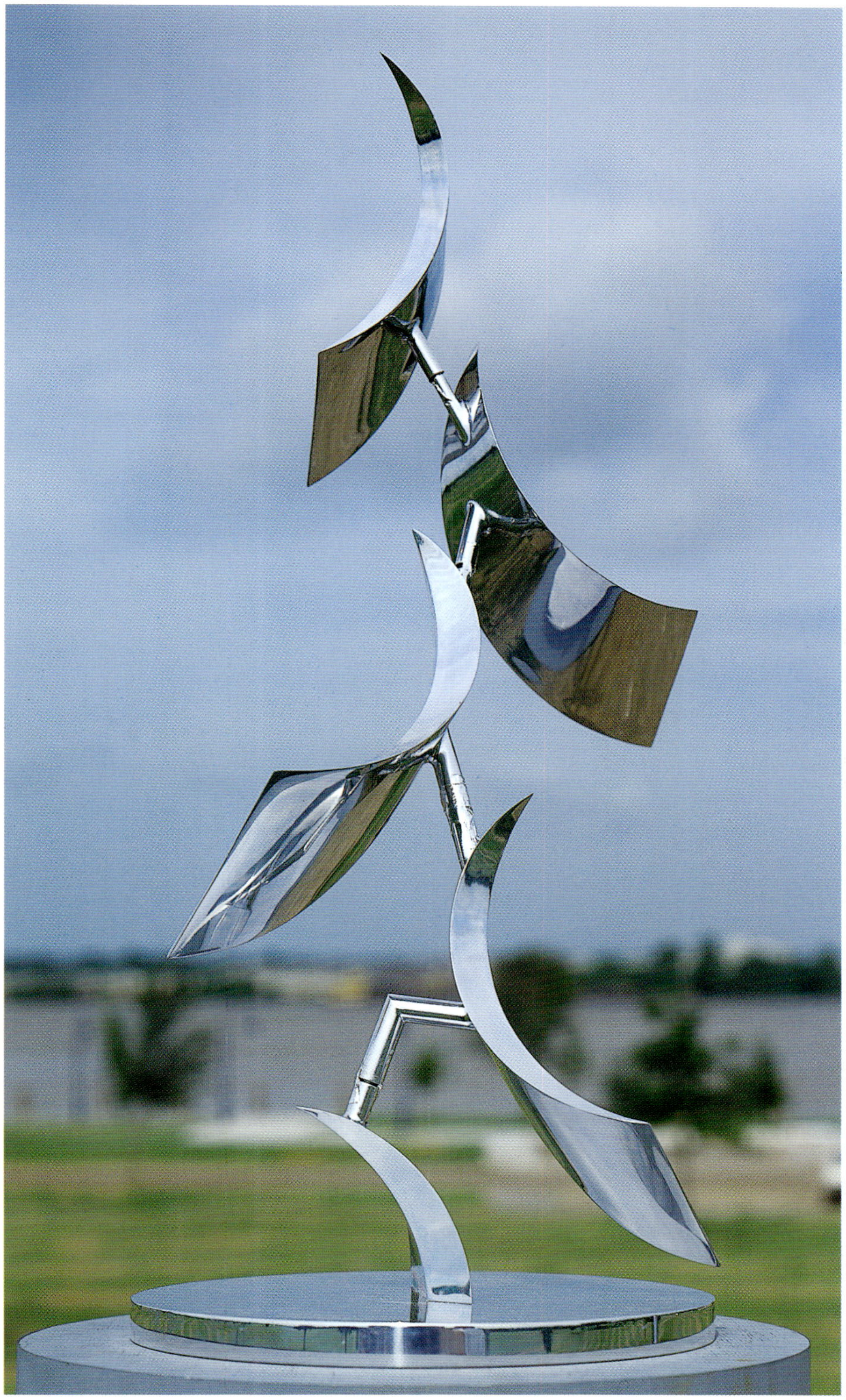

FIG. 5.4 *Lin Emery,* Mobius, *1988. Aluminum, 36 inches, orbit 20 inches (91.4 cm, orbit 50.8 cm). Private collection.*

Lin Emery, Pennant *(model), 1987. Aluminum, 29 inches, orbit 18 inches (73.7 cm, orbit 45.7 cm). Collection of Dr. and Mrs. Warren Gottsegen, New Orleans, LA.*

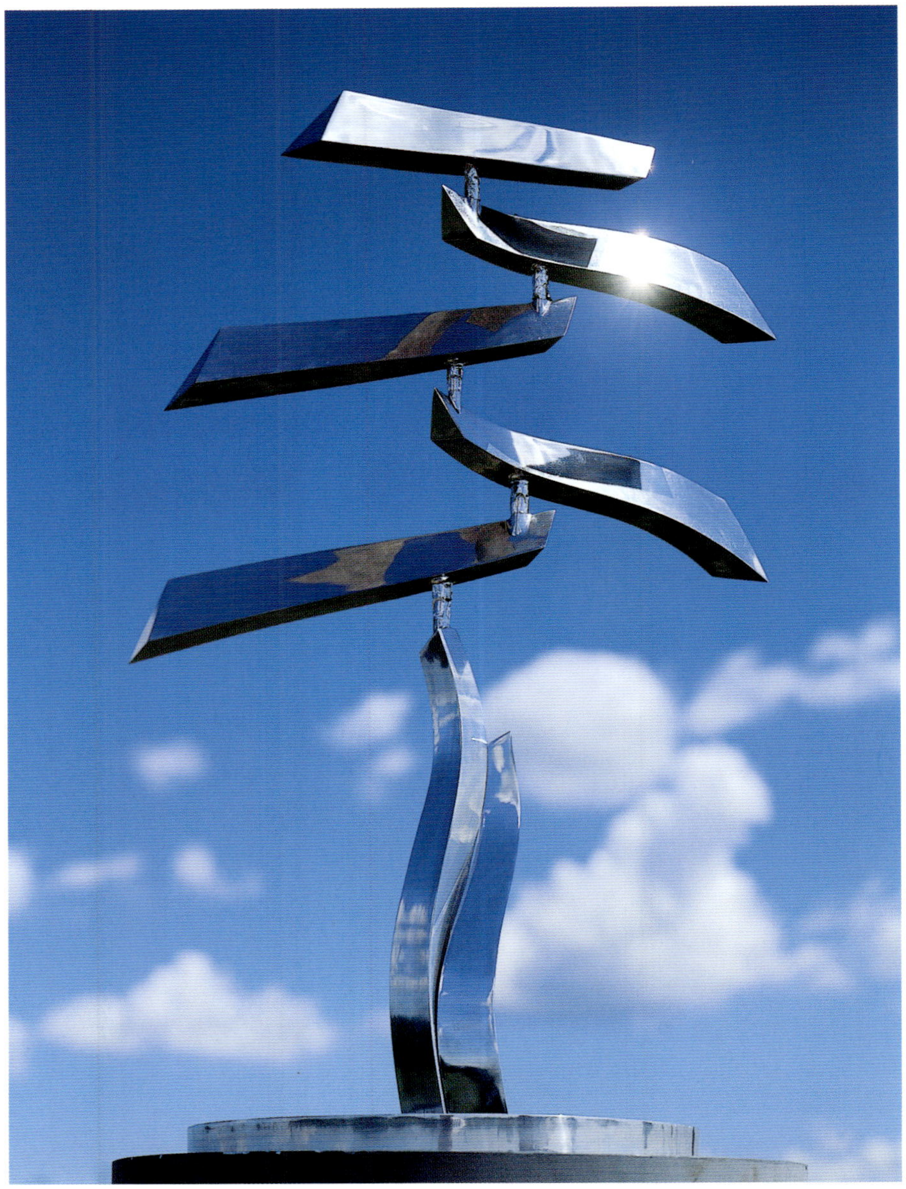

An entirely different conceptual idea and compositional approach is found in another group of Emery's wind-driven sculptures. This aesthetic concept links back to her earliest days in New Orleans, as well as to Paris and her affection for Romanesque art. The title of an abstract work of 1980 gives it away: *Angel* (fig 5.5). In Emery's generously open, pantheistic world, bilateral symmetry, such as the balance of an angel's wings, seems often to be associated with manifestations of the spiritual. The forms of *Phoenix* (fig. 5.6), completed in 1981, could refer to both the legendary bird's plumage and the flames of the fire that consumes it and from which it is reborn. *Deva* (fig. 5.7), completed in 1986, takes the Sanskrit word for deity or angel and could also be identified with the meaning of the word's early origin: "celestial." *Spirit* (fig. 5.8), completed in 1989, partakes of a degree of symmetry, but this spirit also ascends. As these works move in the wind, their symmetry is broken, but when the wind dies they return to their quiet balance.

opposite page

FIG. 5.5 *Lin Emery,* Angel, *1980. Aluminum, 4 feet, orbit 3 feet (1.2 m, orbit 0.9 m). Collection of Mrs. James Coleman, New Orleans, LA.*

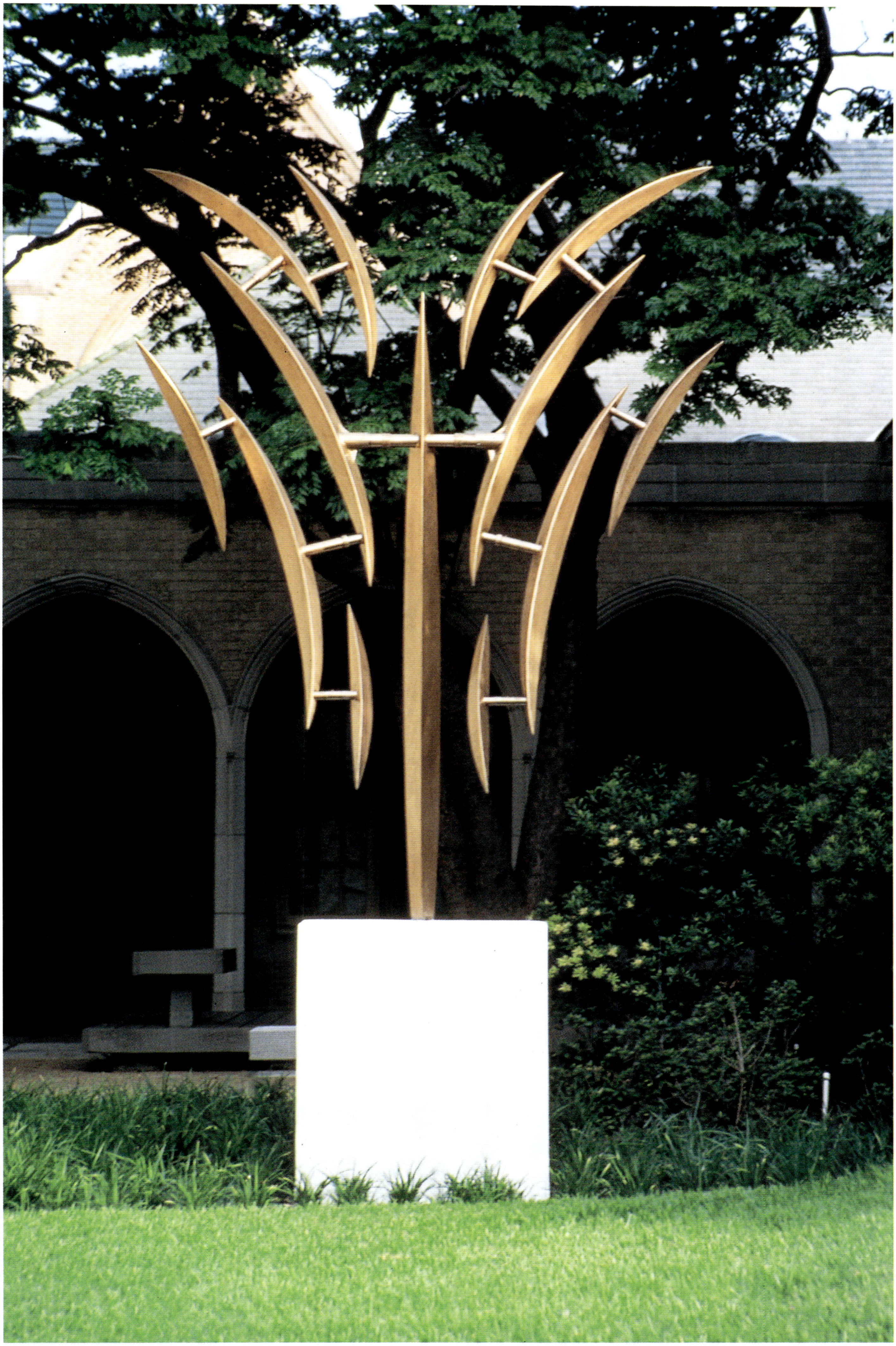

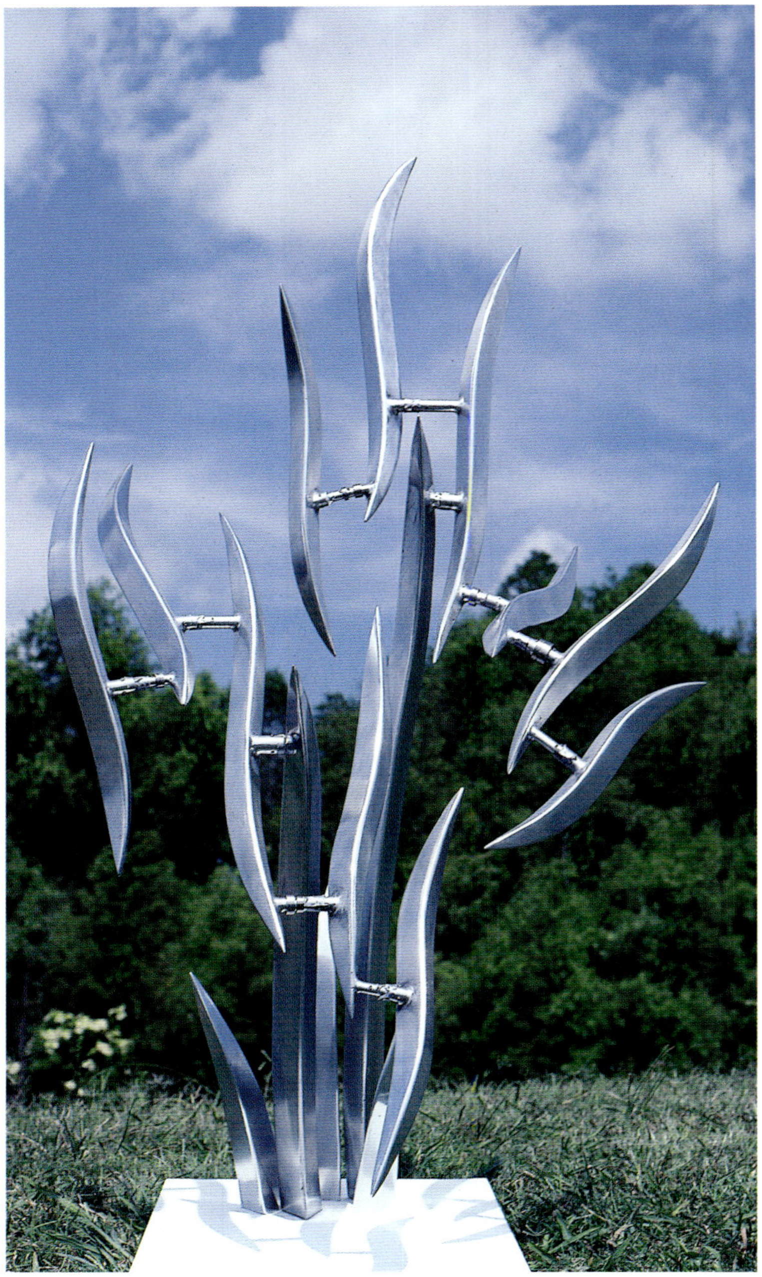

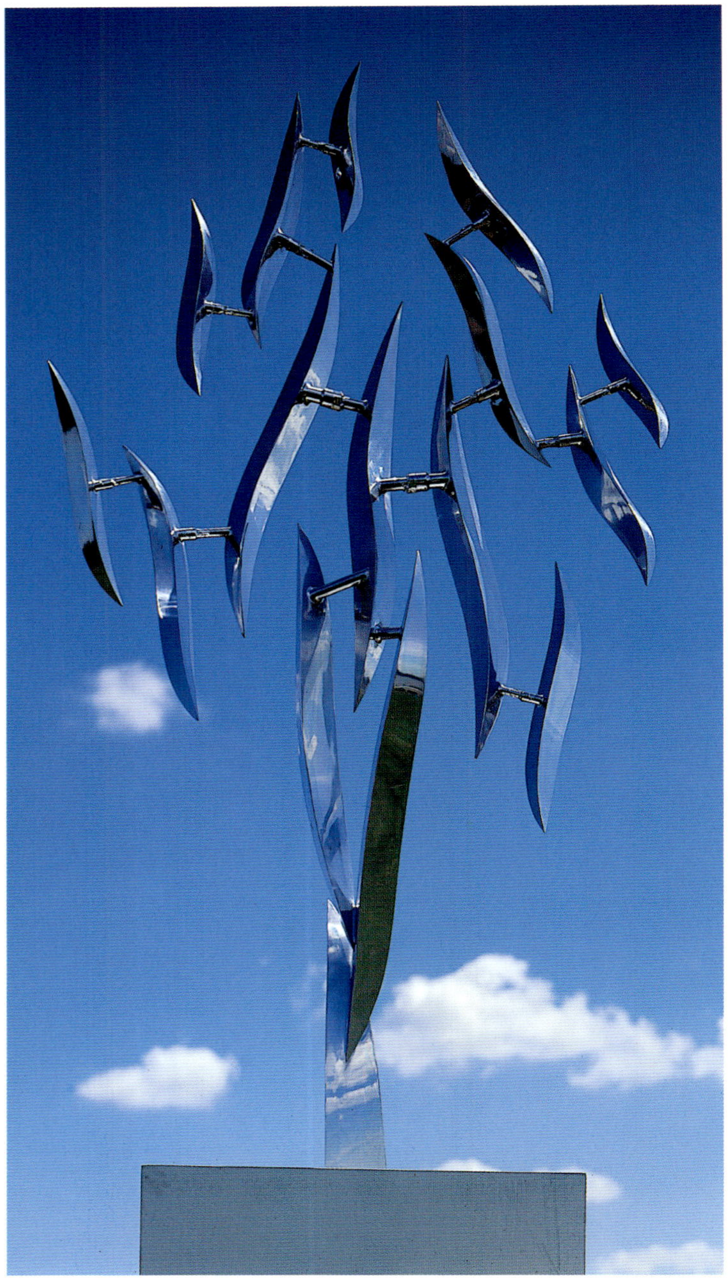

FIG. 5.6 *Lin Emery,* Phoenix, *1981. Aluminum, 48 x 32 x 6 inches (121.9 x 81.3 x 15.2 cm). Private collection.*

FIG. 5.7 *Lin Emery,* Deva, *1986. Aluminum, 28 x 14 x 10 feet (8.5 x 4.2 x 3 m). Marina Centre, Singapore.*

opposite page
FIG. 5.8 *Lin Emery,* Spirit, *1989. Aluminum, 5 x 3 x 2 feet (1.5 x 0.9 x 0.6 m). Collection of Mr. and Mrs. Joseph Carmichael, New Orleans, LA.*

Another category of Emery's wind-driven work was initiated in 1989 when, for the first time, she added color to a wind-driven sculpture. Emery is partially color-blind, but not for red, and the color she chose from a book of automotive paints was an intense red of the kind loved by Ferrari owners. She still likes that initial color and uses it often. Up to that time, her wind-driven sculptures, with their polished aluminum surfaces, had a complex visual presence; looking at them, you saw reflections of sky, clouds, or lights as much as you saw metal surfaces. When she painted those surfaces the visual experience became dramatically different. The sculpture became an object in itself rather than a reflection of the world around it. In practice, whenever Emery painted surfaces, others were left clean, so the visual

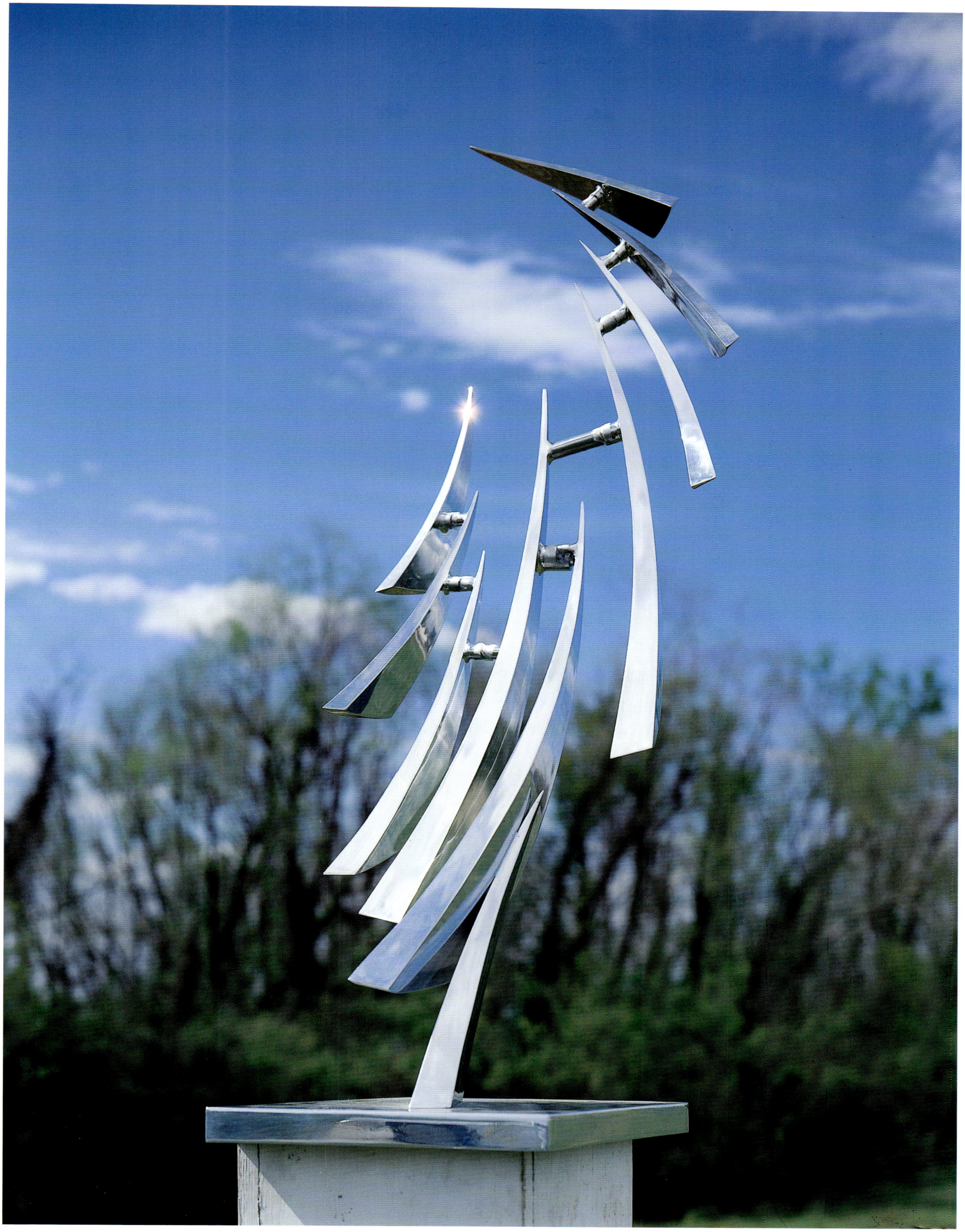

Lin Emery, Hana, *1997. Aluminum and paint, 22 feet, orbit 22 feet (6.7 m, orbit 6.7 m). Izumisano Municipal Hospital, Izumisano, Japan.*

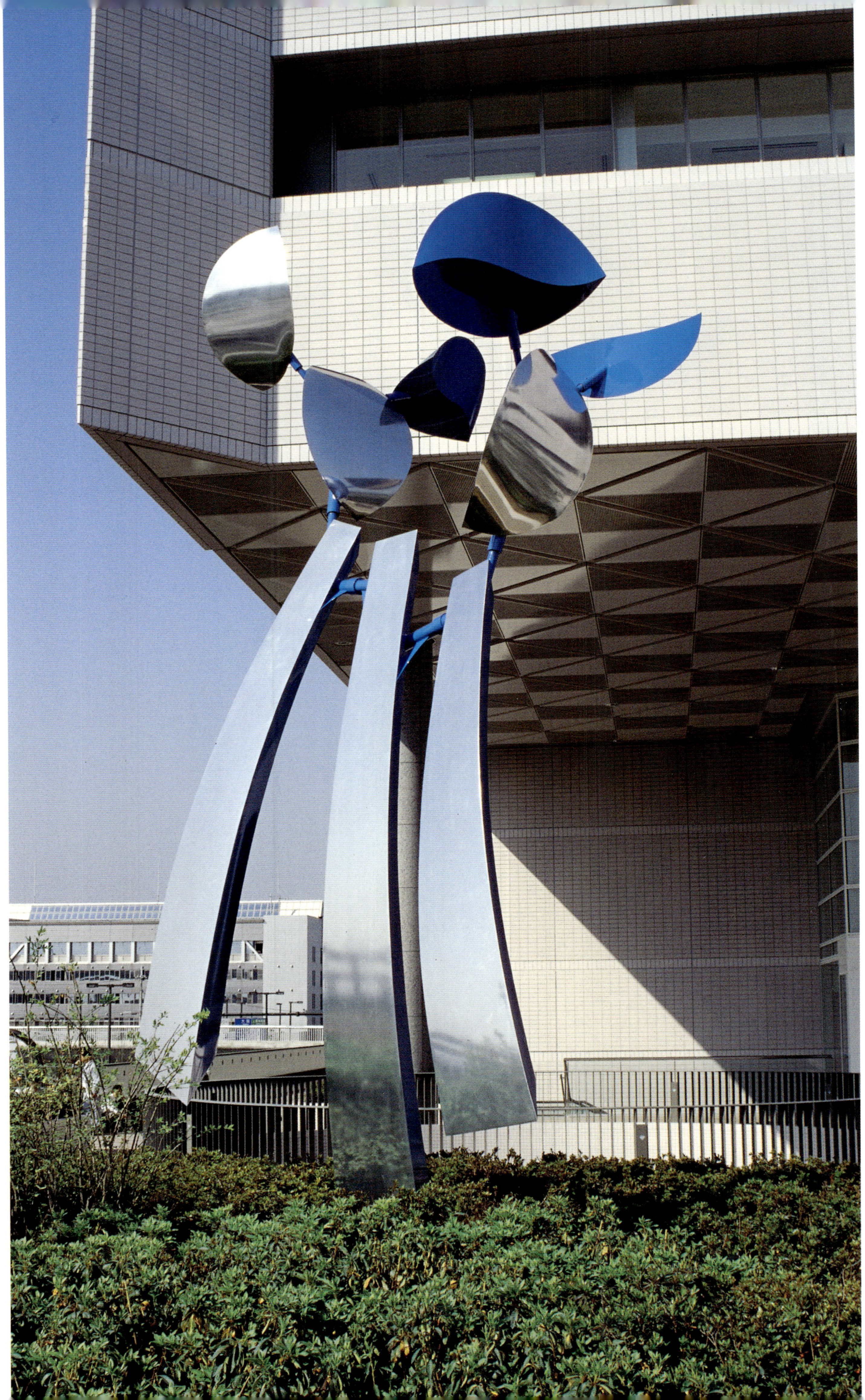

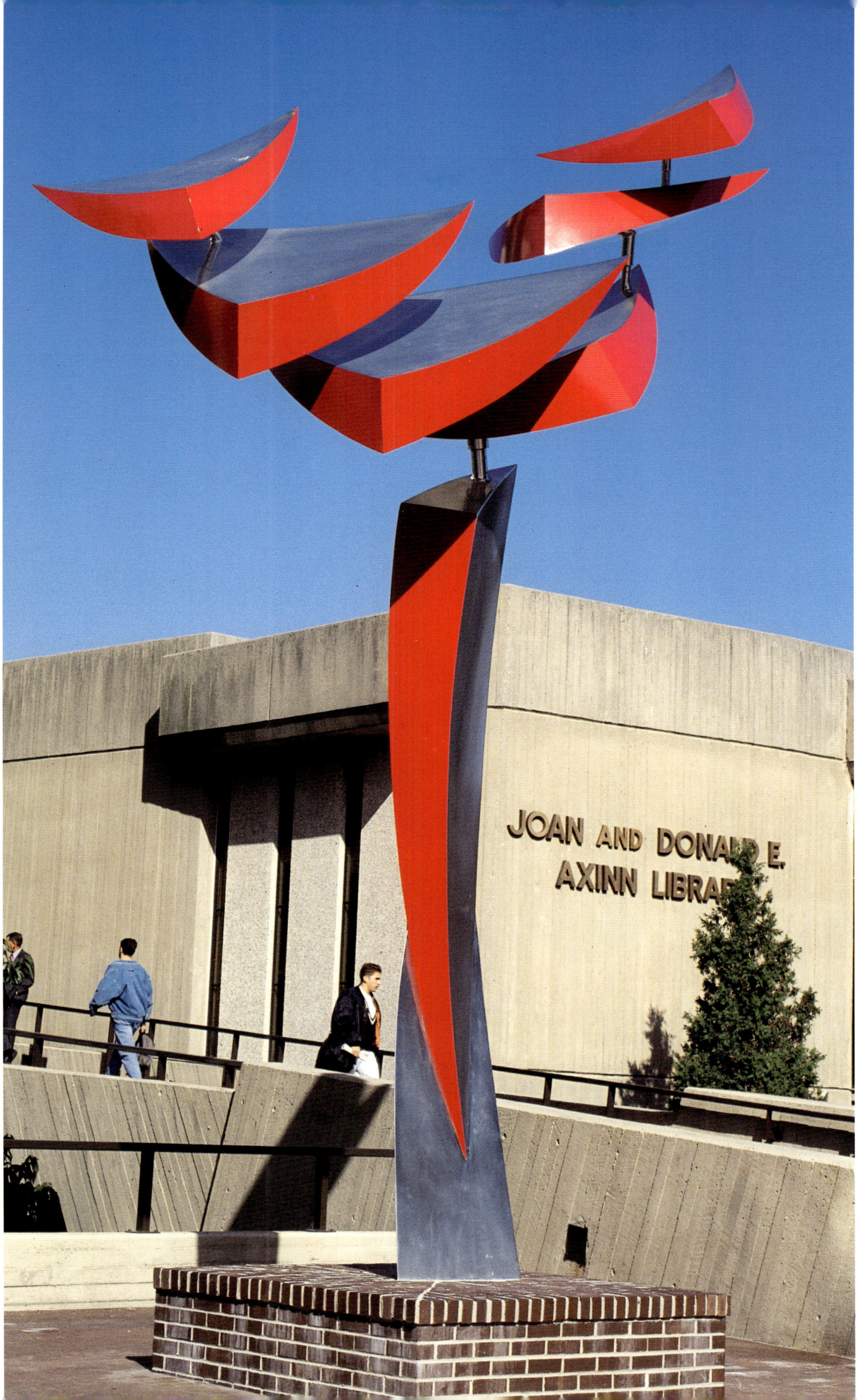

Lin Emery, Tree Dance, *1990. Aluminum and paint, 60 inches, orbit 35 inches (152.4 cm, orbit 88.9 cm). Dr. and Mrs. Harold Stokes, New Orleans, LA.*

Lin Emery, Tree Dance, *1990. Aluminum, stainless steel, and paint, 21 feet, orbit 16 feet (6.4 m, orbit 4.8 m). Hofstra University, Hempstead, NY.*

opposite page
Lin Emery, Flowering, *1994. Aluminum and paint, 22 feet, orbit 16 feet (6.7 m, orbit 4.8 m). Neiman Marcus, Short Hills, NJ.*

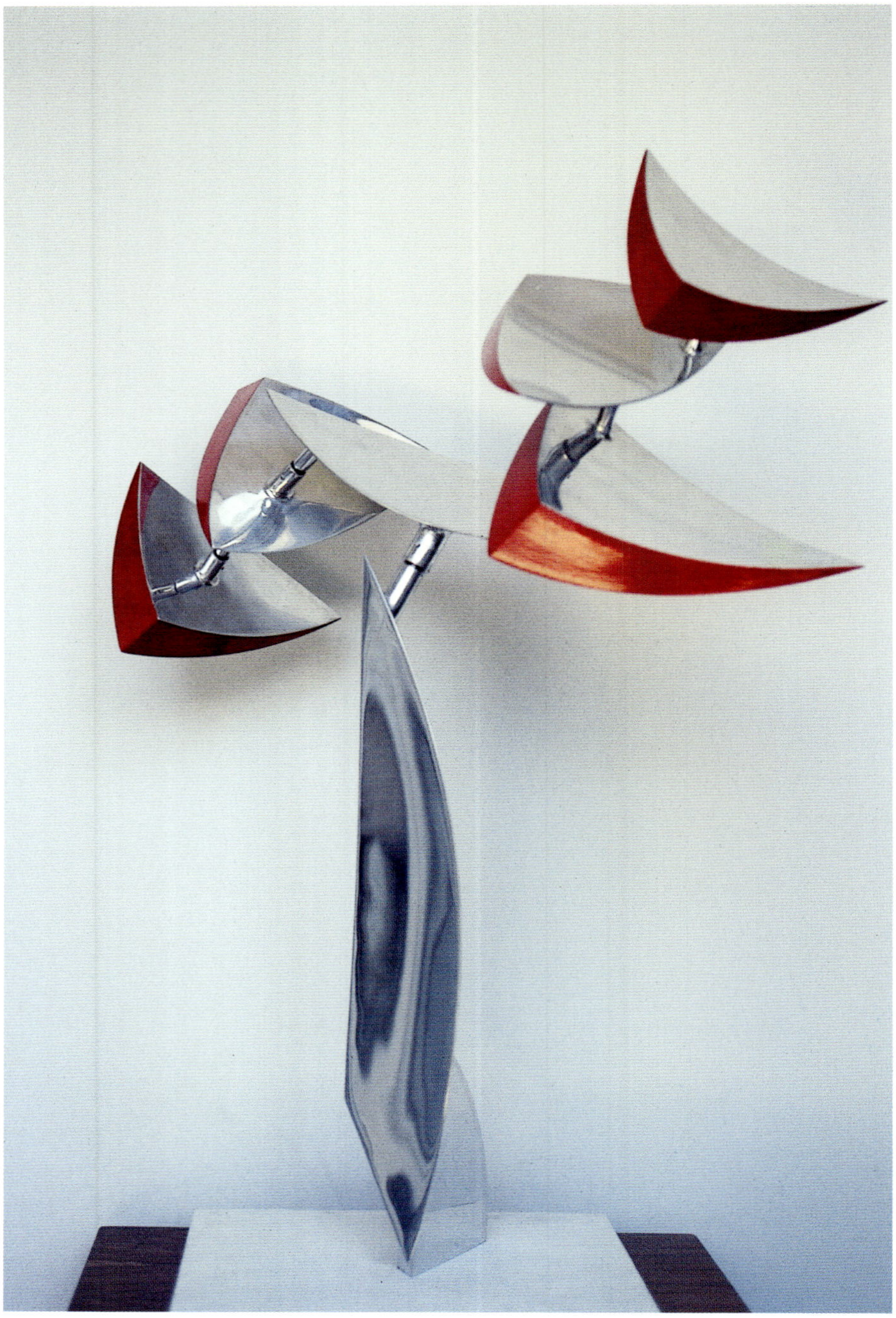

experience is a combination of flatness and reflected depth. She is not above playing visual games with her reflective surfaces. In *Amli* (fig. 5.9), she painted only a few edges, so the color seems to be a reflection of something red in the surroundings, what she calls an optical illusion. *Bright Petals* (fig. 5.10) is designed so that the red, toning to orange, on each petal's undersurface is reflected in the upper surfaces of the petals below. Keep in mind that all of these works move, driven by the wind, interior air currents, or a gentle push. What we see in photographs is only a suggestion of their lively selves. Imagine the elements of *Bright Petals* all rotating independently, surfaces sparkling, with little exclamations of red livening up the event.

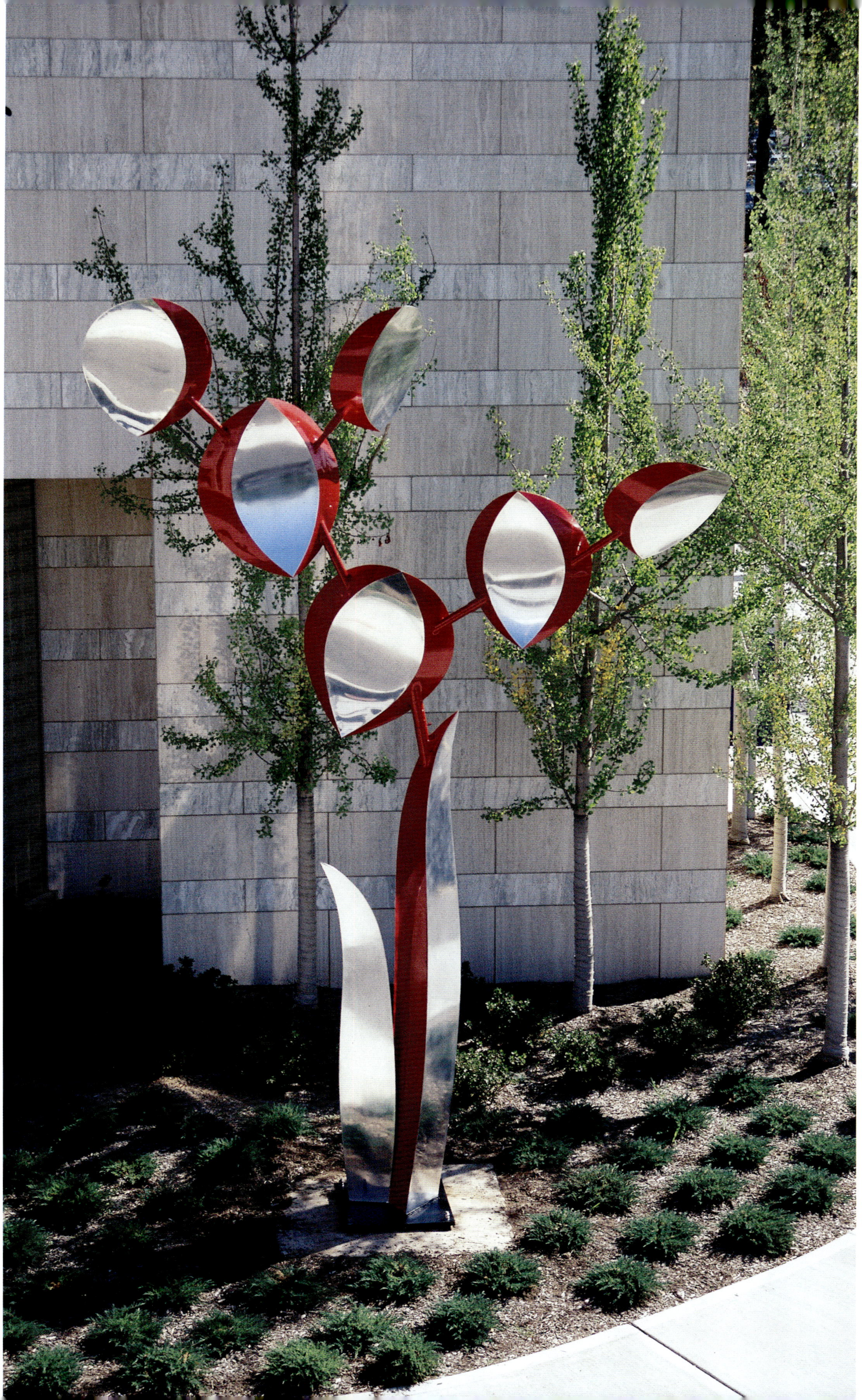

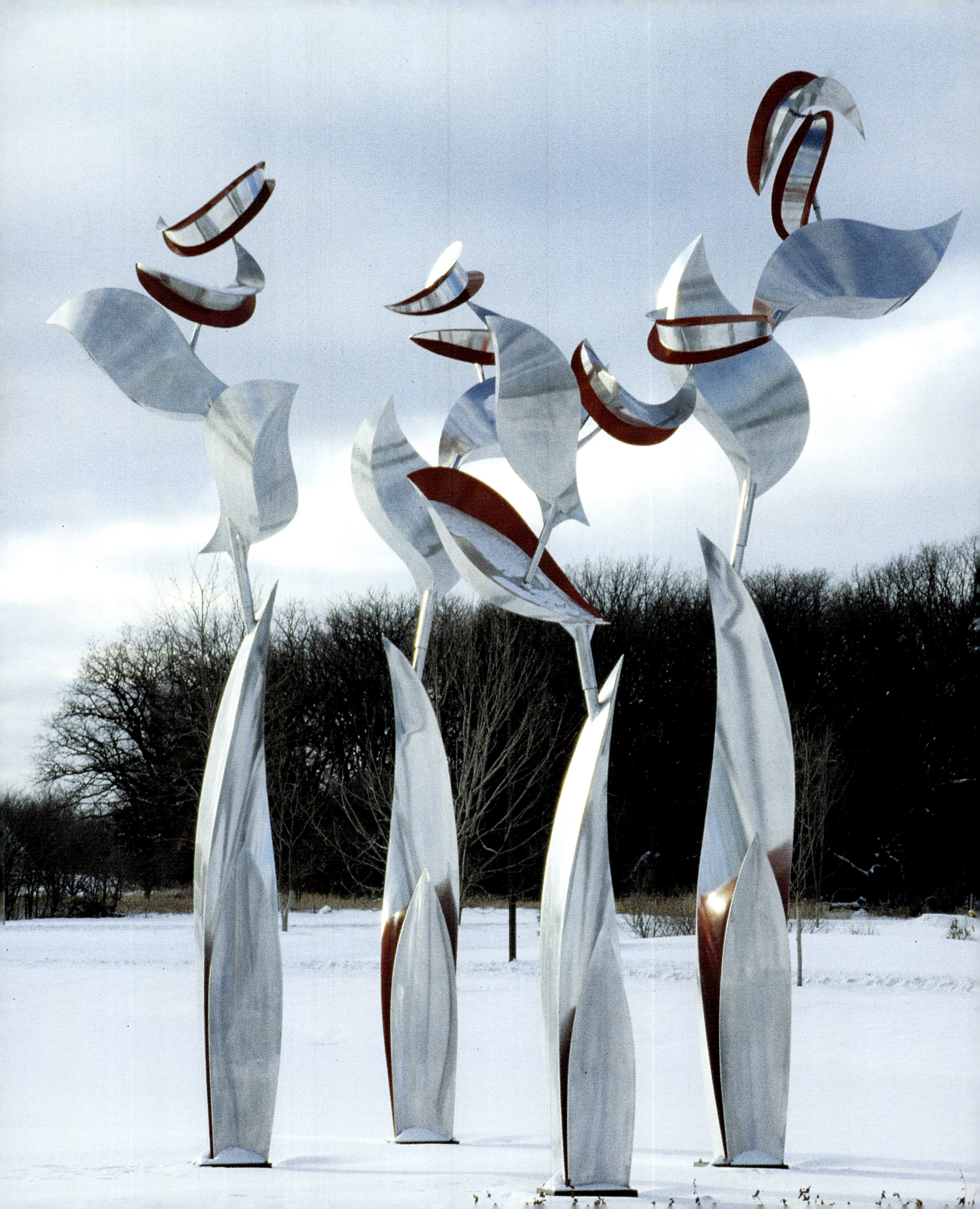

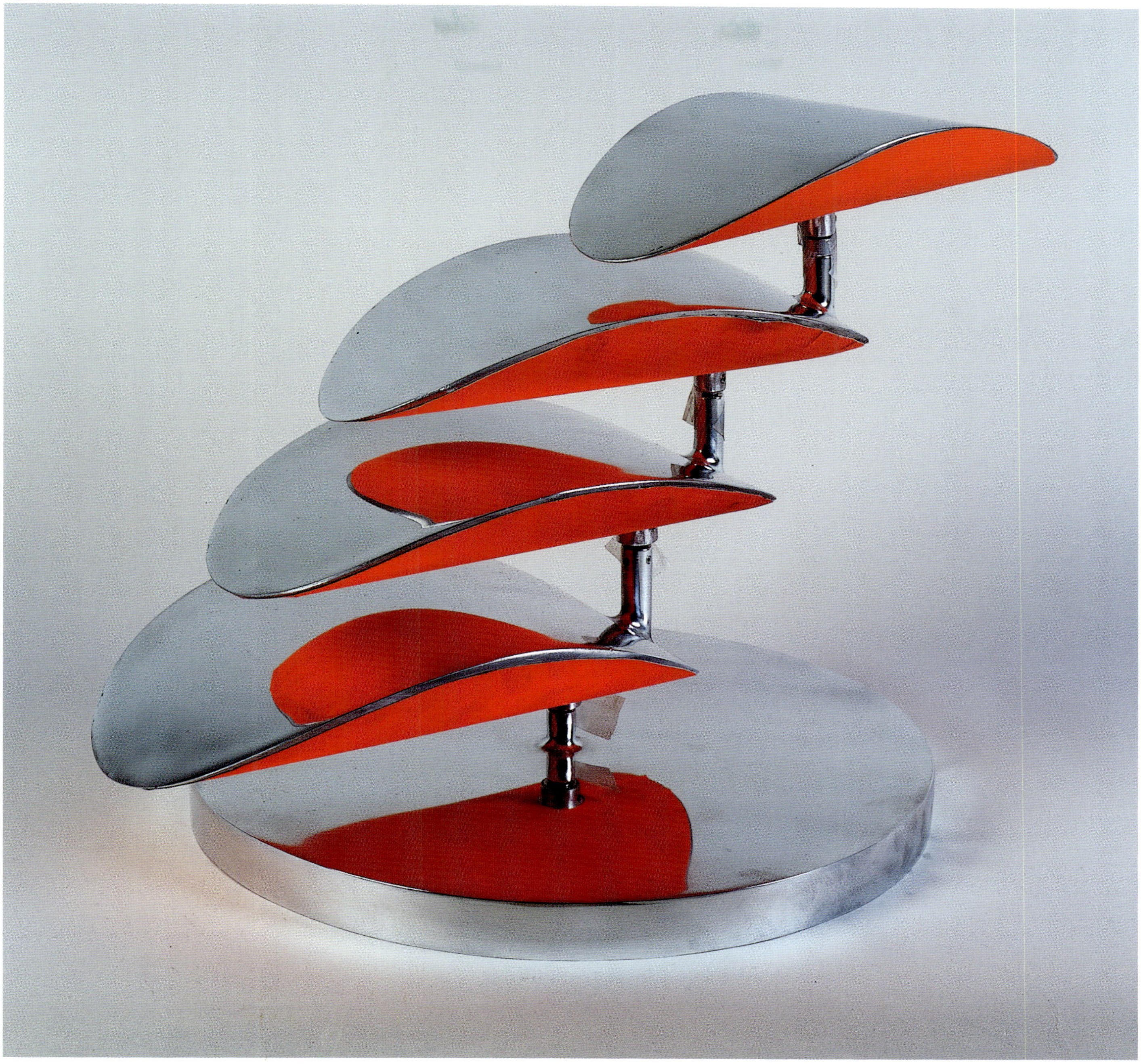

When Emery places her sculptures in groups, they take on extended meaning. It is striking to see a cluster of such individual works, with such idiosyncratic but similar movements. The implications have to do with family resemblance, community, and sympathetic interaction.

At times, Emery has returned to her interest in water, revealing the symbiotic relationship between her forms, their movement, and that liquid medium. In fig. 5.11, *Dulles (Birds in Flight)*, completed in 1987 and commissioned by the developer of an office building complex near the Dulles, Virginia, airport, she captures the impression of a flock of birds skimming over a body of water.

opposite page
FIG. 5.9 *Lin Emery,* Amli, *1990. Aluminum and paint, 36 x 36 x 30 feet (10.9 x 10.9 x 9.1 m). Amhurst Lake Park, Waukegan, IL.*

above
FIG. 5.10 *Lin Emery,* Bright Petals, *2000. Aluminum and paint, 20 x 36 x 8 inches (50.8 x 91.4 x 20.3 cm). Collection of Mr. and Mrs. Don Sanders, Houston, TX.*

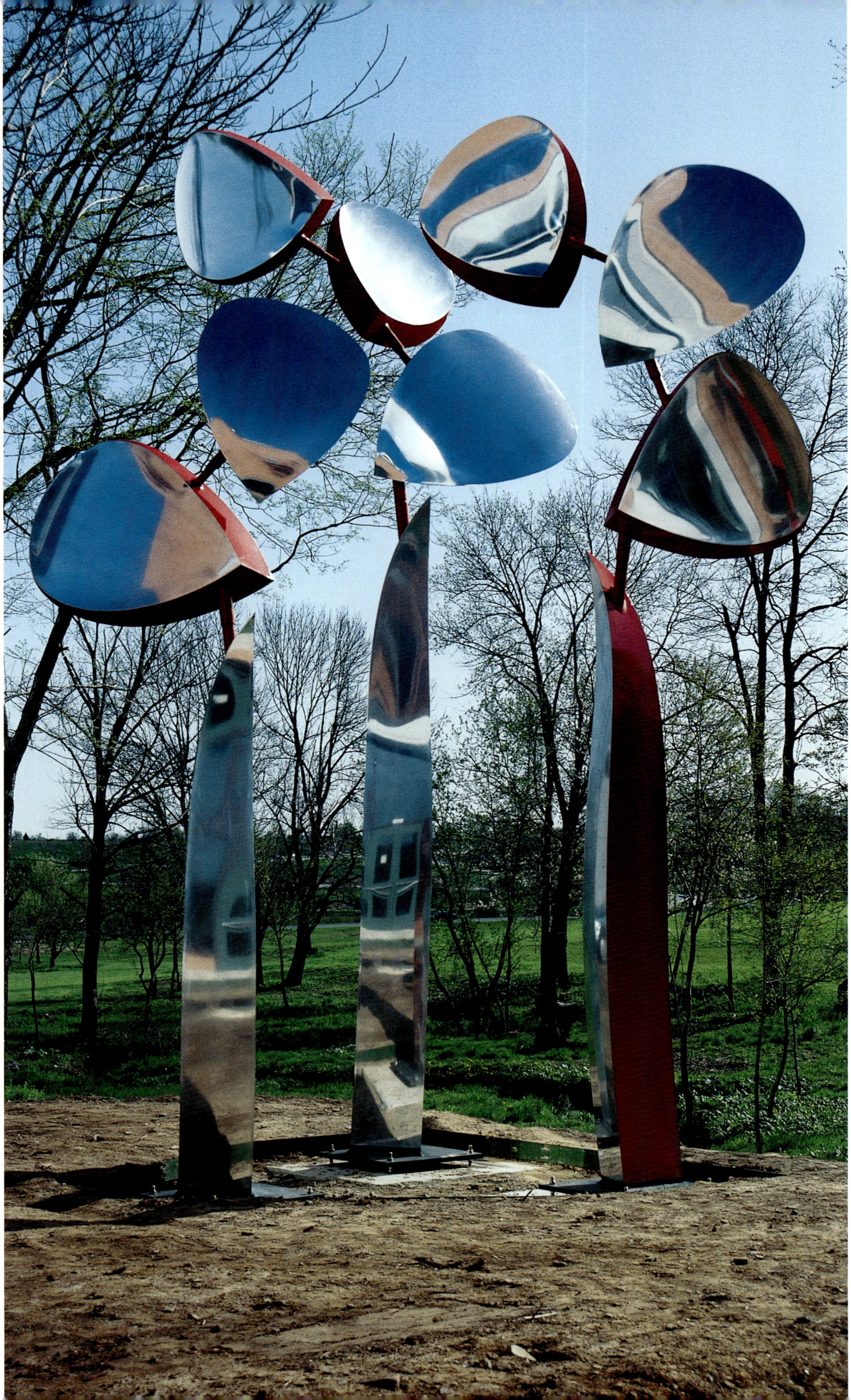

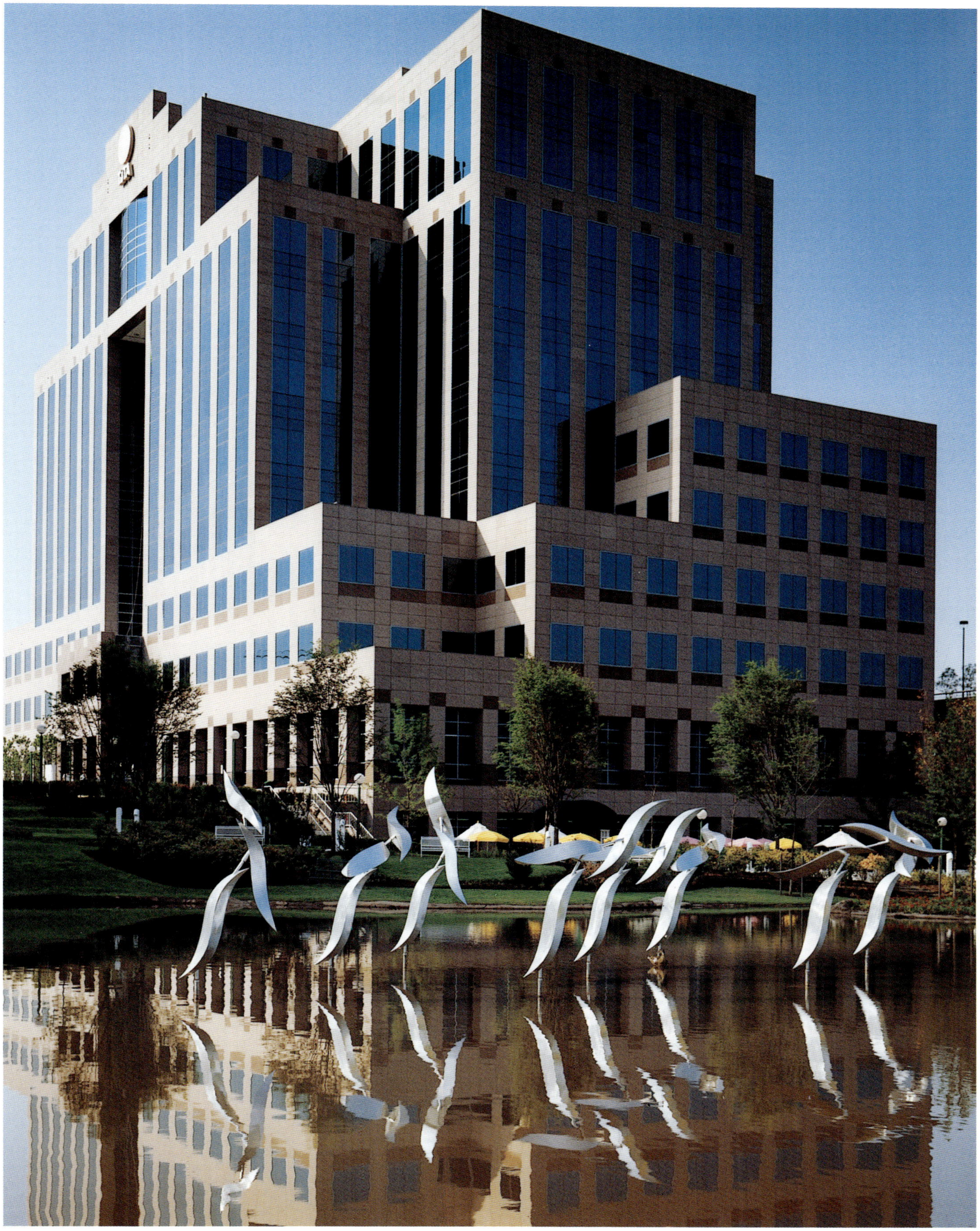

FIG. 5.11 *Lin Emery,* Dulles (Birds in Flight), *1987. Aluminum, 8 x 24 x 12 feet (2.4 x 7.3 x 3.6 m). Dulles Park, VA.*

opposite page

Lin Emery, Untitled, *1992. Aluminum and paint, 22 x 18 x 18 feet (6.7 x 5.4 x 5.4 m). Sterling Park, Collegeville, PA.*

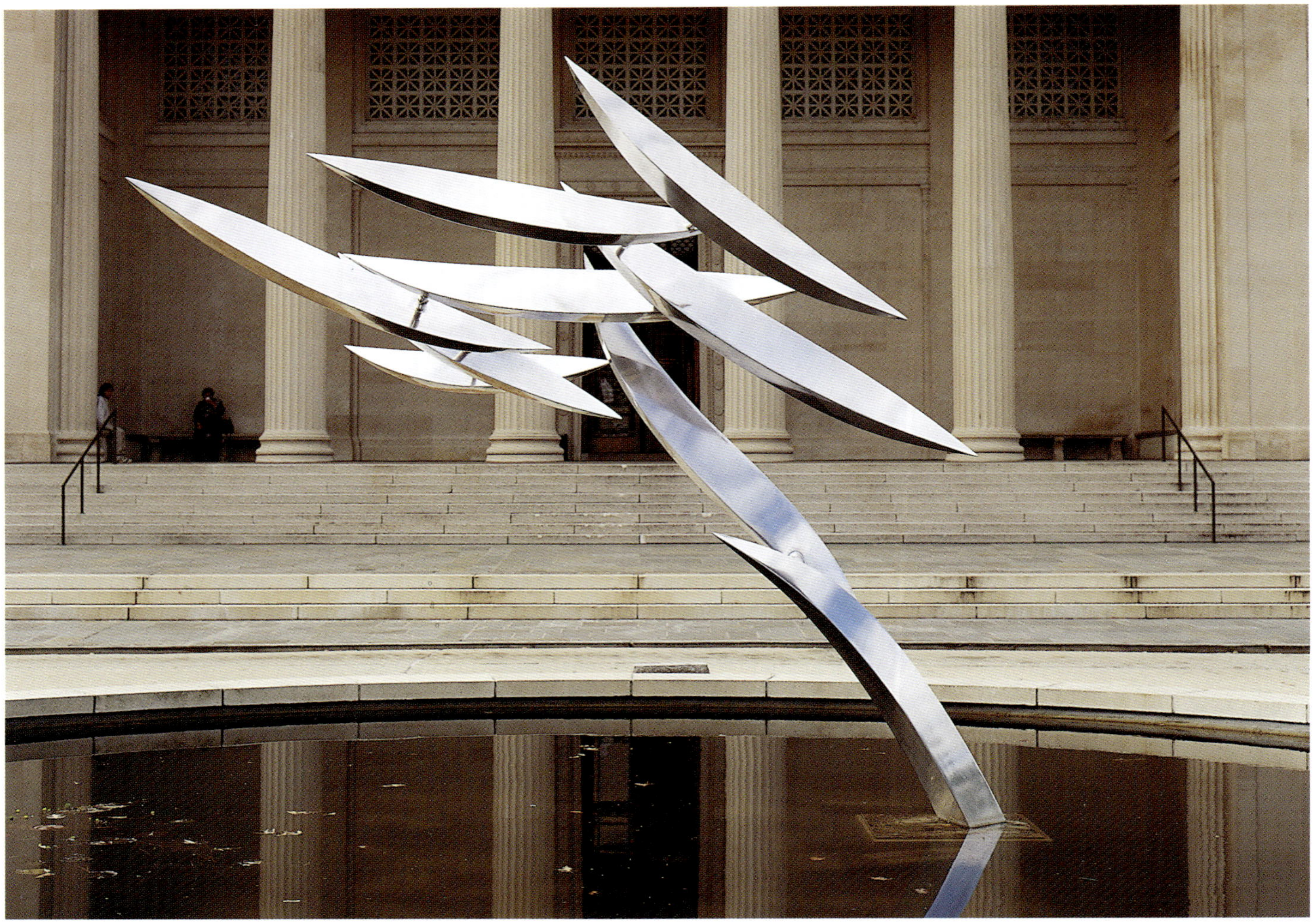

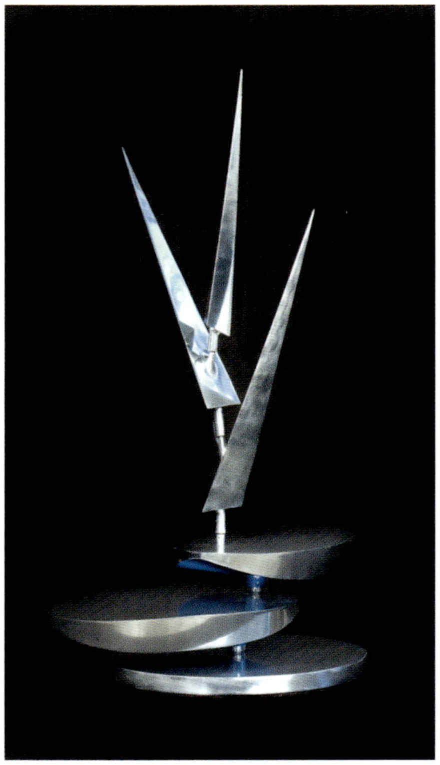

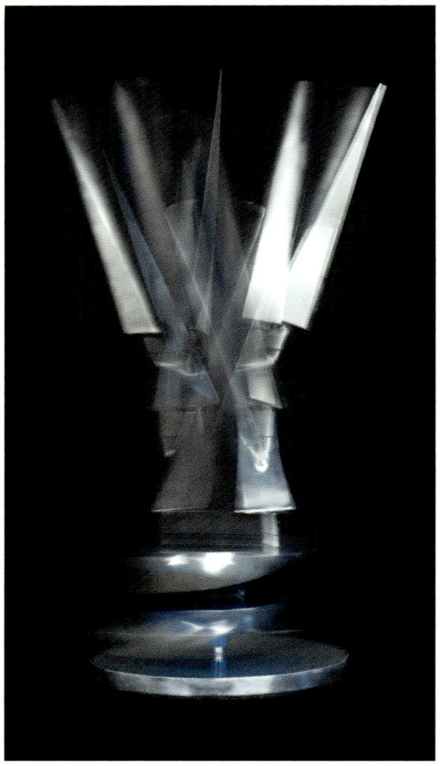

Lin Emery, Wave, *1985. Aluminum, 12 feet, orbit 8 feet (3.6 m, orbit 2.4 m). New Orleans Museum of Art, New Orleans, LA.*

Lin Emery, Water Flower (still), *1998. Aluminum, 42 x 25 x 18 inches (106.7 x 63.5 x 45.7 cm). Artist's studio.*

Lin Emery, Water Flower (in motion), *1998. Aluminum, 42 x 25 x 18 inches (106.7 x 63.5 x 45.7 cm). Artist's studio.*

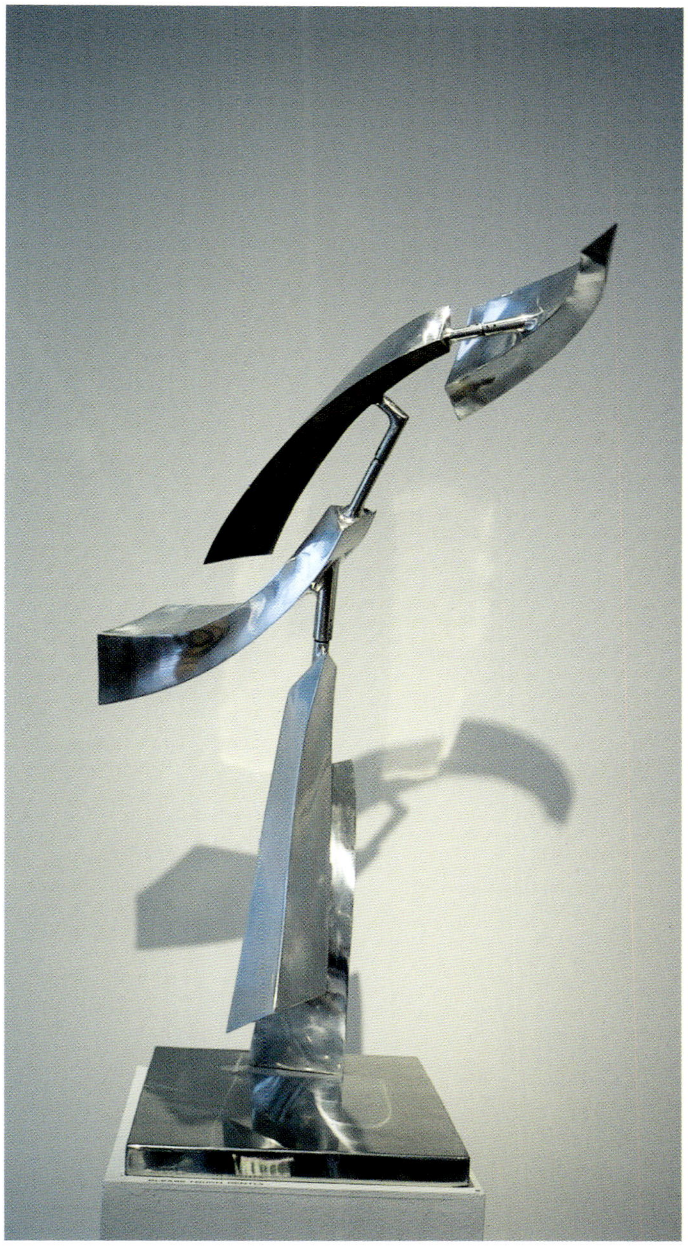

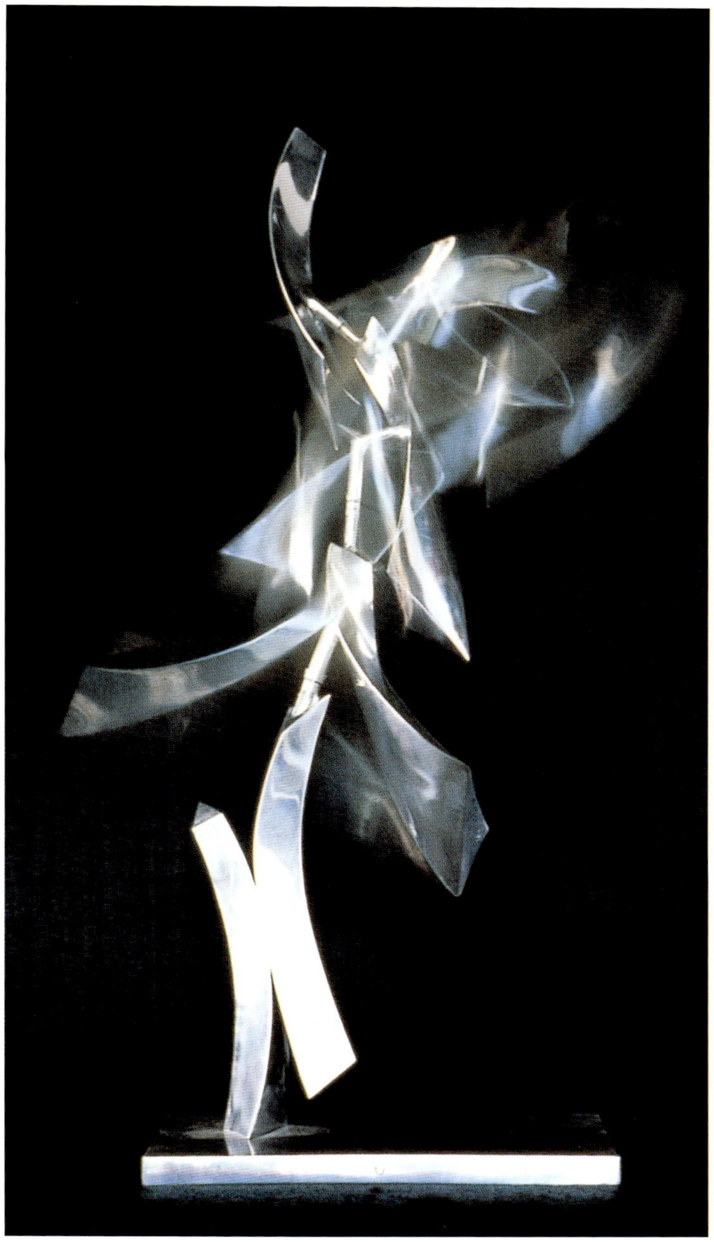

Emery often says that she borrows the forces of nature. She also borrows the forms of nature and its movements. That is why, when you see one of her large sculptures outside gracefully moving in the breeze, it seems to belong. When its shiny surfaces reflect the sky, it seems as though the sky is part of the sculpture, and the sculpture part of the sky. While they seem most natural in the company of trees, flowers, and sky, Emery's large works are openly gregarious. With their industrial materials and superb craftsmanship, they hold their own and harmonize with classic buildings, such as the New Orleans Museum, or the Sterling Commerce Building (the site of *Untitled*, fig. 5.12, circa 2000). They also soften modern architecture, mediating between the vocabulary of brick, concrete, and glass and that of nature. They speak both languages.

Lin Emery, Helix *(still), 1986. Aluminum, 20 inches, orbit 18 inches (50.8 cm, orbit 45.7 cm). Private collection.*

Lin Emery, Helix *(in motion), 1986. Aluminum, 20 inches, orbit 18 inches (50.8 cm, orbit 45.7 cm). Private collection.*

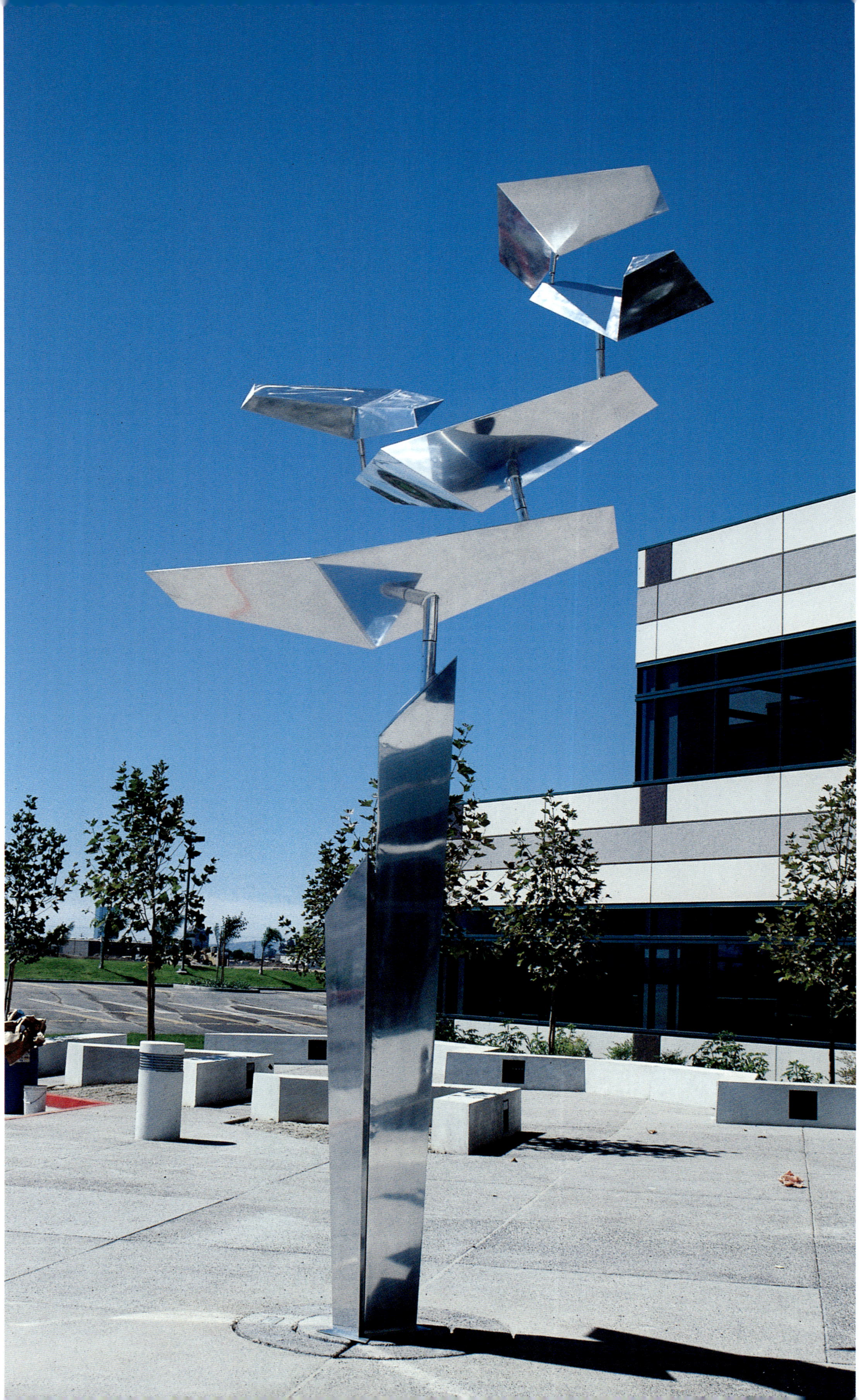

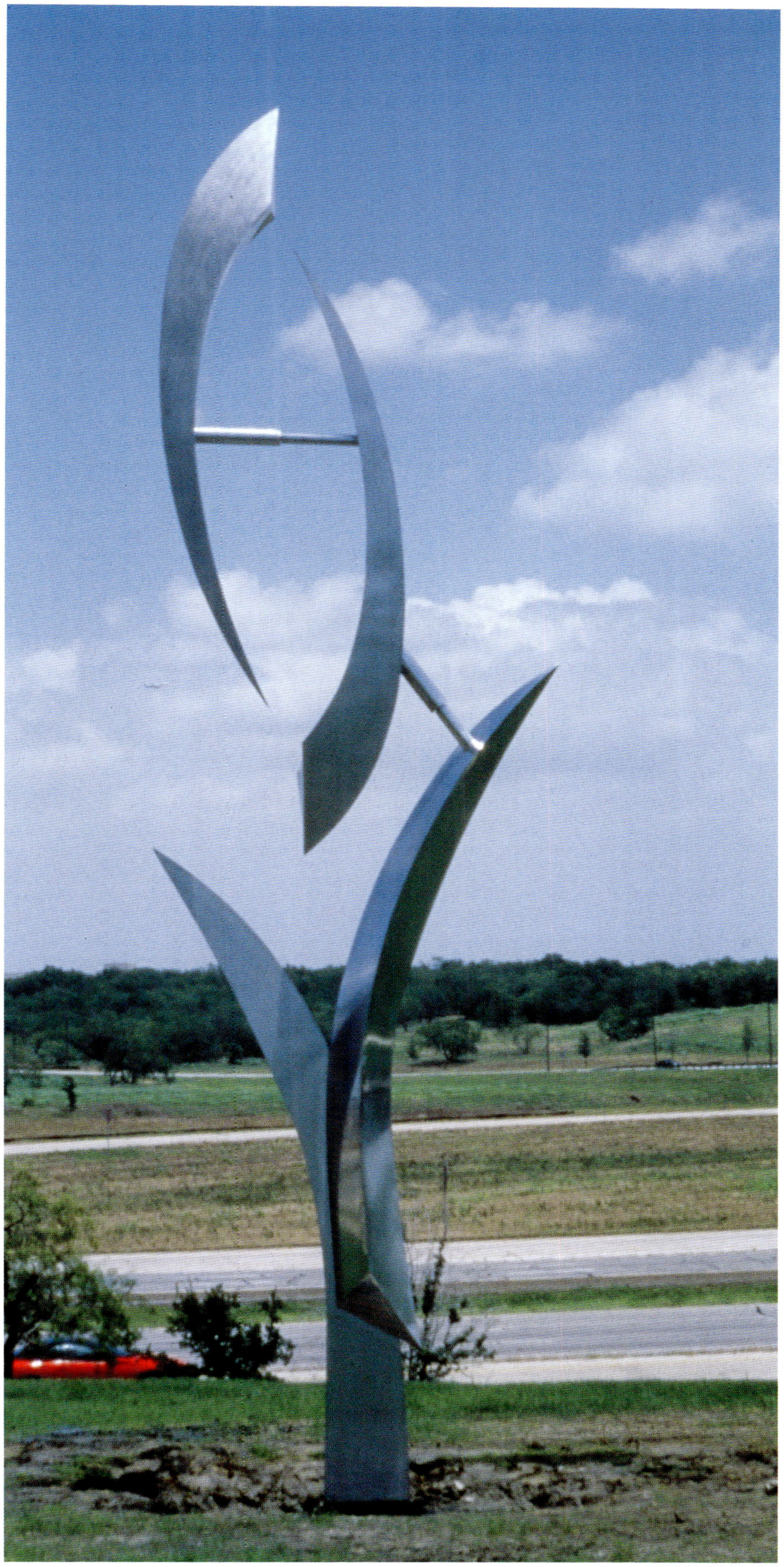

opposite page

Lin Emery, Chevron, *1989. Aluminum, 16 feet, orbit 12 feet (4.8 m, orbit 3.6 m). City of Oxnard, Oxnard, CA.*

left

FIG. 5.12 *Lin Emery,* Untitled, *c. 2000. Aluminum, 22 feet, orbit 14 feet (6.7 m, orbit 4.2 m). Sterling Commerce Building, Dallas, TX.*

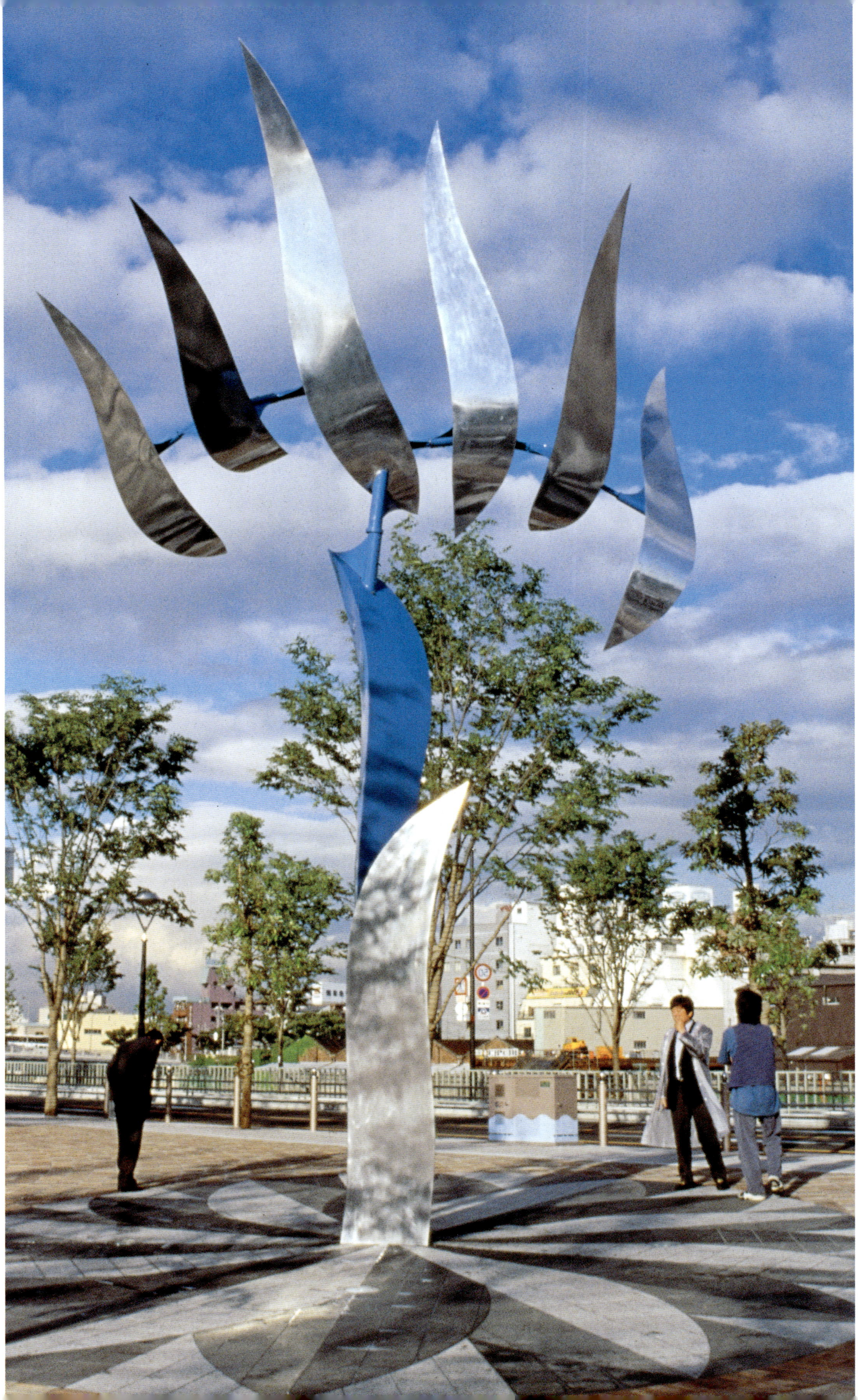

The combined attributes of Emery's monumental wind-driven sculptures, their art-historical stature, their popular appeal, and their compatibility with architecture and nature have made them favorites of architects, municipalities, and developers. By the mid-1980s, Emery's reputation was such that she could be selective in accepting the commissions she was most interested in undertaking. Her stately, sparkling, gracefully moving sculptures animate spaces on university campuses and in shopping malls, airports, and industrial parks from California to New York. One has been installed at a hospital in Japan, another in a marina in Singapore. In 1997, her 36-foot-high *Honoo-no-ki* (*Dance of the Tree*) (fig. 5.13), installed in front of the Osaka Dome, was awarded the Grand Prize for Public Sculpture by the Osaka Prefecture.

At times, Emery will diverge from her use of simplified natural forms to employ more geometric shapes. She did so in some of her fountains, such as *Untitled*, 1974 (see fig. 3.12), at the University of South Carolina, and she has done so recently in some of her smaller works. But whatever the forms of the individual elements, the movements are always fluid, with a Bach fugue's combination of surprise and inevitability.

opposite page

FIG. 5.13 *Lin Emery,* Honoo-no-ki (Dance of the Tree), *1997. Aluminum, 36 x 22 x 18 feet (10.9 x 6.7 x 5.4 m). Osaka Dome, Japan.*

below

Lin Emery, Acrobat *(still), 2001. Aluminum, 16 inches, orbit 12 inches (40.6 cm, orbit 30.5 cm). Private collection.*

Lin Emery, Acrobat *(in motion), 2001. Aluminum, 16 inches, orbit 12 inches (40.6 cm, orbit 30.5 cm). Private collection.*

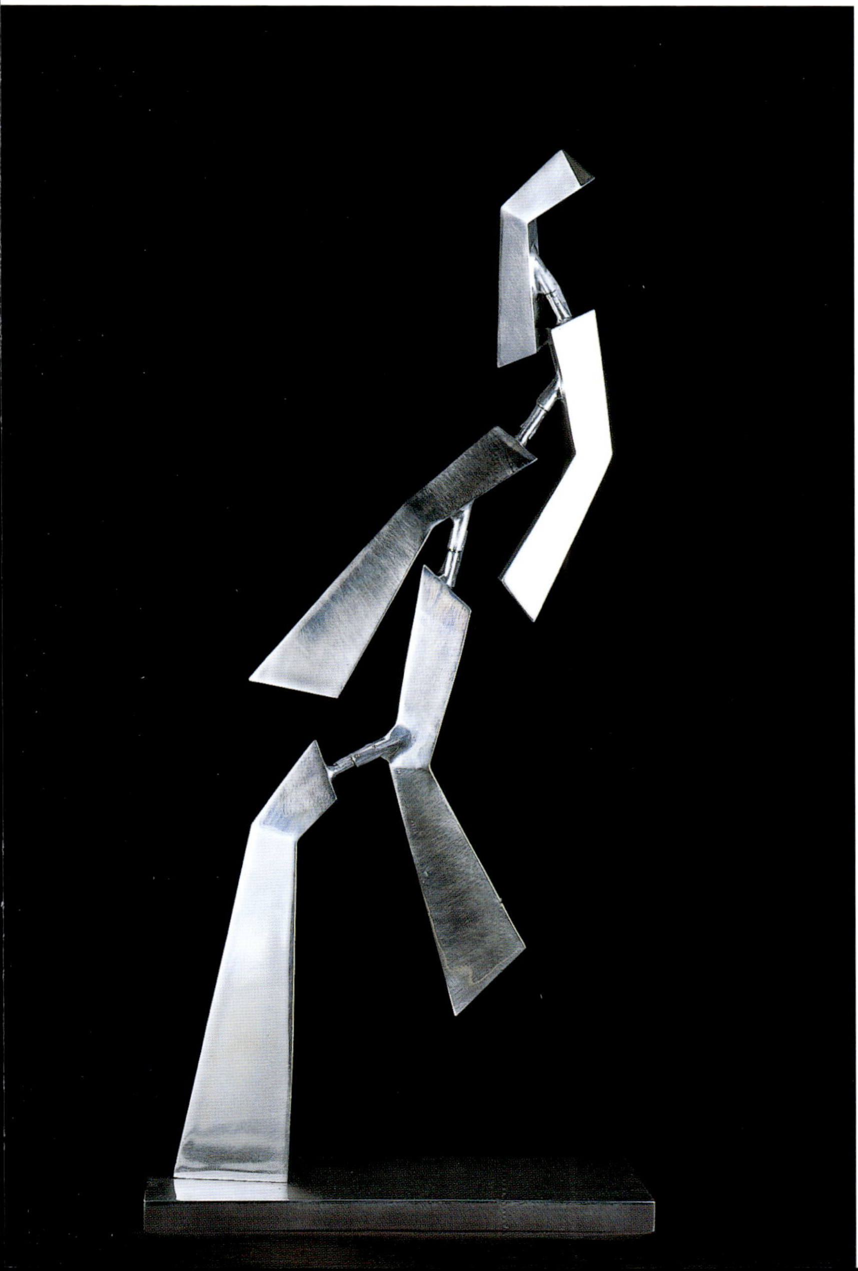

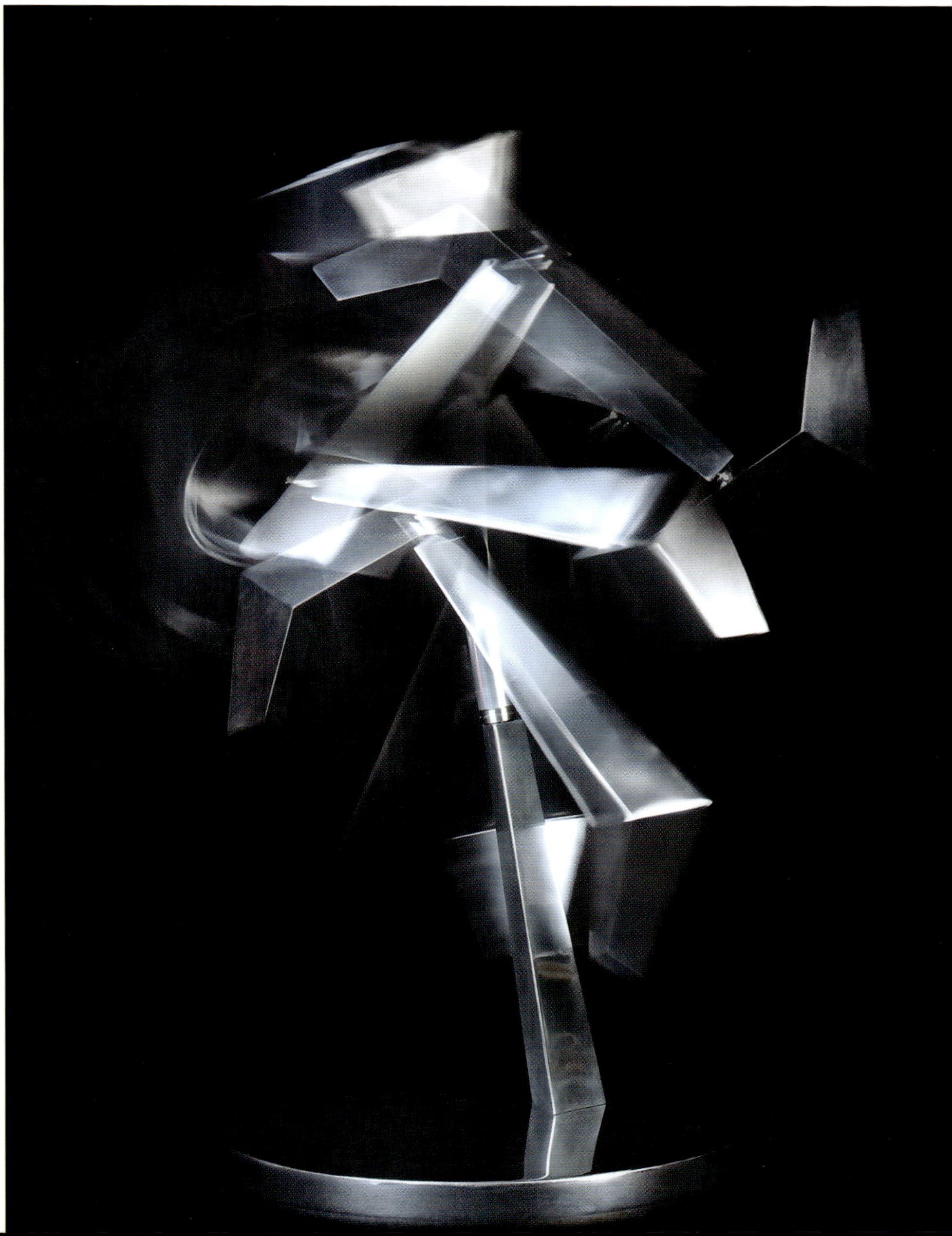

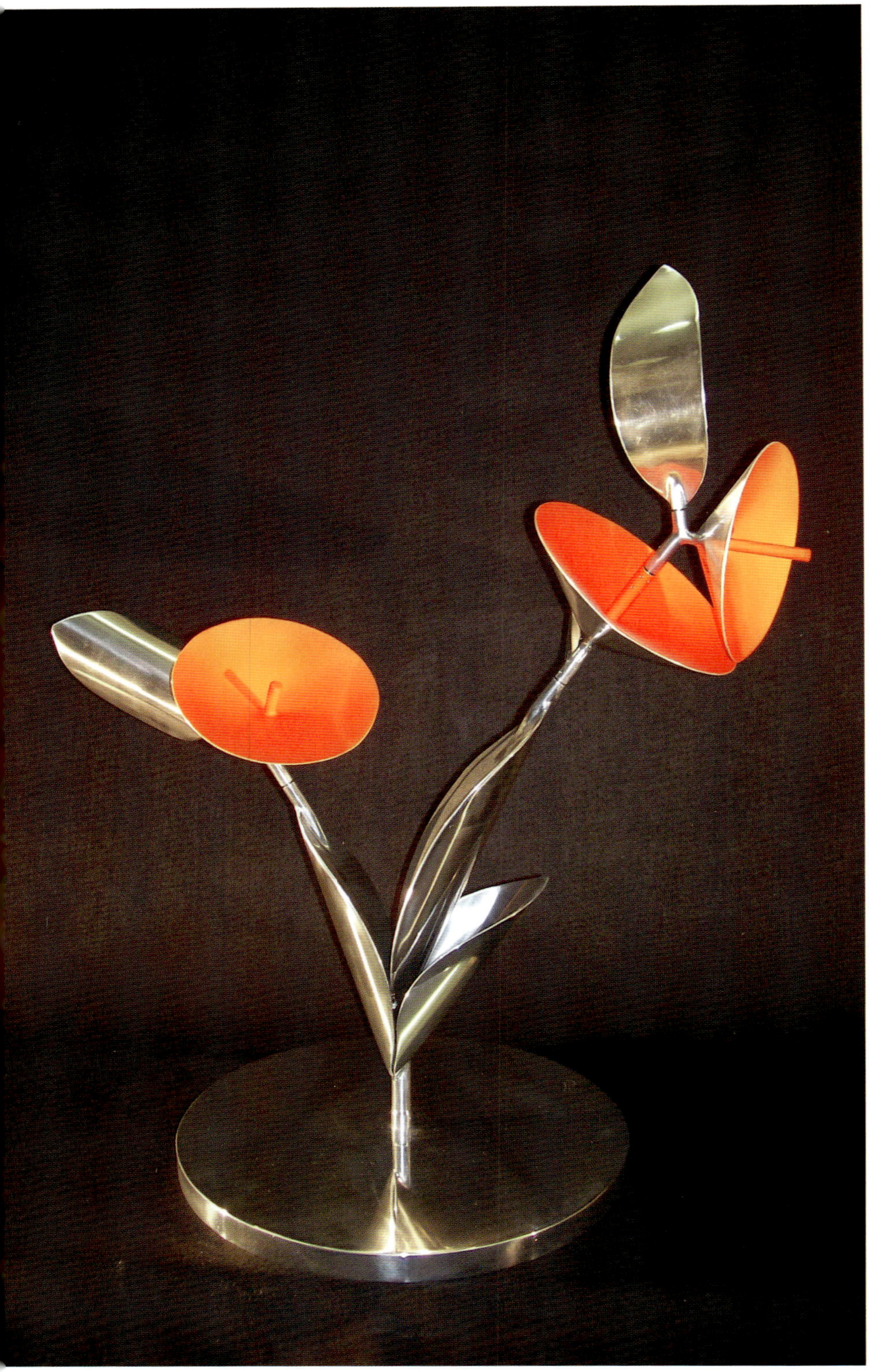

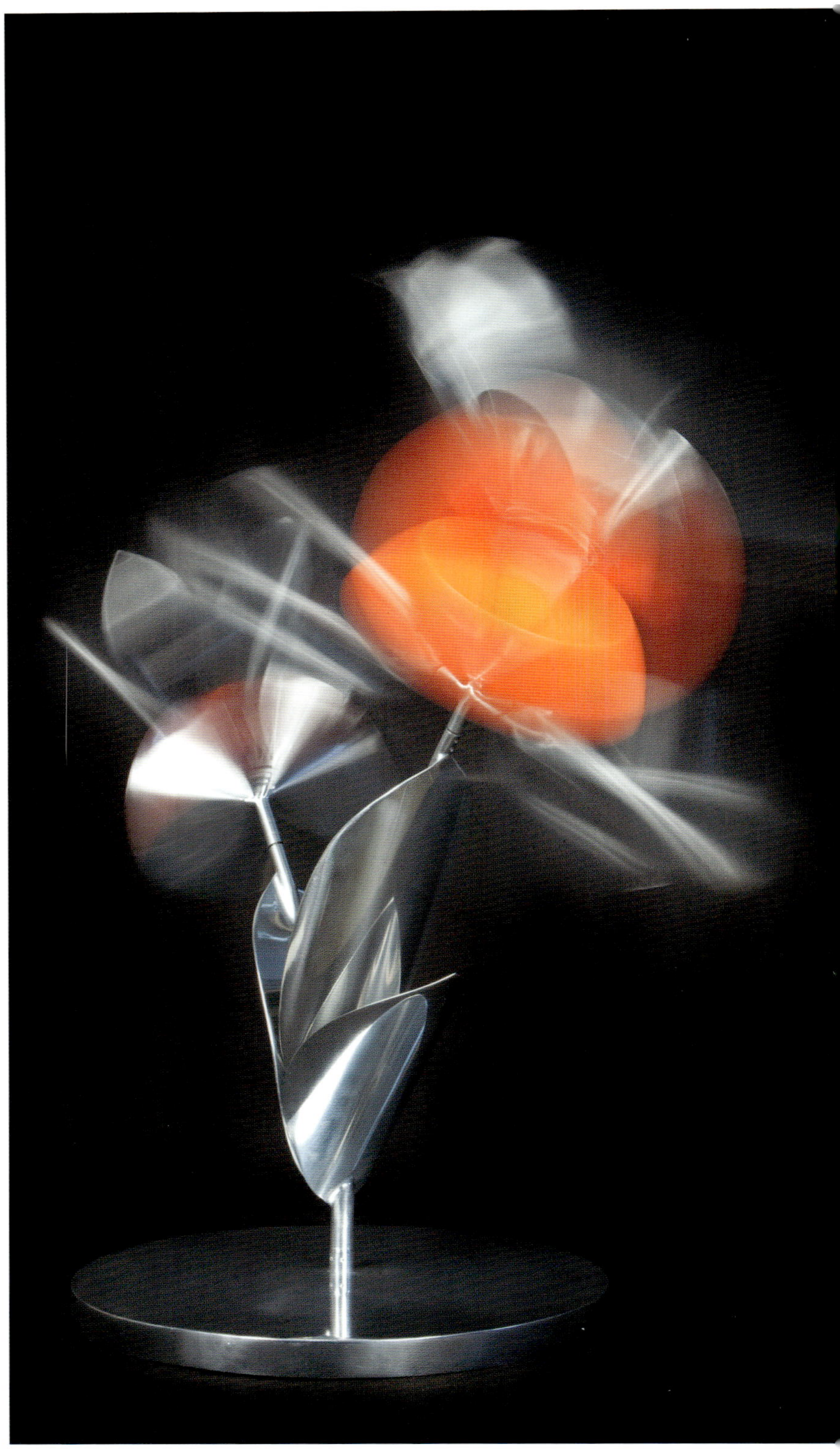

Lin Emery, Sunflower *(still), 2009. Aluminum and paint, 32 inches, orbit 14 inches (81.3 cm, orbit 35.6 cm). Artist's studio.*

Lin Emery, Sunflower *(in motion), 2009. Aluminum and paint, 32 inches, orbit 14 inches (81.3 cm, orbit 35.6 cm). Artist's studio.*

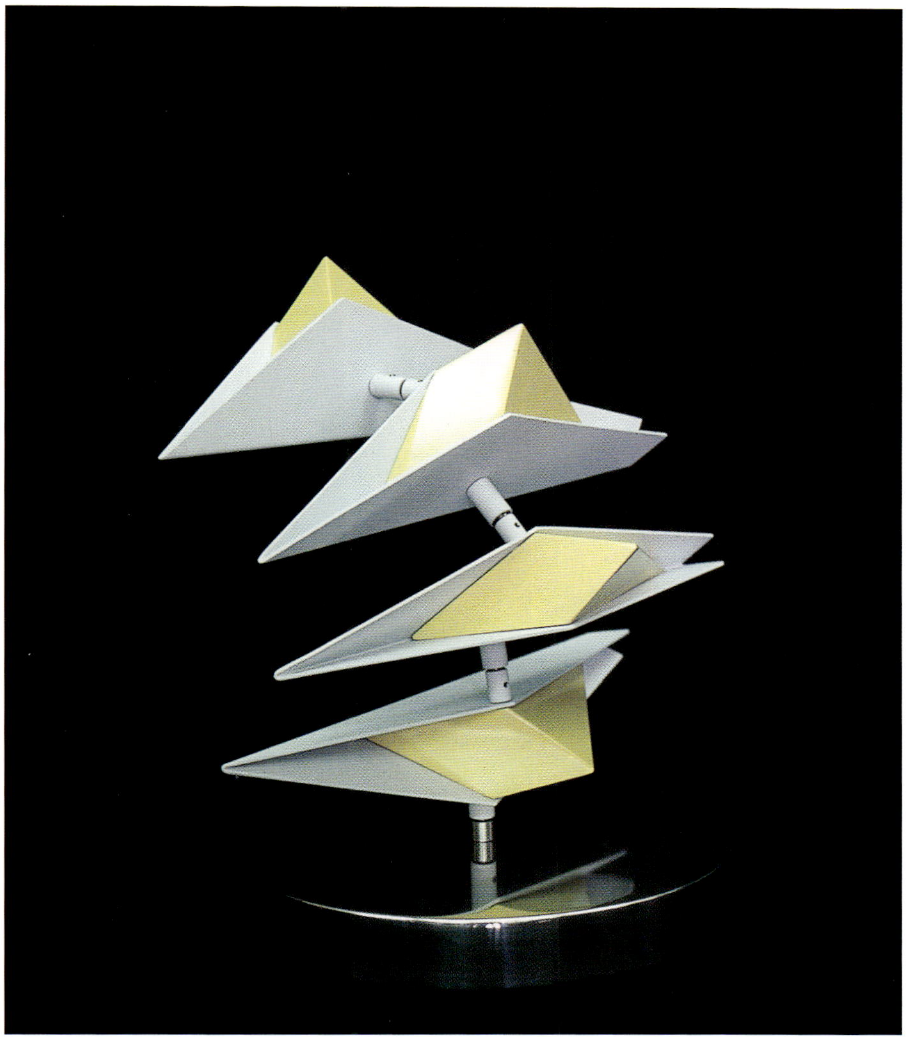

Lin Emery, Origami, *2008. Aluminum and paint, 13 x 12 x 4 inches (33 x 30.5 x 10.2 cm). Private collection.*

It is unusual for Emery to commemorate an event through her sculpture, but Hurricane Katrina had a powerful effect on her and she felt a need to express her own and her city's distress. The meaning of *Katrina* (fig. 5.14) deepens if you know something of Emery's earlier work. The three lower elements of the sculpture are forms that Emery has used to represent water, but now they are partially painted black, with that black reflected in their shiny surfaces. Water is still the primordial source of life, but now it is also the source of death. The balance of the work is still delicate, but now it is life that is precarious. The two upper elements represent people crying for help during and after the storm. In *Katrina*, Emery manages to use her personal artistic vocabulary to convey a message of anguish, pain, and sympathy without compromising the artistic integrity of her sculpture.

Martin Heiddeger suggested that the essence of a sculpture is not simply the object itself but how it came into being, the "generative power that makes a thing what it is."[6] Emery's sculptures are both machines and works of art. Their integrity is a result of the complete integration of two temperaments in the sculptor, that of the engineer/technician and that of the artist. Throughout her career, from the early days of learning to weld, to her pouring metal in her own foundry and shaping of aluminum on an English wheel in her studio, Emery has savored the mechani-

FIG. 5.14 *Lin Emery,* Katrina *(right: still; opposite page: in motion), 2008. Aluminum and paint, 27½ inches, orbit 18 inches (69.9 cm, orbit 45.7 cm). Private collection.*

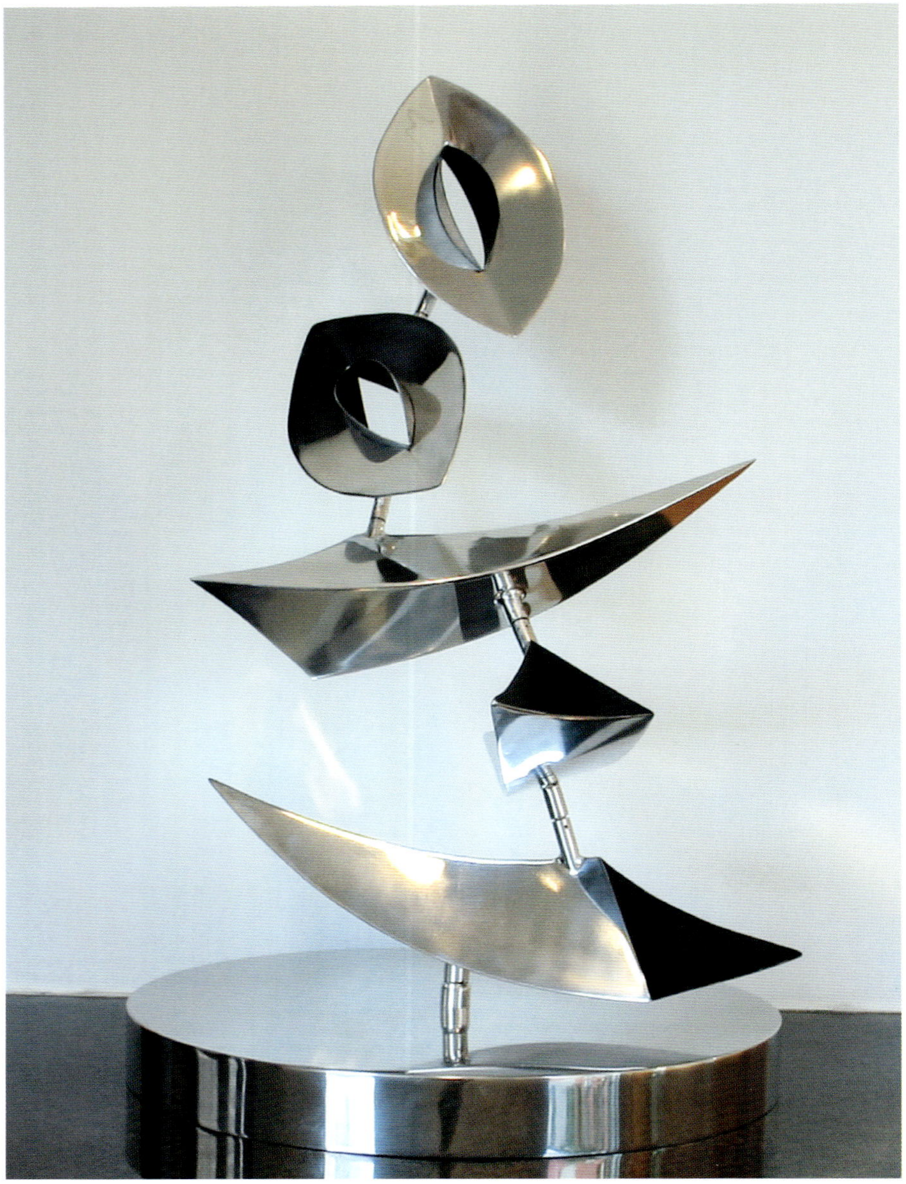

cal aspects of creating sculpture. Machines are a passion. Once, when her mother gave her a mink coat for Christmas, Emery traded it for a band saw. In 2009, she took delight in showing a visitor her Christmas present to herself, a fancy German tilting-bed milling machine.

As she conceives of a new sculpture, Emery does not sketch on a pad but engages in literal cutting and pasting. She first cuts out a roughly 8-inch-high paper version of the work, with the elements connected with straight pins. She uses poster board to cut and paste together a model, 16–18 inches high, connecting the elements with plastic straws within straws, which allows them to move. In these little white models, the basic movements of the work are approximated. In a process that Arthur Roger, who represents Emery in his eponymous gallery in New Orleans, calls creating while materializing, she then uses that model to create a 2–3-foot-high

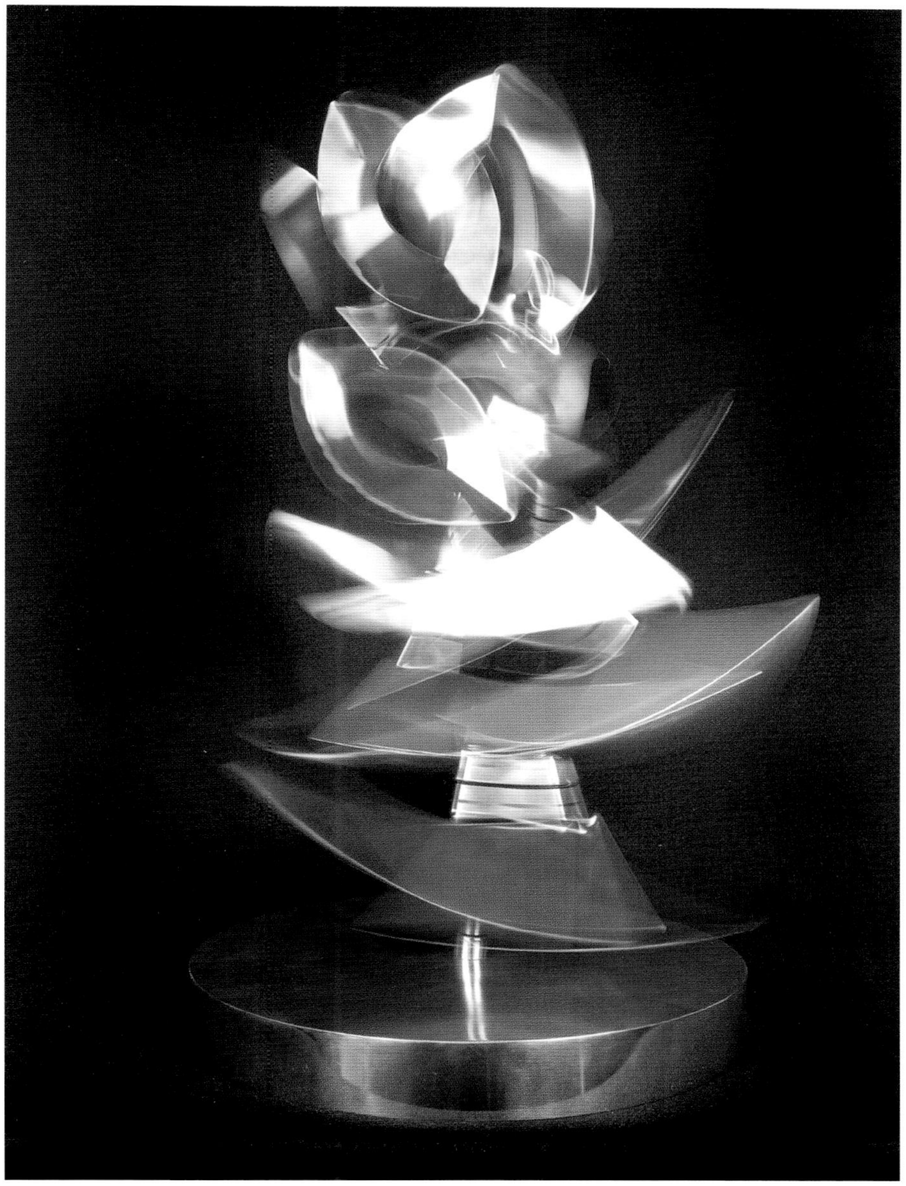

maquette in polished aluminum. It is at this stage that Emery thinks through the exact three-dimensional shapes of all the elements and all of the movements of the final work. This involves finding the exact balance points and global center of gravity of the piece, in order to create an easy, natural movement. In addition to being a step toward a large outdoor work, this is a fully executed sculpture that Emery will sell from one of the commercial galleries representing her. If the outdoor piece is particularly large, say, 35 feet high or more, she will produce a half-scale version as a step toward the final work. Except for the final stages of some of her largest pieces that won't fit in her studio, Emery is engaged with every step of the fabrication of each new work. She designs all of the bearing assemblies, the key mechanical components containing the ball bearings that connect the forms and allow them to move independently.

Sketch of bearing assembly. Photograph by Lin Emery.

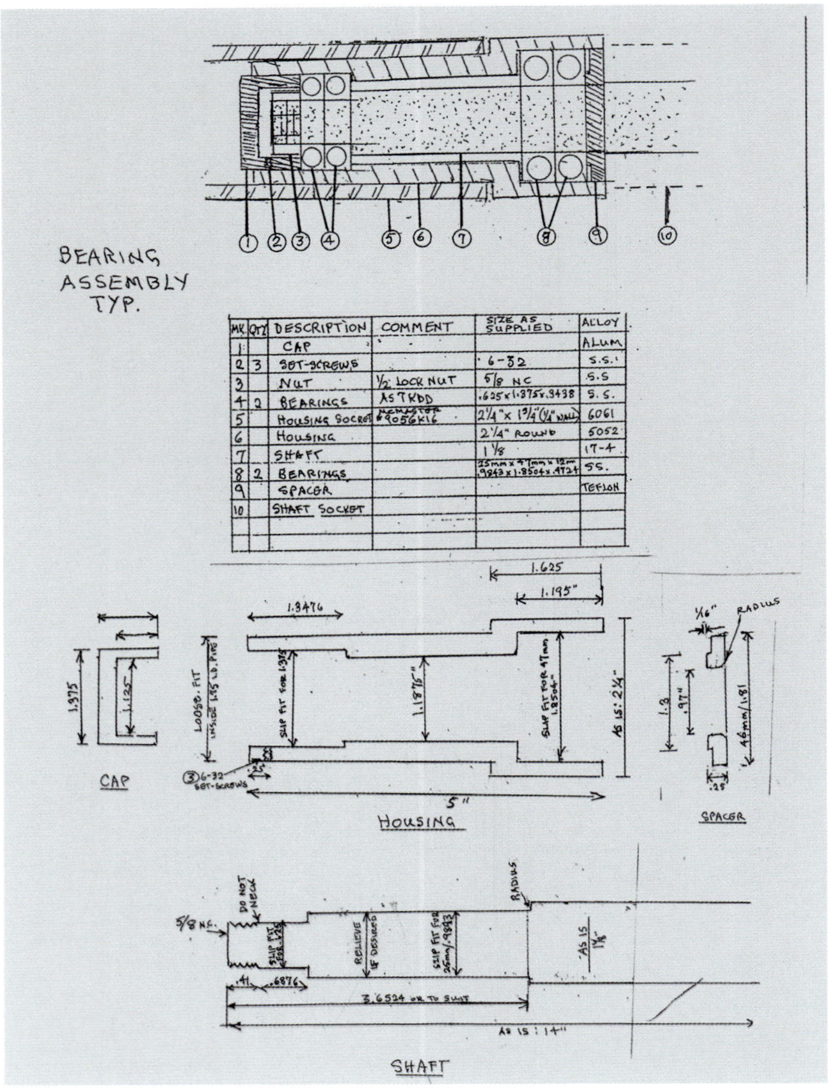

Photo of bearings. Photograph by Lin Emery.

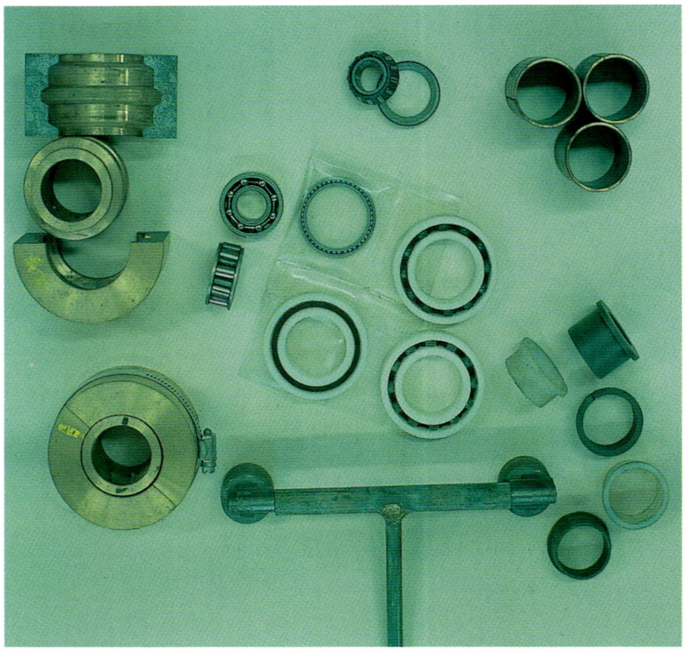

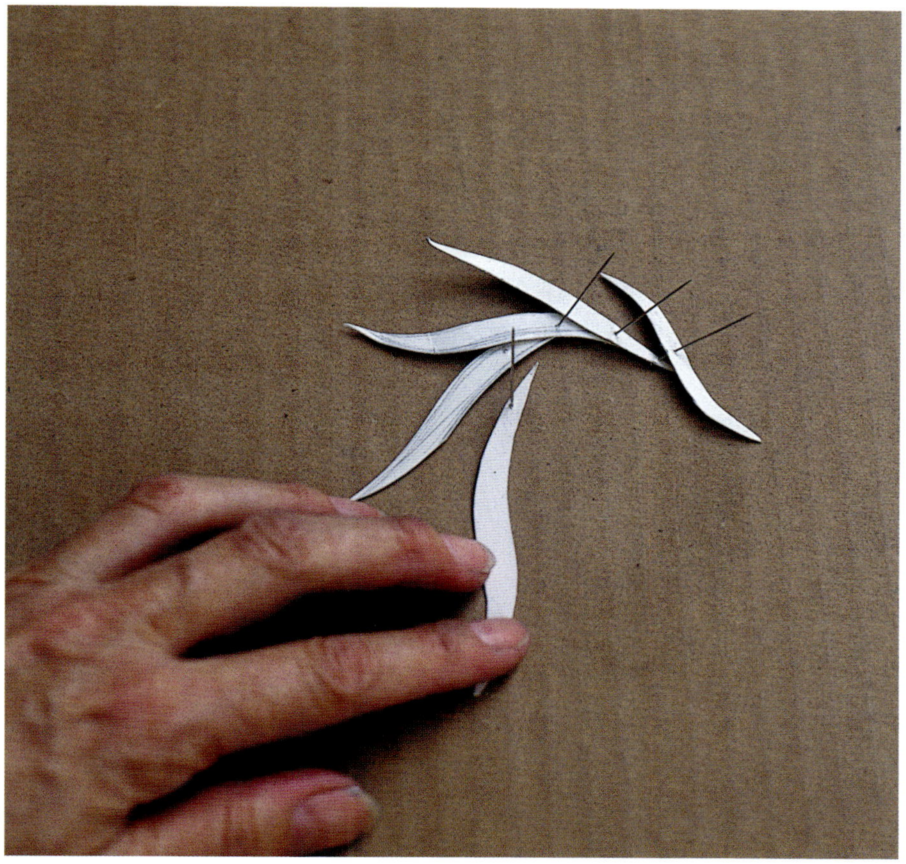

The first steps: paper cutouts and cardboard models. Photograph by Lin Emery.

There are a number of ways in which sculptures can be enlarged from a size measured in inches to one measured in feet. The traditional method is to use a "pointing machine," a sort of three-dimensional pantograph that has now been modernized by the use of lasers. Sculptures such as Emery's aluminum works, which are fabricated rather than cast or carved, are more often scaled up by the use of templates. A piece of paper is cut to the shape of each surface and then enlarged photographically to produce the template for cutting the final sheet of metal.

It is remarkable how many major commissions Emery has been able to undertake in recent years, considering the personal involvement she has in each of her sculptures. Despite their popularity, when all of her costs are considered, Emery does not make money on her large commissions, so the sale of her smaller works is important financially.

Emery has two studios. One, where she works on larger pieces and complex works, is a salvaged former movie theater on Apple Street in the Holly Grove section of the city. But the place where most of her sculptural ideas are transformed into reality is a studio attached to her house in Uptown New Orleans. It is there that she does the initial work on a new piece: the design, creating the poster-board sketch, and fabricating the aluminum maquette. The space reflects the concept-rich orderliness of Emery's mind. The work tables are piled with mechanical sketches; there are sculptures about in various stages of completion, and machines to cut, drill, shape, weld, and polish metal. It is a space pure in its single purpose: the

Dominican Street studio.
Photograph by Lin Emery.

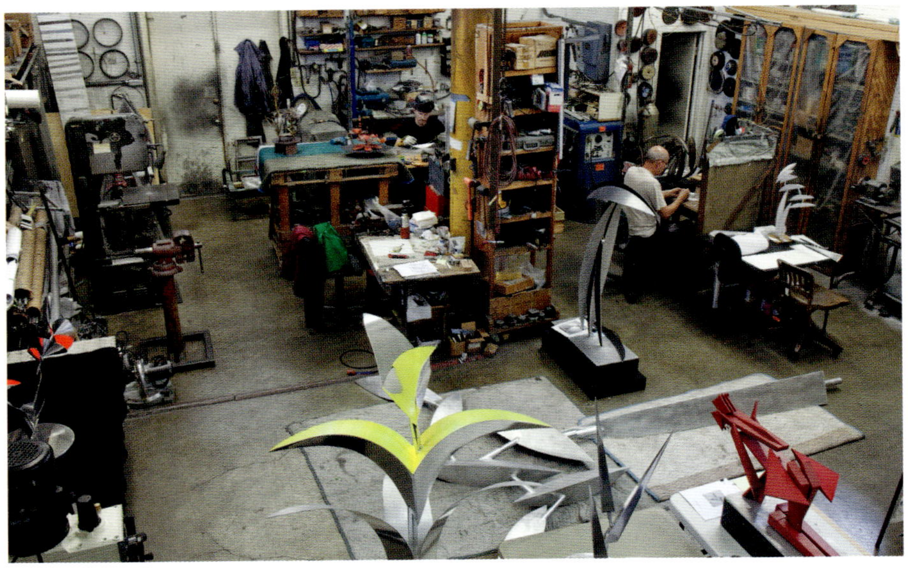

middle and bottom
Apple Street studio (old Ashton Theater).
Photograph by Lin Emery.

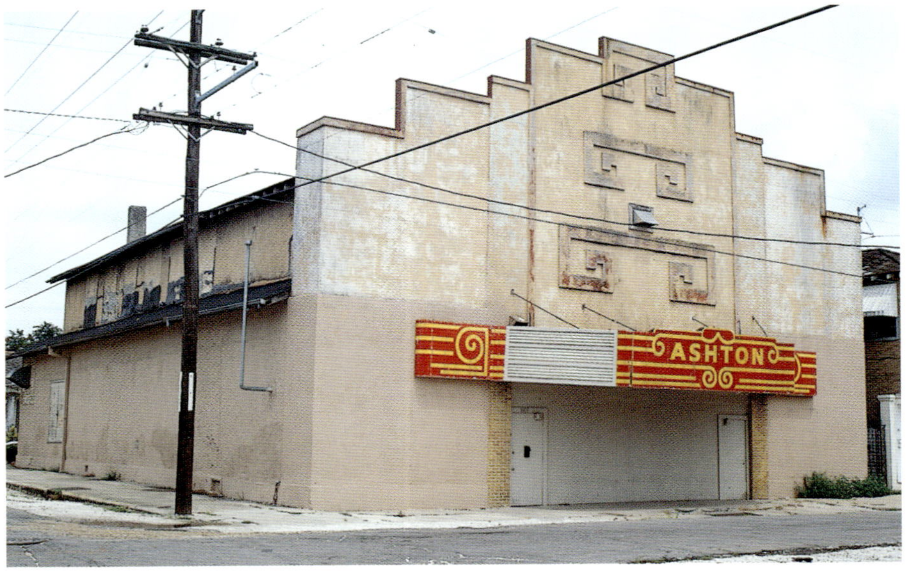

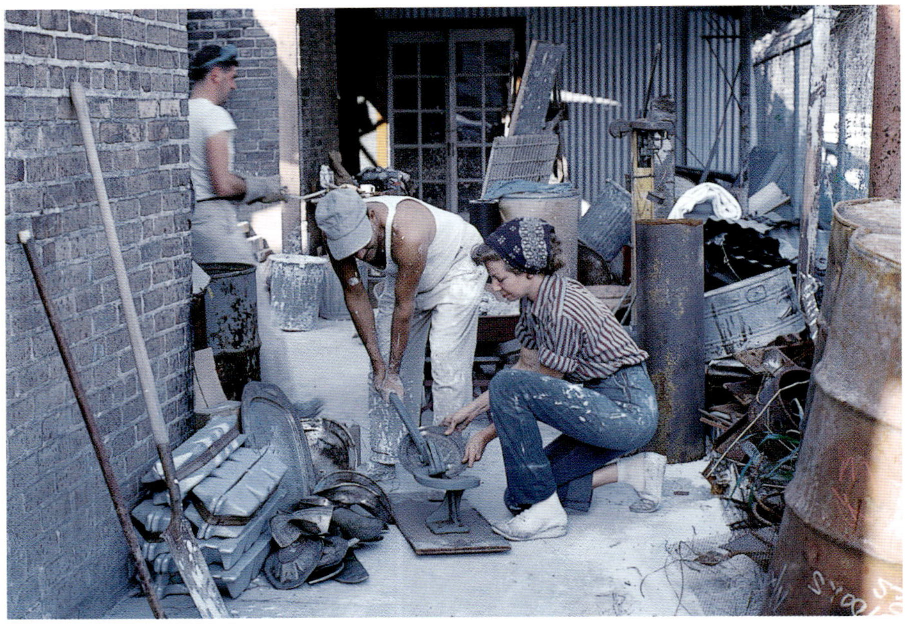

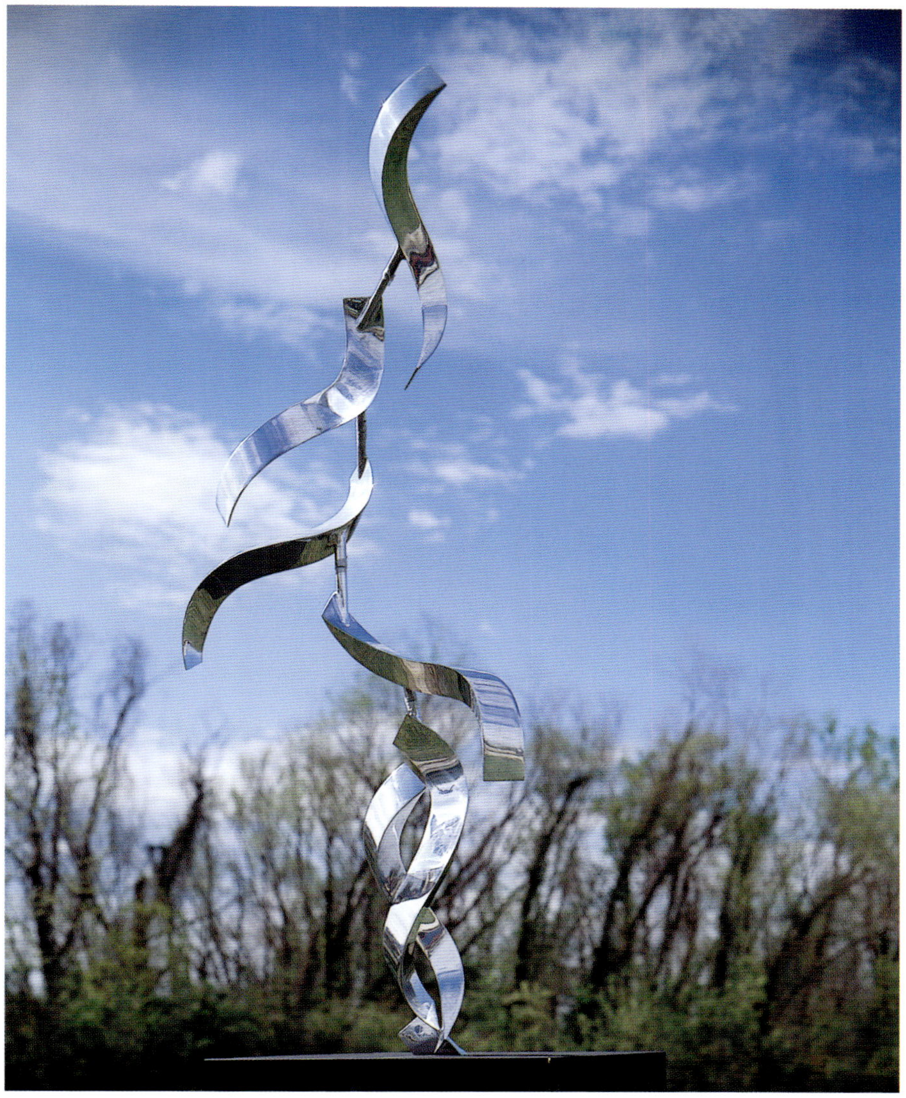

Lin Emery, Hyperbole*, 1989. Aluminum, 60 inches, orbit 30 inches (152.4 cm, orbit 76.2 cm). Private collection.*

transformation of artistic ideas into gracefully moving aluminum shapes. In that space, Emery is the quietly confident master of that transformation, acting as though it is the most natural thing in the world to convert tubes, ball bearings, and pieces of metal into objects of fluid beauty.

NOTES

1. Edward Albee, "Moving," in *Lin Emery*, exhibition catalogue, Alexandria Museum of Art and Kouros Gallery, October–December 1989.

2. W.G.C. Byvanck, *Un Hollandais à Paris en 1891*, as quoted by Frederic V. Grunfeld, *Rodin: A Biography* (New York: Henry Holt and Co., 1987), p. 29.

3. Washington Irving, *The Legend of Sleepy Hollow*, in *The Complete Tales of Washington Irving* (New York: Da Capo Press, 1998), p. 41 (first published 1819).

4. The evolutionary basis for our taste in art is discussed by Dennis Dutton in *The Art Instinct* (New York: Bloomsbury Press, 2009).

5. Kenneth Clark, *Looking at Pictures* (Boston: Beacon Press, 1960), p. 16.

6. F. David Martin, *Sculpture and Enlivened Space: Aesthetics and History* (Lexington, KY: The University Press of Kentucky, 1981), p. 12.

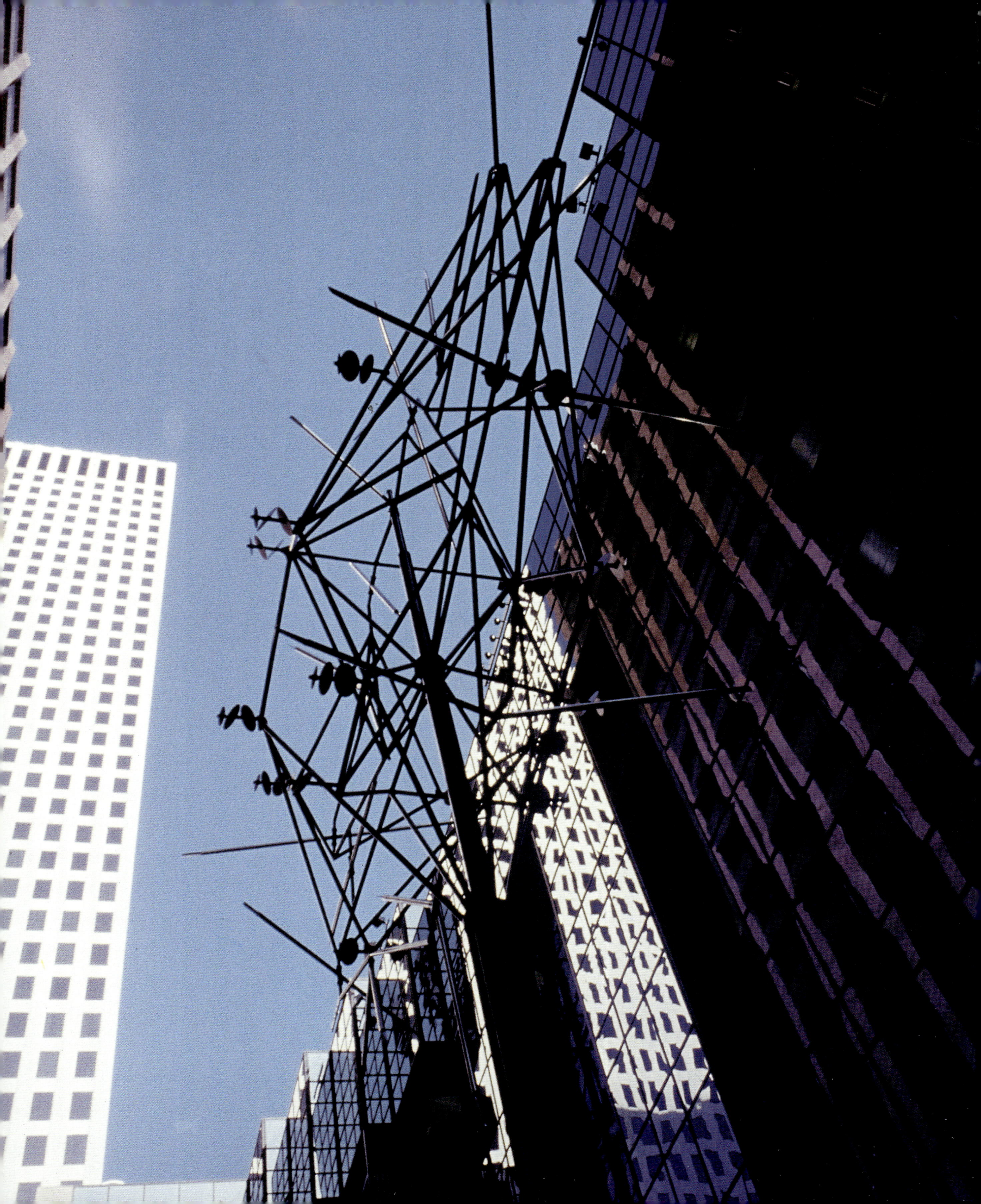

CHAPTER VI

Sculpture as Theater

Kinetic art has wiped out the border between the plastic and the performing arts.

—Harry Kramer[1]

Although sculpture is at the center of Emery's universe, she has an eclectic, exploratory cast of mind in things intellectual and artistic. Even before she discovered sculpture, Emery had an interest in theater, which she nurtured during her stay in Mexico with Mrs. Oliver and at the Goodman School of Drama in Chicago (now the Theatre School at DePaul University). When she returned from Paris in 1950 and settled in New Orleans, in addition to producing sculpture in a range of styles she designed and made sets for the local TV station. And in 1957, she

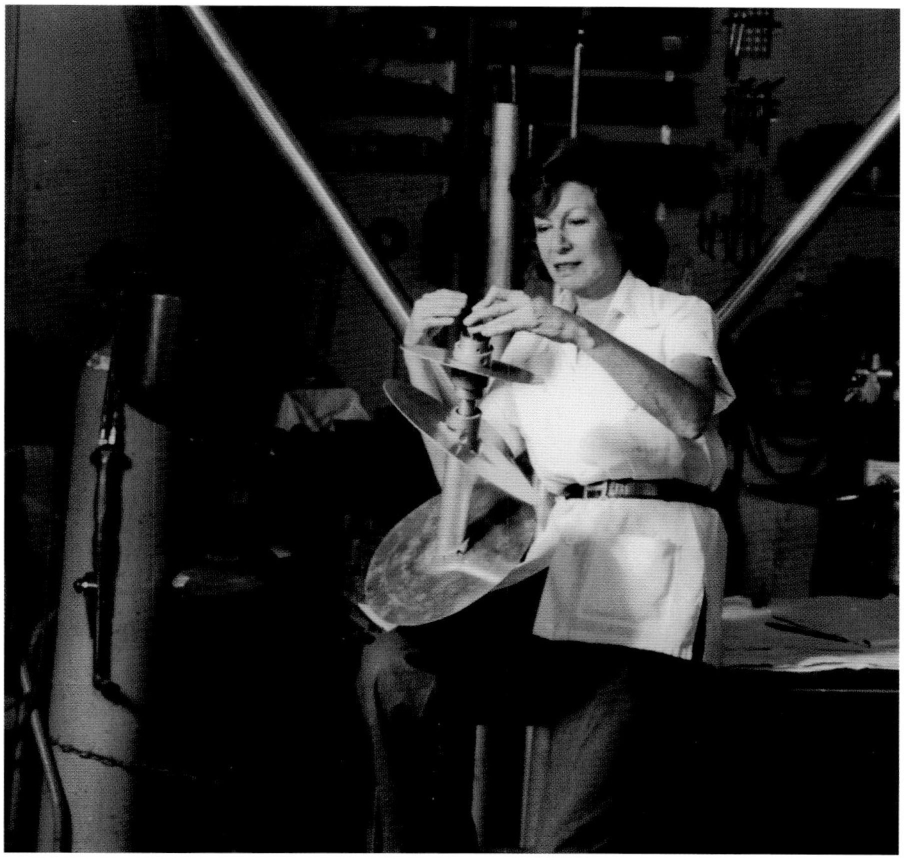

left
Lin Emery assembling kinetic elements for Anamorphic Grid.

opposite page
FIG. 6.1 *Lin Emery, trees for* Anamorphic Grid, *1982–1983. Steel and aluminum, 56 x 40 x 18 feet (17 x 12.1 x 5.4 m). InterContinental Hotel, New Orleans, LA.*

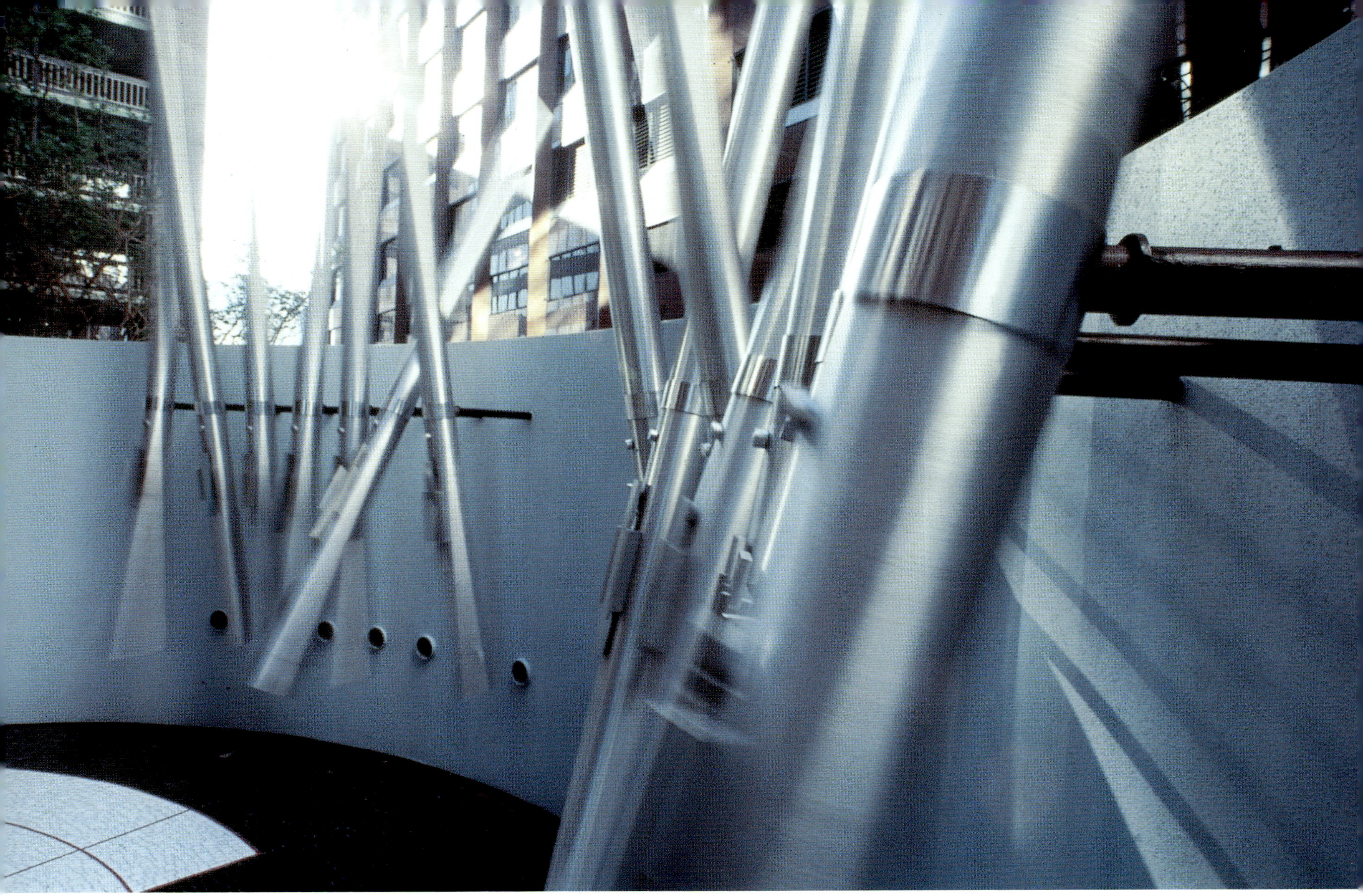

FIG. 6.2 *Lin Emery,* Wind Kinesones, *1983. Aluminum and mixed-media mechanisms, 10 x 20 x 3 feet (3 x 6 x 0.9 m). InterContinental Hotel, New Orleans, LA.*

designed the sets for a production of *Kaleidoscope* at the Provincetown Playhouse in New York. So it was quite natural, as her sculptures evolved into large moving objects in the 1970s, that she thought of them in a theatrical context. Her thinking was propelled in 1982 by an invitation from the architect Steven Bingler to participate in a multidisciplinary project for the InterContinental Hotel in New Orleans. In addition to Emery, Bingler's group included a physicist, Robert Morriss; a mosaic artist, Patricia Whitty-Johnson; and a composer, James Drew. For this multifarious project, *Anamorphic Grid* (fig. 6.1), sited in a fifth-storey atrium-courtyard of the hotel, Emery designed a pair of abstract aluminum trees that rose an additional five stories. In any breeze, the trees seemed alive with twirling leaves and swaying branches. Emery also created a novel, wind-activated, sculptural musical instrument, *Wind Kinesones* (fig. 6.2), consisting of a wall of fourteen 5-inch-diameter aluminum tubes of different lengths and tuned to different notes. Each contains an internal hammer that strikes a metal bar as it moves in the wind. The tube then amplifies and sustains the note. At the time, Emery was a fervent admirer of the sculptural musical instruments of François and Bernard Baschet, as well as the novel instruments of the composer Harry Partch, but she aimed at simpler forms for her sculptural orchestra.

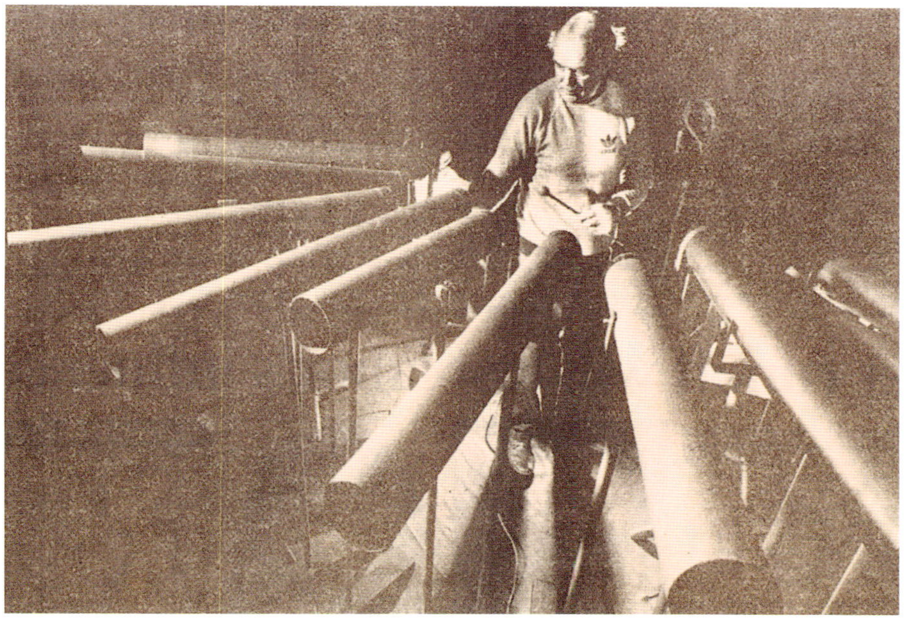

James Drew, composer, and Kinesones.

Soon after the InterContinental Hotel project, Emery designed another set of musical instruments for James Drew and the concert hall. Then Drew suggested a more ambitious project. Inspired by T.S. Eliot's *Murder in the Cathedral*, he had long wanted to compose a work on the story of Thomas à Becket. The confidant of King Henry II of England, Becket rose to the position of Archbishop of Canterbury, only to clash with the king over the relationship between the church and the crown. The king is said to have cried out in frustration to his court, "Who will rid me of this troublesome priest?" Set to Drew's score, Emery's five-minute work, *Becket: The Final Moments* (fig. 6.3), depicts the moment in 1170 when four knights, responding to the king's entreaty, hacked Becket to death with their swords at the altar of Canterbury Cathedral. The action takes place in a stylized interpretation of the cathedral and is set in motion by a viewer pushing a button and thereby acting as the king. The four robotic knights, ominous black-felt figures accompanied by dirgelike music, glide haltingly toward an abstracted white Becket standing at the foot of a large cross of Lorraine. Their swords fall, Becket collapses to the floor, and the knights retreat into the cathedral's apse.

This brief work took Emery two years to accomplish, with the help of her studio assistants, Jim Farrell and Bryan Mavor. Given Emery's distaste for the predictable, the movements of the knights have some randomness built into their driving mechanisms. With Drew, who has perfect pitch, listening and advising at the other end of the phone, she honed metal bars incorporated into the robots to produce the four desired tones. Emery knew from the beginning that *Becket* would not make money, but she could not resist such a creative adventure. The project clearly represented a concept of importance to her. For one thing, it placed consequential human action and drama at the center of art. It also broke down barriers between the arts and reflected her open-minded eclecticism in the arts as in things philosophical and spiritual.

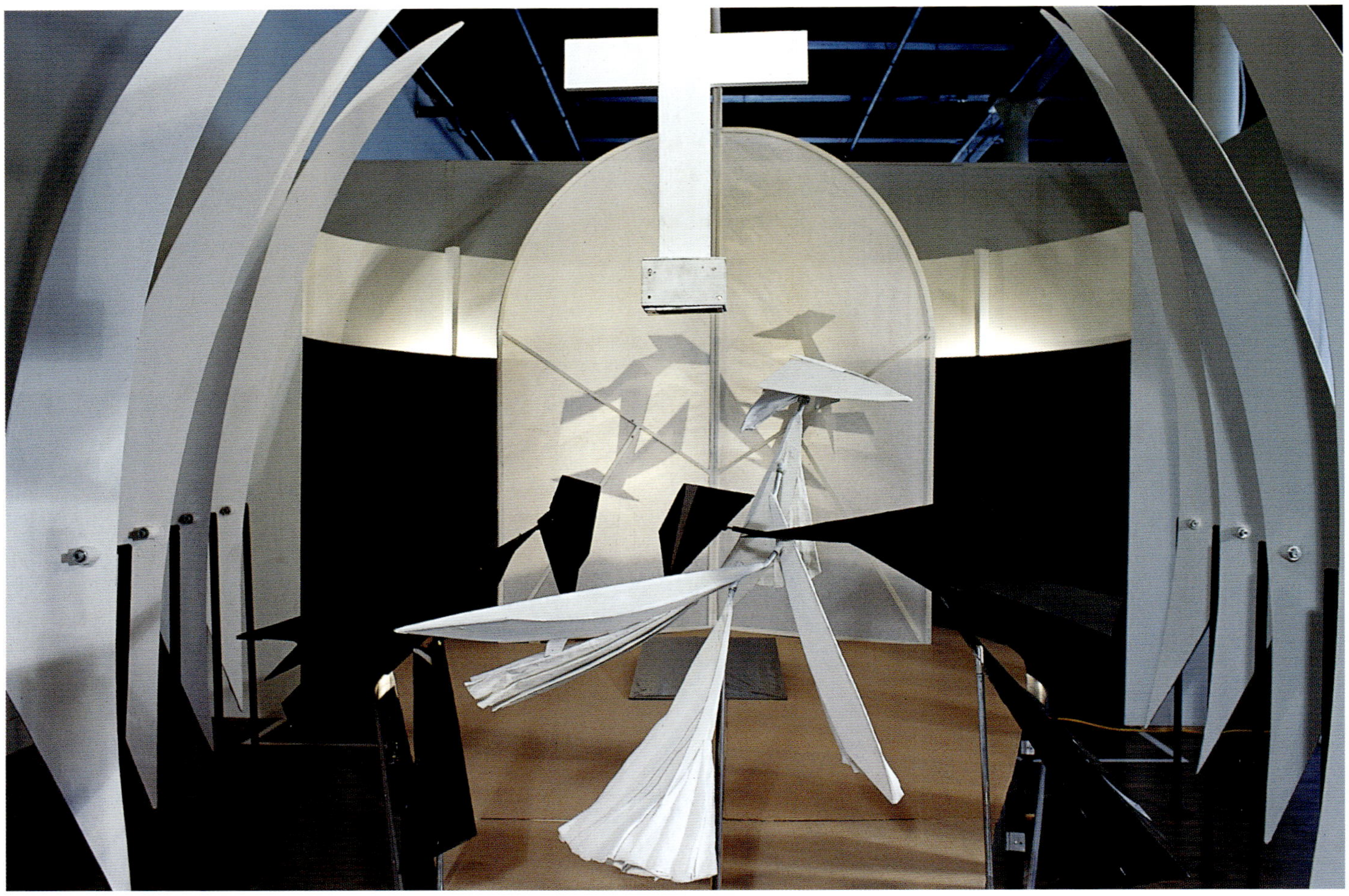

FIG. 6.3 *Lin Emery,* Becket: The Final Moments, *1985. Mixed-media theater piece, dimensions variable. Music by James Drew. Max Hutchinson Gallery, New York, NY; Alexandria Museum of Art, Alexandria, LA; Contemporary Arts Center, New Orleans, LA.*

opposite page
Lin Emery, Sanctum, *1987–1992. Mixed media, dimensions variable. New Orleans Museum of Art and Arthur Roger Gallery, New Orleans, LA.*

Becket has been shown in many venues. When it was presented at the Max Hutchinson Gallery in New York in 1984, Grace Glueck wrote a review for the *New York Times* saying that "it achieves a brilliant synthesis of space and movement," and calling the work "a piece of Expressionist theater in Bauhaus garb."[2] Glueck's reference to the Bauhaus could just as well have been to the Russian Constructivists, who contributed significantly to the concept of the Bauhaus. It is not that Emery was directly influenced by the Constructivists or the Bauhaus in her theater works; the ancient spectacles of Hero of Alexandria, who initially inspired her water-based works, were a more overt inspiration. But Emery shared with the Constructivists a common set of instincts and interests—of sculpture in a broader architectural and social context as well as the use of industrial materials. She also shared the Constructivists' and the Bauhaus's interest in imaginative collaborative theatrical enterprises.

Emery's next theater piece evolved over several years. It started in 1987 as a piece of abstract realism, a room-sized space created by semitransparent black fabric walls. The walls of the room gradually change from a square to an elongated and angled shape, disorienting the viewer inside. This installation, *Acolytes* (fig. 6.4), engaged the visceral attention of the viewer-participant even more deeply

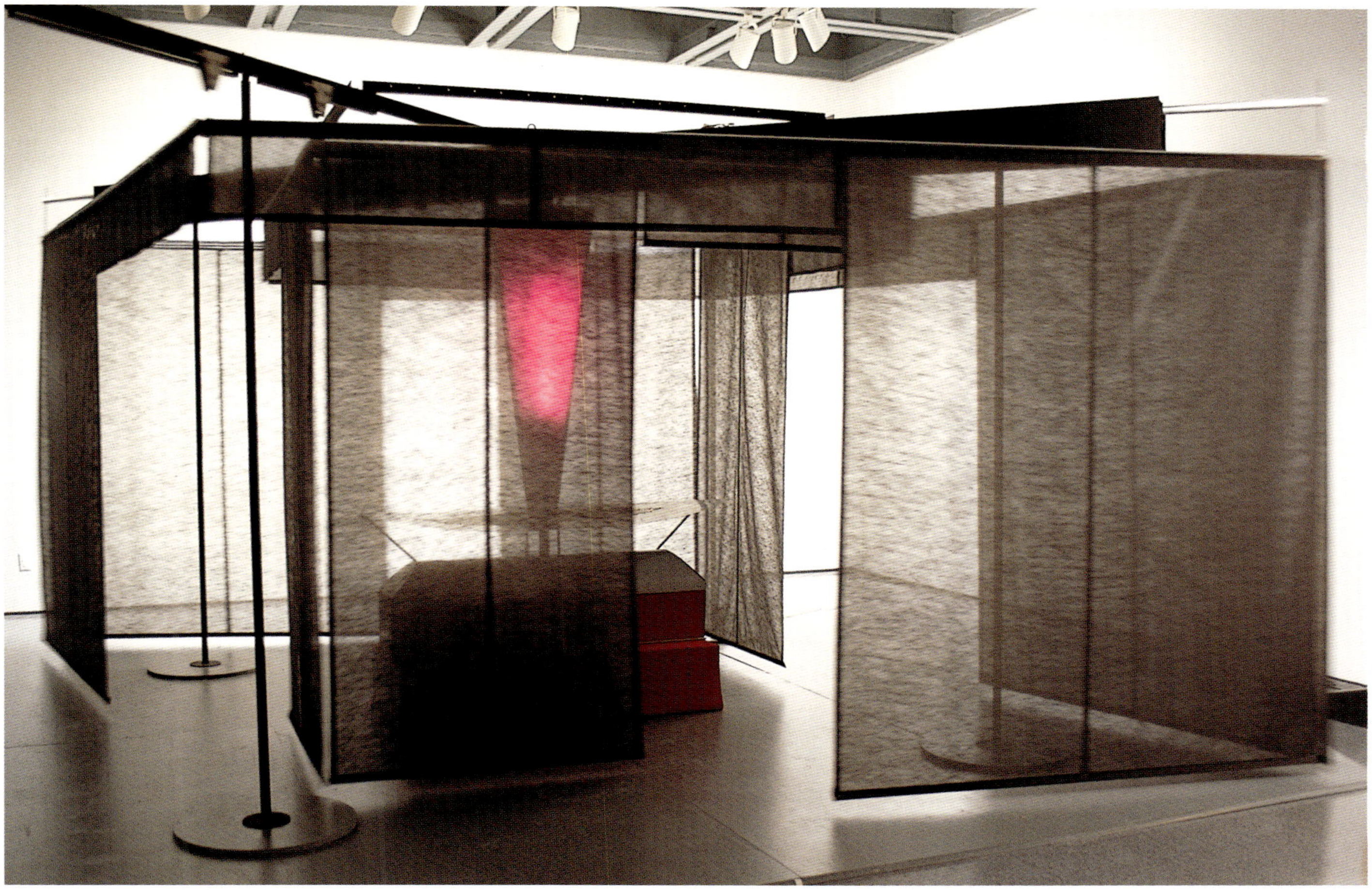

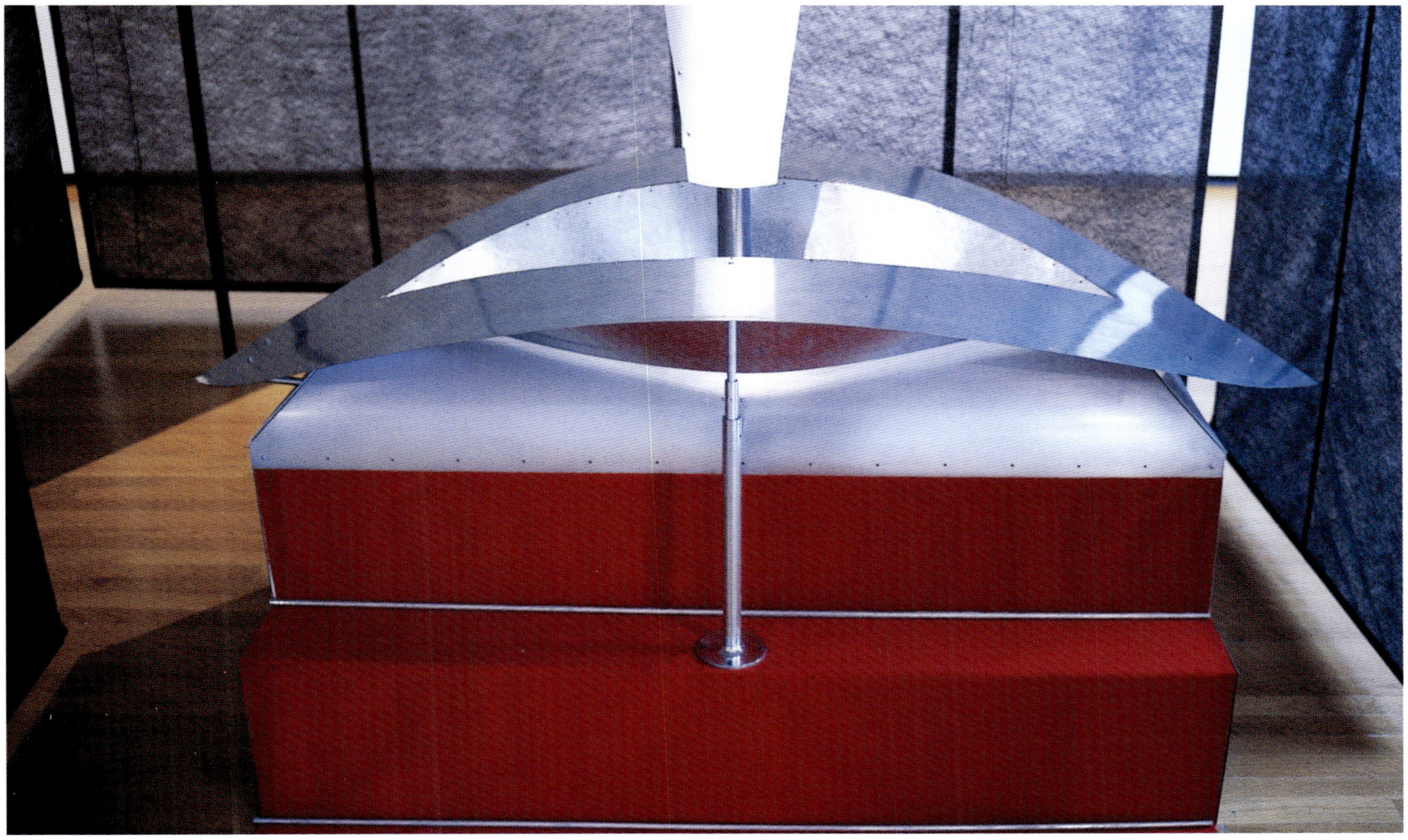

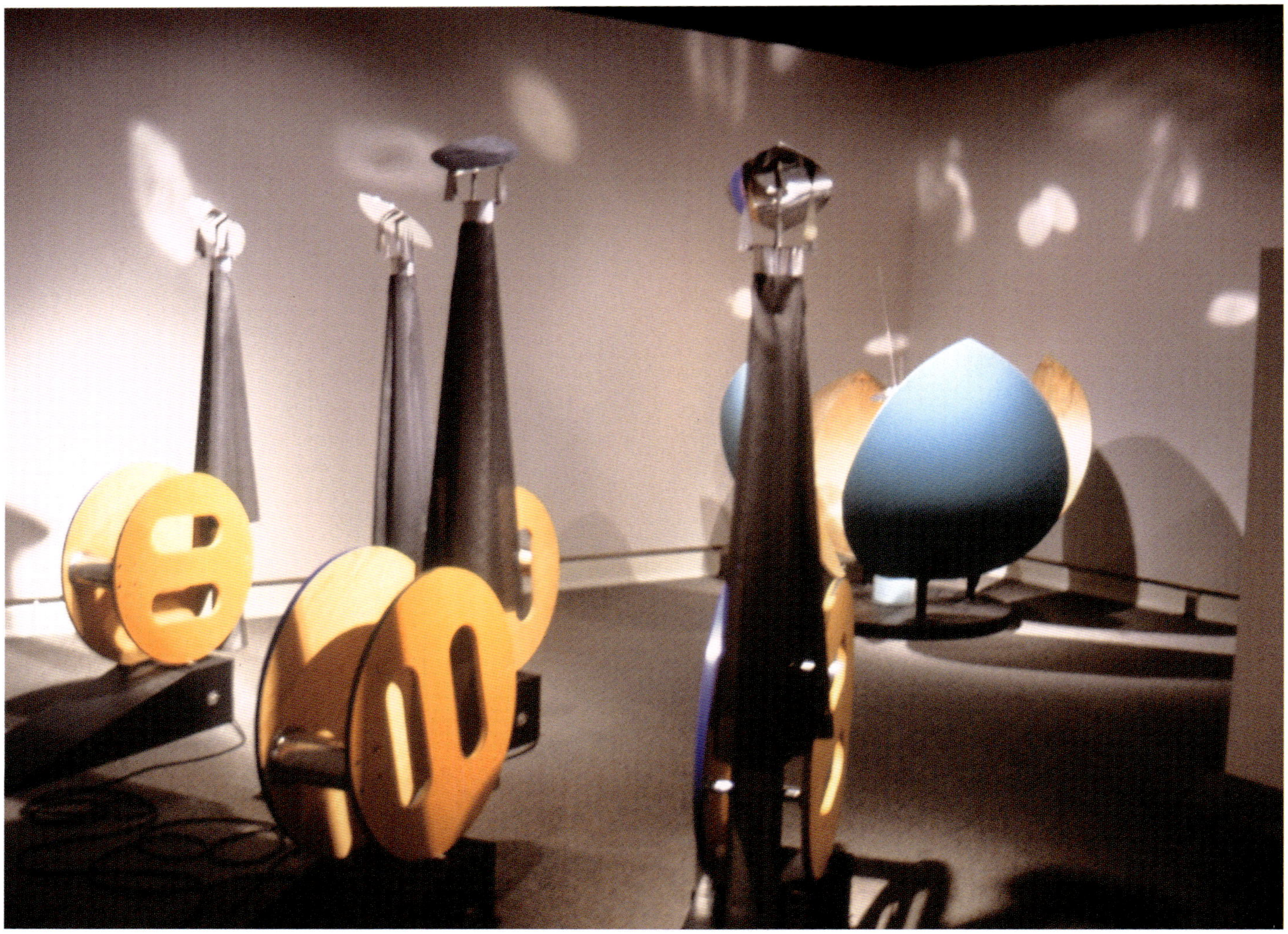

FIG. 6.4 *Lin Emery,* Acolytes, *1990–1992. Mixed media, dimensions variable. Pensacola Museum of Art, Pensacola, FL; Leepa-Rattner Museum of Art, Tarpon Springs, FL.*

than Emery's wind-driven works. She next added an abstracted altar at the center of the fabric room. Inspired by Mayan sacrificial altars, her aluminum altar opens to expose an oval cleft and then closes. A shaft at the center represents both sacrifice and phallus. The complex work is completed by a set of abstracted robotic acolytes on the outside of the room, each an intricate construction of wood, aluminum, and black fabric, advancing and bobbing, with bangles shimmering. This individualistic and challenging work was first exhibited at the Arthur Roger Gallery in New Orleans in 1996.[3] The acolytes are sometimes shown independently.

Emery expressed her concern for the fragile Louisiana environment in her 2000 work *Landscape* (fig. 6.5). Darkly disturbing black disks (obscured suns?) rotate slowly behind reedlike, musical aluminum rods sprouting from a field of matted Spanish moss. Despite its puzzling iconography, *Landscape* manages to convey an aura of mysterious significance.

Emery's most recent robotic theater piece was a product of her reaction to Israel's invasion of Hebron in April 2002. Involving three groups of small robotic

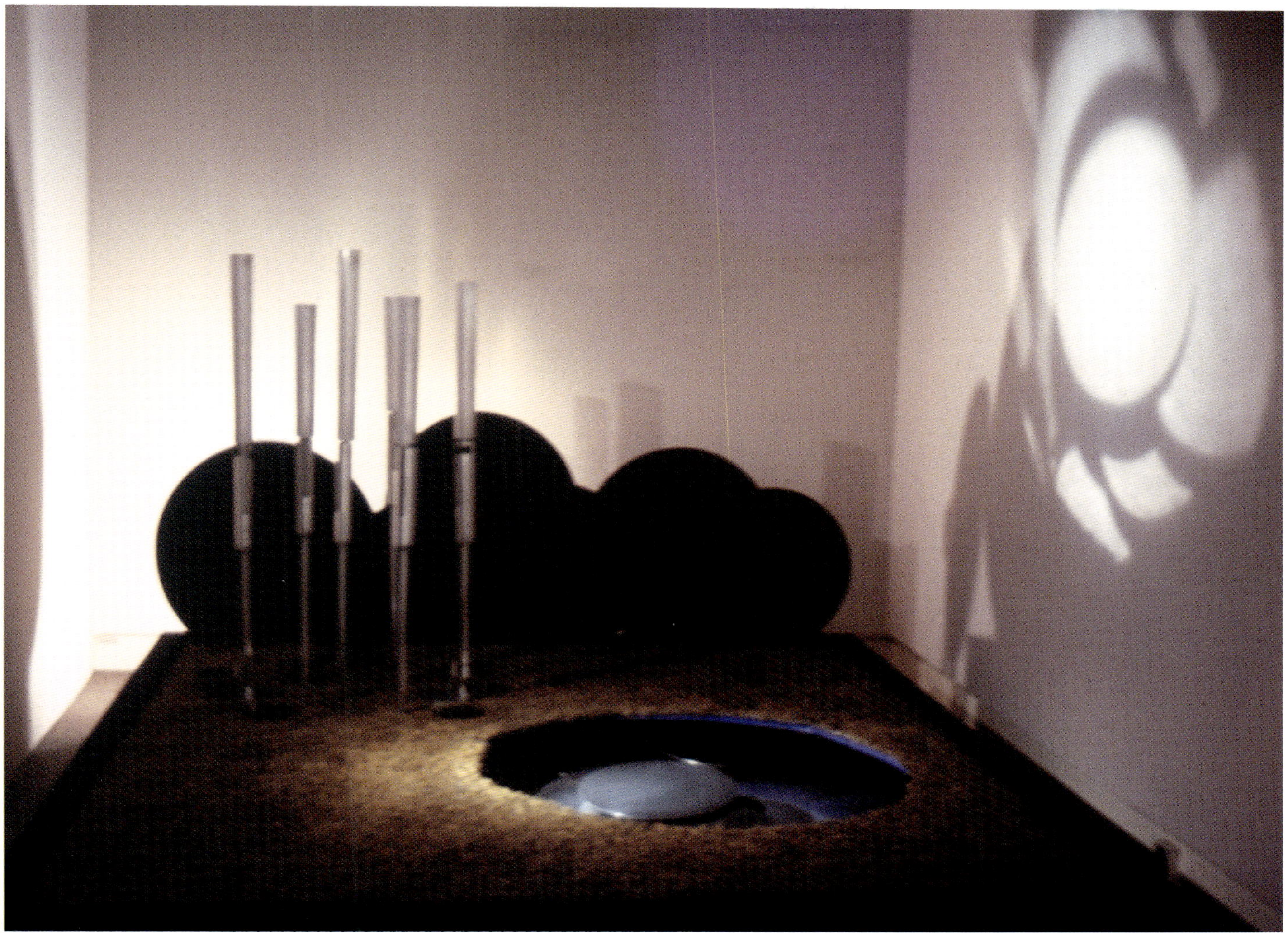

figures, *Breaking News* (fig. 6.6) is about the cynical ineffectualness of the journalists observing the killing of Palestinians by the Israeli army. The work is mechanically and conceptually complex, and it was only in 2008 that Emery felt it had developed sufficiently to be exhibited. She continues to work on it.

When *Breaking News* was first shown at the Arthur Roger Gallery, Emery was disappointed in the fact that nobody seemed to understand it. Inevitably, the challenge of communication in Emery's theater works is far greater than in kinetic sculpture, in part because of the originality of her vocabulary. By distancing herself from conventions (or, what amounts to the same thing, by using ancient but forgotten conventions), Emery sets herself a daunting challenge in these works. However, what is clearly demonstrated by these meticulously crafted works is her ability to translate imaginative concepts into kinetic form and her dedication to dramatically creative exploration.

FIG. 6.5 *Lin Emery,* Landscape, *2000. Mixed media, dimensions variable. Masur Museum of Art, Monroe, LA; Meadows Museum, Shreveport, LA; Kouros Gallery, New York, NY.*

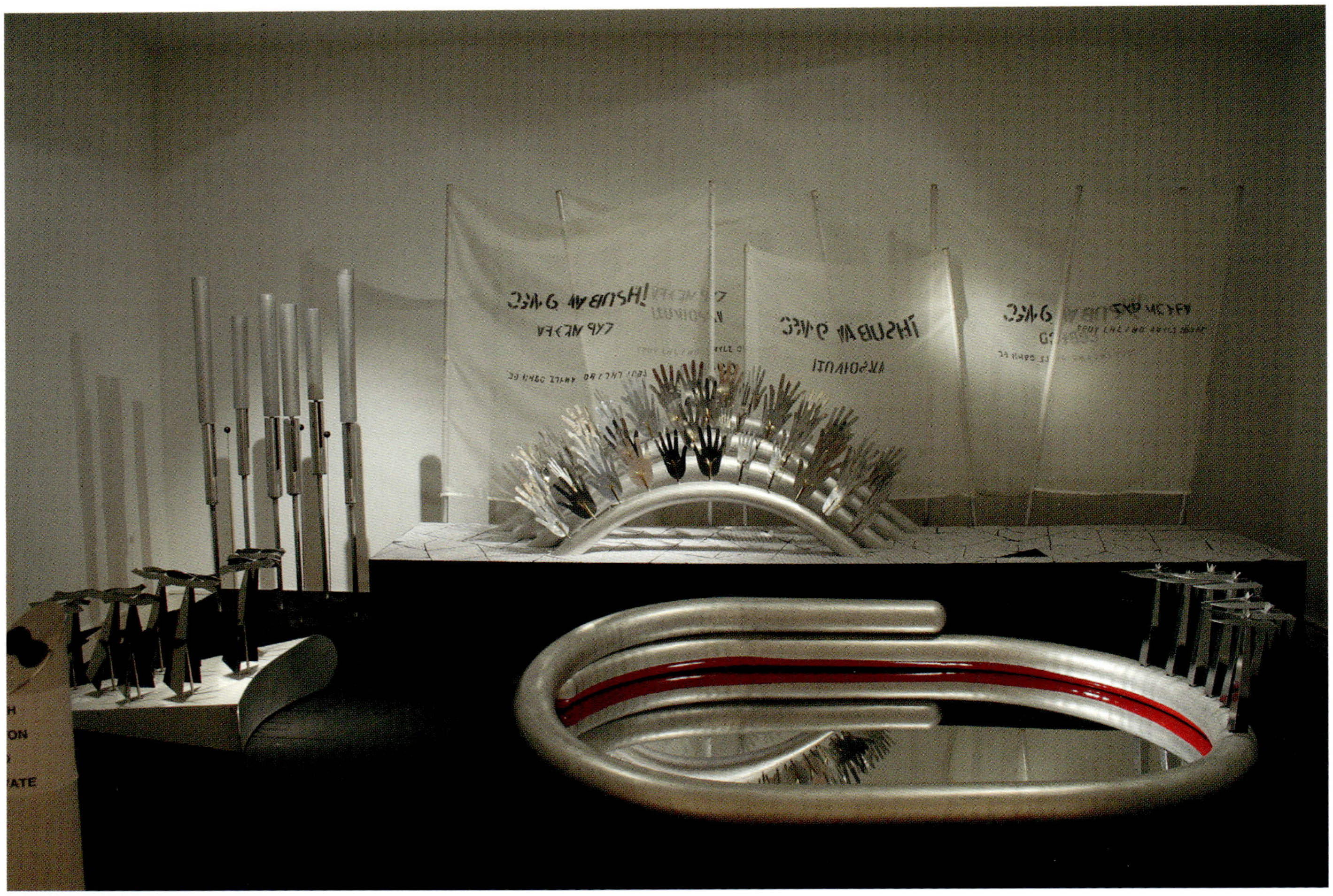

FIG. 6.6 *Lin Emery,* Breaking News, *2002. Mixed media, dimensions variable. Arthur Roger Gallery, New Orleans, LA.*

NOTES

1. Harry Kramer, quoted in Peter Selz, *Directions in Kinetic Sculpture*, catalogue, Berkeley Art Museum, University of California, 1966.

2. Grace Glueck, *New York Times*, December 21, 1984.

3. A video of *Sanctum* can be seen at arthurrogergallery.com/dynamic/video.asp?ExhibitID=116.

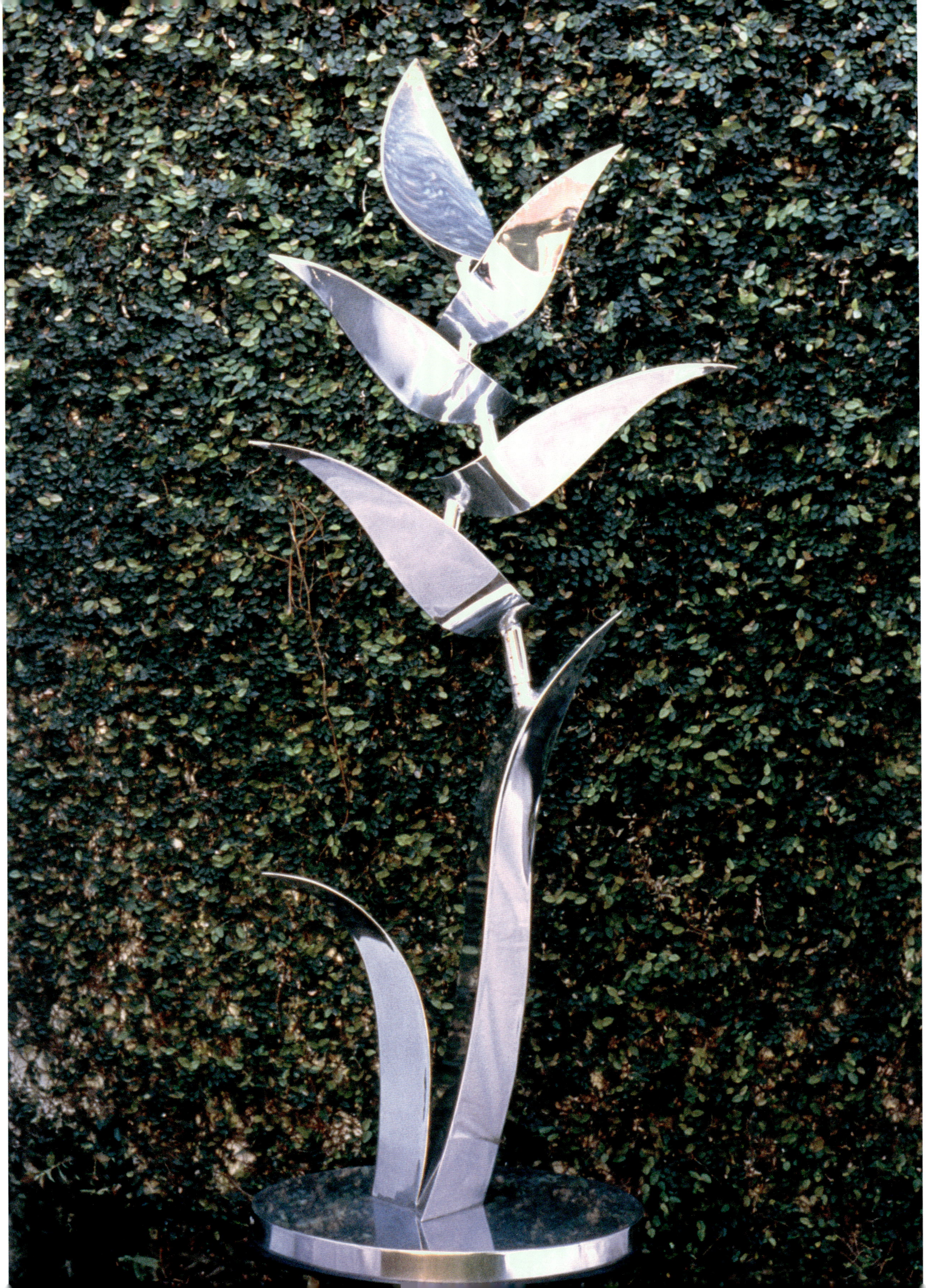

CHAPTER VII

The Historical Context and Beyond

The reason for artists' existence is to reveal the beauties of the world.

—Constantin Brancusi[1]

In its quality, individuality, and range, the body of work that Lin Emery has produced over the past four decades has a distinctive place in the history of modern sculpture. Its character is illuminated by the traditions of which it is a part, and by the ways in which it stands apart from those traditions.

Emery's art has many predecessors, ranging from Hero of Alexandria through Leonardo to Picasso. But some of the most dominant genes in her artistic DNA descend from the Constructivists, who not only set out abstraction and modern materials as the first requirements for sculpture but declared the central importance of movement. While there are many tributaries to modernism, the Constructivist movement in Russia established the first confident and complete program for abstract art. The Realistic Manifesto, written in 1920 by Naum Gabo and also signed by his brother, Antoine Pevsner, was its Magna Carta. In those heady days when revolution was transforming into social engineering, artists felt themselves to be a part of the creation of a new society, one that demanded a radically new form of art that played an entirely new role. The concept of sculpture was transformed from the lofty object on a pedestal to something purposeful—a machine or a building—and sculptors employed the materials from which the new society would be built. The manifesto boldly renounced mass as the essence of sculpture and insisted that it be dynamic:

> *We renounce the thousand-year-old delusion in art that held the static rhythms as the only elements of the plastic and pictorial arts. We affirm in these arts a new element the kinetic rhythms as the basic forms of our perception of real time.*[2]

The case could be made that when Marcel Duchamp mounted a bicycle wheel on a stool in 1913 and set it spinning, he created the first modern kinetic sculpture. But Duchamp's work is in a category of its own, as much a provocative jeu d'esprit as a work of sculpture. The motor-driven rotating sculptures that used the painted glass he made in the 1920s also count as isolated experiments.

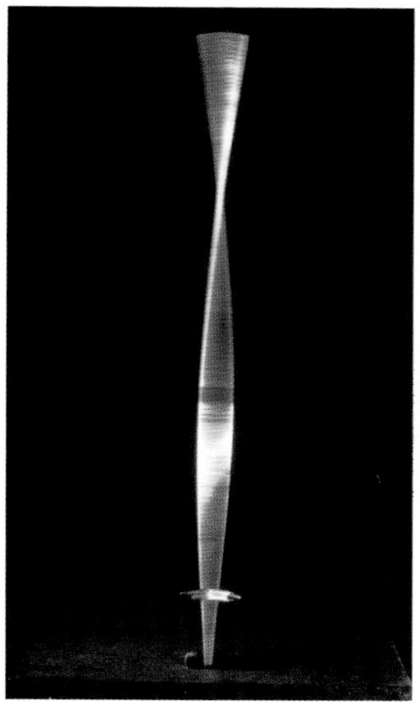

FIG. 7.1 *Naum Gabo (American, b. Russia, 1890–1977),* Kinetic Construction (Standing Wave), *1919–1920; replica, 1985. Metal, painted wood, and electrical mechanism, 24¼ x 9½ x 7½ inches (61.5 x 24.1 x 19 cm). Presented by the artist through the American Federation of Arts, 1966. The Works of Naum Gabo © Nina and Graham Williams. Photograph © 2011 Tate London.*

opposite page
Lin Emery, Lily, *1998. Aluminum and stainless steel, 86 inches, orbit 36 inches (218.4 cm, orbit 91.4 cm). Loyola University Sculpture Garden, New Orleans, LA.*

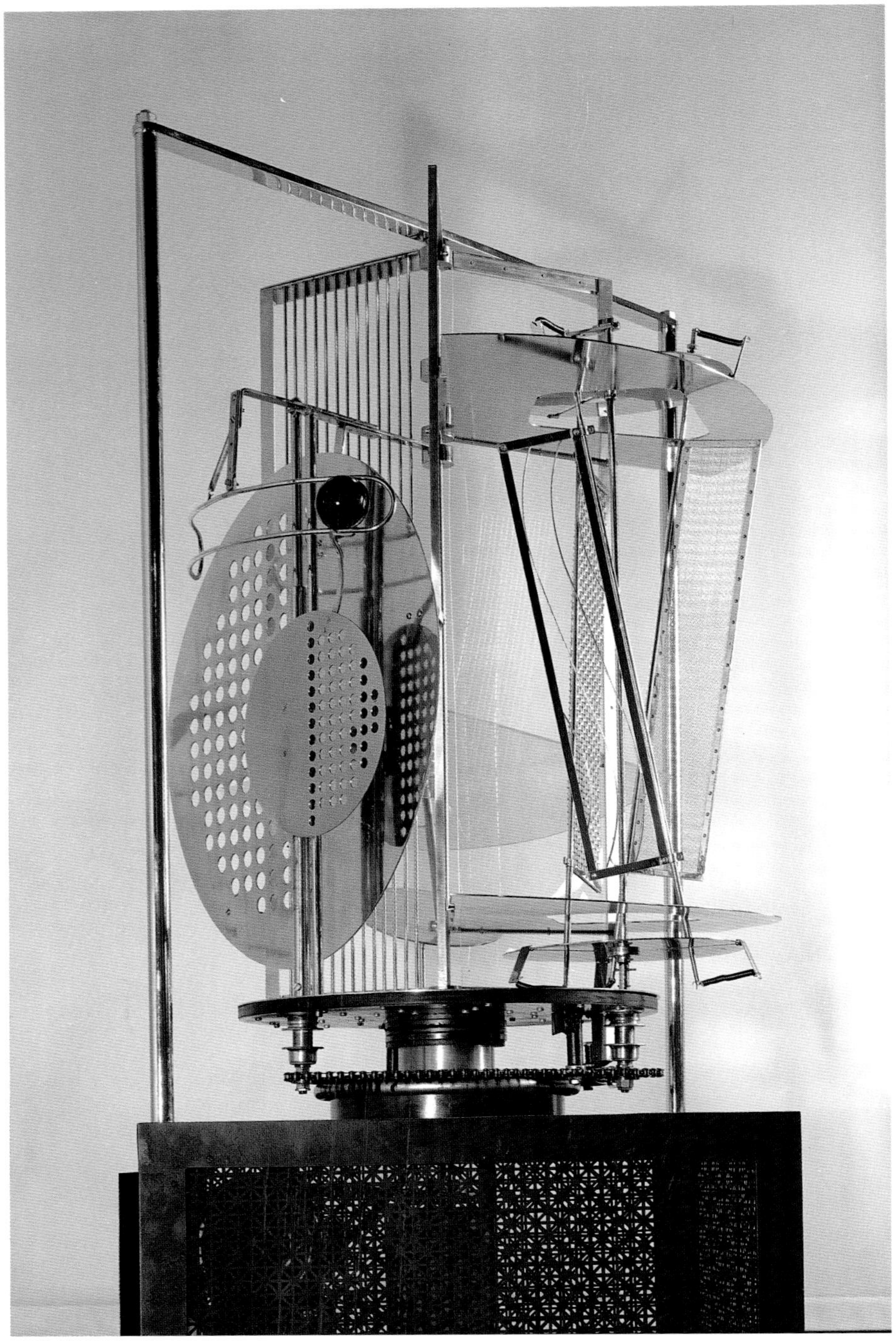

FIG. 7.2 *László Moholy-Nagy (American, b. Hungary, 1895–1946),* Light Prop for an Electric Stage (Light-Space Modulator), *1930. Aluminum, steel, nickel-plated brass, other metals, plastic, wood, and electric motor, 59½ x 27½ x 27½ inches (151.1 x 69.9 x 69.9 cm). Harvard Art Museums, Busch-Reisinger Museum. Gift of Sibyl Moholy-Nagy, BR56.5. Photograph by Junius Beebe, © President and Fellows of Harvard College. © 2011 Artists Rights Society (ARS), New York/VG Bild-Kunst, Bonn.*

Despite the manifesto's advocacy of movement, there were few kinetic Constructivist sculptures. A notable exception was created by Gabo himself, his *Kinetic Construction (Standing Wave)* of 1920, which consisted of a single metal rod vibrated by a motor (fig. 7.1). Gabo's work, built as a demonstration for his students, exemplifies how motion can produce perceived volume. In this case, the svelte volume created by the blur of the vibrating rod is like a ghost of Brancusi's *Bird in Space*.

At the other extreme of Constructivist ambition from Gabo's *Kinetic Construction* was Vladimir Tatlin's visionary *Monument to the Third International*, a three-storey building composed of three rooms stacked vertically on a diagonal axis, each rotating at a different speed. Less ambitious but still complex was László Moholy-Nagy's *Light Prop for an Electric Stage* (fig. 7.2). Completed in 1930, this work was referred to by Tatlin as a space kaleidoscope, or a light display machine, for it combines a motor-driven open construction with projection lights. The structure is made of reflective and transparent or semitransparent materials: glass, plastic, wire-mesh, and latticework. As it turns, it is alive with illuminated surfaces and sources of direct and reflected light. After laboring over this work for eight years, Moholy-Nagy thought he understood all its possible appearances, but when it was set in motion for the first time he was startled and said that he was almost led to "believe in magic."[3] Unpredictability and surprise link kinetic sculpture to life itself. The magic of seemingly spontaneous movement is central to the appeal of kinetic sculpture in general, and to that of Lin Emery in particular.

The kinetic works of Gabo, Tatlin, and Moholy-Nagy were bound to the ground or to walls. One of the first Constructivist objects that were suspended, and that depended on air currents for their movement, were Alexander Rodchenko's *Spatial Construction No. 9* (fig. 7.3) of 1920–1921. At about the same time, Man Ray and Kurt Schwitters also suspended abstract objects to move freely in passing breezes. Those innovations became, some twelve years later, the inspiration for Alexander Calder's first kinetic art. At galleries in Paris and New York in 1932,

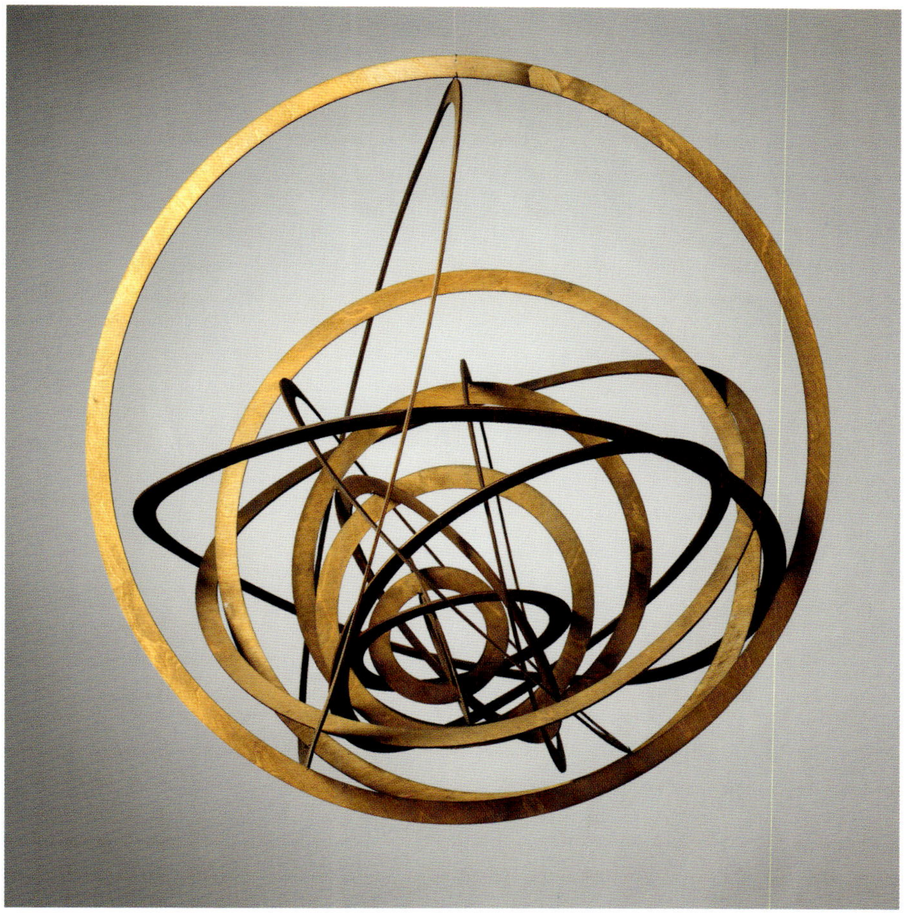

FIG. 7.3 *Alexander Rodchenko (Russian, 1891–1956),* Spatial Construction No. 9, Circle in a Circle, *1920–1921. Plywood of peach wood, 31½ x 31½ x 33½ inches (80 x 80 x 85.1 cm). Donation, Galerie Gmurzynska. Photograph by Moderna Museet/Åsa Lundén, Moderna Museet, Stockholm. Art © Estate of Alexander Rodchenko/RAO, Moscow/VAGA, New York.*

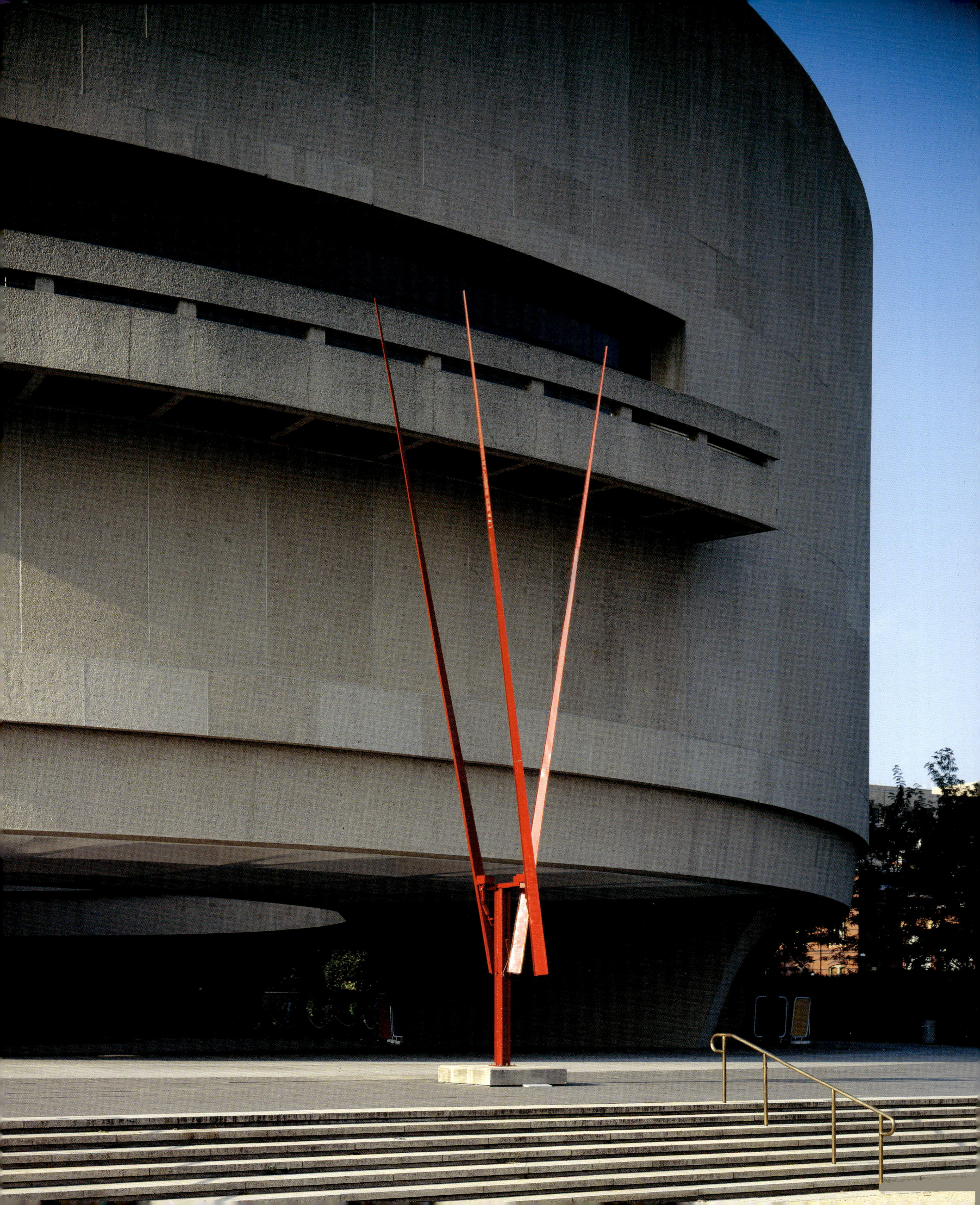

Calder showed works powered by little cranks or motors, which Marcel Duchamp dubbed mobiles. Calder holds a paradoxical place in the history of kinetic sculpture. On the one hand, the immediately appealing nature of his mobiles established the place of kinetic sculpture in the public imagination and, as a result, as public art. On the other hand, the whimsical, romantic spirit of Calder's art, with its affinity to the paintings of Arp and Miro, is quite independent of the spirit of Constructivism. And it was Constructivist principles that formed the core of modernist abstract sculpture, including kinetic sculpture.

Calder's mobiles were less concerned with motion than with collective form and pattern, and thus his works are quite different in spirit from Emery's, which have movement at their heart. That is also the case for George Rickey, who pared down his forms so that motion became the very subject of his sculptures. In the 1930s, while still a painter, Rickey became interested in Calder's kinetic art, but it was Naum Gabo who catalyzed his transition to kinetic sculpture. Rickey became deeply interested in the history of Constructivism and dedicated his book on the subject to Gabo.[4]

Emery came to know Rickey in 1955 when he came to New Orleans to chair the Tulane Art Department. This was a time when Emery was producing her highly popular aquamobiles, as well as abstract bronzes and religious sculptures. Avid in her openness to new ideas, she found in Rickey's work a persuasive case for kinetic sculpture as a serious art form. Not only did Rickey represent a link to the origins of kinetic sculpture, but he also served as an exemplar for Emery in his integration of engineering and art. At that time Rickey's personal artistic philosophy was solidifying, very much influenced by Gabo and his fellow Constructivists.[5] It was also the time when the field of kinetic sculpture was beginning to burgeon; it was in 1955 that Denise René mounted the first commercial exhibition of kinetic art, showing the work of eight artists, including Duchamp and Calder, at her gallery in Paris. By 1961 some seventy-two artists were included in an international exhibition of movement in art that was shown at museums in the Netherlands, Sweden, and Denmark.

The increasing diversity, inventiveness, and popularity of kinetic sculpture in the mid-1960s came face-to-face with upheavals in the concept of what constituted art. Post-Vietnam disillusionment crushed the art object under the heavy antiart weight of conceptual postmodernism. Contemporary aesthetics talked of "the end of art," but the most reasonable interpretation of that concept was simply the end of a single dominating avant-garde path for art, and there eventually emerged a new kind of artistic freedom and tolerance. By the 1990s, kinetic art was flourishing again, with Emery's sculpture having a prominent and respected place in the field. The Kinetic Art Organization (KAO) was established in 2001 and now has well over a thousand members from sixty countries, with the Chinese contingent growing the most rapidly. Emery was an early member and was included in a show organized by KAO at Grounds For Sculpture in Hamilton, New Jersey, in 2007.

In their advocacy of movement as a subject of sculpture, and in their embrace of metal as the quintessentially modern material for sculpture, the Constructivists were ancestors of Emery's art. But her art is, in fundamental ways, also independent

opposite page

George Rickey (American, 1907–2002), Three Red Lines, *1966. Painted stainless steel with hydraulic devices, mounting screws, and braces, 444 x (variable) x 51.3 inches (1,127.8 x [variable] x 130.3 cm). On metal base: 12.1 x 12.1 inches (30.8 x 30.8 cm); on stone base: 55 x 55.6 inches (139.7 x 141.2 cm). Gift of the artist through the Joseph H. Hirshhorn Foundation, 1972. Photograph by Lee Stalsworth, Hirshhorn Museum and Sculpture Garden, Smithsonian Institution. Art © Estate of George Rickey/Licensed by VAGA, New York, NY.*

opposite page
Lin Emery, Buds, *2004. Aluminum, 14 feet, orbit 8 feet (4.2 m, orbit 2.4 m). Private collection.*

following spread
left: *Lin Emery,* Rondelet, *2010. Aluminum, 14 feet, orbit 9 feet (4.2 m, orbit 2.7 m). Private collection.*

right: *Lin Emery,* Terminus, *2009. Aluminum and paint, 30 feet, orbit 12 feet (9.1 m, orbit 3.6 m). Cousins Properties, Atlanta, GA.*

of that tradition and independent of those, like George Rickey, who are close to the spirit of the Constructivists. Emery's sculptures are mechanical devices, as sober in their materials and mechanisms as any Constructivist contraption or work by Rickey. But they derive their forms and movements from nature, elevating those elements into the realm of the ideal. The uniqueness of Emery's lyrical kinetic sculpture resides in an inspired combination of qualities. The elements are pure and minimal; the workings are fine-tuned machines; the movement is baroque—unexpected and bravura; and the evocations are romantic. Each of these characteristics is part of a distinct artistic tradition, but Emery synthesizes them in works of absolute coherence and integrity.

The integrity of Emery's sculptures also results from the melding of multiple aspects of nature. Many of the component forms are derived from nature, using the shapes of pods or leaves or birds. Also, nature's hidden energies are made visible by the sculptures' wind-driven movement. These two aspects of nature are closely related, just as the shapes of a bird's body and wings are dictated by natural forces and the requirements of efficient motion through the air. So, too, in Emery's sculptures, where form and movement are dictated by natural laws.

In addition to reflecting the forms and forces of nature, Emery's wind-driven sculptures express her relationship with nature. "I love the natural movement of the trees on the levees," she once said, "the river and anything in nature,"[6] and her work evokes in us that feeling of well-being when we are out on an early spring day, warmed by the morning sun and cooled by a light breeze. In this context, Emery relates to the tradition of the Romantic landscape, and more directly to the outlook of artists such as Robert Smithson, Walter De Maria, and David Nash, who, in the late 1960s, found not only their inspiration but also their medium in nature. Of all these nature-based artists, the closest in spirit to Emery is perhaps Andy Goldsworthy, who seeks to represent the "lifeblood of nature" in its movement, change, and light.[7]

When Emery says that her work is about the energies moving through nature, she means something deeper than the breezes that move her shining sculptures. In her early years, when she was developing her philosophical outlook on the world, the people and belief systems that attracted her were open rather than dogmatic, universal rather than narrow, systems that sought underlying, deeper commonalities. Similarly, the natural forces that flow through her work are those deeper energies that early civilizations identified with the gods of the earth, the energies that she attempted to suggest in her major water-based work. That is why she noted, as she moved from aquamobiles to wind-driven sculptures, that she did not abandon the energies of flowing water, but carried with her its forms and energies. The result, in her wind-driven work, is a kind of liquefaction of movement.

In Emery's evocations of the deeper flows of nature, her work again relates to that of Isamu Noguchi. In the mid-1960s, concerned about the value of art in a troubled and technological age, Noguchi wrote, "Where all we see is change, I like to think that sculpture may have . . . a special role—as an antidote to impermanence—with newness, yes, but with a quality of enduring freshness relative to that resonant void."[8] The enduring freshness of Emery's sculpture is due in part to the timeless natural energies evoked by and manifested in her work.

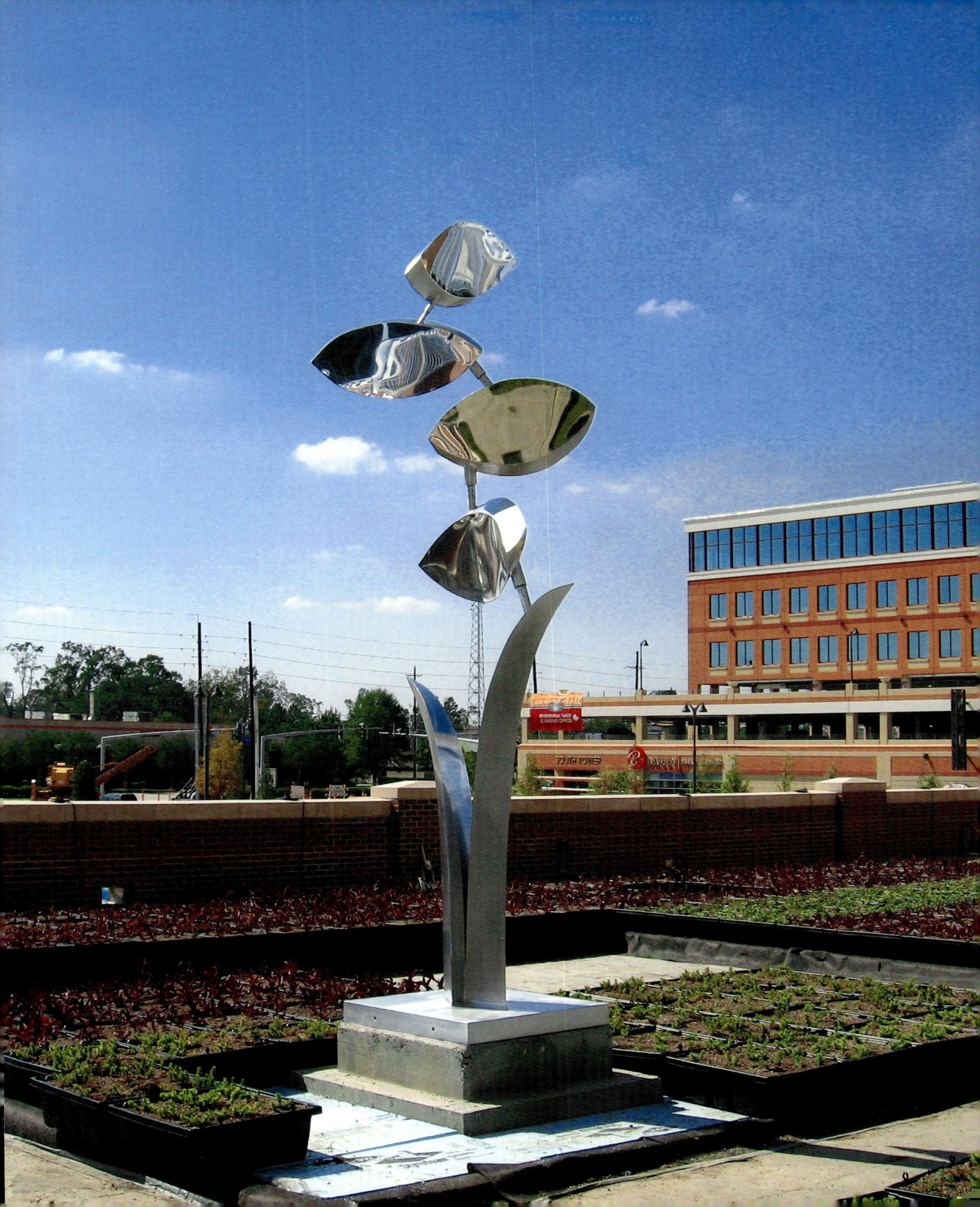
SOUTH TOWER

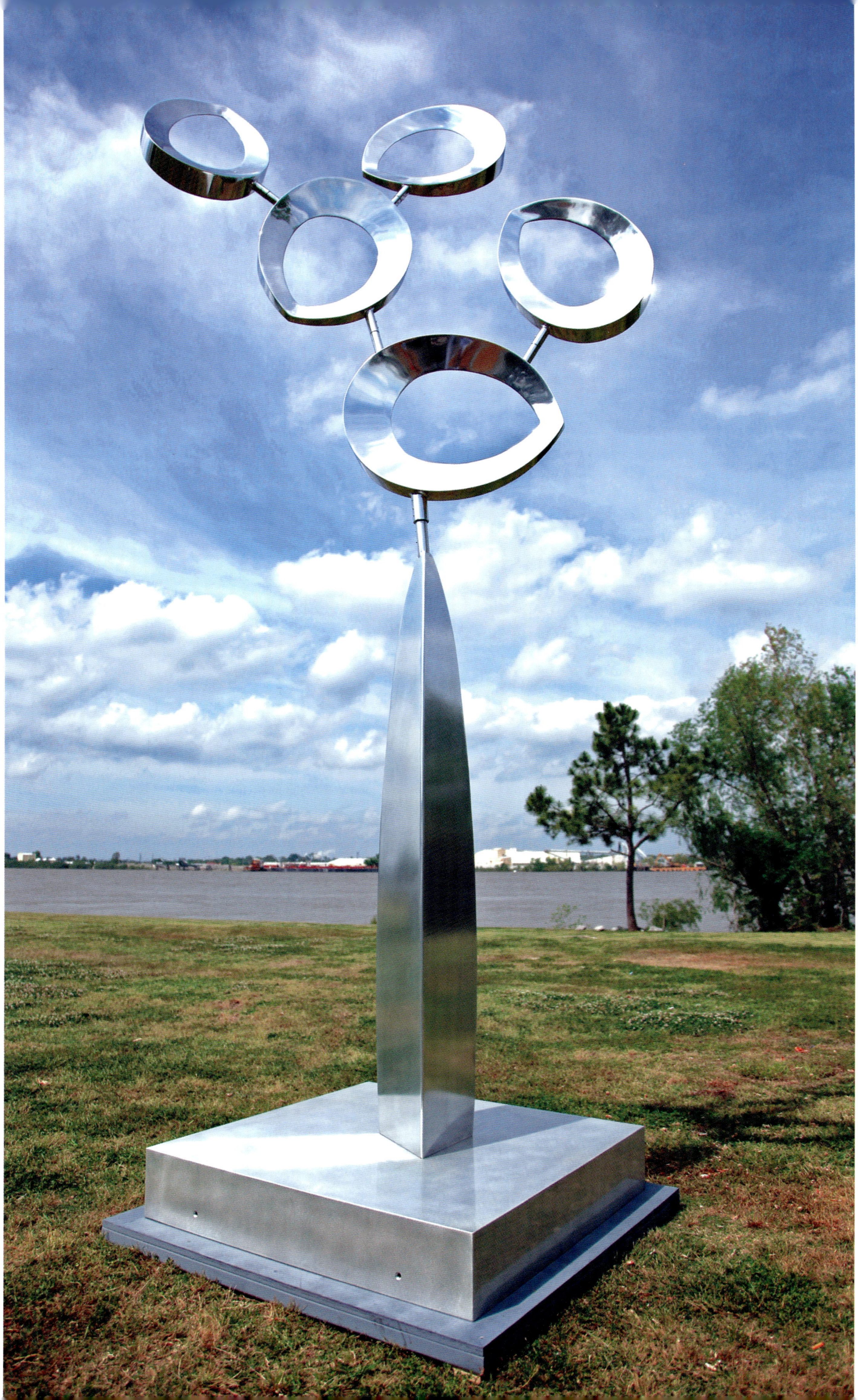

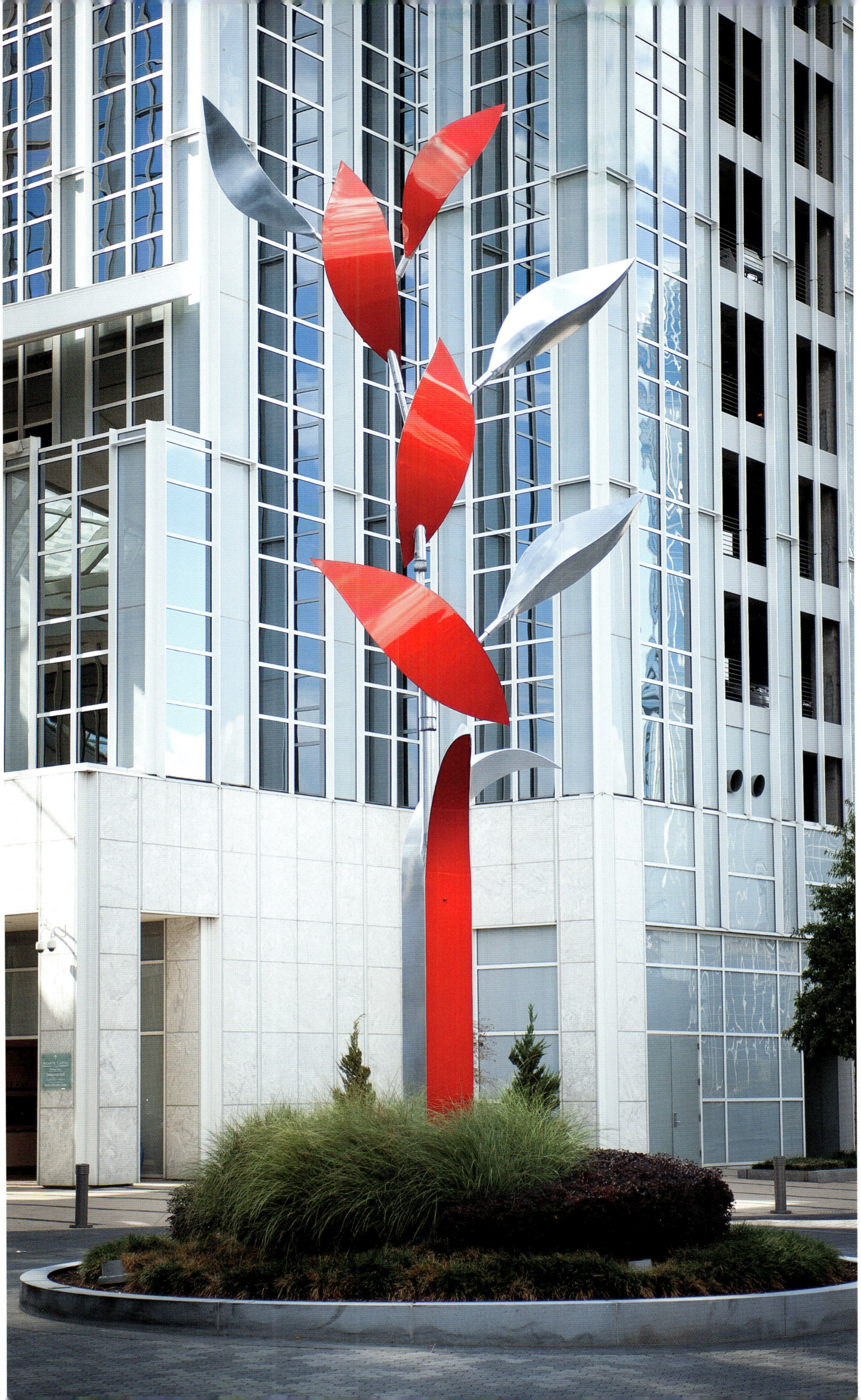

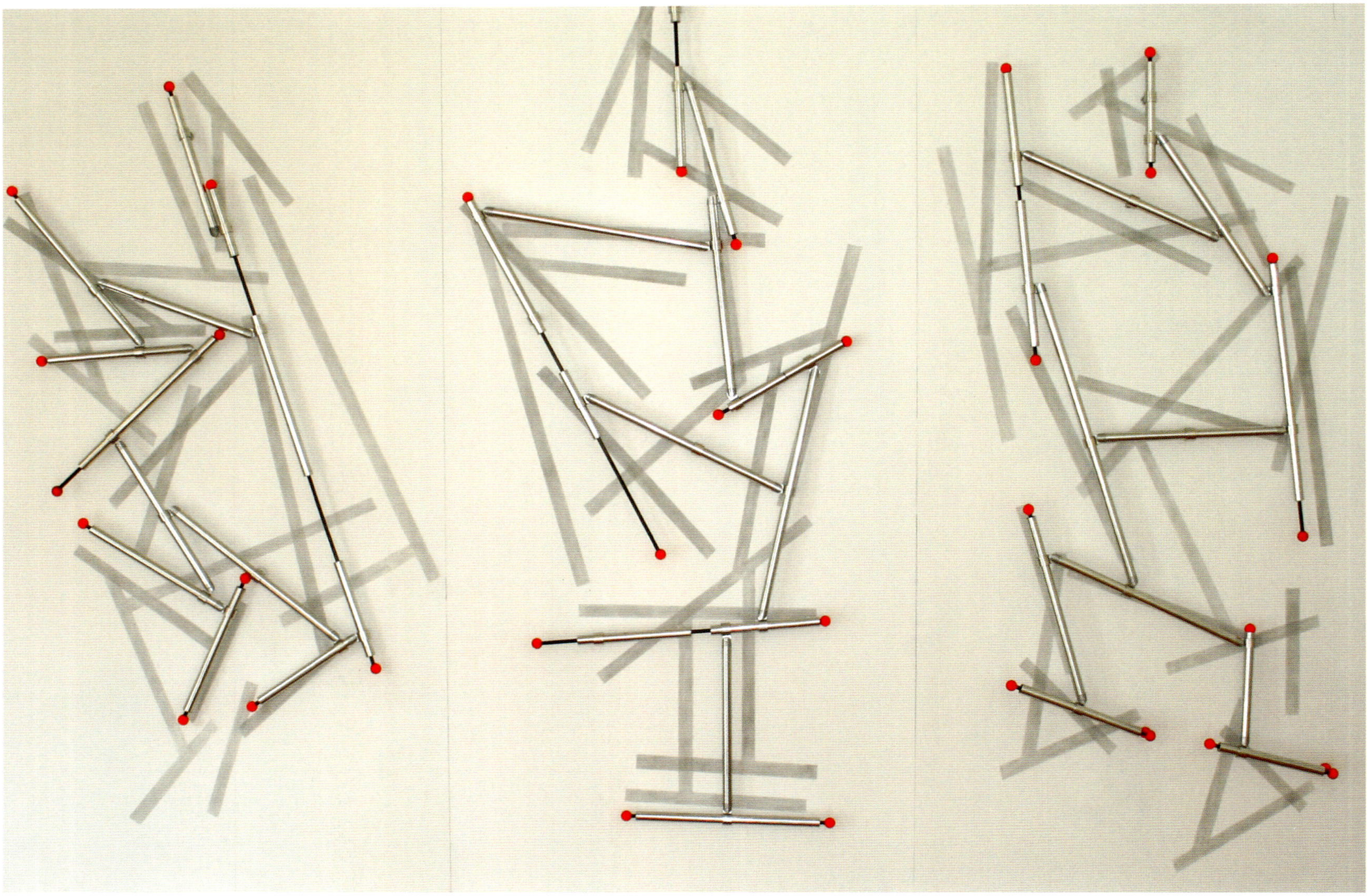

FIG. 7.4 *Lin Emery,* Shadow Wall, *2005. Aluminum, paint, and motors, 8 x 8 x 1 feet (2.4 x 2.4 x 0.3 m). Renaissance Arts Hotel, on loan from Arthur Roger Gallery.*

Every day that she is in New Orleans Emery enters her studio with the same avidity and enthusiasm as ever. She would prefer to work on new concepts and formal ideas rather than staying close to past successes, as new clients would often prefer. Not one to be pigeonholed and always searching for new sculptural concepts, Emery has produced several sculptures over the past few years that are unrelated to natural forms. *Shadow Wall* (fig. 7.4), a major wall sculpture now located in the Renaissance Arts Hotel in New Orleans, involves three groups of thin articulated and connected tubes, with bright red tips. Real and false shadows intertwine on the wall as the elements slowly tilt and turn. A 2007 work evokes the spirit of David Smith (*David Smith*, fig. 7.5). If you visit her home next to her studio you will see on a table a recent small work in the polished aluminum she favors, but in an abstracted human form. Inspired by Japanese anime, this engaging work (*Animé*, fig. 7.6) may lead to a new phase in Emery's art. Or it may not. Such is the way of the active, inquiring artist.

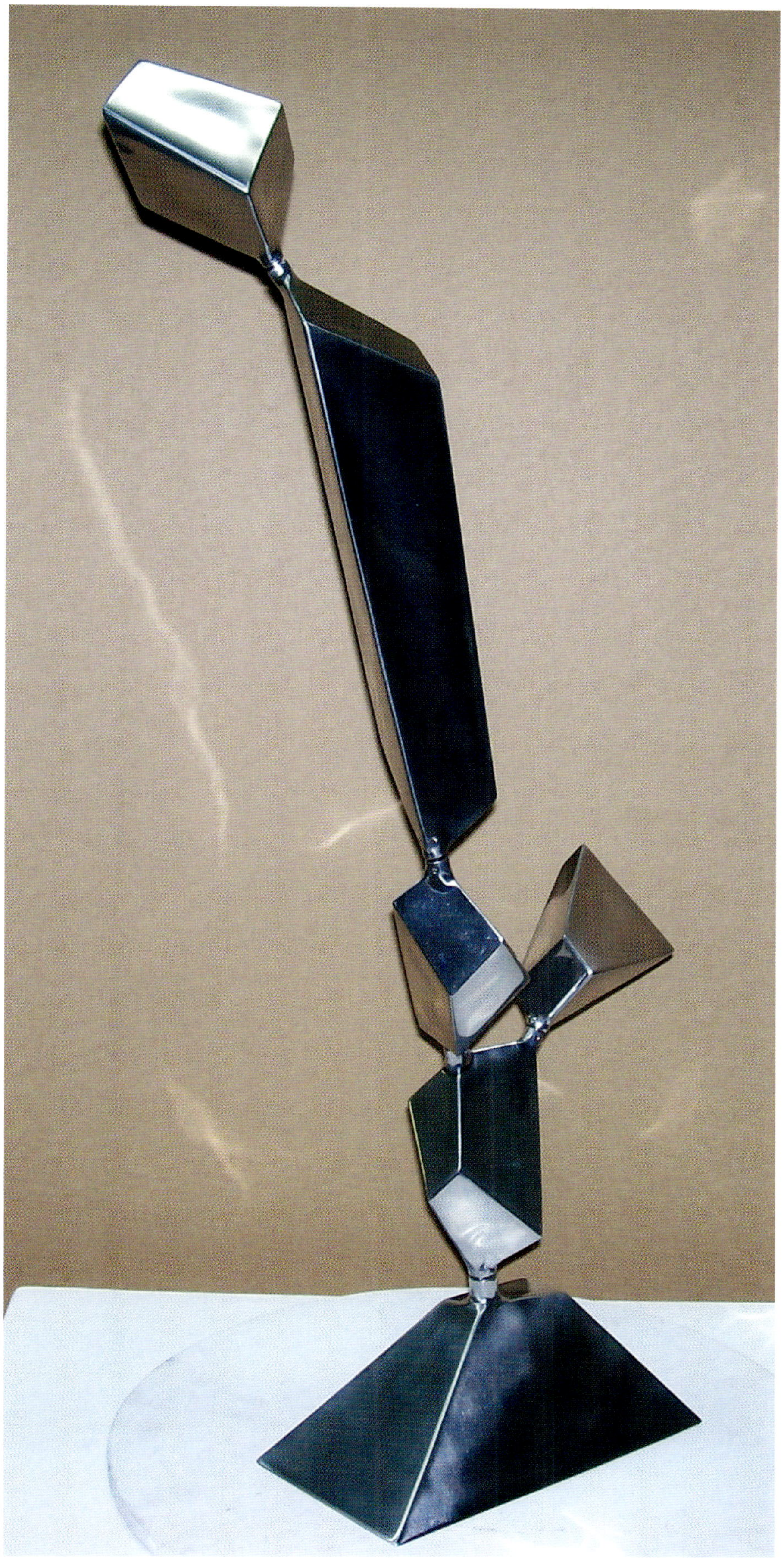

FIG. 7.5 *Lin Emery,* David Smith, *2007. Aluminum, 28 feet, orbit 17 inches (8.5 m, orbit 43.2 cm). Private collection.*

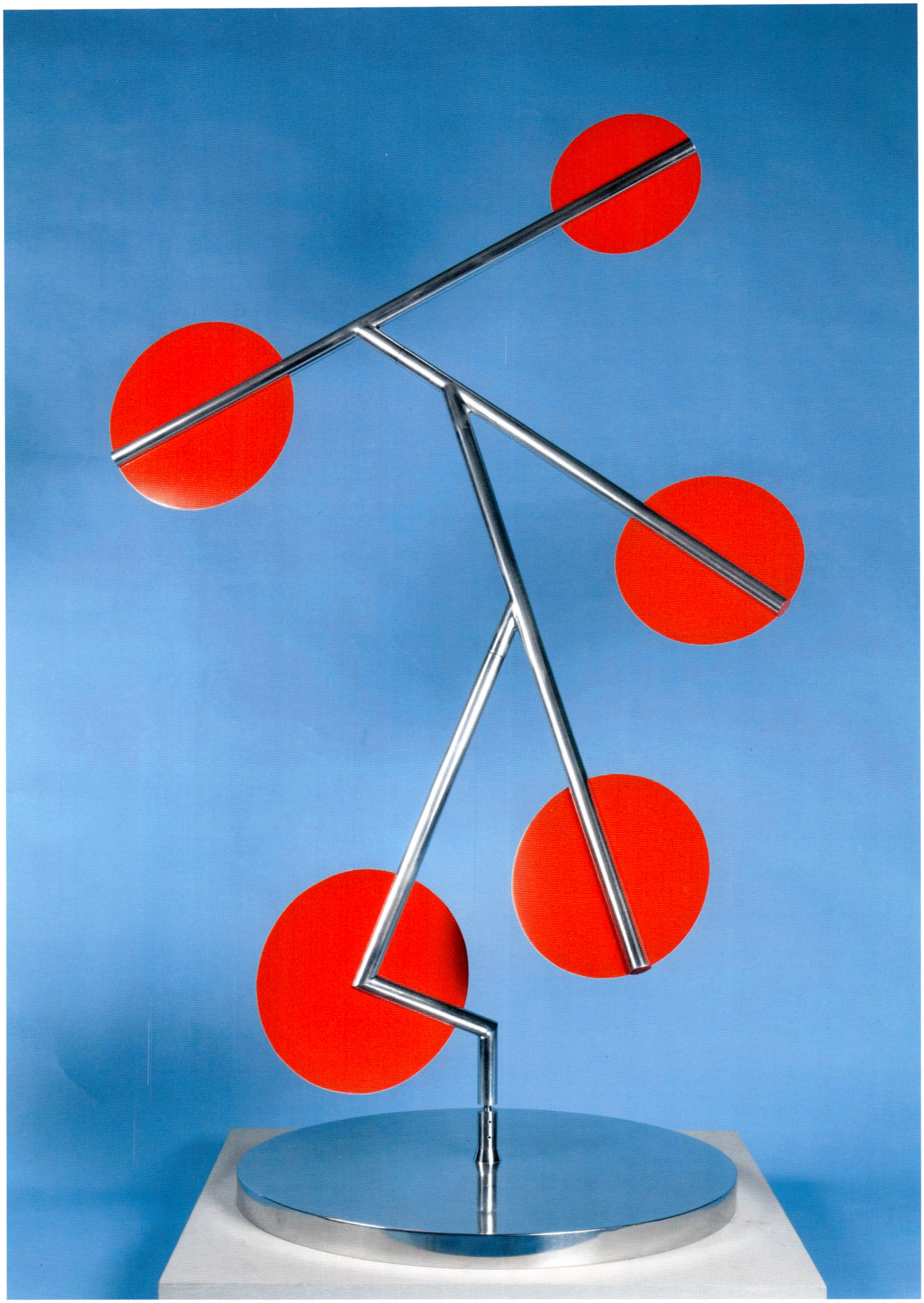

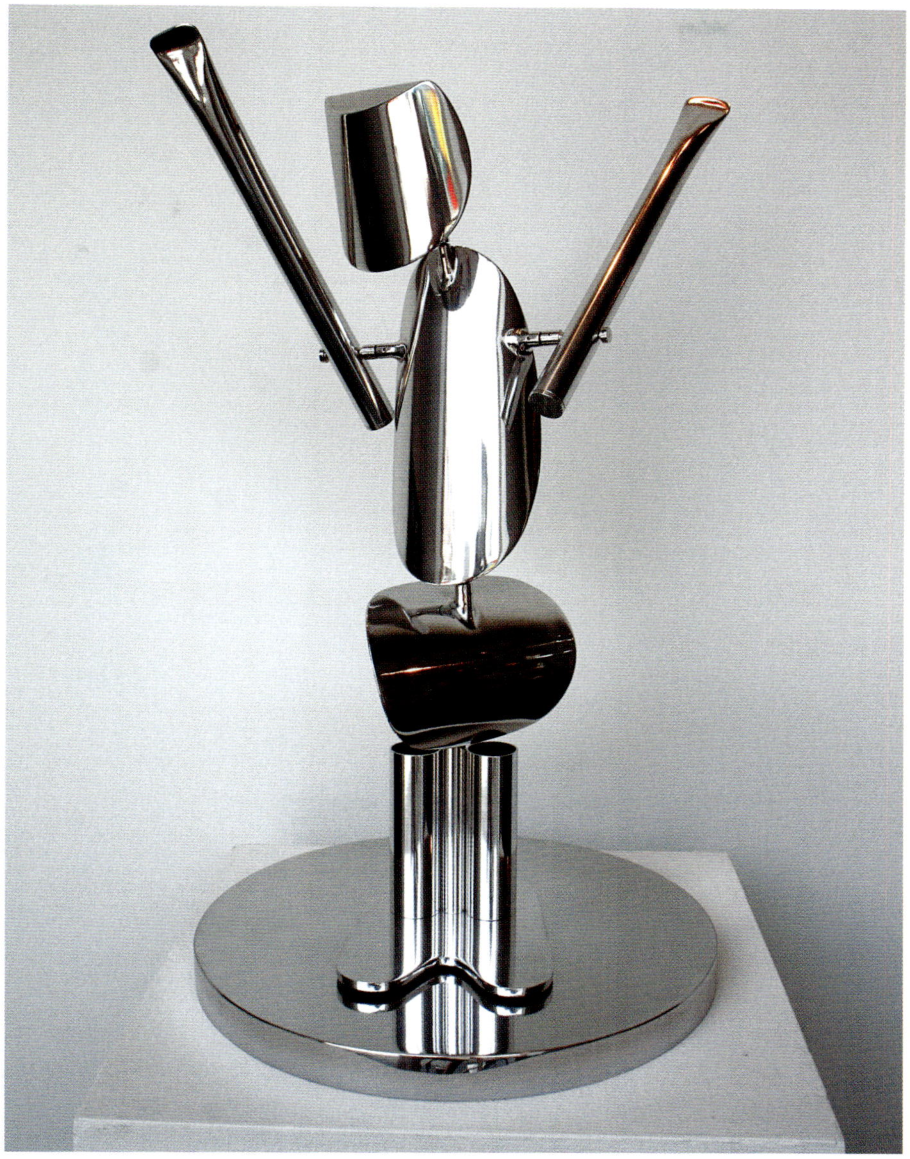

left

FIG. 7.6 *Lin Emery,* Animé, *2009. Aluminum, 17 inches, orbit 12 inches (43.2 cm, orbit 30.5 cm). Artist's studio.*

opposite page

Lin Emery, Circles, *2008. Aluminum and paint, 56 inches, orbit 52 inches (142.2 cm, orbit 132.1 cm). Private collection.*

NOTES

1. Constantin Brancusi, *Românul Brâncuşi* (Sibiu, Romania: Editura Thausib, 1996).

2. Naum Gabo and Antoine Pevsner, the Realistic Manifesto, in Stephen Bann, ed., *The Tradition of Constructivism* (New York: Da Capo Press, 1974), p. 3. First published on August 5, 1920, to accompany an open-air art exhibition in Moscow.

3. László Moholy-Nagy, *The New Vision and Abstract of an Artist* (New York: George Wittenborn, 1947), p. 80.

4. George Rickey, *Constructivism: Origins and Evolution* (New York: George Braziller, revised edition, 1995).

5. George Rickey, "Irrelevant Reflections" in *George Rickey: Kinetic Sculpture and Machines*, exhibition catalogue, Delgado Museum, New Orleans, 1956.

6. Lin Emery, quoted in John R. Kemp, "The Sculpture of Lin Emery," *Louisiana Endowment for the Humanities*, Summer 2007, p. 34.

7. Andy Goldsworthy, *Andy Goldsworthy: A Collaboration with Nature* (New York: Harry Abrams, 1990), p. 1. See also the stiking video directed and edited by Thomas Riedelsheimer, *Rivers and Tides: Andy Goldsworthy Working with Time*, Roxie Releasing, 2004.

8. Isamu Noguchi, *A Sculptor's World* (New York: Harper & Row, 1968), p. 40.

Acknowledgments

It all started on a cruise up the Rhine River. I was delighted to find out that the Lin Emery on the passenger list was indeed the Lin Emery whose sculpture I had known and admired for years, but whom I had never met. By the time we reached Basel at the end of five days of history, art, and Riesling, the possibility of a book had been delicately discussed and over the following weeks on shore it became a committed project. Lin and I were both taking a chance entering into this venture—she more than I. My objective of understanding the relationship between the artist and her sculpture would have been unachievable without the thoughtfulness and candor with which Lin answered my endless questions. My education at her hands included a revelatory introduction to her beloved New Orleans.

Lin and I are both grateful to John Berendt for contributing his insightful introduction. I am also indebted to many people who added important details to the portrait of the artist and her work. Along the way I discovered the advantages of writing about someone who is held in such wide admiration and affection. My thanks go to Willie Birch, artist and New Orleans social activist; Katie Bode, operations manager, the New York Sculpture Center; John Bullard, director, New Orleans Museum of Art; Shirley Corey, director, Louisiana ArtWorks; Ralf Gschwend, president of the Kinetic Art Organization; James Lamantia, architect; Barbara Lekberg, sculptor; Marshall Price, curator of Modern and Contemporary Art, National Academy Museum; and Arthur Roger, owner of Arthur Roger Gallery, which represents Lin in New Orleans.

To date, the most substantial writing on Lin Emery's life and sculpture has been by Edward Lucie-Smith, most notably his essay, "Lin Emery: Borrowing the Forces of Nature," in a catalogue accompanying a retrospective of her work at the New Orleans Museum of Art in 1996. That essay, rich in insights, was a helpful guide at the beginning of my own work.

Publication of the book would not have been possible without a generous grant from the Louisiana Endowment for the Humanities arranged by John Cleveland. Jain Kelly accomplished the task of obtaining photographs and reproduction permissions with thoughtful expertise. It was a pleasure to once again work with Leslie Pell van Breen, executive director of Hudson Hills Press, whose dedication to quality is a writer's and artist's delight.

On that journey up the Rhine, it was my wife Betsy who met Lin and introduced us, a small example of her continuing advice, encouragement, and cheerful support that has allowed me to work on such rewarding projects as this book.

Philip F. Palmedo
St. James, New York, March 2011

Chronology

1926 Born on May 20 in New York City; named Leonor; parents Jean Weill and Cornell Emery.

1929 Cornell Emery, 46, dies; Jean Weill Emery takes Lenore to Miami Beach and meets banker William Reid.

1931 Mrs. Bertha Oliver joins household as governess.

1935 Graduates from fourth grade, Payson School, New Rochelle, New York.

1935–1941 Alternates fall, winter, and spring enrollments at Ursuline Convent School, Palm Beach Private School, Rye Country Day School, and West Palm Beach Public School; also has private tutors in French, Latin, German, and drawing.

1941–1942 Attends Edgewood Rudolf Steiner School, Greenwich, Connecticut; concentrates on innovative program of block studies, three weeks for a single subject and no grades. Changes name to Lin.

1942–1943 Attends Columbia University and Syracuse University.

1943 Joins Mrs. Oliver in New Orleans and Mexico; takes part in summer program at Universidad de Mexico.

1943–1944 Attends Goodman School of Drama, Chicago, Illinois. Works for *Chicago Sun-Times* newspaper; afterward, writes publicity articles and fashion copy.

1944	Attends University of Chicago (Great Books program). Marries Chris Joslyn.
1945	Moves to New Orleans; works as fashion copywriter.
1947	Separates from Chris Joslyn. Takes "tramp steamer" to Paris.
1947–1948	Studies at Cours de la Civilisation Française at the Sorbonne; takes evening drawing sessions at la Grande Chaumière.
1948	Returns to New Orleans and joins Mrs. Oliver in Taos, New Mexico, in the summer; exhibits paintings at Harwood Museum, Taos.
1949–1950	Returns to Paris; first sculpture studies in Ossip Zadkine's studio.
1950	Returns to New Orleans and begins working in clay and plaster.
1951	Enrolls in the Sculpture Center in New York; works in clay and pewter, alongside Dorothy Dehner and Louise Nevelson.
1952	Learns welding and casting in the Sculpture Center; exhibits with Herbert Ferber, David Hare, Seymour Lipton, and David Smith.
1953	Included in the Sculpture Center exhibition *Women Welders*, which launched five artists on long careers. Settles permanently in New Orleans, with visits to New York; converts ground-floor living space into bedroom-studio. Continues figurative clay work for churches as well as welded work; subsidizes income by making sets for WDSU television programs.
1955	Selected for *Art in America* feature "New Talent in the U.S.A," which led to a traveling show in southern museums: Birmingham Museum of Art, Alabama; Hunter Museum of American Art, Chattanooga, Tennessee; Columbia Museum of Art, Columbia, South Carolina; and Norton Museum of Art, Palm Beach, Florida.
1956	Mother, Jean Emery, and William Reid marry.
1956–1970	Joins with six other artists to create Orleans Gallery; first run by the artists and then expanded to be managed as a nonprofit by a board of directors. More local artists became members; the gallery's success prompted new commercial galleries, leading to the closing of the Orleans Gallery.

1957 Designs, fabricates, and installs sets for *Kaleidoscope* (revue), staged at Provincetown Playhouse, New York.

1958 Shares an exhibition with painter James Lamantia in Havana, Cuba; leaves Havana on New Year's Eve, as Fidel Castro was entering the city.

1960 Travels with mother and William Reid on Reid's banking trip to Japan, Singapore, Delhi, and Beirut; continues alone to Cairo and Rome.

1962 Accompanies an Orleans Gallery show, part of a cultural mission from the city of New Orleans, to Tokyo, Hong Kong, and Manila. Learns to speak some Japanese. Marries Shirley Braselman in Mexico City; accompanies him on business trips to Athens, Paris, Brussels, London, and Mexico; helps with the design of a new house, completed in 1964.

1963 Joins two other artists to build the Orleans Workshop, a foundry and ceramic facility; develops bronze and aluminum casting techniques for both investment and full-mold procedures; uses the facility for many subsequent projects.

1964 Moves into new house that won an *Architectural Record* award; builds studio with jib crane next door.

1966–1971 Commissioned by the city of New Orleans to create a memorial to Mayor deLesseps "Chep" Morrison; learns to work with political entities; project includes landscape and pool design, 13 aquamobiles, and a 40-foot column; Kaiser Aluminum provides aluminum for the column and a metallurgist to assist in the construction.

1967 William Reid dies from ocean undertow accident in Palm Beach.

1969 Adopts son, Brooks, born in 1968.

1969–1970 Teaches at Tulane University School of Architecture; benefits from access to engineering department's water lab and machine shop, as well as private instruction.

1972–present Works on large-scale and smaller-size projects and installations, with one or two assistants. All work kinetic—activated by water, magnets, wind, and motors.

1975–1976 Preparation and realization of International Sculpture Conference in New Orleans; involves three universities and large group of local patrons; invited speakers include Isamu Noguchi, Yaacov Agam, Hilton Kramer, Beverly Pepper, Irving Sandler, Seymour Lipton, and George Sugarman.

1979	Chairs studio sessions and activities for College Art Association in New Orleans. Arranges for final celebration, "Meat Market Ball," in newly opened Contemporary Arts Center.
1980	Receives Mayor's Award for Achievement in the Arts, New Orleans, LA.
1983–1984	Works with architect Charles Moore on water designs for the New Orleans World's Fair. Awarded a solo exhibition in the fair; fair opened to excellent reviews, but went bankrupt and closed.
1985	Jean Emery Reid dies from heart disease.
1989	Purchases an abandoned 1925 movie theater and adapts it as a studio with large open space, balcony, and marquis displaying theater's name, "Ashton."
1995–1999	Japanese consortium commissions work for Osaka and Izumisano, and arranges exhibitions in Kyoto. It hosts two trips to Japan; Japanese language study continues.
2001	Receives Governor's Arts Award, Baton Rouge, LA. Shirley Braselman dies after long illness.
2003	Ongoing friendship develops with John Cleveland, an art enthusiast and supporter.
2004	Accepts honorary doctorate, Loyola University of the South. Organizes and directs symposium in New Orleans for the International Sculpture Center with Antony Gormley as keynote speaker.
2005	Hurricane Katrina strikes; stays through the storm, but is forced to leave after five days. Evacuates to New York; allowed to return after three months. Extensive repairs needed to house, studios, and damaged sculptures.
2009	Storm repairs completed and full use of both studios resumed.

SELECTED PUBLIC COLLECTIONS

Museum Collections

Brevard Art Museum, Melbourne, FL
Centennial Art Center, Nashville, TN
Centennial Art Museum, Corpus Christi, TX
Chattahoochee Valley Art Center, LaGrange, GA
Chrysler Museum of Art, Norfolk, VA
Columbia Museum of Art, Columbia, SC
Delaware Art Museum, Wilmington, DE
Farnsworth Art Museum, Rockland, ME
Fine Arts Museum of the South, Mobile, AL
Flint Institute of Arts, Flint, MI
Frederick R. Weisman Art Foundation, Los Angeles, CA
Grounds For Sculpture, Hamilton, NJ
Historic New Orleans Collection, New Orleans, LA
Hunter Museum of American Art, Chattanooga, TN
Huntington Museum of Art, Huntington, WV
J. Patrick Lannan Foundation, Palm Beach, FL
Jule Collins Smith Museum of Fine Art at Auburn University, Auburn, AL
Leepa-Rattner Museum of Art, Tarpon Springs, FL
Longue Vue House and Gardens, New Orleans, LA
Museum of Outdoor Arts, Englewood, CO
National Academy of Design, New York, NY
National Collection of American Art, Washington, DC
National Gallery for Foreign Art, Sofia, Bulgaria
New Orleans Museum of Art, LA
Norton Museum of Art, West Palm Beach, FL
Ogden Museum of Southern Art, New Orleans, LA
Pensacola Museum of Art, Pensacola, FL

Municipal Collections

Allen J. Ellender Federal Building, Houma, LA
Civic Center, Lawrence, KS
Florida State Department of Corrections, Tallahassee, FL
Lisle City Hall, Lisle, IL
The MITRE Corporation, McLean, VA
New Orleans Civic Center, New Orleans, LA
State Library of Louisiana, Baton Rouge, LA

University Collections

Auburn University, Auburn, AL
Hofstra University, Hempstead, NY
Huntingdon College, Montgomery, AL
Sweet Briar College, Sweet Briar, VA
University of South Carolina, Columbia, SC

Collections in Medical Centers

Christiana Care Health System, Wilmington, DE
East Jefferson General Hospital, Metairie, LA
Hospital Corporation of America, Nashville, TN
Izumisano Municipal Hospital, Izumisano, Japan
Menorah Medical Center, Overland Park, KS
The NeuroMedical Center, Baton Rouge, LA
Touro Infirmary, New Orleans, LA

Collections in Religious Centers

Congregation Emanu El, Houston, TX
Emanuel Baptist Church, Alexandria, LA
Father Judge Mission Seminary, Monroe, VA
Grace Episcopal Church, New Orleans, LA
Holy Cross High School, New Orleans, LA
The New Orleans Jewish Community Center, New Orleans, LA
St. Catherine of Siena Church, Metairie, LA
St. Gertrude Catholic Church, Des Allemands, LA
St. James Major Church, New Orleans, LA
St. Patrick's Church, New Orleans, LA
St. Philip Neri Church, Metairie, LA
St. Scholastica Academy, Covington, LA

Selected Corporate Collections

Amhurst Lake Park, Waukegan, IL
Caribbean Corporate Center, Sunnyvale, CA
Chateau Mall, Kenner, LA
Chevron Headquarters Building, Oxnard, CA
Deloitte & Touche, Chicago, IL, and New Orleans, LA

Fidelity Center, Oklahoma City, OK
Financial Guaranty Insurance Company, New York, NY
First National Bank of Atlanta, Atlanta, GA
Germantown Savings Bank, Philadelphia, PA
Guajardo Bottling Company, Monterrey, Mexico
Helmerich Park, Tulsa, OK
Imperial House Restaurant, Tampa, FL
InterContinental Hotel, New Orleans, LA
Joske's of Texas, San Antonio, TX
K&B Plaza, New Orleans, LA
Knight Oil Tools, Lafayette, LA
L.R. Nelson Corporation, Peoria, IL
Linclay Corporation, Cincinnati, OH
Marina Centre, Singapore
Nashville Life and Casualty Tower, Nashville, TN
Neiman Marcus, Short Hills, NJ
Osaka Dome, Osaka, Japan
Pan American Life Center, New Orleans, LA
South Central Bell Building, Birmingham, AL
Southland Corporation, Dallas, TX
Sterling Drug Headquarters, Collegeville, PA
Sterling Corporation, Irving, TX
Texas Instruments, Inc., Dallas, TX
Trammell Crow Company Office Park, Arboretum Lakes, IL

SELECTED SOLO EXHIBITIONS

2011, 2006, 2000, 1989 Kouros Gallery, New York, NY

2010 Leepa-Rattner Museum of Art, Tarpon Springs, FL

2010, 2008, 2005 Arthur Roger Gallery, New Orleans, LA

2007 Century Association, New York, NY

Pensacola Museum of Art, Pensacola, FL

2003 Slidell Arts Center, Slidell, LA

2002 Meadows Museum of Art, Shreveport, LA

2001 Masur Museum of Art, Monroe, LA

1999 Art Life Mitsuhashi Gallery, Kyoto, Japan

Honen-in Temple, Kyoto, Japan

1997 Imperial Calcasieu Museum, Lake Charles, LA

1996	Retrospective, New Orleans Museum of Art, New Orleans, LA; Edward Lucie-Smith, curator
1992	Brevard Art Museum, Melbourne, FL
1991	Art Museum of Southeast Texas, Beaumont, TX
1989	Alexandria Museum of Art, Alexandria, LA
1987	Malton Gallery, Cincinnati, OH
1986	Glass Art Gallery, Toronto, Ontario, Canada
1985	Hunter Museum of American Art, Chattanooga, TN
	Heath Gallery, Atlanta, GA
1984	New Orleans World's Fair, New Orleans, LA
1984, 1982	Max Hutchinson Gallery, New York, NY
1978	Contemporary Arts Center, New Orleans, LA
1977	Lauren Rogers Museum of Art, Laurel, MS
1975	Bodley Gallery, New York, NY
1968, 1967, 1964, 1962	Orleans Gallery, New Orleans, LA
1967	Kiko Galleries, Houston, TX
	Centennial Art Museum, Corpus Christi, TX
1966	Museum of New Mexico, Santa Fe, NM
1965	Gallery of Modern Art, Scottsdale, AZ
1964	Royal-Athena Galleries, New York, NY
1964, 1962	New Orleans Museum of Art, New Orleans, LA
1963	Valley House Gallery & Sculpture Garden, Dallas, TX
	Marble Arch Gallery, Miami, FL
1962	Tennessee Fine Arts Center, Nashville, TN
1962, 1957	Sculpture Center, New York, NY

SELECTED INVITATIONAL EXHIBITIONS

2001	Inaugural exhibition, Bass Museum of Art, Miami Beach, FL
2000	*Welded! Sculpture of the 20th Century*, Neuberger Museum of Art, Purchase, NY
	Contemporary Sculpture at Chesterwood 2000, Stockbridge, MA
	Contemporary Kinetic Sculpture, Contemporary Arts Center, New Orleans, LA

1996	Frankfurt Forum Competition (finalist), Frankfurt, Germany
1990	Fujisankei Biennial, Hakone, Japan
1988	World Expo '88, Brisbane, Australia
1983	International Water Sculpture Competition, Expo 84, New Orleans, LA
1980	International Sculpture Conference, Washington, DC
	Art in Architecture: G.S.A. Projects, National Collection, Washington, DC
	Nine Louisiana Sculptors, Houston Museum of Fine Arts School Gallery, Houston, TX
1977	*Awards Candidates*, American Academy and Institute of Arts and Letters, New York, NY
1976	Fordham University Library at Lincoln Center, New York, NY
	Fine Arts in New Federal Buildings, national tour
1974	*Thirteen Sculptors*, University of New Orleans, New Orleans, LA
1973	*Eight State Exhibition*, Oklahoma Art Center, Oklahoma City, OK
1968	*Art in Louisiana*, German-American Volkfest, Berlin, Germany
1966	*Flint Invitational*, Flint Institute of Arts, Flint, MI
1965	*Fountains in Modern Architecture*, American Federation of Arts & The American Institute of Architects (AIA) (tour)
1964	*Orleans Gallery Group*, Southern Association of Museums (tour)
	Contemporary Sculpture, American–Israel Pavilion, New York World's Fair
1964, 1960	Pennsylvania Academy of the Fine Arts Annuals, Philadelphia, PA
1963	*Outdoor Sculpture*, Bundy Art Gallery, Waitsfield, VT
1962	*Catastrophe*, Raymond Cordier Gallery, Paris, France
	New Directions, American Federation of Arts (tour)
	Garden Exhibition, Allentown Art Museum, Allentown, PA
1961	*Art in the South*, University of Southwestern Louisiana Gallery, Lafayette, LA
	Orleans Gallery Group, Tokyo, Manila, and Hong Kong, under United States Information Agency (USIA) auspices

1960	*Five American Sculptors Interpret Freedom*, American Federation of Arts (tour)
1956	Norton Museum of Art, West Palm Beach, FL (tour under auspices of Delgado Museum, now New Orleans Museum of Art; solo traveling show of aquamobiles)
1955	Columbia Museum of Art, Columbia, SC (tour under auspices of Delgado Museum, now New Orleans Museum of Art; solo traveling show of aquamobiles)
	Birmingham Museum of Art, Birmingham, AL (tour under auspices of Delgado Museum, now New Orleans Museum of Art; solo traveling show of aquamobiles)
1951	*American Sculpture 1951*, The Metropolitan Museum of Art, New York, NY

PUBLIC COMMISSIONS

2011	Sandler Center for the Performing Arts, Virginia Beach, VA: kinetic sculpture, 24 x 20 x 8 feet (7.3 x 6.0 x 2.4 m)
2010	Houston University, Houston TX: kinetic sculpture, 16 feet, orbit 12 feet (4.8 m, orbit 3.6 m)
2008–2009	Terminus development, Atlanta, GA: kinetic sculpture, 30 feet, orbit 18 feet (9.1 m, orbit 5.4 m)
2006	Knight Oil Tools, Lafayette, LA: kinetic sculpture, 24 feet, orbit 14 feet (7.3 m, orbit 4.2 m)
2005	The NeuroMedical Center, Baton Rouge, LA: kinetic sculpture, 15 feet, orbit 8 feet (4.5 m, orbit 2.4 m)
2003	Renaissance Arts Hotel, New Orleans, LA: 5 aquamobiles, 8 x 4 x 1.5 feet each (2.4 x 1.2 x 0.5 m)
2001	The MITRE Corporation, McLean, VA: kinetic sculpture, 21 feet, orbit 14 feet (6.4 m, orbit 4.2 m)
	Schiffer Publishing Company, Atglen, PA: 3 kinetic sculptures, 12–14 feet, orbit 7 feet (3.6–4.2 m, orbit 2.1 m)
1999	Sterling Commerce, Dallas, TX: kinetic sculpture, 19 feet, orbit 14 feet (5.7 m, orbit 4.2 m)
1997	Overland Park Regional Medical Center, Overland Park, KS: kinetic sculpture, 16 feet, orbit 12 feet (4.8 m, orbit 3.6 m)
	L.R. Nelson Corporation, Peoria, IL: kinetic sculpture, 24 feet, orbit 18 feet (7.3 m, orbit 5.4 m)

Izumisano Municipal Hospital, Izumisano, Japan: kinetic sculpture, 23 feet, orbit 24 feet (7 m, orbit 7.3 m)

Osaka Dome, Osaka, Japan: kinetic sculpture (awarded Grand Prize for Public Sculpture), 36 feet, orbit 22 feet (10.9 m, orbit 6.7 m)

1994 Neiman Marcus, Short Hills, NJ: kinetic sculpture, 22 feet, orbit 16 feet (6.7 m, orbit 4.8 m)

Financial Guaranty Insurance Company, New York, NY: suspended mobile, 23 x 14 x 10 feet (7.0 x 4.2 x 3.0 m)

1992 Sterling Drug Park, Collegeville, PA: three kinetic sculptures, each 20 feet, orbit 12 feet (6 m, orbit 3.6 m)

Congregation Emanu El, Houston, TX: kinetic sculpture, 16 feet, orbit 8 feet (4.8 m, orbit 2.4 m)

Daytona Beach Airport, Daytona Beach, FL: kinetic sculpture, 22 feet, orbit 16 feet (6.7 m, orbit 4.8 m)

1990 Hofstra University, Hempstead, NY: kinetic sculpture, 21 feet, orbit 16 feet (6.4 m, orbit 4.8 m)

Amhurst Lake Park, Waukegan, IL: four kinetic sculptures, each 36 feet, orbit 22 feet (10.9 m, orbit 6.7 m)

1989 Brevard Art Museum, Melbourne, FL: kinetic sculpture, 16 feet, orbit 12 feet (4.8 m, orbit 3.6 m)

City of Oxnard, CA: kinetic sculpture for Chevron Corporation, 18 feet, orbit 16 feet (5.4 m, orbit 4.8 m)

1988 City of Virginia Beach, VA: kinetic sculpture for Central Library (awarded Laszlo Aranyi Award for Public Sculpture), 28 feet, orbit 22 feet (8.5 m, orbit 6.7 m)

1987 Delaware Art Museum, Wilmington, DE: kinetic sculpture, 15 feet, orbit 12 feet (4.5 m, orbit 3.6 m)

Central Park, Dulles, VA: kinetic sculpture, 8 x 30 x 15 feet (2.4 x 9.1 x 4.5 m)

1986 Arboretum Lakes, Lisle, IL: kinetic sculpture, 18 feet, orbit 16 feet (5.4 m, orbit 4.8 m)

Marina Centre, Singapore: kinetic sculpture, 28 x 14 x 14 feet (8.5 x 4.2 x 4.2 m)

1984 Chateau Mall, Kenner, LA: aquamobile, 20 x 8 x 8 feet (6 x 2.4 x 2.4 m)

Linclay Executive Plaza, Cincinnati, OH: kinetic sculpture, 16 feet, orbit 12 feet (4.8 m, orbit 3.6 m)

	InterContinental Hotel, New Orleans, LA: musical wall, 10 x 18 feet (3 x 5.4 m)
1983	InterContinental Hotel, New Orleans, LA: two kinetic sculptures, each 56 x 52 feet (17 x 15.8 m)
1982	City of Lawrence, KS: kinetic sculpture for City Hall, 22 feet, orbit 20 feet (6.7 m, orbit 6 m)
	State Library of Louisiana, Baton Rouge, LA: kinetic sculpture, 18 feet, orbit 12 feet (5.4 m, orbit 3.6 m)
1981	Sweet Briar College, Sweet Briar, VA: kinetic sculpture, 10 x 8 x 8 feet (3 x 2.4 x 2.4 m)
1980	Emanuel Baptist Church, Alexandria, LA: kinetic sculpture, 18 feet (5.4 m)
1979	The New Orleans Jewish Community Center, New Orleans, LA: kinetic relief, 20 x 17 x 2 feet (6 x 5.1 x 0.6 m)
1977	G.S.A. Arts in Federal Buildings Program, Houma, LA: kinetic sculpture, 8 x 28 x 3 feet (2.4 x 8.5 x 0.9 m)
	Helmerich Park, Tulsa, OK: aquamobile, 16 x 20 x 20 feet (4.8 x 6 x 6 m)
1974	John Welsh Humanities Center, University of South Carolina, Columbia, SC: aquamobile, 8 x 20 x 18 feet (2.4 x 6 x 5.4 m)
	Germantown Savings Bank, Philadelphia, PA: aquamobile, 8 x 10 x 7 feet (2.4 x 3 x 2.1 m)
1973	South Central Bell Building, Birmingham, AL: magnetmobile, 30 x 12 x 10 feet (9.1 x 3.6 x 3 m)
1972	Fidelity Center, Oklahoma City, OK: aquamobile, 20 x 12 x 12 feet (6 x 3.6 x 3.6 m)
1966–1970	Civic Center, New Orleans, LA: memorial column, 40 feet; aquamobile, 5 x 20 x 22 feet (12.1 m; 1.5 x 6 x 6.7 m)
1960	Imperial House Restaurant, Tampa, FL: aquamobile, 9 x 5 x 5 feet (2.7 x 1.5 x 1.5 m)
	Father Judge Mission Seminary, Monroe, VA: baldachino, aluminum, 14 x 11 x 11 feet (4.2 x 3.3 x 3.3 m)
	Father Judge Mission Seminary, Monroe, VA: Stations of the Cross, terra-cotta, 14 x 14 inches (35.6 x 35.6 cm)
1957	St. Catherine of Siena Church, Metairie, LA: tabernacle supports, bronze, 3 x 3 x 2 feet (0.9 x 0.9 x 0.6 m)
1956	St. Scholastica Academy, Covington, LA: exterior figure, 10 x 3 x 2 feet (3.0 x 0.9 x 0.6 m)

	St. Gertrude Catholic Church, Des Allemands, LA: exterior figure, 9 x 3 x 2 feet (2.7 x 0.9 x 0.6 m)
1955	Holy Cross High School, New Orleans, LA: two figures, 8 x 6 x 2 feet (2.4 x 1.8 x 0.6 m)

LECTURES AND SEMINARS

2004	Master class, National Foundation for Advancement in the Arts, Miami, FL
2002	Speaker, Fellows program, International Women's Forum, Beijing, China
2001	Panelist, "Kinetic Sculpture," 19th International Sculpture Conference, Pittsburgh, PA
	Speaker, "Art Luncheon," Century Association, New York, NY
2000	Lecturer, Longue Vue House and Gardens, New Orleans, LA
1998	Lecturer, Contemporary Arts Center, New Orleans, LA
1992	Panelist, Chesterwood Museum, Stockbridge, MA
1990	Lecturer, New Orleans Museum of Art, New Orleans, LA
1988	Visiting artist and lecturer, The University of Maine, Orono, ME
	Lecturer, New Orleans Center for Creative Arts, New Orleans, LA
1986	Panelist, "Women Sculptors," Soho Gallery, New York, NY
	Lecturer, University of New Orleans, New Orleans, LA
1985	Visiting artist and lecturer, Louisiana State University, Baton Rouge, LA
	Visiting artist and lecturer, Art Academy of Cincinnati, Cincinnati, OH
1983	Visiting artist and juror, Foothills Art Center, Golden, CO
	Panelist, "Symposium on Imagination," New Orleans, LA
1982	Panelist, "Sculptors & Architects," 12th International Sculpture Conference, Washington, DC
1980	Visiting artist, Tulane University, New Orleans, LA
	Moderator, panels for 11th International Sculpture Conference, Washington, DC
	Slide presentation, LaGrange College, LaGrange, GA
1978	Moderator, "Fountain Technology," 10th International Sculpture Conference, Toronto, Canada

1977	Panelist, "Contemporary Women Artists," The University of Texas at Austin, Austin, TX
	Slide presentation, Lauren Rogers Museum of Art, Laurel, MS
	Speaker, "Kinetic Sculpture," physics department, Tulane University, New Orleans, LA
	"Technology of Sculpture," American Society of Metals, New Orleans, LA
1969–1970	Visiting critic, Tulane University School of Architecture, New Orleans, LA
1968	Speaker, "Monumental and Fountain Sculpture," American Institute of Architects, Louisiana chapter, Tulane University, New Orleans, LA

SELECTED TELEVISION FEATURES AND INTERVIEWS

2005	WDSU-TV, New Orleans, interview
2003	WWNO-TV (PBS), New Orleans, "Louisiana Artist," 10-minute feature
1999	Jan Jander, New Orleans, "It's Dancing," 28-minute documentary
1996	WYES-TV, New Orleans, "Lin Emery," 15-minute feature
	WWL-TV, New Orleans, "Remoulade: Moving Art," 5-minute feature
	Loyola University, New Orleans, "Retrospective," 12-minute documentary
1989	WDSU-TV, New Orleans, "Profile," feature
1987	WVUE-TV, New Orleans, "First Person," 30-minute interview
1985	*PM* magazine, "Lin Emery Exhibition, Atlanta"
1984	McNeil-Lehrer Report, interview and studio visit
1981	WYES-TV (PBS), "Spaces at an Exhibition," 28-minute documentary
1977	WWL-TV, New Orleans, interview and studio visit
1970	WDSU-TV, New Orleans, "Morrison Memorial"
1967	WDSU-TV, New Orleans, "Lin Emery," 15-minute program

HONORS

2005	Sidney Simon Sculpture Award, National Academy Museum, New York, NY
2004	Honorary doctorate, Order of St. Lazarus Companionate of Merit, Loyola University of the South, New Orleans, LA
2003	"Role Model," Young Leadership Council award, New Orleans, LA
2001	Governor's Arts Award, capitol, Baton Rouge, LA
1998	Grand Prize for Public Sculpture, Osaka Prefecture, Japan
1997	Delgado Society Award for Artistic Excellence, New Orleans Museum of Art, New Orleans, LA
1990	Laszlo Aranyi Award of Honor for Public Art, Central Library, Virginia Beach, VA
1989	"Role Model," YWCA award, Sheraton Hotel, New Orleans, LA
1988	Distinguished Louisiana Artist award, New Orleans Center for Creative Arts (NOCCA), New Orleans, LA
1987	Sweet Arts Award, Contemporary Arts Center, New Orleans, LA
1984	Louisiana Women of Achievement Award, *Louisiana Endowment for the Humanities* publication, New Orleans, LA
1983	InterArts grant, National Endowment for the Arts publication, Washington, DC
1981	Fellow, Virginia Center for Creative Arts, Amherst, VA
1980	Mayor's Award for Achievement in the Arts, New Orleans, LA

Honorary Associations (by election)

Century Association, New York, NY
International Women's Forum, Washington, DC
National Academy of Design, New York, NY
Royal British Society of Sculptors (past international member), London, England
Sculptors Guild, New York, NY

Advisory Appointments

2004	Chair, International Sculpture Center Symposium, New Orleans, LA
2000–2004	Board member, International Sculpture Center, Hamilton, NJ
2000–2001	Campaign cabinet, Louisiana ArtWorks, New Orleans, LA

1999	Advisory board member, New Orleans Video Access Center, New Orleans, LA
1998–1999	Mentor, New Orleans Center for Creative Arts, New Orleans, LA
1997–1999	Advisor, ArtWorks project, Arts Council of New Orleans, LA
1994–2000	Board member, Contemporary Arts Center, New Orleans, LA
1993–1998	Loyola University Visual Arts Committee, Chicago, IL
1992	Co-chair, riverfront design, New Orleans city planning, New Orleans, LA
1991–1992	Program committee chair, International Sculpture Conference, Philadelphia, PA
1990–1991	Board member, Sculpture Center, New York, NY
1988	Consultant, robotics display, Gulf South Research Institute, University of Louisiana, Baton Rouge, LA
1987–1990	Member, New Orleans Percent for Art Committee, New Orleans, LA
1986	Advisory committee, National Sculpture Conference: Works by Women, Cincinnati, OH
1983	Advisory committee for Louisiana Exposition Hall Art Plan, Architecture School, Tulane University, New Orleans, LA
	Consultant, Charles Moore & Associates, Louisiana World Exposition, New Orleans, LA
1981–1983, 1990	Board member, Arts Council of New Orleans, New Orleans, LA
1980	Steering committee, Mayor's Task Force for the Arts, New Orleans, LA
1979	Chair, Studio Sessions, College Art Association, New Orleans, LA
	Co-chair, Mayor's Committee for Duncan Plaza, New Orleans, LA
1977–1982, 1984–1986	Board member, Contemporary Arts Center, New Orleans, LA
1976	Chair, 9th International Sculpture Conference, New Orleans, LA
1973–1979	Board member, National Sculpture Center, The University of Kansas, Lawrence, KS

COLLABORATIVE PROJECTS

1988	Design proposal with Redstone Architects for Mt. Elliott Park, Detroit, MI
1987	Design proposal with Concordia Architects for Concord Square, Concord, CA (award)

1983–1984	Water-feature designs with architect Charles Moore for 1984 World's Fair, New Orleans, LA
1983	Installation/performance with composer James Drew, Contemporary Arts Center, New Orleans, LA
1982	InterContinental Hotel courtyard with architect Steven Bingler, physicist Robert Morriss, mathematician Ron Knill, mosaic artist Patricia Whitty-Johnson, and composer James Drew, New Orleans, LA
	Newport Marina art plan with architect Ivan Mandich, Mississippi Gulf Coast
	Vatican Pavilion proposal for Louisiana World Expo with architects at Mathes Group, New Orleans, LA
	Fountains with artist Emery Clark, Touro Medical Office Building, New Orleans, LA
1981	Installation with sculptor Helen Escobedo, Contemporary Arts Center, New Orleans, LA

AUDIO-KINETIC INSTALLATIONS

2008	*Breaking News*, Arthur Roger Gallery, New Orleans, LA
2000	*Landscape*, Kouros Gallery, New York, NY; Louisiana museums tour
1999	*After the Garden*, Arthur Roger Gallery, New Orleans, LA
1996	*Passages*, New Orleans Museum of Art, New Orleans, LA
1992	*Sanctum*, Arthur Roger Gallery, New Orleans, LA; Meadows Museum of Art, Shreveport, LA
1987–1988	*First Sanctum*, Contemporary Arts Center, New Orleans, LA
1984–1985	*Becket: The Final Moments*, Max Hutchinson Gallery, New York, NY; Contemporary Arts Center, New Orleans, LA; Alexandria Museum of Art, Alexandria, LA; New Orleans Museum of Art, New Orleans, LA
1983	Musical instruments, *Kinesones*, for performance by James Drew, New Orleans Symphony, New Orleans, LA
1980	*Reflexions: A Play with Water*, Jefferson Parish levee (funded by Louisiana Division of the Arts), New Orleans, LA
	Flim-Flambeau, Mardi Gras parade float, street event (funded by Louisiana Division of the Arts), New Orleans, LA
1978	*Waterways: A Louisiana Environment*, Contemporary Arts Center, New Orleans, LA

Bibliography

General

Aujourd'hui: Art et Architecture, 46 (April 1962): 94.

Bishop, Minor L. *Fountains in Contemporary Architecture*. New York: The American Federation of Arts, 1965.

Boehm, Arlene P. *Jack in Search of Art*. Boulder, CO: Roberts Rinehart Publishers, 1998.

Calas, Terrington. "Modernist Style, Spiritual Message." *Lagniappe*, May 29, 1992, 17.

Cameron, Dan. *Then & Now*. New Orleans, LA: Contemporary Arts Center, 2011, 16–17.

"Casting Reviews." *Casting Engineering Magazine* (July/August 1971): 8.

Clark, Linda F. "Lawrence Kansas—Genuine Community Involvement." *Public Art Connections*, 1, no. 1 (1982): 4.

Cocke, Edward J. *Monumental New Orleans*. New Orleans, LA: LaFayette Publishers, 1968.

"Collaborative Sculpture in New Orleans." *Public Art Connections*, 1, no. 4 (1983).

Collins, Jim L. *Women Artists in America II*. Chattanooga, TN: The University of Tennessee at Chattanooga, 1973, 64–65.

Collischan, Judy. *Welded Sculpture of the Twentieth Century*. New York: Hudson Hills Press, 2000, 56.

"The Culture." *Middle South 1967 Annual Report*, 1967, 23.

De Marsche, Michael. *Katrina: Catastrophe and Catharsis*. Colorado Springs, CO: The Colorado Springs Fine Art Center, 2007, 19.

"Eleven New U.S. Churches." *Architectural Forum* (December 1953): 100.

Emery, Lin. "Bronze Casting." *Modern Casting* (December 1975): 40–43.

Feldman, Edmund Burke. *Art as Image and Idea*. Englewood Cliffs, NJ: Prentice-Hall Inc., 1967, 390.

"Fountains." *Art in America*, 52, no. 6 (December 1964): 46.

"Gallery Previews in New York." *Pictures on Exhibit*, 20, no. 5 (February 1957): 10–11.

Genauer, Emily. "Behind the Bars." *House & Garden* (July 1958): p. 6.

Gerber, Allison, and Bobbie Jo Hedrick. *What Is Art? What Is an Artist?* Sweet Briar, VA: Department of Art History at Sweet Briar College, 1998.

Golightly, Bill. "Tubular Bells." *Horizon* (April 1985): 32–33.

Gould, Dudley C. "Art Casting in America Today." *Modern Casting*, 58, no. 1 (July 1970): 45.

Green, Roger. "Art to Be Installed at NOMA, Tulane." *The Times-Picayune*, December 14, 1988, sec. E, p. 14.

———. "Subdivision Sculpture." *The Times-Picayune/The States-Item*, August 21, 1984.

Hale, Nathan Cabot. *Welded Sculpture*. New York: Watson-Guptill Publications, 1968, 172.

Hennessy, Jefferson. "The Dream of Eddy Knight." *Acadiana Profile* (April 2006): 31, 36.

"Highlights." *National Sculpture Review* (Fall 1971): 5.

Intermezzo Magazine (November 1975): 17.

Jotterand, Franck. "Le Carnet." *Gazette de Lausanne*, Paris, November 25, 1960.

Kemp, John R. "Crafting a Comeback." *American Style*, New Orleans (October 2006): 61–62.

———. "Studio Session: Angels in Flight." *Art & Antiques* (May 2006): 55–57.

Kingsley, Karen. "Urban Sculpture: A Shot in the Public Eye." *New Orleans Magazine*, 19, no. 1 (October 1984): 52, 54.

Lansford, Alonzo. "The South: Four New Artists." *Art in America* (February 1955): 72–74.

Lauer, David A. *Design Basics*. 2nd ed. New York: Holt, Rinehart, and Winston, including CBS College Publishing, 1985, 217.

Leitner, Cynthia Madden. *Collection: The Museum of Outdoor Arts*. Englewood, CO: The Museum of Outdoor Arts, 2008, 9.

Lucie-Smith, Edward. *Art Today: From Abstract Expressionism to Superrealism*. Oxford: Phaidon, 1977.

———. *New Art in an Old City/2*. New Orleans, LA: Virlane Foundation and K&B Corporation Collections, 1994, 113–114.

McCarthy, Jane, and K. Laurily Eputein. *Sculpture Parks & Gardens*. New York: Michael Kesend Publishing, Ltd., 1996, 19, 20, 76–78, 188.

Merkel, Joseph. *Art Speak* (November 1986): 11.

Micmacker, Brigitte. *Sculpture in Motion: Art Choreographed by Nature, at the Atlanta Botanical Garden*. San Francisco, 2008.

"A Monument for New Orleans." *Architectural Record* (September 1971): 37.

"Monument Planned for New Orleans." *Architectural Record* (July 1965): 214.

"New Orleans." *Holiday*, 30, no. 5 (1961): 58.

"New Orleans Parish Expands." *Church Property Administration*, 18, no. 2 (March/April 1954): 37.

"People Who Do Things: Welding Women." *Mechanix Illustrated*, 53, no. 6 (June 1957): 60–61.

Redstone, Louis G., and Ruth P. Redstone. *Public Art: New Directions*. New York: McGraw Hill Book Co., 1981.

Rickey, George. *Constructivism: Origins and Evolution*. New York: George Braziller, Inc., 1967, 207.

Rubinstein, Charlotte Streifer. *American Women Artists: From Early Indian Times to Present*. Boston: G.K. Hall & Co., 1982, 366–367.

———. *American Women Sculptors: A History of Women Working in Three Dimensions*. Boston: G.K. Hall & Co., 1990, 389–390.

Schwab, Priscilla. "Art." *Nation's Business* (November 1977): 100.

"Sculpture Installations: Thirty-Three Galleries Present a Portfolio of Forty-Seven Sculptures." *Art in America* (April 1983): 76.

Seckler, Dorothy Gees. "Gallery Notes: Preview 1957." *Art in America* (Winter 1956–1957): 59–60.

"Section News and Events." *Welding Journal*, 44, no. 12 (December 1965): 1064.

Smith, Herbert L., Jr. "Braselman House, New Orleans, Louisiana." *Architectural Record: Record of Houses 1969*, 145, no. 6 (mid-May 1969): 58–61.

Thalacker, Donald W. *The Place of Art in the World of Architecture.* New York: Chelsea House Publishers, 1980, 64–65.

"Three Sculptors of the Americas." *International Textiles Interior*, no. 3 (Tri-Annual, 1978): 79–81.

Vogt, Paul. *Standplastiken aus Stahl*. Düsseldorf, Germany: Verlag Stahleisen mbH, 1962.

Volkmar, Karl F. "Mechanical Biota, Chromatic Scales." *New Orleans Art Review* (Spring/Summer 2008).

Watson-Jones, Virginia. *Contemporary American Women Sculptors*. Phoenix, AZ: The Oryx Press, 1986, 152–153.

Wiggington, Antoinette, and Virginia Biddle Allen. "Metal that Moves as Sculpture." *Louisiana Magazine*, 1, no. 6 (July/August 1967): 4–7.

Williams, Arthur. *Beginning Sculpture*. Worcester, MA: Davis Publications, Inc., 2005, 19.

———. *The Sculpture Reference Illustrated*. Gulfport, MS: Sculpture Books Publishing, 2005, 36, 227, 443.

Lin Emery Specific

Albee, Edward. "Moving," in *Emery*, exhibition catalogue, 1989. Alexandria Museum of Art, Alexandria, Louisiana, and Kouros Gallery, New York.

"Aquamobiles by Lin Emery." *Interiors* (September 1962).

Bennet, Lennie. "Leepa-Rattner Museum Presents 'Sculpture in Motion: Lin Emery, a Retrospective.'" *St. Petersburg Times*, November 28, 2010.

Bookhardt, D. Eric. "Lin Emery: New Work." *Gambit Weekly*, April 22, 2008.

———. *LoneStar Visions—Lin Emery: Kinetic Sculpture*. Beaumont, TX: Art Museum of Southeast Texas, 1991.

———. "War and Leaves: Sculpture by Lin Emery." *Gambit Weekly*, May 25, 1999.

Bullard, E. John. *Lin Emery*. Atlanta, GA: Heath Gallery, Inc., 1985.

———. *Lin Emery: The Kinetic Sculpture of Lin Emery*. New York: Max Hutchinson Gallery, 1982.

Butler, Madeleine L. "Lin Emery." *Art Voices/South*, 1, no. 3 (May/June 1978): 15.

"Copper – Tin Alloy + GTAW = Aquamobile in Tulsa's Helmerich Park." *Welding Journal*, 57, no. 1 (January 1978): 44–46.

Emery, Lin, and Robert Morriss. "Kinesone I: A Kinetic Sound Sculpture." *Leonardo*, 19, no. 3 (1986): 207–210.

Glueck, Grace. "Lin Emery." *The New York Times*, December 22, 1984.

Green, Roger. "The Kinetic Sculpture of Lin Emery." *Arts Magazine*, 54, no. 4 (December 1979): 106–107.

Kemp, John R. "Grace, Form and Motion: The Sculptures of Lin Emery." *Louisiana Cultural Vistas*, New Orleans (Summer 2007): 34–42.

———. "Reviews: National—Lin Emery." *ARTnews*, 105, no. 3 (March 2006): 145, 151.

Kodera, Nobuo. *Lin Emery—Kinetic World*. Japan: Zeus Art Produce, 1998.

Lin Emery: Wave. New Orleans, LA: New Orleans Museum of Art, 1998.

Lucie-Smith, Edward. *Lin Emery*. Shreveport, LA: Meadows Museum of Art at Centenary College, 2002.

———. "Lin Emery: Borrowing the Forces of Nature," in *Lin Emery*, exhibition monograph, 1996. New Orleans Museum of Art.

"Merchandise Cues: Aquamobiles by Lin Emery." *Interiors*, 122, no. 2 (September 1962): 160.

"Off Center: Audio-Kinetic Becket." *International Sculpture* (April/May 1985): 5.

"Outdoor Sculptures: Lin Emery, 1980." *The Great Big Book about New Orleans*, vol. 1. New Orleans, LA: Gambit Publications, Inc., 1984, 12.

"Panoply: Ohio Outdoor Sculpture." Cleveland, OH: The Sculpture Center, 1994.

Pierce, James Smith. "Lin Emery's Aquamobiles." *Art International*, 13, no. 1 (January 1969): 34–35.

Price, Marshall N. "Lin Emery," in *The Abstract Impulse: Fifty Years of Abstraction at the National Academy, 1956–2006*, exhibition catalogue, 2007. New York: National Academy, 46.

Ratterree, LeClare. "Lin Emery Sculpture." *New Orleans* (May 1968): 44.

"Reviews and Previews: Lin Emery." *ARTnews*, 55, no. 10 (February 1957): 56.

Rub, Timothy F. "Arts Reviews: Lin Emery." *Arts Magazine*, 57, no. 4 (December 1982): 34.

Solomon, Jay. *Cane Dance—Lin Emery*. Houma, LA: General Services Administration, Allen J. Ellender Federal Building and Post Office, 1977.

Strachan, Sue. "Pace Persona: Sculptor Lin Emery Breaks the Mold." *New Orleans Magazine* (July 2006): 16–18.

Volkmar, Karl F. "Musica Kinetika: Lin Emery Sculptures." *New Orleans Art Review* (May/June 1999).

Waddington, Chris. "Emery's Kinetic Sculptures Hold Sway at NOMA." *The Times-Picayune*, June 7, 1996.

———. "Lin Emery's Sculptures Sizzle with Kinetic Energy." *The Times-Picayune*, June 16, 1995.

Whitelaw, R. Lynn, and Philip F. Palmedo. *Sculpture in Motion, Lin Emery: A Retrospective*. St. Petersburg, FL: Leepa-Rattner Museum of Art at St. Petersburg College, 2010.

Index

Page numbers in *italics* refer to illustrations.

Unless otherwise indicated, all photographs are courtesy of the artist's studio.

First Edition

Published in the United States by Hudson Hills Press, LLC
P.O. Box 205, 3556 Main Street, Manchester, Vermont 05254

Distributed in the United States, its territories and possessions, and Canada by National Book Network, Inc.
Distributed outside of North America by Antique Collectors' Club, Ltd.

Publisher and Executive Director: Leslie Pell van Breen
Production Manager: David Skolkin
Design: David Skolkin / S+C Studio, Santa Fe
Editor: Deborah Thompson
Proofreader: Karen Stough
Production Editor: Marisa Crumb
Indexer: Karla Knight
Printed and bound by Toppan Leefung
Founding Publisher: Paul Anbinder

Manufactured in China

Library of Congress Cataloging-in-Publication Data
Palmedo, Philip F.
Lin Emery / by Philip F. Palmedo ; introduction by John Berendt.
p. cm.
Includes bibliographical references and index.
ISBN 978-1-55595-369-0
1. Emery, Lin, 1926---Themes, motives. 2. Kinetic sculpture--United States. I. Emery, Lin, 1926- II. Title.
NB237.E53P35 2011
730.92--dc22
2011018049

Cover: Lin Emery, Sunflower *(in motion), 2009 (detail). Aluminum and paint, 32 inches, orbit 14 inches (81.3 cm, orbit 35.6 cm). Artist's studio.*

Frontispiece: Lin Emery, Acrobat *(in motion), 2001 (detail). Aluminum, 16 inches, orbit 12 inches (40.6 cm, orbit 30.5 cm). Private collection.*

Errata

LOUISIANA ENDOWMENT FOR THE HUMANITIES

This publication was made possible through a grant from Louisiana Endowment for the Humanities, state affiliate of the National Endowment for the Humanities.

Photography Credits

Ann Sherman, p. 56

C. Wolff, p. 88

Courtesy of Albright-Knox Art Gallery/Art Resource, NY, p. 35

Courtesy of Alinari Archives/The Image Works, p. 28

Courtesy of Arthur Lavine/JPMorgan Chase, p. 50

Courtesy of Farnsworth Art Museum, p. 42

Courtesy of Gjon Mili/Time & Life Pictures/Getty Images, p. 19

Courtesy of Hervé Champollion/akg-images/The Image Works, p. 28

Courtesy of Hiromi Faibisch, p. 52

Courtesy of Junius Beebe, p. 124

Courtesy of Moderna Museet/Åsa Lundén, Moderna Museet, Stockholm, p. 125

Courtesy of Smithsonian American Art Museum, p. 72

Courtesy of Tate London, p. 123

David Smith, p. 33

Donn Young, pp. 114, 115

Jeff Thompson, p. 30

Jeremiah Russell, pp. 30, 36

John Kuhlman, p. 25

Judy Cooper, p. 39

Lee Stalsworth, pp. 18, 127

Mike Smith, cover, frontispiece, pp. 4, 6, 10, 12, 28, 43 (*Flight*, 1961), 47 (*Mixed Quartet*), 60, 64 (*Leaf Play*), 98 (*Water Flower*), 103 (*Acrobat*), 104, 106, 107

Myles De Russy, p. 30

Neal Auction, p. 46

Owen Murphy, pp. 26, 117

Stuart Lynn, pp. 31, 39

Tom W. Meyer, pp. 131, 132